INTRODUCTION TO THE
SCIENCE OF SOCIOLOGY

THE HERITAGE OF SOCIOLOGY

A Series Edited by Morris Janowitz

Robert E. Park
and Ernest W. Burgess

INTRODUCTION TO THE
SCIENCE OF SOCIOLOGY

*including an index to basic
sociological concepts*

Student Edition

Abridged and with a New Preface by

MORRIS JANOWITZ

THE UNIVERSITY OF CHICAGO PRESS

CHICAGO AND LONDON

This Student Edition of Park and
Burgess's *Introduction to the Science of Sociology* is
an abridgment of the original (Copyright 1921, 1924 by
The University of Chicago) and includes the Introduction
added when the volume was reissued in 1969.

International Standard Book Number: 0-226-64606-8
Library of Congress Catalog Card Number: 71-126075

Published 1970
Printed in the United States of America

CONTENTS

CHAPTER IV. SOCIAL CONTACTS

CHAPTER V. SOCIAL INTERACTION

CHAPTER VI. COMPETITION

PREFACE TO THE STUDENT EDITION

In 1969, almost a quarter of a century after it went out of print, *Introduction to the Science of Sociology*, by Robert E. Park and Ernest W. Burgess, was republished. This third edition, together with the original index to basic sociological concepts, included the full text and was designed to make the book available to libraries and research scholars. The "green bible," as the original volume was described in its day, was an important document reflecting a major aspect of the early conceptual apparatus of the "Chicago school" of sociology. Robert E. L. Faris in *Chicago Sociology, 1920–1932*, has described the circumstances under which the book was prepared.

Since 1921, when the book first appeared, a major part of its contents obviously have become outdated. Therefore an abridged student edition, containing what is most lasting and relevant for the use and interests of students, is now called for.

The book as originally prepared consisted essentially of a series of introductory essays written by Park and Burgess plus selections of what were then contemporary writings. My criteria for abridgment were that original material was to be given priority, and that among the selections, outmoded and peripheral materials were to be excluded. Wherever possible, the original index to basic sociological concepts was also to be kept intact. Although I conferred with a number of colleagues while working on this edition, I am sure there are other sociologists who will disagree with the judgments that went into the abridgment—even with the idea of any abridgment at all. Of course, I accept full responsibility for the final decisions. My hope is that if the present edition accomplishes nothing else, it will serve many students as a bridge to the complete edition, which will remain in the Heritage of Sociology series.

In abridging I found it possible to eliminate a few conceptual sections. These included isolation, social forces, and progress. The term *isolation* was the counterpoint to *social contact* in the analysis of interaction. In the few pages devoted to this concept, however, it was underdeveloped as compared with other categories. *Social forces* was treated more extensively, but it is a concept that has passed from sociological analysis. In effect, in the analysis of social control much of the same material is presented in more systematic fashion.

The section on *progress* is by no means a simplistic or naïve treatment of the history and the sociological import of the term. This section might well have been retained, but the language is outmoded although the issues are relevant. These men were progressives and meliorists of their day, but they were realists and skeptics as well. It is hardly surprising that they challenged mechanical and evolutionary notions of progress. "Every new mechanical device, every advance in business organization or in science, which makes the world more tolerable for most of us, makes it impossible for others." (3d ed., p. 954). In fact, they sought to be as explicit as possible. For the 10 percent of the population whom they described as "the inferior, incompetent, and unfortunate, unable to keep pace with progress, the more rapid advance of the world means disease, despair, and death" (p. 955).

In dealing with progress, they anticipated current concern with social indicators, indicators not only of economic, but of social progress in its humanistic aspects. Park and Burgess were careful and restless searchers for any aspect of scholarship or research that would contribute to sociological understanding. Students of social indicators may note that they identify the work of Walter F. Willcox, "A Statistician's Idea of Progress," published appropriately in the *International Journal of Ethics* in 1913, as one of the earliest attempts at quantitative research in this direction. Their programmatic statements are indeed contemporary because of the focus on attitudes and values. They state, for example, "The securing of indices which will measure satisfactorily even such social values as are generally accepted is difficult" (p. 1003).

In the 1960s, critics of sociology, especially students, raised the question whether sociology was not unduly concerned with "consensus" and static analysis. Therefore, I hope that this student edition will accurately convey the notion that the study of conflict and social control was at the very heart of the work of Park and Burgess.

MORRIS JANOWITZ

The University of Chicago
February 1970

INTRODUCTION

For twenty years after its publication in 1921, *Introduction to the Science of Sociology* by Robert E. Park and Ernest W. Burgess was the leading textbook in the discipline. But it was a volume which conformed to the older format of a textbook and a treatise at the same time. There was no conscious effort at popularization of an academic specialty to reach a wider undergraduate audience. It contained no photographs or wide margins as has become the practice for social science textbooks. There was no doubt that it was designed for the classroom and the increasing numbers of undergraduates enrolled in courses offered by the Department of Sociology at the University of Chicago. As a treatise, it was simultaneously addressed to graduate students throughout the country for whom it became known as "the green bible" as they prepared for their doctoral examinations and research endeavors. Park and Burgess thought of it as a reasoned statement of the theoretical state of the discipline, and they were prepared to have it evaluated as such by mature scholars in the field. In fact, it also served to present sociological thinking to the related faculties of the social science community.

It is now over a quarter of a century since the book went out of print and became a collector's item. A great many of the specific selections included in the volume have, of course, become outdated. But the decision to reprint the volume in its entirety is thought to be more than a contribution to the history of the development of sociology. Many of the concepts presented and illustrated in the *Introduction to the Science of Sociology,* especially those concerning collective behavior (which has experienced a renewed interest in sociology), are remarkably up to date, and their presentation is indeed penetrating. For example, one is struck that the concept of "institutionalization," which plays such an important part in contemporary structural functional analysis, had by 1921 already sociological currency. Thus, the contemporary student of sociology will find in this treatise a wide range of concepts that remain viable because of their present utility, and he will be able to note how Park and Burgess sought to handle these concepts. Of particular relevance is the careful analytic index which supplies a guide to the conceptualizations in the volume.

The collaboration between Robert E. Park and Ernest W. Burgess was a fortunate and fruitful one. While there is no need to deprecate Burgess' contribution, it was clear to all including Burgess himself that the volume represented the theoretical impact of Robert E. Park, who, in effect, was drawing upon and modifying the ideas of W. I. Thomas. In responding to an inquiry from Ralph H. Turner shortly before his death, Ernest Burgess stated in a brief handwritten letter that "the leadership in the preparation of the book *Introduction to the Science of Sociology*" was taken on by Dr. Park. "He came to the project with a conceptual framework of sociology. He and I shared the task of looking up the reading selections, we went through hundreds of volumes to make the selections."

It does appear that the first draft of chapter 1 was under the sole authorship of Robert Park since it had appeared previously in the form of three articles in the *American Journal of Sociology*. For the bulk of the book, chapters 2 through 11, Burgess indicated that "in writing the introduction and the statements of further research for each chapter, we typically talked these over and I wrote the first draft which Dr. Park edited." From chapter 12 on, dealing with social control and collective behavior, Burgess stated that Robert Park wrote the introductions.

The *Introduction to the Science of Sociology* rapidly came to represent the Chicago school of sociology wherever sociology was taught or debated. The scope of the treatise is remarkably comprehensive in the range of the problems and concepts it presented. However, neither Park nor Burgess were system builders and were content to present a loose collection of concepts. In this sense, the volume is an unfortunate and unrepresentative perspective of the intellectual interests subsumed under the Chicago school of sociology. The work of W. I. Thomas or that of William Ogburn represented a much more systematic effort to present an integrated approach to sociology. No doubt the very eclecticism of the Park and Burgess volume made for its popularity as a textbook and its usefulness as a reference volume to the sociology fraternity concerned with developing empirical research.

Its impact and success were almost instantaneous. E. A. Ross, professor of sociology and social psychology at the University of Wisconsin, removed from the intellectual and social life of the Midway and in opposition to many of its social values, reviewed it for the *American Journal of Sociology* (November 1921) and declared "this handsome, wieldy volume will prove a Godsend to teachers of sociology. . . . This ripe and scholarly volume is the last word of perfection in source books for the classroom, no teacher of sociology can afford to be without it. No doubt it will contribute much to the expansion of social studies in our colleges."

At that time, to produce a book of over a thousand pages was a major enterprise for a university press if the book was devoted to sociological materials. However, from 1921 until it was declared out of print in June 1943, over thirty thousand copies were sold. By contemporary standards this seems modest. It was indeed impressive for that period. In the absence of planned obsolescence by continuous minor revisions, secondhand copies passed back and forth from student generation to student generation. It was translated into various foreign languages as foreign students completed their education at Chicago and returned home.

As a footnote in the changing social history of the university professor the income derived from royalties was not viewed by Park and especially by Ernest Burgess as a regular part of their standard of living. It was something extraordinary and special. In the case of Ernest W. Burgess it was carefully husbanded in order to underwrite research and ultimately after his death turned over to the Department of Sociology to make possible a generous scholarship fund.

The format of the treatise was a direct replication of W. I. Thomas' earlier influential volume which appeared in 1908 under the title *Source Book for Social Origins: Ethnological Materials, Psychological Standpoint, Classified and Annotated Bibliographies for the Interpretation of Savage Societies*. Both volumes represented the Chicago school's concern with fusing theory and empirical data. Each was not only a voluminous collection of essential source materials but included careful introductions and conceptual commentaries as well as bibliographic annotations. This format is still widely used in sociological textbooks, even though they are no longer treatises.

Park and Burgess were dedicated to the energetic application of the scientific method to those human phenomena which they saw as part of sociology. And yet, not for a moment did they believe that the generalizations being sought by the social scientists would dispense with the importance of concrete detail. It was out of this sensitivity that the tradition of interplay between concept and social detail developed, as represented in the research monographs about the urban community and the social worlds of the metropolis of their students. These men believed that sociology had to have a special genre, and subsequent generations of empirical researchers clung to this tradition.

At the conceptual level, Park and Burgess represented the view of the Chicago empirical school that fused sociology into the classical problems of social philosophy. They sought to understand the social order or, in their language, the processes of social control. There was no hesitation; it was abundantly evident that society, the social organism, was in a never-ending process of flux. As a result this volume reflects their underlying intellectual orientation. It focuses on categories of social processes. At the heart of their analysis is a set of process categories which have become classical in describing social change, namely, competition, conflict, and accommodation. All of these are elements of social control. For them collective behavior was not a distinct aspect of sociological analysis but an essential element in the processes of social change. They were interested in the study of social contagion, crowds, mass movements, and public opinion, topics which remain contemporary in a period of explosive social tensions.

But their very concern with social process limited their identification of the essential stratification features of an industrial society and weakened their analysis of social structure. Instead of examining the macrostructures of society, at points they used such vague formulations as "social forces." This is not to deny their awareness of the political process that penetrated the local community. Rather they viewed these political elements as derivative or epiphenomenological. They could not see political institutions as having independent consequences.

Nevertheless, this volume is a powerful refutation of the argument that the American sociological tradition avoided a concern with the analysis of conflict. In the approach that Park and Burgess were striving to construct, the notion of interaction is crucial. It is the counterpart of Parsons' theory of action. It is not merely a social psychological term connected with the subjective definition of the self, as derived from the writings of George Herbert Mead. Interaction is a process to be seen at all the levels of sociological analysis: ecological, social organizational, and the normative as well.

In turn, the more specific processes of competition, conflict, accommodation, and assimilation cut through the variety of structures that are to be found in organized society. The positive benefits of conflict which are so much at the core of contemporary conflict theory were already identified in an undifferentiated way by Park and Burgess. More precisely there is a Hobbesian overtone throughout the volume. The term social organization has come to be neutrally defined as an abstracted entity involving either patterns of roles or patterns of influence among social groups. There was no such academic attachment in the thinking of Park and Burgess. Their view of the ecological substructure of society led them to see an unending competition and conflict of interests. The development of forms of social organization was already essentially an accommodation of differences through the transformation or limitation of conflicts. "Social organization, with the exception of the order based on competition and adaptation, is essentially an accommodation of differences through conflicts" (p. 664).

Their interest in the ecological order led them to focus the bulk of their own writings at the community level. The human community was the object of analysis that interested them. But community was loosely fused with society. Through the fundamental processes of social transformation "a community assumes the form of a society" (p. 786). They did not highlight the structures and the mechanisms by which the parts related to the whole. The absence of an explicit macrosociology was a source of intellectual and analytic weakness. The collection of the statistical trend data about the national arena stimulated by their quantitative colleagues such as William F. Ogburn served to introduce a better balance but failed to stimulate them to concern with societal structures.

They were deeply aware of nationalism. Their frequent references to the collective representation stimulated by the writings of Emile Durkheim attest to their awareness of the social system level of analysis. But again national authority and legitimacy were not central concerns of theirs. This was seen by the relative absence of reference to the work of Max Weber.

It was not far-fetched to point out that much of what has come to be described as phenomenology is part of their concern. Repeatedly, page after page and section after section, whether one is reading the original contributions of Park and Burgess or included selections, there is an expression of the subjective definition of social behavior and social institutions. Thus, for example, the discussion of prestige encompasses the nonrational and mystical aspects of this concept. If in effect prestige can be reduced to the concrete measures of income and education then there is something subjective left over. In turn, contemporary analysis of the presentation of individual self has its earlier analogy in concepts dealing with ceremonialism, individual control, and the like. Furthermore, one has only to read the analysis of collective behavior and public opinion to realize the extent to which their categories are relevant in a period of rapid social change. They emphasized myth, ritual, dogma, and propaganda.

One of the most dramatic aspects of the volume is the concluding section on the idea of progress. The notion that Chicago sociology under the impact of empiricism was devoid of value concerns is hardly documented by the contents of this volume. The idea that American sociologists got their interests in social goals from Europe is simply incorrect. Of course, these men were aware of eighteenth- and nineteenth-century European social philosophers. For them, the study of human values was an essential part of the subject matter of sociology. And more important, they believed in the last analysis that sociology had to deal with policy and problem issues. Their terminology centered on definitions, including sociological definitions of progress and the conditions for achieving progress and its consequences.

Park and Burgess were men of great insight who sought to extend their knowledge by the use of specific concepts. Contemporary sociologists are more concerned with systems of concepts in order to present a more integrated overview.

There is no doubt that if they were alive today they would participate in the efforts at new formulations in sociology. But they would not have abandoned their commitment to concrete and specific data. Thus, it is well to point out their fundamental viewpoint: "It has been the dream of philosophers that theoretical and abstract science could and some day would succeed in putting into formulae and into general terms all that was significant in the concrete facts of life. It has been the tragic mistake of the so-called intellectuals, who have gained their knowledge from textbooks rather than from observation and research, to assume that science had already realized its dream. But there is no indication that science has begun to exhaust the sources or significance of concrete experience."

MORRIS JANOWITZ

CHAPTER I

SOCIOLOGY AND THE SOCIAL SCIENCES[1]

I. SOCIOLOGY AND "SCIENTIFIC" HISTORY

Sociology first gained recognition as an independent science with the publication, between 1830 and 1842, of Auguste Comte's *Cours de philosophie positive.* Comte did not, to be sure, create sociology. He did give it a name, a program, and a place among the sciences.

Comte's program for the new science proposed an extension to politics and to history of the positive methods of the natural sciences. Its practical aim was to establish government on the secure foundation of an exact science and give to the predictions of history something of the precision of mathematical formulae.

We have to contemplate social phenomena as susceptible of prevision, like all other classes, within the limits of exactness compatible with their higher complexity. Comprehending the three characteristics of political science which we have been examining, prevision of social phenomena supposes, first, that we have abandoned the region of metaphysical idealities, to assume the ground of observed realities by a systematic subordination of imagination to observation; secondly, that political conceptions have ceased to be absolute, and have become relative to the variable state of civilization, so that theories, following the natural course of facts, may admit of our foreseeing them; and, thirdly, that permanent political action is limited by determinate laws, since, if social events were always exposed to disturbance by the accidental intervention of the legislator, human or divine, no scientific prevision of them would be possible. Thus, we may concentrate the conditions of the spirit of positive social philosophy on this one great attribute of scientific prevision.[2]

Comte proposed, in short, to make government a technical science and politics a profession. He looked forward to a time when legislation, based on a scientific study of human nature, would

[1] From Robert E. Park, "Sociology and the Social Sciences," *American Journal of Sociology*, XXVI (1920–21), 401–24; XXVII (1921–22), 1–21; 169–83.

[2] Harriet Martineau, *The Positive Philosophy of Auguste Comte*, freely translated and condensed (London, 1893). II, 61.

assume the character of natural law. The earlier and more elementary sciences, particularly physics and chemistry, had given man control over external nature; the last science, sociology, was to give man control over himself.

Men were long in learning that Man's power of modifying phenomena can result only from his knowledge of their natural laws; and in the infancy of each science, they believed themselves able to exert an unbounded influence over the phenomena of that science. . . . . Social phenomena are, of course, from their extreme complexity, the last to be freed from this pretension: but it is therefore only the more necessary to remember that the pretension existed with regard to all the rest, in their earliest stage, and to anticipate therefore that social science will, in its turn, be emancipated from the delusion. . . . . It [the existing social science] represents the social action of Man to be indefinite and arbitrary, as was once thought in regard to biological, chemical, physical, and even astronomical phenomena, in the earlier stages of their respective sciences. . . . . The human race finds itself delivered over, without logical protection, to the ill-regulated experimentation of the various political schools, each one of which strives to set up, for all future time, its own immutable type of government. We have seen what are the chaotic results of such a strife; and we shall find that there is no chance of order and agreement but in subjecting social phenomena, like all others, to invariable natural laws, which shall, as a whole, prescribe for each period, with entire certainty, the limits and character of political action: in other words, introducing into the study of social phenomena the same positive spirit which has regenerated every other branch of human speculation.[1]

In the present anarchy of political opinion and parties, changes in the existing social order inevitably assume, he urged, the character, at the best, of a mere groping empiricism; at the worst, of a social convulsion like that of the French Revolution. Under the direction of a positive, in place of a speculative or, as Comte would have said, metaphysical science of society, progress must assume the character of an orderly march.

It was to be expected, with the extension of exact methods of investigation to other fields of knowledge, that the study of man and of society would become, or seek to become, scientific in the sense in which that word is used in the natural sciences. It is interesting, in this connection, that Comte's first name for sociology

[1] Harriet Martineau, *op. cit.*, II, 59–61.

was *social physics*. It was not until he had reached the fourth volume of his *Positive Philosophy* that the word sociological is used for the first time.

Comte, if he was foremost, was not first in the search for a positive science of society, which would give man that control over men that he had over external nature. Montesquieu, in his *The Spirit of Laws*, first published in 1747, had distinguished in the organization of society, between form, "the particular structure," and forces, "the human passions which set it in motion." In his preface to this first epoch-making essay in what Freeman calls "comparative politics," Montesquieu suggests that the uniformities, which he discovered beneath the wide variety of positive law, were contributions not merely to a science of law, but to a science of mankind.

I have first of all considered mankind; and the result of my thoughts has been, that amidst such an infinite diversity of laws and manners, they are not solely conducted by the caprice of fancy.[1]

Hume, likewise, put politics among the natural sciences.[2] Condorcet wanted to make history positive.[3] But there were, in the period between 1815 and 1840 in France, conditions which made the need of a new science of politics peculiarly urgent. The Revolution had failed and the political philosophy, which had directed and justified it, was bankrupt. France, between 1789 and 1815, had adopted, tried, and rejected no less than ten different constitutions. But during this period, as Saint-Simon noted, society, and the human beings who compose society, had not changed. It was evident that government was not, in any such sense as the philosophers had assumed, a mere artefact and legislative construction. Civilization, as Saint-Simon conceived it, was a part of nature. Social change was part of the whole cosmic process. He proposed, therefore, to make politics a science as positive as physics. The subject-matter of political science, as he conceived it, was not so

---

[1] Montesquieu, Baron M. de Secondat, *The Spirit of Laws*, translated by Thomas Nugent (Cincinnati, 1873), I, xxxi.

[2] David Hume, *Inquiry Concerning Human Understanding*, Part II, sec. 7.

[3] Condorcet, *Esquisse d'un tableau historique des progrès de l'esprit humain* (1795), 292. See Paul Barth, *Die Philosophie der Geschichte als Sociologie* (Leipzig, 1897), Part I, pp. 21–23.

much political forms as social conditions.   History had been literature.   It was destined to become a science.[1]

Comte called himself Saint-Simon's pupil.   It is perhaps more
correct to say Saint-Simon formulated the problem for which Comte,
in his *Positive Philosophy*, sought a solution.   It was Comte's notion
that with the arrival of sociology the distinction which had so long
existed, and still exists, between philosophy, in which men define
their wishes, and natural science, in which they describe the existing
order of nature, would disappear.   In that case ideals would be defined
in terms of reality, and the tragic difference between what men want
and what is possible would be effaced.   Comte's error was to mistake
a theory of progress for progress itself.   It is certainly true that as
men learn what is, they will adjust their ideals to what is possible.
But knowledge grows slowly.

Man's knowledge of mankind has increased greatly since 1842.
Sociology, "the positive science of humanity," has moved steadily
forward in the direction that Comte's program indicated, but it has
not yet replaced history.   Historians are still looking for methods of
investigation which will make history "scientific."

No one who has watched the course of history during the last generation
can have felt doubt of its tendency.   Those of us who read Buckle's first
volume when it appeared in 1857, and almost immediately afterwards, in
1859, read the *Origin of Species* and felt the violent impulse which Darwin
gave to the study of natural laws, never doubted that historians would follow
until they had exhausted every possible hypothesis to create a science of
history.   Year after year passed, and little progress has been made.   Perhaps
the mass of students are more skeptical now than they were thirty years ago
of the possibility that such a science can be created.   Yet almost every successful historian has been busy with it, adding here a new analysis, a new
generalization there; a clear and definite connection where before the rupture
of idea was absolute; and, above all, extending the field of study until it
shall include all races, all countries, and all times.   Like other branches of
science, history is now encumbered and hampered by its own mass, but its
tendency is always the same, and cannot be other than what it is.   That
the effort to make history a science may fail is possible, and perhaps probable; but that it should cease, unless for reasons that would cause all science
to cease, is not within the range of experience.   Historians will not, and

---

[1] *Œuvres de Saint-Simon et d'Enfantin* (Paris, 1865–78), XVII, 228.   Paul
Barth, *op. cit.*, Part I, p. 23.

even if they would they can not, abandon the attempt. Science itself would admit its own failure if it admitted that man, the most important of all its subjects, could not be brought within its range.[1]

Since Comte gave the new science of humanity a name and a point of view, the area of historical investigation has vastly widened and a number of new social sciences have come into existence—ethnology, archaeology, folklore, the comparative studies of cultural materials, i.e., language, mythology, religion, and law, and in connection with and closely related with these, folk-psychology, social psychology, and the psychology of crowds, which latter is, perhaps, the forerunner of a wider and more elaborate political psychology. The historians have been very much concerned with these new bodies of materials and with the new points of view which they have introduced into the study of man and of society. Under the influences of these sciences, history itself, as James Harvey Robinson has pointed out, has had a history. But with the innovations which the new history has introduced or attempted to introduce, it does not appear that there have been any fundamental changes in method or ideology in the science itself.

Fifty years have elapsed since Buckle's book appeared, and I know of no historian who would venture to maintain that we had made any considerable advance toward the goal he set for himself. A systematic prosecution of the various branches of social science, especially political economy, sociology, anthropology, and psychology, is succeeding in explaining many things; but history must always remain, from the standpoint of the astronomer, physicist, or chemist, a highly inexact and fragmentary body of knowledge. . . . . History can no doubt be pursued in a strictly scientific spirit, but the data we possess in regard to the past of mankind are not of a nature to lend themselves to organization into an exact science, although, as we shall see, they may yield truths of vital importance.[2]

History has not become, as Comte believed it must, an exact science, and sociology has not taken the place of History in the social sciences. It is important, however, for understanding the mutations which have taken place in sociology since Comte to

[1] Henry Adams, *The Degradation of the Democratic Dogma* (New York, 1919), p. 126.

[2] James Harvey Robinson, *The New History, Essays Illustrating the Modern Historical Outlook* (New York, 1912), pp. 54–55.

remember that it had its origin in an effort to make history exact. This, with, to be sure, considerable modifications, is still, as we shall see, an ambition of the science.

II. HISTORICAL AND SOCIOLOGICAL FACTS

Sociology, as Comte conceived it, was not, as it has been characterized, "a highly important point of view," but a fundamental science, i.e., a method of investigation and "a body of discoveries about mankind."[1] In the hierarchy of the sciences, sociology, the last in time, was first in importance. The order was as follows: mathematics, astronomy, physics, chemistry, biology including psychology, sociology. This order represented a progression from the more elementary to the more complex. It was because history and politics were concerned with the most complex of natural phenomena that they were the last to achieve what Comte called the positive character. They did this in sociology.

Many attempts have been made before and since Comte to find a satisfactory classification of the sciences. The order and relation of the sciences is still, in fact, one of the cardinal problems of philosophy. In recent years the notion has gained recognition that the difference between history and the natural sciences is not one of degree, but of kind; not of subject-matter merely, but of method. This difference in method is, however, fundamental. It is a difference not merely in the interpretation but in the *logical character* of facts.

Every historical fact, it is pointed out, is concerned with a unique event. History never repeats itself. If nothing else, the mere circumstance that every event has a *date* and *location* would give historical facts an individuality that facts of the abstract sciences do not possess. Because historical facts always are located and dated, and cannot therefore be repeated, they are not subject to experiment and verification. On the other hand, a fact not subject to verification is not a fact for natural science. History, as distinguished from natural history, deals with individuals, i.e., individual events, persons, institutions. Natural science is concerned, not with individuals, but with classes, types, species. All the assertions that are valid for natural science concern classes. An illustration will make this distinction clear.

[1] James Harvey Robinson, *op. cit.*, p. 83.

Sometime in October, 1838, Charles Darwin happened to pick up and read Malthus' book on *Population*. The facts of "the struggle for existence," so strikingly presented in that now celebrated volume, suggested an explanation of a problem which had long interested and puzzled him, namely, the origin of species.

This is a statement of a historical fact, and the point is that it is not subject to empirical verification. It cannot be stated, in other words, in the form of a hypothesis, which further observation of other men of the same type will either verify or discredit.

On the other hand, in his *Descent of Man*, Darwin, discussing the rôle of sexual selection in evolution of the species, makes this observation: "Naturalists are much divided with respect to the object of the singing of birds. Few more careful observers ever lived than Montagu, and he maintained that the 'males of song-birds and of many others do not in general search for the female, but, on the contrary, their business in spring is to perch on some conspicuous spot, breathing out their full and amorous notes, which, by instinct, the female knows and repairs to the spot to choose her mate.'"

This is a typical statement of a fact of natural history. It is not, however, the rather vague generality of the statement that makes it scientific. It is its representative character, the character which makes it possible of verification by further observation which makes it a scientific fact.

It is from facts of this kind, collected, compared, and classified, irrespective of time or place, that the more general conclusions are drawn, upon which Darwin based his theory of the "descent of man." This theory, as Darwin conceived it, was not an *interpretation* of the facts but an *explanation*.

The relation between history and sociology, as well as the manner in which the more abstract social sciences have risen out of the more concrete, may be illustrated by a comparison between history and geography. Geography as a science is concerned with the visible world, the earth, its location in space, the distribution of the land masses, and of the plants, animals, and peoples upon its surface. The order, at least the fundamental order, which it seeks and finds among the objects it investigates is *spatial*. As soon as the geographer begins to compare and classify the plants, the animals, and the peoples with which he comes in contact, geography passes over into the special sciences, i.e., botany, zoölogy, and anthropology.

History, on the other hand, is concerned with a world of events. Not everything that happened, to be sure, is history, but every event that ever was or ever will be significant is history.

Geography attempts to reproduce for us the visible world as it exists in space; history, on the contrary, seeks to re-create for us in the present the significance of the past. As soon as historians seek to take events out of their historical setting, that is to say, out of their time·and space relations, in order to compare them and classify them; as soon as historians begin to emphasize the typical and representative rather than the unique character of events, history ceases to be history and becomes sociology.

The differences here indicated between history and sociology are based upon a more fundamental distinction between the historical and the natural sciences first clearly defined by Windelband, the historian of philosophy, in an address to the faculty of the University of Strassburg in 1894.

The distinction between natural science and history begins at the point where we seek to convert facts into knowledge. Here again we observe that the one (natural science) seeks to formulate laws, the other (history) to portray events. In the one case thought proceeds from the description of particulars to the general relations. In the other case it clings to a genial depiction of the individual object or event. For the natural scientist the object of investigation which cannot be repeated never has, as such, scientific value. It serves his purpose only so far as it may be regarded as a type or as a special instance of a class from which the type may be deduced. The natural scientist considers the single case only so far as he can see in it the features which serve to throw light upon a general law. For the historian the problem is to revive and call up into the present, in all its particularity, an event in the past. His aim is to do for an actual event precisely what the artist seeks to do for the object of his imagination. It is just here that we discern the kinship between history and art, between the historian and the writer of literature. It is for this reason that natural science emphasized he abstract; the historian, on the other hand, is interested mainly in the concrete.

The fact that natural science emphasizes the abstract and history the concrete will become clearer if we compare the results of the researches of the two sciences. However finespun the conceptions may be which the historical critic uses in working over his materials, the final goal of such study is always to create out of the mass of events a vivid portrait of the past. And what history offers us is pictures of men and of human life, with all the wealth of their individuality, reproduced in all their characteristic vivacity. Thus do the peoples and languages of the past, their forms and beliefs, their struggles for power and freedom, speak to us through the mouth of history.

How different it is with the world which the natural sciences have created for us! However concrete the materials with which they started, the goal of these sciences is theories, eventually mathematical formulations of laws of change. Treating the individual, sensuous, changing objects as mere unsubstantial appearances (phenomena), scientific investigation becomes a search for the universal laws which rule the timeless changes of events. Out of this colorful world of the senses, science creates a system of abstract concepts, in which the true nature of things is conceived to exist—a world of colorless and soundless atoms, despoiled of all their earthly sensuous qualities. Such is the triumph of thought over perception. Indifferent to change, science casts her anchor in the eternal and unchangeable. Not the change as such but the unchanging form of change is what she seeks.

This raises the question: What is the more valuable for the purposes of knowledge in general, a knowledge of law or a knowledge of events? As far as that is concerned, both scientific procedures may be equally justified. The knowledge of the universal laws has everywhere a practical value in so far as they make possible man's purposeful intervention in the natural processes. That is quite as true of the movements of the inner as of the outer world. In the latter case knowledge of nature's laws has made it possible to create those tools through which the control of mankind over external nature is steadily being extended.

Not less for the purposes of the common life are we dependent upon the results of historical knowledge. Man is, to change the ancient form of the expression, the animal who has a history. His cultural life rests on the transmission from generation to generation of a constantly increasing body of historical memories. Whoever proposes to take an active part in this cultural process must have an understanding of history. Wherever the thread is once broken—as history itself proves—it must be painfully gathered up and knitted again into the historical fabric.

It is, to be sure, true that it is an economy for human understanding to be able to reduce to a formula or a general concept the common characteristics of individuals. But the more man seeks to reduce facts to concepts and laws, the more he is obliged to sacrifice and neglect the individual. Men have, to be sure, sought, in characteristic modern fashion, "to make of history a natural science." This was the case with the so-called philosophy of history of positivism. What has been the net result of the laws of history which it has given us ? A few trivial generalities which justify themselves only by the most careful consideration of their numerous exceptions.

On the other hand it is certain that all interest and values of life are concerned with what is unique in men and events. Consider how quickly our appreciation is deadened as some object is multiplied or is regarded as one case in a thousand. "She is not the first" is one of the cruel passages in *Faust*. It is in the individuality and the uniqueness of an object that all our sense of value has its roots. It is upon this fact that Spinoza's doctrine of the conquest of the passions by knowledge rests, since for him knowledge is the submergence of the individual in the universal, the "once for all" into the eternal.

The fact that all our livelier appreciations rest upon the unique character of the object is illustrated above all in our relations to persons. Is it not an unendurable thought, that a loved object, an adored person, should have existed at some other time in just the form in which it now exists for us ? Is it not horrible and unthinkable that one of us, with just this same individuality should actually have existed in a second edition ?

What is true of the individual man is quite as true of the whole historical process: it has value only when it is unique. This is the principle which the Christian doctrine successfully maintained, as over against Hellenism in the Patristic philosophy. The middle point of their conception of the world was the fall and the salvation of mankind as a unique event. That was the first and great perception of the inalienable metaphysical right of the historian to preserve for the memory of mankind, in all their uniqueness and individuality, the actual events of life.[1]

Like every other species of animal, man has a natural history. Anthropology is the science of man considered as one of the animal species, *Homo sapiens*. History and sociology, on the other hand, are concerned with man as a person, as a "political animal," participating with his fellows in a common fund of social traditions and cultural ideals. Freeman, the English historian, said that history was "past politics" and politics "present history." Freeman uses

[1] Wilhelm Windelband, *Geschichte und Naturwissenschaft, Rede zum Antritt des Rectorats der Kaiser-Wilhelms Universität Strassburg* (Strassburg, 1900). The logical principle outlined by Windelband has been further elaborated by Heinrich Rickert in *Die Grenzen der naturwissenschaftlichen Begriffsbildung, eine logische Einleitung in die historischen Wissenschaften* (Tübingen u. Leipzig, 1902). See also Georg Simmel, *Die Probleme der Geschichtsphilosophie. eine erkenntnistheoretische Studie* (2d ed., Leipzig, 1915), and Benedetto Croce, *History*. Its theory and practice (New York, 1921).

the word politics in the large and liberal sense in which it was first used by Aristotle. In that broad sense of the word, the political process, by which men are controlled and states governed, and the cultural process, by which man has been domesticated and human nature formed, are not, as we ordinarily assume, different, but identical, procedures.

All this suggests the intimate relations which exist between history, politics, and sociology. The important thing, however, is not the identities but the distinctions. For, however much the various disciplines may, in practice, overlap, it is necessary for the sake of clear thinking to have their limits defined. As far as sociology and history are concerned the differences may be summed up in a word. Both history and sociology are concerned with the life of man as man. History, however, seeks to reproduce and interpret concrete events as they actually occurred in time and space. Sociology, on the other hand, seeks to arrive at natural laws and generalizations in regard to human nature and society, irrespective of time and of place.

In other words, history seeks to find out what actually happened and how it all came about. Sociology, on the other hand, seeks to explain, on the basis of a study of other instances, the nature of the process involved.

By nature we mean just that aspect and character of things in regard to which it is possible to make general statements and formulate laws. If we say, in explanation of the peculiar behavior of some individual, that it is natural or that it is after all "simply human nature," we are simply saying that this behavior is what we have learned to expect of this individual or of human beings in general. It is, in other words, a law.

Natural law, as the term is used here, is any statement which describes the behavior of a class of objects or the character of a class of acts. For example, the classic illustration of the so-called "universal proposition" familiar to students of formal logic, "all men are mortal," is an assertion in regard to a class of objects we call men. This is, of course, simply a more formal way of saying that "men die." Such general statements and "laws" get meaning only when they are applied to particular cases, or, to speak again in the terms of formal logic, when they find a place in a syllogism, thus: "Men are mortal. This is a man." But such syllogisms may always be stated in the form of a hypothesis. If this is a man, he is mortal. If *a* is *b*, *a* is also *c*. The statement, "Human nature is a product of social contact," is a general assertion familiar to students of sociology. This law or, more correctly, hypothesis, applied to an individual case explains the so-called feral man. Wild men, in the proper sense of the word, are not the so-called savages, but the men who have never been domesticated, of which an individual example is now and then discovered.

To state a law in the form of a hypothesis serves to emphasize the fact that laws—what we have called natural laws at any rate—are subject to verification and restatement. Under the circumstances the exceptional instance, which compels a restatement of the hypothesis, is more important for the purposes of science than other instances which merely confirm it.

Any science which operates with hypotheses and seeks to state facts in such a way that they can be compared and verified by further observation and experiment is, so far as method is concerned, a natural science.

III.   HUMAN NATURE AND LAW

One thing that makes the conception of natural history and natural law important to the student of sociology is that in the field of the social sciences the distinction between natural and moral law has from the first been confused. Comte and the social philosophers in France after the Revolution set out with the deliberate purpose of superseding legislative enactments by laws of human nature, laws which were to be positive and "scientific." As a matter of fact, sociology, in becoming positive, so far from effacing, has rather emphasized the distinctions that Comte sought to abolish. Natural law may be distinguished from all other forms of law by the fact that it aims at nothing more than a description of the behavior of certain types or classes of objects. A description of the way in which a class, i.e., men, plants, animals, or physical objects, may be expected under ordinary circumstances to behave, tells us what we may in a general way expect of any individual member of that class. If natural science seeks to predict, it is able to do so simply because it operates with concepts or class names instead, as is the case with history, with concrete facts and, to use a logical phrase, "existential propositions."

That the chief end of science is descriptive formulation has probably been clear to keen analytic minds since the time of Galileo, especially to the great discoverers in astromony, mechanics, and dynamics. But as a definitely stated conception, corrective of misunderstandings, the view of science as essentially descriptive began to make itself felt about the beginning of the last quarter of the nineteenth century, and may be associated with the names of Kirchhoff and Mach. It was in 1876 that Kirchhoff defined the task of mechanics as that of "describing completely and in the simplest manner the motions which take place in nature." Widening this a little, we may say that the aim of science is to describe natural phenomena and occurrences as exactly as possible, as simply as possible, as completely as possible, as consistently as possible, and always in terms which are communicable and verifiable. This is a very different rôle from that of solving the riddles of the universe, and it is well expressed in what Newton said in regard to the law of gravitation: "So far I have accounted for the phenomena presented to us by the heavens and the sea by means of the force of gravity, but I have as yet assigned no cause to this gravity. . . . . I have not been able to deduce from phenomena the *raison d'être* of the properties of gravity and I have not set up hypotheses." (Newton, *Philosophiae naturalis principia Mathematica*, 1687.)

"We must confess," said Prof. J. H. Poynting (1900, p. 616), "that physical laws have greatly fallen off in dignity. No long time ago they were quite commonly described as the Fixed Laws of Nature, and were supposed sufficient in themselves to govern the universe. Now we can only assign to them the humble rank of mere descriptions, often erroneous, of similarities which we believe we have observed. . . . . A law of nature explains nothing, it has no governing power, it is but a descriptive formula which the careless have sometimes personified." It used to be said that "the laws of Nature are the thoughts of God"; now we say that they are the investigator's formulae summing up regularities of recurrence.[1]

If natural law aims at prediction it tells us what we can do. Moral laws, on the other hand, tell us, not what we can, but what we ought to do.[2] The civil or municipal law, finally, tells us not what we can, nor what we ought, but what we must do. It is very evident that these three types of law may be very intimately related.

[1] J. Arthur Thomson, *The System of Animate Nature* (New York, 1920), pp. 8–9. See also Karl Pearson, *The Grammar of Science* (2d ed.; London, 1900), chap. iii.

[2] See Max Weber, *Gesammelte Aufsätze zur Wissenschaftslehre.* "Die 'Objektivität' sozialwissenschaftlicher und sozialpolitischer Erkenntnis," pp. 146–214. Tübingen, 1922.

We do not know what we ought to do until we know what we can do; and we certainly should consider what men can do before we pass laws prescribing what they must do. There is, moreover, no likelihood that these distinctions will ever be completely abolished. As long as the words "can," "ought," and "must" continue to have any meaning for us the distinctions that they represent will persist in science as well as in common sense.

The immense prestige which the methods of the natural sciences have gained, particularly in their application to the phenomena of the physical universe, has undoubtedly led scientific men to over-estimate the importance of mere conceptual and abstract knowledge. It has led them to assume that history also must eventually become "scientific" in the sense of the natural sciences. In the meantime the vast collections of historical facts which the industry of historical students has accumulated are regarded, sometimes even by historians themselves, as a sort of raw material, the value of which can only be realized after it has been worked over into some sort of historical generalization which has the general character of scientific and ultimately, mathematical formula.

"History," says Karl Pearson, "can never become science, can never be anything but a catalogue of facts rehearsed in a more. or less pleasing language until these facts are seen to fall into sequences which can be briefly resumed in scientific formulae."[1] And Henry Adams, in a letter to the American Historical Association already referred to, confesses that history has thus far been a fruitless quest for "the secret which would transform these odds and ends of philosophy into one self-evident, harmonious, and complete system."

You may be sure that four out of five serious students of history who are living today have, in the course of their work, felt that they stood on the brink of a great generalization that would reduce all history under a law as clear as the laws which govern the material world. As the great writers of our time have touched one by one the separate fragments of admitted law by which society betrays its character as a subject for science, not one of them can have failed to feel an instant's hope that he might find the secret which would transform these odds and ends of philosophy into one self-evident, harmonious, and complete system. He has seemed to have it, as the Spanish say, in his inkstand. Scores of times he must have dropped his pen to think how one short step, one sudden inspiration, would show all human knowledge; how, in these thickset forests of history, one corner

[1] Karl Pearson, *op. cit.*, p. 359.

turned, one faint trail struck, would bring him on the highroad of science. Every professor who has tried to teach the doubtful facts which we now call history must have felt that sooner or later he or another would put order in the chaos and bring light into darkness. Not so much genius or favor was needed as patience and good luck. The law was certainly there, and as certainly was in places actually visible, to be touched and handled, as though it were a law of chemistry or physics. No teacher with a spark of imagination or with an idea of scientific method can have helped dreaming of the immortality that would be achieved by the man who should successfully apply Darwin's method to the facts of human history.[1]

The truth is, however, that the concrete facts, in which history and geography have sought to preserve the visible, tangible, and, generally speaking, the experiential aspects of human life and the visible universe, have a value irrespective of any generalization or ideal constructions which may be inferred from or built up out of them. Just as none of the investigations or generalizations of individual psychology are ever likely to take the place of biography and autobiography, so none of the conceptions of an abstract sociology, no scientific descriptions of the social and cultural processes, and no laws of progress are likely, in the near future at any rate, to supersede the more concrete facts of history in which are preserved those records of those unique and never fully comprehended aspects of life which we call *events*.

It has been the dream of philosophers that theoretical and abstract science could and some day perhaps would succeed in putting into formulae and into general terms all that was significant in the concrete facts of life. It has been the tragic mistake of the so-called intellectuals, who have gained their knowledge from textbooks rather than from observation and research, to assume that science had already realized its dream. But there is no indication that science has begun to exhaust the sources or significance of concrete experience. The infinite variety of external nature and the inexhaustible wealth of personal experience have thus far defied, and no doubt will continue to defy, the industry of scientific classification, while, on the other hand, the discoveries of science are constantly making accessible to us new and larger areas of experience.

What has been said simply serves to emphasize the instrumental character of the abstract sciences. History and geography, all of

[1] Henry Adams, *op. cit.*, p. 127.

the concrete sciences, can and do measurably enlarge our experience of life. Their very purpose is to arouse new interests and create new sympathies; to give mankind, in short, an environment so vast and varied as will call out and activate all his instincts and capacities.

The more abstract sciences, just to the extent that they are abstract and exact, like mathematics and logic, are merely methods and tools for converting experience into knowledge and applying the knowledge so gained to practical uses.

IV. HISTORY, NATURAL HISTORY, AND SOCIOLOGY

Although it is possible to draw clear distinctions in theory between the purpose and methods of history and sociology, in practice the two forms of knowledge pass over into one another by almost imperceptible gradations.

The sociological point of view makes its appearance in historical investigation as soon as the historian turns from the study of "periods" to the study of institutions. The history of institutions, that is to say, the family, the church, economic institutions, political institutions, etc., leads inevitably to comparison, classification, the formation of class names or concepts, and eventually to the formulation of law. In the process, history becomes natural history, and natural history passes over into natural science. In short, history becomes sociology.

Westermarck's *History of Human Marriage* is one of the earliest attempts to write the natural history of a social institution. It is based upon a comparison and classification of marriage customs of widely scattered peoples, living under varied physical and social conditions. What one gets from a survey of this kind is not so much history as a study of human behavior. The history of marriage, as of any other institution, is, in other words, not so much an account of what certain individuals or groups of individuals did at certain times and certain places, as it is a description of the responses of a few fundamental human instincts to a variety of social situations. Westermarck calls this kind of history sociology.[1]

---

[1] Professor Robertson Smith (*Nature*, XLIV, 270), criticizing Westermarck's *History of Human Marriage*, complains that the author has confused history with natural history. "The history of an institution," he writes, "which is controlled by public opinion and regulated by law is not natural history. The true history of

It is in the firm conviction that the history of human civilization should be made an object of as scientific a treatment as the history of organic nature that I write this book. Like the phenomena of physical and psychical life those of social life should be classified into certain groups and each group investigated with regard to its origin and development. Only when treated in this way can history lay claim to the rank and honour of a science in the highest sense of the term, as forming an important part of Sociology, the youngest of the principal branches of learning.

Descriptive historiography has no higher object than that of offering materials to this science.[1]

Westermarck refers to the facts which he has collected in his history of marriage as phenomena. For the explanation of these phenomena, however, he looks to the more abstract sciences.

The causes on which social phenomena are dependent fall within the domain of different sciences—Biology, Psychology, or Sociology. The reader will find that I put particular stress upon the psychological causes, which have often been deplorably overlooked, or only imperfectly touched upon. And more especially do I believe that the mere instincts have played a very important part in the origin of social institutions and rules.[2]

Westermarck derived most of his materials for the study of marriage from ethnological materials. Ethnologists, students of folklore (German Völkerkunde), and archaeology are less certain than the historians of institutions whether their investigations are historical or sociological.

Jane Harrison, although she disclaims the title of sociologist, bases her conception of the origin of Greek religion on a sociological theory, the theory namely that "among primitive peoples religion reflects collective feeling and collective thinking." Dionysius, the

---

marriage begins where the natural history of pairing ends. . . . . To treat these topics (polyandry, kinship through the female only, infanticide, exogamy) as essentially a part of the natural history of pairing involves a tacit assumption that the laws of society are at bottom mere formulated instincts, and this assumption really underlies all our author's theories. His fundamental position compels him, if he will be consistent with himself, to hold that every institution connected with marriage that has universal validity, or forms an integral part of the main line of development, is rooted in instinct, and that institutions which are not based on instinct are necessarily exceptional and unimportant for scientific history."

[1] Edward Westermarck, *The History of Human Marriage* (London, 1901), p. 1.

[2] *Ibid.*, p. 5.

god of the Greek mysteries, is according to her interpretation a product of the group consciousness.

The mystery-god arises out of those instincts, emotions, desires which attend and express life; but these emotions, desires, instincts, in so far as they are religious, are at the outset rather of a group than of individual consciousness. . . . . It is a necessary and most important corollary to this doctrine, that the form taken by the divinity reflects the social structure of the group to which the divinity belongs. Dionysius is the Son of his Mother because he issues from a matrilinear group.[1]

This whole study is, in fact, merely an application of Durkheim's conception of "collective representations."

Robert H. Lowie, in his recent volume, *Primitive Society*, refers to "ethnologists and other historians," but at the same time asks: "What kind of an historian shall the ethnologist be?"

He answers the question by saying that, "If there are laws of social evolution, he [the ethnologist] must assuredly discover them," but at any rate, and first of all, "his duty is to ascertain the course civilization has *actually* followed. . . . . To strive for the ideals of another branch of knowledge may be positively pernicious, for it can easily lead to that factitious simplification which means falsification."

In other words, ethnology, like history, seeks to tell what actually happened. It is bound to avoid abstraction, "over-simplification," and formulae, and these are the ideals of another kind of scientific procedure. As a matter of fact, however, ethnology, even when it has attempted nothing more than a description of the existing cultures of primitive peoples, their present distribution and the order of their succession, has not freed itself wholly from the influence of abstract considerations. Theoretical problems inevitably arise for the solution of which it is necessary to go to psychology and sociology. One of the questions that has arisen in the study, particularly the comparative study, of cultures is: how far any existing cultural trait is borrowed and how far it is to be regarded as of independent origin.

In the historical reconstruction of culture the phenomena of distribution play, indeed, an extraordinary part. If a trait occurs everywhere, it might veritably be the product of some universally operative social law. If it is

[1] Jane Ellen Harrison, *Themis, A Study of the Social Origins of Greek Religion* (Cambridge, 1912), p. ix.

found in a restricted number of cases, it may still have evolved through some such instrumentality acting under specific conditions that would then remain to be determined by analysis of the cultures in which the feature is embedded. . . . . Finally, the sharers of a cultural trait may be of distinct lineage but through contact and borrowing have come to hold in common a portion of their cultures. . . . .

Since, as a matter of fact, cultural resemblances abound between peoples of diverse stock, their interpretation commonly narrows to a choice between two alternatives. Either they are due to like causes, whether these can be determined or not; or they are the result of borrowing. A predilection for one or the other explanation has lain at the bottom of much ethnological discussion in the past; and at present influential schools both in England and in continental Europe clamorously insist that all cultural parallels are due to diffusion from a single center. It is inevitable to envisage this moot-problem at the start, since uncompromising championship of either alternative has far-reaching practical consequences. For if every parallel is due to borrowing, then sociological laws, which can be inferred only from independently developing likenesses, are barred. Then the history of religion or social life or technology consists exclusively in a statement of the place of origin of beliefs, customs and implements, and a recital of their travels to different parts of the globe. On the other hand, if borrowing covers only part of the observed parallels, an explanation from like causes becomes at least the ideal goal in an investigation of the remainder.[1]

An illustration will exhibit the manner in which problems originally historical become psychological and sociological. Tylor in his *Early History of Mankind* has pointed out that the bellows used by the negro blacksmiths of continental Africa are of a quite different type from those used by natives of Madagascar. The bellows used by the Madagascar blacksmiths, on the other hand, are exactly like those in use by the Malays of Sumatra and in other parts of the Malay Archipelago. This indication that the natives of Madagascar are of Malay origin is in accordance with other anthropological and ethnological data in regard to these peoples, which prove the fact, now well established, that they are not of African origin.

Similarly Boas' study of the Raven cycle of American Indian mythology indicated that these stories originated in the northern part of British Columbia and traveled southward along the coast.

[1] Robert H. Lowie, *Primitive Society* (New York, 1920), pp. 7–8.

One of the evidences of the direction of this progress is the gradual diminution of complexity in the stories as they traveled into regions farther removed from the point of origin.

All this, in so far as it seeks to determine the point of origin, direction, speed, and character of changes that take place in cul-' tural materials in the process of diffusion, is clearly history and ethnology.

Other questions, however, force themselves inevitably upon the attention of the inquiring student. Why is it that certain cultural materials are more widely and more rapidly diffused than others? Under what conditions does this diffusion take place and why does it take place at all? Finally, what is the ultimate source of customs, beliefs, languages, religious practices, and all the varied technical devices which compose the cultures of different peoples? What are the circumstances and what are the processes by which cultural traits are independently created? Under what conditions do cultural fusions take place and what is the nature of this process?

These are all fundamentally problems of human nature, and as human nature itself is now regarded as a product of social intercourse, they are problems of sociology.

The cultural processes by which languages, myth, and religion have come into existence among primitive peoples have given rise in Germany to a special science. Folk-psychology (*Völkerpsychologie*) had its origin in an attempt to answer in psychological terms the problems to which a comparative study of cultural materials has given rise.

From two different directions ideas of folk-psychology have found their way into modern science. First of all there was a demand from the different social sciences [*Geisteswissenschaften*] for a psychological explanation of the phenomena of social life and history, so far as they were products of social [*geistiger*] interaction. In the second place, psychology itself required, in order to escape the uncertainties and ambiguities of pure introspection, a body of objective materials.

Among the social sciences the need for psychological interpretation first manifested itself in the studies of language and mythology. Both of these had already found outside the circle of the philological studies independent fields of investigation. As soon as they assumed the character of comparative sciences it was inevitable that they should be driven to recognize that in addition to the historical conditions, which everywhere determines the concrete form of these phenomena, there had been certain fundamental psychical forces at work in the development of language and myth.[1]

The aim of folk-psychology has been, on the whole, to explain the genesis and development of certain cultural forms, i.e., language, myth, and religion. The whole matter may, however, be regarded from a quite different point of view. Gabriel Tarde, for example, has sought to explain, not the genesis, but the transmission and diffusion of these same cultural forms. For Tarde, communication (transmission of cultural forms and traits) is the one central and significant fact of social life. "Social" is just what can be transmitted by imitation. Social groups are merely the centers from which new ideas and inventions are transmitted. Imitation is the social process.

There is not a word that you say, which is not the reproduction, now unconscious, but formerly conscious and voluntary, of verbal articulations reaching back to the most distant past, with some special accent due to your immediate surroundings. There is not a religious rite that you fulfil, such as praying, kissing the icon, or making the sign of the cross, which does not reproduce certain traditional gestures and expressions, established through imitation of your ancestors. There is not a military or civil requirement that you obey, nor an act that you perform in your business, which has not been taught you, and which you have not copied from some living model. There is not a stroke of the brush that you make, if you are a painter, nor a verse that you write, if you are a poet, which does not conform to the customs or the prosody of your school, and even your very originality itself is made up of accumulated commonplaces, and aspires to become commonplace in its turn. Thus, the unvarying characteristic of every social fact whatsoever is that it is imitative. And this characteristic belongs exclusively to social facts.[2]

Tarde's theory of transmission by imitation may be regarded, in some sense, as complementary, if not supplementary, to Wundt's

[1] Wilhelm Wundt, *Völkerpsychologie, eine Untersuchung der Entwicklungsgesetze von Sprache, Mythus und Sitte.* Erster Band, *Die Sprache*, Erster Theil (Leipzig, 1900), p. 13. The name folk-psychology was first used by Lazarus and Steinthal, *Zeitschrift für Völkerpsychologie und Sprachwissenschaft*, I, 1860. Wundt's folk-psychology is a continuation of the tradition of these earlier writers.

[2] G. Tarde, *Social Laws, An Outline of Sociology*, translated from the French by Howard C. Warren (New York, 1899), pp. 40–41.

theory of origins, since he puts the emphasis on the fact of transmission rather than upon genesis. In a paper, "Tendencies in Comparative Philology," read at the Congress of Arts and Sciences at the St. Louis Exposition in 1904, Professor Hanns Oertel, of Yale University, refers to Tarde's theory of imitation as an alternative explanation to that offered by Wundt for "the striking uniformity of sound changes" which students of language have discovered in the course of their investigation of phonetic changes in widely different forms of speech.

It seems hard to maintain that the change in a syntactical construction or in the meaning of a word owes its universality to a simultaneous and independent primary change in all the members of a speech-community. By adopting the theory of imitative spread, all linguistic changes may be viewed as one homogeneous whole. In the second place, the latter view seems to bring linguistic changes into line with the other social changes, such as modifications in institutions, beliefs, and customs. For is it not an essential characteristic of a social group that its members are not co-operative in the sense that each member actively participates in the production of every single element which goes to make up either language, or belief, or customs? Distinguishing thus between *primary* and *secondary* changes and between the *origin* of a change and its *spread*, it behooves us to examine carefully into the causes which make the members of a social unit, either consciously or unconsciously, willing to accept the innovation. What is it that determines acceptance or rejection of a particular change? What limits one change to a small area, while it extends the area of another? Before a final decision can be reached in favor of the second theory of imitative spread it will be necessary to follow out in minute detail the mechanism of this process in a number of concrete instances; in other words to fill out the picture of which Tarde (*Les lois de l'imitation*) sketched the bare outlines. If his assumptions prove true, then we should have here a uniformity resting upon other causes than the physical uniformity that appears in the objects with which the natural sciences deal. It would enable us to establish a second group of uniform phenomena which is psycho-physical in its character and rests upon the basis of social suggestion. The uniformities in speech, belief, and institutions would belong to this second group.[1]

What is true of the comparative study of languages is true in every other field in which a comparative study of cultural materials

[1] Hanns Oertel, "Some Present Problems and Tendencies in Comparative Philology," *Congress of Arts and Science, Universal Exposition, St. Louis, 1904* (Boston, 1906), III, 59.

has been made. As soon as these materials are studied from the point of view of their similarities rather than from the point of view of their historical connections, problems arise which can only be explained by the more abstract sciences of psychology or sociology. Freeman begins his lectures on *Comparative Politics* with the statement that "the comparative method of study has been the greatest intellectual achievement of our time. It has carried light and order into whole branches of human knowledge which before were shrouded in darkness and confusion. It has brought a line of argument which reaches moral certainty into a region which before was given over to random guess-work. Into matters which are for the most part incapable of strictly external proof it has brought a form of strictly internal proof which is more convincing, more unerring."

Wherever the historian supplements *external* by *internal* proof, he is in a way to substitute a sociological explanation for historical interpretation. It is the very essence of the sociological method to be comparative. When, therefore, Freeman uses, in speaking of comparative politics, the following language he is speaking in sociological rather than historical terms:

For the purposes then of the study of Comparative Politics, a political constitution is a specimen to be studied, classified, and labelled, as a building or an animal is studied, classified, and labelled by those to whom buildings or animals are objects of study. We have to note the likenesses, striking and unexpected as those likenesses often are, between the political constitutions of remote times and places; and we have, as far as we can, to classify our specimens according to the probable causes of those likenesses.[1]

Historically sociology has had its origin in history. It owes its existence as a science to the attempt to apply exact methods to the explanation of historical facts. In the attempt to achieve this, however, it has become something quite different from history. It has become like psychology with which it is most intimately related, a natural and relatively abstract science, and auxiliary to the study of history, but not a substitute for it. The whole matter may be summed up in this general statement: history interprets, natural science explains. It is upon the interpretation of the facts of experience that we formulate our creeds and found our faiths. Our

[1] Edward A. Freeman, *Comparative Politics* (London, 1873), p. 23.

explanations of phenomena, on the other hand, are the basis for technique and practical devices for controlling nature and human nature, man and the physical world.

V.   THE SOCIAL ORGANISM: HUMANITY OR LEVIATHAN?

After Comte the first great name in the history of sociology is Spencer. It is evident in comparing the writings of these two men that, in crossing the English Channel, sociology has suffered a sea change. In spite of certain similarities in their points of view there are profound and interesting differences. These differences exhibit themselves in the different ways in which they use the term "social organism."

Comte calls society a "collective organism" and insists, as Spencer does, upon the difference between an organism like a family, which is made up of independent individuals, and an organism like a plant or an animal, which is a physiological unit in which the different organs are neither free nor conscious. But Spencer, if he points out the differences between the social and the biological organisms, is interested in the analogy. Comte, on the other hand, while he recognizes the analogy, feels it important to emphasize the distinctions.

Society for Comte is not, as Lévy-Bruhl puts it, "a polyp." It has not even the characteristics of an animal colony in which the individuals are physically bound together, though physiologically independent. On the contrary, "this 'immense organism' is especially distinguished from other beings in that it is made up of separable elements of which each one can feel its own co-operation, can will it, or even withhold it, so long as it remains a direct one."[1]

On the other hand, Comte, although he characterized the social *consensus* and solidarity as "collective," nevertheless thought of the relations existing between human beings in society—in the family, for example, which he regards as the unit and model of all social relations—as closer and more intimate than those which exist between the organs of a plant or an animal. The individual, as Comte expressed it, is an abstraction. Man exists as man only by participation in the life of humanity, and "although the individual

[1] L. Lévy-Bruhl, *The Philosophy of Auguste Comte*, authorized translation; an Introduction by Frederic Harrison (New York, 1903), p. 337.

elements of society appear to be more separable than those of a living being, the social *consensus* is still closer than the vital."[1]

Thus the individual man was, in spite of his freedom and independence, in a very real sense "an organ of the Great Being" and the great being was humanity. Under the title of humanity Comte included not merely all living human beings, i.e., the human race, but he included all that body of tradition, knowledge, custom, cultural ideas and ideals, which make up the social inheritance of the race, an inheritance into which each of us is born, to which we contribute, and which we inevitably hand on through the processes of education and tradition to succeeding generations. This is what Comte meant by the social organism.

If Comte thought of the social organism, the great being, somewhat mystically as itself an individual and a person, Herbert Spencer, on the other hand, thought of it realistically as a great animal, a leviathan, as Hobbes called it, and a very low-order leviathan at that.[2]

Spencer's manner of looking at the social organism may be illustrated in what he says about growth in "social aggregates."

When we say that growth is common to social aggregates and organic aggregates, we do not thus entirely exclude community with inorganic aggregates. Some of these, as crystals, grow in a visible manner; and all of them on the hypothesis of evolution, have arisen by integration at some time or other. Nevertheless, compared with things we call inanimate, living bodies and societies so conspicuously exhibit augmentation of mass, that we may fairly regard this as characterizing them both. Many organisms grow throughout their lives; and the rest grow throughout considerable

---

[1] *Ibid.*, p. 234.

[2] Hobbes's statement is as follows: "For by art is created that great *Leviathan* called a *Commonwealth*, or *State*, in Latin *Civitas*, which is but an artificial man; though of greater stature and strength than the natural, for whose protection and defence it was intended; and in which the *sovereignty* is an artificial *soul*, as giving life and motion to the whole body; the *magistrates*, and other *officers* of judicature, artificial *joints; reward* and *punishment*, by which fastened to the seat of the sovereignty every joint and member is moved to perform his duty, are the *nerves*, that do the same in the body natural." Spencer criticizes this conception of Hobbes as representing society as a "factitious" and artificial rather than a "natural" product. Herbert Spencer, *The Principles of Sociology* (London, 1893), I, 437, 579–80. See also chap. iii, "Social Growth," pp. 453–58.

parts of their lives. Social growth usually continues either up to times when the societies divide, or up to times when they are overwhelmed.

Here, then, is the first trait by which societies ally themselves with the organic world and substantially distinguish themselves from the inorganic world.[1]

In this same way, comparing the characteristic general features of "social" and "living bodies," noting likeness and differences, particularly with reference to complexity of structure, differentiation of function, division of labor, etc., Spencer gives a perfectly naturalistic account of the characteristic identities and differences between societies and animals, between sociological and biological organizations. It is in respect to the division of labor that the analogy between societies and animals goes farthest and is most significant.

This division of labour, first dwelt upon by political economists as a social phenomenon, and thereupon recognized by biologists as a phenomenon of living bodies, which they called the "physiological division of labour," is that which in the society, as in the animal, makes it a living whole. Scarcely can I emphasize enough the truth that in respect of this fundamental trait, a social organism and an individual organism are entirely alike.[2]

The "social aggregate," although it is "discrete" instead of "concrete"—that is to say, composed of spatially separated units—is nevertheless, because of the mutual dependence of these units upon one another as exhibited in the division of labor, to be regarded as a living whole. It is "a living whole" in much the same way that the plant and animal communities, of which the ecologists are now writing so interestingly, are a living whole; not because of any intrinsic relations between the individuals who compose them, but because each individual member of the community, finds in the community as a whole, a suitable milieu, an environment adapted to his needs and one to which he is able to adapt himself.

Of such a society as this it may indeed be said, that it "exists for the benefit of its members, not its members for the benefit of society. It has ever to be remembered that great as may be the efforts made for the prosperity of the body politic, yet the claims of the body politic are nothing in themselves, and become something

---

[1] Herbert Spencer, op. cit., I, 437.

[2] Ibid., p. 440.

only in so far as they embody the claims of its component individuals."[1]

In other words, the social organism, as Spencer sees it, exists
not for itself but for the benefit of the separate organs of which it is
composed, whereas, in the case of biological organism the situation
is reversed. There the parts manifestly exist for the whole and not
the whole for the parts.

Spencer explains this paradoxical conclusion by the reflection
that in social organisms sentience is not localized as it is in biological
organisms. This is, in fact, the cardinal difference between the two.
There is no *social sensorium*.

In the one (the individual), consciousness is concentrated in a small
part of the aggregate. In the other (society), it is diffused throughout the
aggregate: all the units possess the capacities for happiness and misery, if
not in equal degrees, still in degrees that approximate. As then, there is no
social sensorium, the welfare of the aggregate, considered apart from that of
the units, is not an end to be sought. The society exists for the benefit
of its members; not its members for the benefit of the society.[2]

The point is that society, *as distinct from the individuals* who
compose it, has no apparatus for feeling pain or pleasure. There
are no *social* sensations. Perceptions and mental imagery are individual and not social phenomena. Society lives, so to speak, only
in its separate organs or members, and each of these organs has its
own brain and organ of control which gives it, among other things,
the power of independent locomotion. This is what is meant when
society is described as a collectivity.

VI.   SOCIAL CONTROL AND SCHOOLS OF THOUGHT

The fundamental problem which Spencer's paradox raises is
that of social control. How does a mere collection of individuals
succeed in acting in a corporate and consistent way? How in the
case of specific types of social group, for example an animal herd,
a boys' gang, or a political party, does the group control its individual
members; the whole dominate the parts? What are the specific
sociological differences between plant and animal communities and
human society? What kind of differences are *sociological differences*,

---

[1] *Ibid.*, p. 450.   [2] *Ibid.*, pp. 449–50.

and what do we mean in general by the expression "sociological" anyway ?

Since Spencer's essay on the social organism was published in 1860,[1] this problem and these questions, in one form or another, have largely absorbed the theoretical interest of students of society.   The attempts to answer them may be said to have created the existing schools into which sociologists are divided.

A certain school of writers, among them Paul Lilienfeld, Albert Schaeffle, and René Worms, have sought to maintain, to extend, or modify the biological analogy first advanced by Spencer.   In doing so they have succeeded sometimes in restating the problem but have not solved it.   René Worms has been particularly ingenious in discovering identities and carrying out the parallelism between the social and the biological organizations.   As a result he has reached the conclusion that, as between a social and a biological organism, there is no difference of kind but only one of degree.   Spencer, who could not find a "social sensorium," said that society was conscious only in the individuals who composed it.   Worms, on the other hand, declares that we must assume the existence of a social consciousness, even without a sensorium, because we see everywhere the evidence of its existence.

Force manifests itself by its effects.   If there are certain phenomena that we can only make intelligible, provided we regard them as the products of collective social consciousness, then we are bound to assume the existence of such a consciousness.   There are many illustrations . . . . the attitude for example, of a crowd in the presence of a crime.   Here the sentiment of indignation is unanimous.   A murderer, if taken in the act, will get summary justice from the ordinary crowd.   That method of rendering justice, "lynch law," is deplorable, but it illustrates the intensity of the sentiment which, at the moment, takes possession of the social consciousness.

Thus, always in the presence of great and common danger the collective consciousness of society is awakened; for example France of the Valois after the Treaty of Troyes, or modern France before the invasion of 1791 and before the German invasion in 1870; or Germany, herself, after the victories of Napoleon I.   This sentiment of national unity, born of resistance to the stranger. goes so far that a large proportion of the members of society do not hesitate to give their lives for the safety and glory of the state; at such a moment the individual comprehends that he is only a small part of

[1] *Westminster Review*, January, 1860.

a large whole and that he belongs to the collectivity of which he is a member. The proof that he is entirely penetrated by the social consciousness is the fact that in order to maintain its existence he is willing to sacrifice his own.[1]

There is no question that the facts of crowd excitement, of class, caste, race, and national consciousness, do show the way in which the individual members of a group are, or seem to be, dominated, at certain moments and under certain circumstances, by the group as a whole. Worms gives to this fact, and the phenomena which accompany it, the title "collective consciousness." This gives the problem a name, to be sure, but not a solution. What the purpose of sociology requires is a description and an explanation. Under what conditions, precisely, does this phenomenon of collective consciousness arise? What are the mechanisms—physical, physiological, and social—by which the group imposes its control, or what seems to be control, upon the individual members of the group?

This question had arisen and been answered by political philosophers, in terms of political philosophy, long before sociology attempted to give an objective account of the matter. Two classic phrases, Aristotle's "Man is a political animal" and Hobbes's "War of each against all," *omnes bellum omnium*, measure the range and divergence of the schools upon this topic.

According to Hobbes, the existing moral and political order— that is to say the organization of control—is in any community a mere artefact, a control resting on consent, supported by a prudent calculation of consequences, and enforced by an external power. Aristotle, on the other hand, taught that man was made for life in society just as the bee is made for life in the hive. The relations between the sexes, as well as those between mother and child, are manifestly predetermined in the physiological organization of the individual man and woman. Furthermore, man is, by his instincts and his inherited dispositions, predestined to a social existence beyond the intimate family circle. Society must be conceived, therefore, as a part of nature, like a beaver's dam or the nests of birds.

As a matter of fact, man and society present themselves in a double aspect. They are at the same time products of nature and

[1] René Worms, *Organisme et Société*, "Bibliothèque Sociologique Internationale" (Paris, 1896), pp. 210–13.

of human artifice. Just as a stone hammer in the hand of a savage may be regarded as an artificial extension of the natural man, so tools, machinery, technical and administrative devices, including the formal organization of government and the informal "political machine," may be regarded as more or less artificial extensions of the natural social group.

So far as this is true, the conflict between Hobbes and Aristotle is not absolute. Society is a product both of nature and of design, of instinct and of reason. If, in its formal aspect, society is therefore an artefact, it is one which connects up with and has its roots in nature and in human nature.

This does not explain social control but simplifies the problem of corporate action. It makes clear, at any rate, that as members of society, men act as they do elsewhere from motives they do not fully comprehend, in order to fulfil aims of which they are but dimly or not at all conscious. Men are activated, in short, not merely by interests, in which they are conscious of the end they seek, but also by instincts and sentiments, the source and meaning of which they do not clearly comprehend. Men work for wages, but they will die to preserve their status in society, or commit murder to resent an insult. When men act thus instinctively, or under the influence of the mores, they are usually quite unconscious of the sources of the impulses that animate them or of the ends which are realized through their acts. Under the influence of the mores men act typically, and so representatively, not as individuals but as members of a group.

The simplest type of social group in which we may observe "social control" is in a herd or a flock. The behavior of a herd of cattle is, to be sure, not so uniform nor so simple a matter as it seems to the casual observer, but it may be very properly taken as an illustration of the sort of follow-the-leader uniformity that is more or less characteristic of all social groups. We call the disposition to live in the herd and to move in masses, gregariousness, and this gregariousness is ordinarily regarded as an instinct and undoubtedly is pretty regally determined in the original nature of gregarious animals.

There is a school of thought which seeks in the so-called gregarious instincts an explanation of all that is characteristically social in the behavior of human beings.

The cardinal quality of the herd is homogeneity. It is clear that the great advantage of the social habit is to enable large numbers to act as one, whereby in the case of the hunting gregarious animal strength in pursuit and attack is at once increased to beyond that of the creatures preyed upon, and in protective socialism the sensitiveness of the new unit to alarms is greatly in excess of that of the individual member of the flock.

To secure these advantages of homogeneity, it is evident that the members of the herd must possess sensitiveness to the behaviour of their fellows. The individual isolated will be of no meaning, the individual as a part of the herd will be capable of transmitting the most potent impulses. Each member of the flock tending to follow its neighbour and in turn to be followed, each is in some sense capable of leadership; but no lead will be followed that departs widely from normal behaviour. A lead will be followed only from its resemblance to the normal. If the leader go so far ahead as definitely to cease to be in the herd, he will necessarily be ignored.

The original in conduct, that is to say, resistiveness to the voice of the herd, will be suppressed by natural selection; the wolf which does not follow the impulses of the herd will be starved; the sheep which does not respond to the flock will be eaten.

Again, not only will the individual be responsive to impulses coming from the herd, but he will treat the herd as his normal environment. The impulse to be in and always to remain with the herd will have the strongest instinctive weight. Anything which tends to separate him from his fellows, as soon as it becomes perceptible as such, will be strongly resisted.[1]

According to sociologists of his school, public opinion, conscience, and authority in the state rest upon the natural disposition of the animal in the herd to conform to "the decrees of the herd."

Conscience, then, and the feelings of guilt and of duty are the peculiar possessions of the gregarious animal. A dog and a cat caught in the commission of an offence will both recognize that punishment is coming; but the dog, moreover, knows that he has done *wrong*, and he will come to be punished, unwillingly it is true, and as if dragged along by some power outside him, while the cat's sole impulse is to escape. The rational recognition of the sequence of act and punishment is equally clear to the gregarious and to the solitary animal, but it is the former only who understands that he has committed a *crime*, who has, in fact, the *sense of sin*.[2]

[1] W. Trotter, *Instincts of the Herd in Peace and War* (New York, 1916), pp. 29–30.

[2] *Ibid.*, pp. 40–41.

The concept upon which this explanation of society rests is *homogeneity*. If animals or human beings act under all circumstances in the same way, they will act or seem to act, as if they had a common purpose. If everybody follows the crowd, if everyone wears the same clothes, utters the same trite remarks, rallies to the same battles cries and is everywhere dominated, even in his most characteristically individual behavior, by an instinctive and passionate desire to conform to an external model and to the wishes of the herd, then we have an explanation of everything characteristic of society— except the variants, the nonconformists, the idealists, and the rebels. The herd instinct may be an explanation of conformity but it does not explain variation.   Variation is an important fact in society as it is in nature generally.

Homogeneity and like-mindedness are, as explanations of the social behavior of men and animals, very closely related concepts. In "like response to like stimulus," we may discern the beginning of "concerted action" and this, it is urged, is the fundamental social fact.   This is the "like-mindedness" theory of society which has been given wide popularity in the United States through the writings of Professor Franklin Henry Giddings.   He describes it as a "developed form of the instinct theory, dating back to Aristotle's aphorism that man is a political animal."

Any given stimulus may happen to be felt by more than one organism, at the same or at different times.   Two or more organisms may respond to the same given stimulus simultaneously or at different times.   They may respond to the same given stimulus in like or in unlike ways; in the same or in different degrees; with like or with unlike promptitude; with equal or with unequal persistence.   I have attempted to show that in like response to the same given stimulus we have the beginning, the absolute origin, of all concerted activity—the inception of every conceivable form of co-operation; while in unlike response, and in unequal response, we have the beginning of all those processes of individuation, of differentiation, of competition, which in their endlessly varied relations to combination, to co-operation, bring about the infinite complexity of organized social life.[1]

Closely related, logically if not historically, to Giddings' conception of "like-mindedness" is Gabriel Tarde's conception of

[1] Franklin Henry Giddings, *The Concepts and Methods of Sociology*, Congress of Arts and Science, Universal Exposition (St. Louis, 1904), pp. 789–90.

"imitation." If for Giddings "like response to like stimulus" is the fundamental social fact, for Tarde "imitation" is the process through which alone society exists. Society, said Tarde, exists in imitation. As a matter of fact, Tarde's doctrine may be regarded as a corollary to Giddings'. Imitation is the process by which that like-mindedness, by which Giddings explains corporate action, is effected. Men are not born like-minded, they are made so by imitation.

This minute inter-agreement of minds and wills, which forms the basis of the social life, even in troublous times—this presence of so many common ideas, ends, and means, in the minds and wills of all members of the same society at any given moment—is not due, I maintain, to organic heredity, which insures the birth of men quite similar to one another, nor to mere identity of geographical environment, which offers very similar resources to talents that are nearly equal; it is rather the effect of that suggestion-imitation process which, starting from one primitive creature possessed of a single idea or act, passed this copy on to one of its neighbors, then to another, and so on. Organic needs and spiritual tendencies exist in us only as potentialities which are realizable under the most diverse forms, in spite of their primitive similarity; and, among all these possible realizations, the indications furnished by some first initiator who is imitated determine which one is actually chosen.[1]

In contrast with these schools, which interpret action in terms of the herd and the flock—i.e., men act together because they act alike—is the theory of Émile Durkheim who insists that the social group has real corporate existence and that, in human societies at least, men act together not because they have like purposes but a *common purpose*. This common purpose imposes itself upon the individual members of a society at the same time as an ideal, a wish and an obligation. Conscience, the sense of obligation which members of a group feel only when there is conflict between the wishes of the individual and the will of the group, is a manifestation, *in* the individual consciousness, of the collective mind and the group will. The mere fact that in a panic or a stampede, human beings will sometimes, like the Gadarene swine, rush down a steep place into the sea, is a very positive indication of like-mindedness but not an evidence of a common purpose. The difference between an animal herd and a human crowd is that the crowd, what Le Bon calls the "organized crowd," the crowd "in being" to use a nautical term, is dominated by

[1] G. Tarde, *op. cit.*, pp. 38–39.

an impulse to achieve a purpose that is common to every member of the group. Men in a state of panic, on the other hand, although equally under the influence of the mass excitement, act not corporately but individually, each individual wildly seeking to save his own skin. Men in a state of panic have like purposes but no common purpose. If the "organized crowd," "the psychological crowd," is a society "in being," the panic and the stampede is a society "in dissolution."

Durkheim does not use these illustrations nor does he express himself in these terms. The conception of the "organized" or "psychological" crowd is not his, but Le Bon's. The fact is that Durkheim does not think of a society as a mere sum of particulars. Neither does he think of the sentiments nor the opinions which dominate the social group as private and subjective. When individuals come together *under certain circumstances*, the opinions and sentiments which they held as individuals are modified and changed under the influence of the new contacts. Out of the fermentation which association breeds, a new something (*autre chose*) is produced, an opinion and sentiment, in other words, that is not the sum of, and not like, the sentiments and opinions of the individuals from which it is derived. This new sentiment and opinion is public, and social, and the evidence of this is the fact that it imposes itself upon the individuals concerned as something more or less external to them. They feel it either as an inspiration, a sense of personal release and expansion, or as an obligation, a pressure and an inhibition. The characteristic social phenomenon is just this control by the group as a whole of the individuals that compose it. This fact of control, then, is the fundamental social fact.

Now society also gives the sensation of a perpetual dependence. Since it has a nature which is peculiar to itself and different from our individual nature, it pursues ends which are likewise special to it; but, as it cannot attain them except through our intermediacy, it imperiously demands our aid. It requires that, forgetful of our own interests, we make ourselves its servitors, and it submits us to every sort of inconvenience, privation and sacrifice, without which social life would be impossible. It is because of this that at every instant we are obliged to submit ourselves to rules of conduct and of thought which we have neither made nor desired, and which are sometimes even contrary to our most fundamental inclinations and instincts.

Even if society were unable to maintain these concessions and sacrifices from us except by a material constraint, it might awaken in us only the idea of a physical force to which we must give way of necessity, instead of that of a moral power such as religions adore. But as a matter of fact, the empire which it holds over consciences is due much less to the physical supremacy of which it has the privilege than to the moral authority with which it is invested. If we yield to its orders, it is not merely because it is strong enough to triumph over our resistance; it is primarily because it is the object of a venerable respect.

Now the ways of action to which society is strongly enough attached to impose them upon its members, are, by that very fact, marked with a distinctive sign provocative of respect. Since they are elaborated in common, the vigour with which they have been thought of by each particular mind is retained in all the other minds, and reciprocally. The representations which express them within each of us have an intensity which no purely private states of consciousness could ever attain; for they have the strength of the innumerable individual representations which have served to form each of them. It is society who speaks through the mouths of those who affirm them in our presence; it is society whom we hear in hearing them; and the voice of all has an accent which that of one alone could never have. The very violence with which society reacts, by way of blame or material suppression, against every attempted dissidence, contributes to strengthening its empire by manifesting the common conviction through this burst of ardour. In a word, when something is the object of such a state of opinion, the representation which each individual has of it gains a power of action from its origins and the conditions in which it was born, which even those feel who do not submit themselves to it. It tends to repel the representations which contradict it, and it keeps them at a distance; on the other hand it commands those acts which will realize it, and it does so, not by a material coercion or by the perspective of something of this sort, but by the simple radiation of the mental energy which it contains.[1]

But the same social forces, which are found organized in public opinion, in religious symbols, in social convention, in fashion, and in science—for "if a people did not have faith in science all the scientific demonstrations in the world would be without any influence whatsoever over their minds"—are constantly re-creating the old order, making new heroes, overthrowing old gods, creating new myths, and imposing new ideals. And this is the nature of the cultural process of which sociology is a description and an explanation.

[1] Émile Durkheim, *Elementary Forms of Religious Life* (New York, 1915), pp. 206–8.

VII. SOCIAL CONTROL AND THE COLLECTIVE MIND

Durkheim is sometimes referred to, in comparison with other contemporary sociologists, as a realist. This is a reference to the controversy of the medieval philosophers in regard to the nature of concepts. Those who thought a concept a mere class-name applied to a group of objects because of some common characteristics were called nominalists. Those who thought the concept was *real*, and not the name of a mere collection of individuals, were realists. In this sense Tarde and Giddings and all those writers who think of society as a collection of actually or potentially *like-minded* persons would be nominalists, while other writers like Simmel, Ratzenhofer, and Small, who think of society in terms of interaction and social process may be called realists. They are realist, at any rate, in so far as they think of the members of a society as bound together in a system of mutual influences which has sufficient character to be described as a process.

Naturally this process cannot be conceived of in terms of space or physical proximity alone. Social contacts and social forces are of a subtler sort but not less real than physical. We know, for example, that vocations are largely determined by personal competition; that the solidarity of what Sumner calls the "in" or "we" group is largely determined by its conflict with the "out" or "other" groups. We know, also, that the status and social position of any individual inside any social group is determined by his relation to all other members of that group and eventually of all other groups. These are illustrations of what is meant concretely by social interaction and social process and it is considerations of this kind which seem to justify certain writers in thinking of individual persons as "parts" and of society as a "whole" in some other sense than that in which a dust heap is a whole of which the individual particles are parts.

Society not only continues to exist *by* transmission, *by* communication, but it may fairly be said to exist *in* transmission, *in* communication. There is more than a verbal tie between the words common, community, and communication.[1]

Communication, if not identical with, is at least a form of, what has been referred to here as social interaction. But communication

[1] John Dewey, *Democracy and Education* (New York, 1916), p. 5.

as Dewey has defined the term, is something more and different than what Tarde calls "inter-stimulation." Communication is a process by which we "transmit" an experience from an individual to another but it is also a process by which these same individuals get a common experience.

Try the experiment of communicating, with fullness and accuracy, some experience to another, especially if it be somewhat complicated, and you will find your own attitude toward your experience changing; otherwise you resort to expletives and ejaculations. Except in dealing with common-places and catch phrases one has to assimilate, imaginatively, something of another's experience in order to tell him intelligently of one's own experience. All communication is like art.[1]

Not only does communication involve the creation, out of experiences that are individual and private, of an experience that is common and public but such a common experience becomes the basis for a common and public existence in which every individual, to greater or less extent, participates and is himself a part. Furthermore, as a part of this common life, there grows up a body of custom, convention, tradition, ceremonial, language, social ritual, public opinion, in short all that Sumner includes under the term "mores" and all that ethnologists include under the term "culture."

The thing that characterizes Durkheim and his followers is their insistence upon the fact that all cultural materials, and expressions, including language, science, religion, public opinion, and law, since they are the products of social intercourse and social interaction, are bound to have an objective, public, and social character such as no product of an individual mind either has or can have. Durkheim speaks of these mental products, individual and social, as representations. The characteristic product of the individual mind is the percept, or, as Durkheim describes it, the "individual representation." The percept is, and remains, a private and an individual matter. No one can reproduce, or communicate to another, subjective impressions or the mental imagery in the concrete form in which they come to the individual himself. My neighbor may be able to read my "thoughts" and understand the motives that impel me to action better than I understand myself, but he cannot reproduce the images, with just the fringes of sense and feeling with which they come to my mind.

[1] *Ibid.*, pp. 6–7.

The characteristic product of a group of individuals, in their efforts to communicate is, on the other hand, something objective and understood, that is, a gesture, a sign, a symbol, a word, or a concept in which an experience or purpose that was private becomes public. This gesture, sign, symbol, concept, or representation in which a common object is not merely indicated, but in a sense created, Durkheim calls a "collective representation."

Dewey's description of what takes place in communication may be taken as a description of the process by which these collective representations come into existence. "To formulate an experience," as Dewey says, "requires getting outside of it, seeing it as another would see it, considering what points of contact it has with the life of another so that it may be gotten into such form that he can appreciate its meaning." The result of such a conscious effort to communicate an experience is to transform it. The experience, after it has been communicated, is not the same for either party to the communication. To publish or to give publicity o an event is to make of that event something other than it was before publication. Furthermore, the event as published is still something different from the event as reflected in the minds of the individuals to whom the publication is addressed.

It will be evident upon reflection that public opinion is not the opinion of all, nor even of a majority of the persons who compose a public. As a matter of fact, what we ordinarily mean by public opinion is never the opinion of anyone in particular. It is composite opinion, representing a general tendency of the public as a whole. On the other hand, we recognize that public opinion exists, even when we do not know of any individual person, among those who compose the public, whose private and personal opinion exactly coincides with that of the public of which he or she is a part.

Nevertheless, the private and personal opinion of an individual who participates in making public opinion is influenced by the opinions of those around him, and by public opinion. In this sense every opinion is public opinion.

Public opinion, in respect to the manner in which it is formed and the manner in which it exists—that is to say relatively independent of the individuals who co-operate to form it—has the characteristics of collective representation in general. Collective representations are objective, in just the sense that public opinion is objective, and they impose themselves upon the individual as public opinion does, as relatively but not wholly external forces—stabilizing, standardizing, conventionalizing, as well as stimulating, extending, and generalizing individual representations, percepts.

The collective representations are exterior to the individual consciousness because they are not derived from the individuals taken in isolation but from their convergence and union (concours). . . . . Doubtless, in the elaboration of the common result, each (individual) bears his due share; but the private sentiments do not become social except by combining under the action of the forces *sui generis* which association develops. As a result of these combinations, and of the mutual alterations which result therefrom, they (the private sentiments) become something else (*autre chose*). A chemical synthesis results, which concentrates, unifies, the elements synthetized, and by that very process transforms them. . . . . The resultant derived therefrom extends then beyond (*deborde*) the individual mind as the whole is greater than the part. To know really what it is, one must take the aggregate in its totality. It is this that thinks, that feels, that wills, although it may not be able to will, feel, or act save by the intermediation of individual consciousnesses.[1]

This, then, after nearly a century of criticism, is what remains of Comte's conception of the social organism. If society is, as the realists insist, anything more than a collection of like-minded individuals, it is so because of the existence (1) of a social process and (2) of a body of tradition and opinion—the products of this process—which has a relatively objective character and imposes itself upon the individual as a form of control, social control. This process and its product are the social consciousness. The social consciousness, in its double aspect as process and product, is the social organism. The controversy between the realists and the nominalists reduces itself apparently to this question of the objectivity of social tradition and of public opinion. For the present we may let it rest there.

Meanwhile the conceptions of the social consciousness and the social mind have been adopted by writers on social topics who are not at all concerned with their philosophical implications or legitimacy.

[1] Émile Durkheim, "Représentations individuelles et représentations collectives," *Revue métaphysique*, VI (1898), 295. Quoted and translated by Charles Elmer Gehlke, "Émile Durkheim's Contributions to Sociological Theory." *Studies in History, Economics, and Public Law*, LXIII, 29–30.

We are just now seeing the first manifestations of two new types of sociology which call themselves, the one rural and the other urban sociology. Writers belonging to these two schools are making studies of what they call the "rural" and the "urban" minds. In using these terms they are not always quite certain whether the mind of which they are thinking is a collective mind, in Durkheim's realistic sense of the word, or whether it is the mind of the typical inhabitant of a rural or an urban community, an instance of "like-mindedness," in the sense of Giddings and the nominalists.

A similar usage of the word "mind," "the American mind," for example, is common in describing characteristic differences in the attitudes of different nations and their "nationals."

The origin of the phrase, "the American mind," was political. Shortly after the middle of the eighteenth century, there began to be a distinctly American way of regarding the debatable question of British Imperial control. During the period of the Stamp Act agitation our colonial-bred politicians and statesmen made the discovery that there was a mode of thinking and feeling which was native—or had by that time become a second nature—to all the colonists. Jefferson, for example, employs those resonant and useful words "the American mind" to indicate that throughout the American colonies an essential unity of opinion had been developed as regards the chief political question of the day.[1]

Here again, it is not quite clear, whether the American mind is a name for a characteristic uniformity in the minds of individual Americans; whether the phrase refers rather to an "essential unity of opinion," or whether, finally, it is intended to cover both the uniformity and the unity characteristic of American opinion.

Students of labor problems and of the so-called class struggle, on the other hand, use the term "psychology" in much the same way that the students of rural and urban sociology use the term "mind." They speak of the "psychology" of the laboring class, the "psychology" of the capitalistic class, in cases where psychology seems to refer indifferently either to the social attitudes of the members of a class, or to attitude and morale of the class as a whole.

The terms "class-conscious" and "class-consciousness," "national" and "racial" consciousness are now familiar terms to students although they seem to have been used, first of all, by the so-called

[1] Bliss Perry, *The American Mind* (Boston, 1912), p. 47.

"intelligentsia", who have been the leaders in the various types of mass movement to which these terms apply. "Consciousn﹐ ﹐s," in the sense in which it is here used, has a similar, though somewhat different, connotation than the word "mind" when applied to a group. It is a name not merely for the attitudes characteristic of certain races or classes, but for these attitudes when they are in the focus of attention of the group, in the "fore-consciousness" to use a Freudian term. In this sense "conscious" suggests not merely the submergence of the individual and the consequent solidarity of the group, but it signifies a mental mobilization and preparedness of the individual and of the group for collective or corporate action. To be class-conscious is to be prepared to act in the sense of that class.

There is implicit in this rather ambiguous popular usage of the terms "social mind" and "social consciousness" a recognition of the dual aspect of society and of social groups. Society may be regarded at the same time from an individualistic and a collectivistic point of view. Looking at it from the point of view of the individual, we regard as social just that character of the individual which has been imparted to, and impressed upon, him as a result of his participation in the life of the group. Social psychology, from Baldwin's first studies of the development of personality in the child to Ellwood's studies of the society in its "psychological aspects" has been mainly concerned with the investigation of the effects upon the individual of his contacts with other individuals.[1]

On the other hand, we have had, in the description of the crowd and the public by Le Bon, Tarde, Sighele, and their successors, the beginnings of a study of collective behavior and "corporate action." In these two points of view we seem to have again the contrast and the opposition, already referred to, between the nominalistic and realistic conceptions of society. Nominalism represented by social psychology emphasizes, or seems to emphasize, the independence of the individual. Realism, represented by collective psychology, emphasizes the control of the group over the individual, of the whole over the part.

[1] James Mark Baldwin, *Mental Development in the Child and the Race* (New York and London, 1895); Charles A. Ellwood, *Sociology in Its Psychological Aspects* (New York and London, 1912).

While it is true that society has this double aspect, the individual and the collective, it is the assumption of this volume that the touchstone of society, the thing that distinguishes a mere collection of individuals from a society is not like-mindedness, but corporate action. We may apply the term social to any group of individuals which is capable of consistent action, that is to say, action, consciously or unconsciously, directed to a common end. This existence of a common end is perhaps all that can be legitimately included in the conception "organic" as applied to society.

From this point of view social control is the central fact and the central problem of society. Just as psychology may be regarded as an account of the manner in which the individual organism, as a whole, exercises control over its parts or rather of the manner in which the parts co-operate together to carry on the corporate existence of the whole, so sociology, speaking strictly, is a point of view and a method for investigating the processes by which individuals are inducted into and induced to co-operate in some sort of permanent corporate existence which we call society.

To put this emphasis on corporate action is not to overlook the fact that through this corporate action the individual member of society is largely formed, not to say created. It is recognized, however, that if corporate action tends to make of the individual an instrument, as well as an organic part, of the social group, it does not do this by making him "like" merely; it may do so by making him "different." The division of labor, in making possible an ever larger and wider co-operation among men, has indirectly multiplied individual diversities. What like-mindedness must eventually mean, if it is to mean anything, is the existence of so much of a consensus among the individuals of a group as will permit the group to act. This, then, is what is meant here by society, the social organism and the social group.

Sociology, so far as it can be regarded as a fundamental science and not mere congeries of social-welfare programs and practices, may be described as the science of collective behavior. With this definition it is possible to indicate in a general and schematic way its relation to the other social sciences.

Historically, sociology has had its origin in history. History has been and is the great mother science of all the social sciences. Of history it may be said nothing human is foreign to it. Anthropology, ethnology, folklore, and archaeology have grown up largely, if not wholly, to complete the task which history began and answer the questions which historical investigation first raised. In history and the sciences associated with it, i.e., ethnology, folklore, and archaeology, we have the concrete records of that human nature and experience which sociology has sought to explain. In the same sense that history is the concrete, sociology is the abstract, science of human experience and human nature.

On the other hand, the technical (applied) social sciences, that is, politics, education, social service, and economics—so far as economics may be regarded as the science of business—are related to

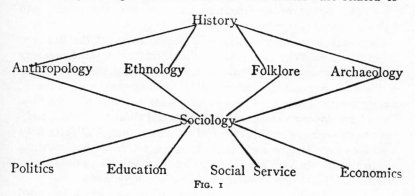

FIG. 1

sociology in a different way. They are, to a greater or lesser extent, applications of principles which it is the business of sociology and of psychology to deal with explicitly. In so far as this is true, sociology may be regarded as fundamental to the other social sciences.

VIII. SOCIOLOGY AND SOCIAL RESEARCH

Among the schools which, since Comte and Spencer, have divided sociological thinking between them the realists have, on the whole, maintained the tradition of Comte; the nominalists, on the other hand, have preserved the style and manner, if not the substance, of Spencer's thought. Later writers, however, realist as well as nominalist, have directed their attention less to society than to societies, i.e., social groups; they have been less interested in social progress than in social process; more concerned with social problems than with social philosophy.

This change marks the transformation of sociology from a philosophy of history to a science of society. The steps in this transition are periods in the history of the science, that is:

1. The period of Comte and Spencer; sociology, conceived in the grand style, is a philosophy of history, a "science" of progress (evolution).

2. The period of the "schools"; sociological thought, dispersed among the various schools, is absorbed in an effort to define its point of view and to describe the kinds of facts that sociology must look for to answer the questions that sociology asks.

3. The period of investigation and research, the period into which sociology is just now entering.

Sociological research is at present (1921) in about the situation in which psychology was before the introduction of laboratory methods, in which medicine was before Pasteur and the germ theory of disease. A great deal of social information has been collected merely for the purpose of determining what to do in a given case. Facts have not been collected to check social theories. Social problems have been defined in terms of common sense, and facts have been collected, for the most part, to support this or that doctrine, not to test it. In very few instances have investigations been made, disinterestedly, to determine the validity of a hypothesis.

Charles Booth's studies of poverty in London, which extended over eighteen years and were finally embodied in seventeen volumes, is an example of such a disinterested investigation. It is an attempt to put to the test of fact the popular conception of the relation between wages and welfare. He says:

My object has been to attempt to show the numerical relation which poverty, misery, and depravity bear to regular earnings and comparative comfort, and to describe the general conditions under which each class lives.

If the facts thus stated are of use in helping social reformers to find remedies for the evils which exist, or do anything to prevent the adoption of false remedies, my purpose is answered. It was not my intention to bring forward any suggestions of my own, and if I have ventured here and there, and especially in the concluding chapters, to go beyond my programme, it has been with much hesitation.

With regard to the disadvantages under which the poor labour, and the evils of poverty, there is a great sense of helplessness: the wage earners are helpless to regulate their work and cannot obtain a fair equivalent for the labour they are willing to give; the manufacturer or dealer can only work within the limits of competition; the rich are helpless to relieve want without stimulating its sources. To relieve this helplessness a better stating of the problems involved is the first step. . . . . In this direction must be sought the utility of my attempt to analyze the population of a part of London.[1]

This vast study did, indeed, throw great light, not only upon poverty in London, but upon human nature in general. On the other hand, it raised more questions than it settled and, if it demonstrated anything, it was the necessity, as Booth suggests, for a restatement of the problem.

Sociology seems now, however, in a way to become, in some fashion or other, an experimental science. It will become so as soon as it can state existing problems in such a way that the results in one case will demonstrate what can and should be done in another. Experiments are going on in every field of social life, in industry, in politics, and in religion. In all these fields men are guided by some implicit or explicit theory of the situation, but this theory is not often stated in the form of a hypothesis and subjected to a test of the negative instances. We have, if it is permitted to make a distinction between them, investigation rather than research.

What, then, in the sense in which the expression is here used, is social research? A classification of problems will be a sort of first aid in the search for an answer.

1. *Classification of social problems.*—Every society and every social group, *capable of consistent action*, may be regarded as an organization of the wishes of its members. This means that society rests on, and embodies, the appetites and natural desires of the individual man; but it implies, also, that wishes, in becoming *organized*, are necessarily disciplined and controlled in the interest of the group as a whole.

Every such society or social group, even the most ephemeral, will ordinarily have (*a*) some relatively formal method of defining its aim and formulating its policies, making them explicit, and (*b*) some machinery, functionary, or other arrangement for realizing its aim

[1] *Labour and Life of the People* (London, 1889), I, pp. 6–7.

and carrying its policies into effect. Even in the family there is government, and this involves something that corresponds to legislation, adjudication, and administration.

Social groups, however, maintain their organizations, agencies, and all formal methods of behavior on a basis and in a setting of instinct, of habit, and of tradition which we call human nature. Every social group has, or tends to have, its own culture, what Sumner calls "folkways," and this culture, imposing its patterns upon the natural man, gives him that particular individuality which characterizes the members of groups. Not races merely but nationalities and classes have marks, manners, and patterns of life by which we infallibly recognize and classify them.

Social problems may be conveniently classified with reference to these three aspects of group life, that is to say, problems of (a) organization and administration, (b) policy and polity (legislation), and (c) human nature (culture).

a) Administrative problems are mainly practical and technical. Most problems of government, of business and social welfare, are technical. The investigations, i.e., social surveys, made in different parts of the country by the Bureau of Municipal Research of New York City, are studies of local administration made primarily for the purpose of improving the efficiency of an existing administrative machine and its personnel rather than of changing the policy or purpose of the administration itself.

b) Problems of policy, in the sense in which that term is used here, are political and legislative. Most social investigations in recent years have been made in the interest of some legislative program or for the purpose of creating a more intelligent public opinion in regard to certain local problems. The social surveys conducted by the Sage Foundation, as distinguished from those carried out by the New York Bureau of Municipal Research, have been concerned with problems of policy, i.e., with changing the character and policy of social institutions rather than improving their efficiency. This distinction between administration and policy is not always clear, but it is always important. Attempts at reform usually begin with an effort to correct administrative abuses, but eventually it turns out that reforms must go deeper and change the character of the institutions themselves.

c) Problems of human nature are naturally fundamental to all other social problems. Human nature, as we have begun to conceive it in recent years, is largely a product of social intercourse; it is, therefore, quite as much as society itself, a subject for sociological investigation. Until recent years, what we are now calling the human factor has been notoriously neglected in most social experiments. We have been seeking to reform human nature while at the same time we refused to reckon with it. It has been assumed that we could bring about social changes by merely formulating our wishes, that is, by "arousing" public opinion and formulating legislation. This is the "democratic" method of effecting reforms. The older "autocratic" method merely decreed social changes upon the authority of the monarch or the ruling class. What reconciled men to it was that, like Christian Science, it frequently worked.

The oldest but most persistent form of social technique is that of "ordering-and-forbidding"—that is, meeting a crisis by an arbitrary act of will decreeing the disappearance of the undesirable or the appearance of the desirable phenomena, and the using arbitrary physical action to enforce the decree. This method corresponds exactly to the magical phase of natural technique. In both, the essential means of bringing a determined effect is more or less consciously thought to reside in the act of will itself by which the effect is decreed as desirable and of which the action is merely an indispensable vehicle or instrument; in both, the process by which the cause (act of will and physical action) is supposed to bring its effect to realization remains out of reach of investigation; in both, finally, if the result is not attained, some new act of will with new material accessories is introduced, instead of trying to find and remove the perturbing causes. A good instance of this in the social field is the typical legislative procedure of today.[1]

2. *Types of social group.*—The varied interests, fields of investigation, and practical programs which find at present a place within the limits of the sociological discipline are united in having one common object of reference, namely, *the concept of the social group.* All social problems turn out finally to be problems of group life, although each group and each type of group has its own distinctive

[1] Thomas and Znaniecki, *The Polish Peasant in Europe and America* (Boston, 1918), I, 3.

problems. Illustrations may be gathered from the most widely separated fields to emphasize the truth of this assertion.[1]

Religious conversion may be interpreted from one point of view as a change from one social group to another. To use the language of religious sentiment, the convert "comes out of a life of sin and enters into a life of grace." To be sure, this change involves profound disturbances of the personality, but permanence of the change in the individual is assured by the breaking up of the old and the establishment of new associations. So the process by which the immigrant makes the transition from the old country to the new involves profound changes in thought and habit. In his case the change is likely to take place slowly, but it is not less radical on that account.

The following paragraph from a recent social survey illustrates, from a quite different point of view, the manner in which the group is involved in changes in community life.

In short, the greatest problem for the next few years in Stillwater is the development of a *community consciousness*. We must stop thinking in terms of city of Stillwater, and country outside of Stillwater, and think in terms of *Stillwater Community*. We must stop thinking in terms of small groups and think in terms of the entire community, no matter whether it is industry, health, education, recreation or religion. Anything which is good will benefit the entire community. Any weakness will be harmful to all. Community co-operation in all lines indicated in this report will make this, indeed, the Queen of the St. Croix.[2]

In this case the solution of the community problem was the creation of "community consciousness." In the case of the professional criminal the character of the problem is determined, if we accept the description of a writer in the *Atlantic Monthly*, by the existence among professional criminals of a primary group consciousness:

The professional criminal is peculiar in the sense that he lives a very intense emotional life. He is isolated in the community. He is in it, but not of it. His social life—for all men are social—is narrow; but just because it is narrow, it is extremely tense. He lives a life of warfare and has

[1] Walter B. Bodenhafer, "The Comparative Rôle of the Group Concept in Ward's Dynamic Sociology and Contemporary American Sociology," *American Journal of Sociology*, XXVI (1920–21), 273–314; 425–74; 588–600; 716–43.

[2] *Stillwater, the Queen of the St. Croix*, a report of a social survey, published by The Community Service of Stillwater, Minnesota, 1920, p. 71.

the psychology of the warrior. He is at war with the whole community. Except his very few friends in crime he trusts no one and fears everyone. Suspicion, fear, hatred, danger, desperation and passion are present in a more tense form in his life than in that of the average individual. He is restless, ill-humored, easily roused and suspicious. He lives on the brink of a deep precipice. This helps to explain his passionate hatred, his brutality, his fear, and gives poignant significance to the adage that dead men tell no tales. He holds on to his few friends with a strength and passion rare among people who live a more normal existence. His friends stand between him and discovery. They are his hold upon life, his basis of security.

Loyalty to one's group is the basic law in the underworld. Disloyalty is treason and punishable by death; for disloyalty may mean the destruction of one's friends; it may mean the hurling of the criminal over the precipice on which his whole life is built.

To the community the criminal is aggressive. To the criminal his life is one of defense primarily. The greater part of his energy, of his hopes, and of his successes, centres around escapes, around successful flight, around proper covering-up of his tracks, and around having good, loyal, and trustworthy friends to participate in his activities, who will tell no tales and keep the rest of the community outside. The criminal is thus, from his own point of view—and I am speaking of professional criminals—living a life of defensive warfare with the community; and the odds are heavy against him. He therefore builds up a defensive psychology against it—a psychology of boldness, bravado, and self-justification. The good criminal—which means the successful one, he who has most successfully carried through a series of depradations against the enemy, the common enemy, the public—is a hero. He is recognized as such, toasted and feasted, trusted and obeyed. But always by a little group. They live in a world of their own, a life of their own, with ideals, habits, outlook, beliefs, and associations which are peculiarly fitted to maintain the morale of the group. Loyalty, fearlessness, generosity, willingness to sacrifice one's self, perseverance in the face of prosecution, hatred of the common enemy—these are the elements that maintain the morale, but all of them are pointed against the community as a whole.[1]

The manner in which the principle of the primary group was applied at Sing Sing in dealing with the criminal within the prison walls is a still more interesting illustration of the fact that social problems are group problems.[2]

[1] Frank Tannenbaum, "Prison Democracy," *Atlantic Monthly*, October, 1920, pp. 438-39. (Psychology of the criminal group.)

[2] *Ibid.*, pp. 443-46.

Assuming, then, that every social group may be presumed to have its own (*a*) administrative, (*b*) legislative, and (*c*) human-nature problems, these problems may be still further classified with reference to the type of social group. Most social groups fall naturally into one or the other of the following classes:

a) The family.

b) Language (racial) groups.

c) Local and territorial communities: (i) neighborhoods, (ii) rural communities, (iii) urban communities.

d) Conflict groups: (i) nationalities, (ii) parties, (iii) sects, (iv) labor organizations, (v) gangs, etc.

e) Accommodation groups: (i) classes, (ii) castes, (iii) vocational, (iv) denominational groups.

The foregoing classification is not quite adequate nor wholly logical. The first three classes are more closely related to one another than they are to the last two, i.e., the so-called "accommodation" and "conflict" groups. The distinction is far-reaching, but its general character is indicated by the fact that the family, language, and local groups are, or were originally, what are known as primary groups, that is, groups organized on intimate, face-to-face relations. The conflict and accommodation groups represent divisions which may, to be sure, have arisen within the primary group, but which have usually arisen historically by the imposition of one primary group upon another.

Every state in history was or is a *state of classes*, a polity of superior and inferior social groups, based upon distinctions either of rank or of property. This phenomenon must, then, be called the "State."[1]

It is the existence at any rate of conflict and accommodation within the limits of a larger group which distinguishes it from groups based on primary relations, and gives it eventually the character described as "secondary."

When a language group becomes militant and self-conscious, it assumes the character of a nationality. It is perhaps true, also, that the family which is large enough and independent enough to be self-conscious, by that fact assumes the character of a clan. Important in this connection is the fact that a group in becoming

[1] Franz Oppenheimer, *The State* (Indianapolis, 1914), p. 5.

group-conscious changes its character.   External conflict has invariably reacted powerfully upon the internal organization of social groups.

Group self-consciousness seems to be a common characteristic of conflict and accommodation groups and distinguishes them from the more elementary forms of society represented by the family and the local community.

3. *Organization and structure of social groups.*—Having a general scheme for the classification of social groups, it is in order to discover methods of analysis that are applicable to the study of all types of groups, from the family to the sect.   Such a scheme of analysis should reveal not only the organization and structure of typical groups, but it should indicate the relation of this organization and structure to those social problems that are actual and generally recognized. The sort of facts which are now generally recognized as important in the stud· .ot merely of society, but the problems of society are:

a) St_ ιcs: numbers, local distribution, mobility, incidence of births, deaths, disease, and crime.

b) Institutions: local distribution, classification (i.e., (i) industrial, (ii) religious, (iii) political, (iv) educational, (v) welfare and mutual aid), communal organization.

c) Heritages: the customs and traditions transmitted by the group, particularly in relation to religion, recreation and leisure time, and social control (politics).

d) Organization of public opinion: parties, sects, cliques, and the press.

4. *Social process and social progress.*—Social process is the name for all changes which can be regarded as changes in the life of the group. A group may be said to have a life when it has a history.   Among social processes we may distinguish (a) the historical, (b) the cultural, (c) the political, and (d) the economic.

a) We describe as historical the processes by which the fund of social tradition, which is the heritage of every permanent social group, is accumulated and transmitted from one generation to another.

History plays the rôle in the group of memory in the individual. Without history social groups would, no doubt, rise and decline, but they would neither grow old nor make progress.

Immigrants, crossing the ocean, leave behind them much of their local traditions.   The result is that they lose, particularly in the second generation, that control which the family and group tradition formerly exercised over them; but they are, for that very reason, all the more open to the influence of the traditions and customs of their adopted country.

b) If it is the function of the historical process to accumulate and conserve the common fund of social experience, it is the function of the cultural process to shape and define the social forms and the social patterns which each preceding generation imposes upon its successors.

The individual living in society has to fit into a pre-existing social world, to take part in the hedonistic, economic, political, religious, moral, aesthetic, intellectual activities of the group. For these activities the group has objective *systems*, more or less complex sets of schemes, organized either by traditional association or with a conscious regard to the greatest possible efficiency of the result, but with only a secondary, or even with no interest in the particular desires, abilities and experiences of the individuals who have to perform these activities.

There is no pre-existing harmony whatever between the individual and the social factors of personal evolution, and the fundamental tendencies of the individual are always in some disaccordance with the fundamental tendencies of social control. Personal evolution is always a struggle between the individual and society—a struggle for self-expression on the part of the individual, for his subjection on the part of society—and it is in the total course of this struggle that the personality—not as a static "essence" but as a dynamic, continually evolving set of activities—manifests and constructs itself.[1]

c) In general, standards of behavior that are in the mores are not the subject of discussion, except so far as discussion is necessary to determine whether this or that act falls under one or the other of the accepted social sanctions. The political as distinguished from the cultural process is concerned with just those matters in regard to which there is division and difference. Politics is concerned with issues.

The Negro, particularly in the southern states, is a constant theme of popular discussion. Every time a Negro finds himself in a new situation, or one in which the white population is unaccustomed to see him, the thing provokes comment in both races. On the other hand, when a southerner asks the question: "Would you want your

[1] Thomas and Znaniecki, *op. cit.*, III, 34–36.

daughter to marry a Negro?" it is time for discussion to cease. Any questions of relations between the races can always be immediately disposed of as soon as it is seen to come, directly or indirectly, under the intolerable formula. Political questions are matters of compromise and expediency. Miscegenation, on the other hand, is contrary to the mores. As such the rule against it is absolute.

The political process, by which a society or social group formulates its wishes and enforces them, goes on within the limits of the mores and is carried on by public discussion, legislation, and the adjudication of the courts.

d) The economic process, so far as it can be distinguished from the production and distribution of goods, is the process by which prices are made and an exchange of values is effected. Most values, i.e., my present social status, my hopes of the future, and memory of the past, are personal and not values that can be exchanged. The economic process is concerned with values that can be treated as commodities.

All these processes may, and do, arise within most but not every society or social group. Commerce presupposes the freedom of the individual to pursue his own profit, and commerce can take place only to the extent and degree that this freedom is permitted. Freedom of commerce is, however, limited on the one hand by the mores and on the other by formal law, so that the economic process takes place ordinarily within limitations that are defined by the cultural and the political processes. It is only where there is neither a cultural nor a political order that commerce is absolutely free.

The areas of (1) the cultural, (2) the political, (3) the economic processes and their relations to one another may be represented by concentric circles.

In this representation the area of widest cultural influences is coterminous with the area of commerce, because commerce in its widest extension is invariably carried on under some restraints of custom and customary law. Otherwise it is not commerce at all, but something predacious outside the law. But if the area of the economic process is almost invariably coterminous with the widest areas of cultural influence, it does not extend to the smaller social groups. As a rule trade does not invade the family. Family interests are always personal even when they are carried on under the forms of commerce. Primitive society, within the limits of the village, is usually communistic. All values are personal, and the relations of individuals to one another, economic or otherwise, are preordained by custom and law.

The impersonal values, values for exchange, seem to be in any given society or social group in inverse relation to the personal values.

The attempt to describe in this large way the historical, cultural, political, and economic processes, is justified in so far as it enables us to recognize that the aspects of social life, which are the subject-matter of the special social sciences, i.e., history, political science, and economics, are involved in specific forms of change that can

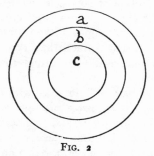

FIG. 2

a = area of most extended cultural influences and of commerce; *b* = area of formal political control; *c* = area of purely personal relationships, communism.

be viewed abstractly, formulated, compared, and related. The attempt to view them in their interrelations is at the same time an effort to distinguish and to see them as parts of one whole.

In contrast with the types of social change referred to there are other changes which are unilateral and progressive; changes which are described popularly as "movements," mass movements. These are changes which eventuate in new social organizations and institutions.

All more marked forms of social change are associated with certain social manifestations that we call social unrest. Social unrest issues, under ordinary conditions, as an incident of new social contacts, and is an indication of a more lively tempo in the process of communication and interaction.

All social changes are preceded by a certain degree of social and individual disorganization. This will be followed ordinarily under normal conditions by a movement of reorganization. All progress implies a certain amount of disorganization. In studying social changes, therefore, that, if not progressive, are at least unilateral, we are interested in:

(1) Disorganization: accelerated mobility, unrest, disease, and crime as manifestations and measures of social disorganization.

(2) Social movements (reorganization) include: (a) crowd movements (i.e., mobs, strikes, etc.); (b) cultural revivals, religious and linguistic; (c) fashion (changes in dress, convention, and social ritual); (d) reform (changes in social policy and administration); (e) revolutions (changes in institutions and the mores).

5. *The individual and the person.*—The person is an individual who has status. We come into the world as individuals. We acquire status, and become persons. Status means position in society. The individual inevitably has some status in every social group of which he is a member. In a given group the status of every member is determined by his relation to every other member of that group. Every smaller group, likewise, has a status in some larger group of which it is a part and this is determined by its relation to all the other members of the larger group.

The individual's self-consciousness—his conception of his rôle in society, his "self," in short—while not identical with his personality is an essential element in it. The individual's conception of himself, however, is based on his status in the social group or groups of which he is a member. The individual whose conception of himself does not conform to his status is an isolated individual. The completely isolated individual, whose conception of himself is in no sense an adequate reflection of his status, is probably insane.

It follows from what is said that an individual may have many "selves" according to the groups to which he belongs and the extent to which each of these groups is isolated from the others. It is true, also, that the individual is influenced in differing degrees and in a specific manner, by the different types of group of which he is a member. This indicates the manner in which the personality of the individual may be studied sociologically.

Every individual comes into the world in possession of certain characteristic and relatively fixed behavior patterns which we call instincts. This is his racial inheritance which he shares with all members of the species. He comes into the world, also, endowed with certain undefined capacities for learning other forms of behavior, capacities which vary greatly in different individuals. These individual differences and the instincts are what is called original nature.[1]

Sociology is interested in "original nature" in so far as it supplies the raw materials out of which individual personalities and the social order are created. Both society and the persons who compose society are the products of social processes working in and through the materials which each new generation of men contributes to it.

Charles Cooley, who was the first to make the important distinction between primary and secondary groups, has pointed out that the intimate, face-to-face associations of primary groups, i.e., the family, the neighborhood, and the village community, are fundamental in forming the social nature and ideals of the individual.[2]

There is, however, an area of life in which the associations are more intimate than those of the primary group as that group is ordinarily conceived. Such are the relations between mother and child, particularly in the period of infancy, and the relations between men and women under the influence of the sexual instinct. These are the associations in which the most lasting affections and the most violent antipathies are formed. We may describe it as the area of touch relationships.

Finally, there is the area of secondary contacts, in which relationships are relatively impersonal, formal, and conventional. It is in this region of social life that the individual gains, at the same time, a personal freedom and an opportunity for distinction that is denied him in the primary group.

As a matter of fact, many, if not most, of our present social problems have their source and origin in the transition of great masses of the population—the immigrants, for example—out of a society

---

[1] Original nature in its relation to social welfare and human progress has been made the subject-matter of a special science, eugenics. For a criticism of the claims of eugenics as a social science see Leonard T. Hobhouse, *Social Evolution and Political Theory* (Columbia University Press, 1917).

[2] Charles H. Cooley, *Social Organization*, p. 28.

based on primary group relationships into the looser, freer, and less controlled existence of life in great cities.

The "moral unrest" so deeply penetrating all western societies, the growing vagueness and indecision of personalities, the, almost complete disappearance of the "strong and steady character" of old times, in short, the rapid and general increase of Bohemianism and Bolshevism in all societies, is an effect of the fact that not only the early primary group controlling all interests of its members on the general social basis, not only the occupational group of the mediaeval type controlling most of the interests of its members on a professional basis, but even the special modern group dividing with many others the task of organizing permanently the attitudes of each of its members, is more and more losing ground. The pace of social evolution has become so rapid that special groups are ceasing to be permanent and stable enough to organize and maintain organized complexes of attitudes of their members which correspond to their common pursuits. In other words, society is gradually losing all its old machinery for the determination and stabilization of individual characters.

Every social group tends to create, from the individuals that compose it, its own type of character, and the characters thus formed become component parts of the social structure in which they are incorporated. All the problems of social life are thus problems of the individual; and all problems of the individual are at the same time problems of the group. This point of view is already recognized in preventive medicine, and to some extent in psychiatry. It is not yet adequately recognized in the technique of social case work.

Further advance in the application of social principles to social practice awaits a more thoroughgoing study of the problems, systematic social research, and an experimental social science.

CHAPTER II

HUMAN NATURE

I. INTRODUCTION

1. Human Interest in Human Nature

The human interest in human nature is proverbial. It is an original tendency of man to be attentive to the behavior of other human beings. Experience heightens this interest because of the dependence of the individual upon other persons, not only for physical existence, but for social life.

The literature of every people is to a large extent but the crystallization of this persistent interest. Old saws and proverbs of every people transmit from generation to generation shrewd generalizations upon human behavior. In joke and in epigram, in caricature and in burlesque, in farce and in comedy, men of all races and times have enjoyed with keen relish the humor of the contrast between the conventional and the natural motives in behavior. In Greek mythology, individual traits of human nature are abstracted, idealized, and personified into gods. The heroes of Norse sagas and Teutonic legends are the gigantic symbols of primary emotions and sentiments. Historical characters live in the social memory not alone because they are identified with political, religious, or national movements but also because they have come to typify human relationships. The loyalty of Damon and Pythias, the grief of Rachel weeping for her children, the cynical cruelty of the egocentric Nero, the perfidy of Benedict Arnold, the comprehending sympathy of Abraham Lincoln, are proverbial, and as such have become part of the common language of all the peoples who participate in our occidental culture.

Poetry, drama, and the plastic arts are interesting and significant only so far as they reveal in new and ever changing circumstances the unchanging characteristics of a fundamental human nature. Illustrations of this naïve and unreflecting interest in the study of mankind are familiar enough in the experience and observation of any of us. Intellectual interest in, and the scientific observation of, human traits and human behavior have their origin in this natural interest and unreflective observation by man of his fellows. History, ethnology, folklore, all the comparative studies of single cultural traits, i.e., of language, of religion, and of law, are but the more systematic pursuit of this universal interest of mankind in man.

2. Definition of Human Nature

The natural history of the expression "human nature" is interesting. Usage has given it various shades of meaning. In defining the term more precisely there is a tendency either unwarrantedly to narrow or unduly to extend and overemphasize some one or another of the different senses of the term. A survey of these varied uses reveals the common and fundamental meaning of the phrase.

The use which common sense makes of the term human nature is significant. It is used in varied contexts with the most divergent implications but always by way of explanation of behavior that is characteristically human. The phrase is sometimes employed with cynical deprecation as, "Oh, that's human nature." Or as often, perhaps, as an expression of approbation, "He's so human."

The weight of evidence as expressed in popular sayings is distinctly in depreciation of man's nature.

> It's human natur', p'raps,—if so,
> Oh, isn't human natur' low,

are two lines from Gilbert's musical comedy "Babette's Love." "To err is human, to forgive divine" reminds us of a familiar contrast. "Human nature is like a bad clock; it might go right now and then, or be made to strike the hour, but its inward frame is to go wrong," is a simile that emphasizes the popular notion that man's behavior tends to the perverse. An English divine settles the question with the statement, "Human nature is a rogue and a scoundrel, or why would it perpetually stand in need of laws and religion?"

Even those who see good in the natural man admit his native tendency to err. Sir Thomas Browne asserts that "human nature knows naturally what is good but naturally pursues what is evil." The Earl of Clarendon gives the equivocal explanation that "if we did not take great pains to corrupt our nature, our nature would never corrupt us." Addison, from the detached position of an observer and critic of manners and men, concludes that "as man is a creature made up of different extremes, he has something in him very great and very mean."

The most commonly recognized distinction between man and the lower animals lies in his possession of reason. Yet familiar sayings tend to exclude the intellectual from the human attributes. Lord Bacon shrewdly remarks that "there is in human nature, generally, more of the fool than of the wise." The phrase "he is a child of nature" means that behavior in social relations is impulsive, simple, and direct rather than reflective, sophisticated, or consistent. Wordsworth depicts this human type in his poem "She Was a Phantom of Delight":

> A creature not too bright or good
> For human nature's daily food;
> For transient sorrows, simple wiles,
> Praise, blame, love, kisses, tears and smiles.

The inconsistency between the rational professions and the impulsive behavior of men is a matter of common observation. "That's not the logic, reason, or philosophy of it, but it's the human nature of it." It is now generally recognized that the older English conception of the "economic man" and the "rational man," motivated by enlightened self-interest, was far removed from the "natural man" impelled by impulse, prejudice, and sentiment, in short, by human nature. Popular criticism has been frequently directed against the reformer in politics, the efficiency expert in industry, the formalist in religion and morals on the ground that they overlook or neglect the so-called "human factor" in the situation. Sir Arthur Helps says:

No doubt hard work is a great police-agent; if everybody were worked from morning till night, and then carefully locked up, the register of crimes might be greatly diminished. But what would become of human nature? Where would be the room for growth in such a system of things? It is through sorrow and mirth, plenty and need, a variety of passions, circumstances, and temptations, even through sin and misery, that men's natures are developed.

Certain sayings already quoted imply that the nature of man is a fact to be reckoned with in controlling his behavior. "There are limits to human nature" which cannot lightly be overstepped.

"Human nature," according to Periander, "is hard to overcome."
Yet we also recognize with Swift that "it is the talent of human
nature to run from one extreme to another." Finally, nothing is
more trite and familiar than the statement that "human nature is
the same all over the world." This fundamental likeness of human
nature, despite artificial and superficial cultural differences, has found
a classic expression in Kipling's line: "The Colonel's Lady an' Judy
O'Grady are sisters under their skins!"

Human nature, then, as distinct from the formal wishes of the
individual and the conventional order of society, is an aspect of
human life that must be reckoned with. Common sense has long
recognized this, but until recently no systematic attempt has been
made to *isolate*, describe, and explain the distinctively human factors
in the life either of the individual or of society.

Of all that has been written on this subject the most adequate
statement is that of Cooley. He has worked out with unusual penetration and peculiar insight an interpretation of human nature as
a product of group life.

By human nature we may understand those sentiments and impulses
that are human in being superior to those of lower animals, and also in the
sense that they belong to mankind at large, and not to any particular race
or time. It means, particularly, sympathy and the innumerable sentiments into which sympathy enters, such as love, resentment, ambition,
vanity, hero-worship, and the feeling of social right and wrong.

Human nature in this sense is justly regarded as a comparatively
permanent element in society. Always and everywhere men seek honor
and dread ridicule, defer to public opinion, cherish their goods and their
children, and admire courage, generosity, and success. It is always safe to
assume that people are and have been human.

Human nature is not something existing separately in the individual,
but a *group nature or primary phase of society*, a relatively simple and
general condition of the social mind. It is something more, on the one
hand, than the mere instinct that is born in us—though that enters into
it—and something less, on the other, than the more elaborate development
of ideas and sentiments that makes up institutions. It is the nature which
is developed and expressed in those simple, face-to-face groups that are
somewhat alike in all societies; groups of the family, the playground, and
the neighborhood. In the essential similarity of these is to be found the
basis, in experience, for similar ideas and sentiments in the human mind.

In these, everywhere, human nature comes into existence. Man does not have it at birth; he cannot acquire it except through fellowship, and it decays in isolation.[1]

3. Classification of the Materials

With the tacit acceptance by biologists, psychologists, and sociologists of human behavior as a natural phenomenon, materials upon human nature have rapidly accumulated. The wealth and variety of these materials are all the greater because of the diversity of the points of view from which workers in this field have attacked the problem. The value of the results of these investigations is enhanced when they are brought together, classified, and compared.

The materials fall naturally into two divisions: (a) "The Original Nature of Man" and (b) "Human Nature and Social Life." This division is based upon a distinction between traits that are inborn and characters socially acquired; a distinction found necessary by students in this field. Selections under the third heading, "Personality and the Social Self" indicate the manner in which the individual develops under the social influences, from the raw material of "instinct" into the social product "the person." Materials in the fourth division, "Biological and Social Inheritance," contrast the method of the transmission of original tendencies through the germ plasm with the communication of the social heritage through education.

a) *The original nature of man.*—No one has stated more clearly than Thorndike that human nature is a product of two factors, (a) tendencies to response rooted in original nature and (b) the accumulated effects of the stimuli of the external and social environment. At birth man is a bundle of random tendencies to respond. Through experience, and by means of the mechanisms of habit and character, control is secured over instinctive reactions. In other words, the original nature of man is, as Comte said, an abstraction. It exists only in the psychic vacuum of antenatal life, or perhaps only in the potentiality of the germ plasm. The fact of observation is that the structure of the response is irrevocably changed in the process of reaction to the stimulus. The *Biography of a Baby* gives a concrete picture of the development of the plastic infant in the environment of the social group.

[1] Charles H. Cooley, *Social Organization*, pp. 28–30.

The three papers on differences between sexes, races, and individuals serve as an introduction into the problem of differentiating the aspects of behavior which are in *original nature* from those that are *acquired* through social experience. Are the apparent differences between men and women, white and colored, John and James, those which arise from differences in the germ plasm or from differences in education and in cultural contacts? The selections must not be taken as giving the final word upon the subject. At best they represent merely the conclusions reached by three investigators. Attempts to arrive at positive differences in favor either of original nature or of education are frequently made in the interest of preconceived opinion. The problem, as far as science is concerned, is to discover what limitations original nature places upon response to social copies, and the ways in which the inborn potentialities find expression or repression in differing types of social environment.

b) Human nature and social life.—Original nature is represented in human responses in so far as they are determined by the *innate structure of the individual organism.* The materials assembled under this head treat of inborn reactions as influenced, modified, and reconstructed by the *structure of the social organization.*

The actual reorganization of human nature takes place in response to the folkways and mores, the traditions and conventions, of the group. So potentially fitted for social life is the natural man, however, so manifold are the expressions that the plastic original tendencies may take, that instinct is replaced by habit, precedent, personal taboo, and good form. This remade structure of human nature, this objective mind, as Hegel called it, is fixed and transmitted in the folkways and mores, social ritual, i.e., *Sittlichkeit*, to use the German word, and convention.

c) Personality and the social self.—The selections upon "Personality and the Social Self" bring together and compare the different definitions of the term. These definitions fall under three heads:

(1) *The organism as personality:* This is a biological statement, satisfactory as a definition only as preparatory to further analysis.

(2) *Personality as a complex:* Personality defined in terms of the unity of mental life is a conception that has grown up in the recent "individual psychology," so called. Personality includes, in this case, not only the memories of the individual and his stream of

consciousness, but also the characteristic organization of mental complexes and trends which may be thought of as a supercomplex. The phenomena of double and multiple personalities occur when this unity becomes disorganized. Disorganization in releasing groups of complexes from control may even permit the formation of independent organizations. Morton Prince's book *The Dissociation of a Personality* is a classic case study of multiple personality. The selections upon "The Natural Person versus the Social and Conventional Person" and "The Divided Self and the Moral Consciousness" indicate the more usual and less extreme conflicts of opposing sentiments and interests within the organization of personality.

(3) *Personality as the rôle of the individual in the group:* The word personality is derived from the Latin *persona*, a mask used by actors. The etymology of the term suggests that its meaning is to be found in the rôle of the individual in the social group. By usage, personality carries the implication of the social expression of behavior. Personality may then be defined as the sum and organization of those traits which determine the rôle of the individual in the group. The following is a classification of the characteristics of the person which affect his social status and efficiency:

(a) physical traits, as physique, physiognomy, etc.;
(b) temperament;
(c) character;
(d) social expression, as by facial expression, gesture, manner, speech, writing, etc.;
(e) prestige, as by birth, past success, status, etc.;
(f) the individual's conception of his rôle.

The significance of these traits consists in the way in which they enter into the rôle of the individual in his social milieu. Chief among these may be considered the individual's conception of the part which he plays among his fellows. Cooley's discriminating description of "the looking-glass self" offers a picture of the process by which the person conceives himself in terms of the attitudes of others toward him.

The reflected or looking-glass self seems to have three principal elements: the imagination of our appearance to the other person; the imagination of his judgment of that appearance; and some sort of self-feeling, such as pride or mortification. The comparison with a looking-glass self hardly suggests the second element, the imagined judgment which is quite essential. The thing that moves us to pride or shame is not the mere mechanical reflection of ourselves, but an imputed sentiment, the imagined effect of this reflection upon another's mind. This is evident from the fact that the character and weight of that other, in whose mind we see ourselves, makes all the difference with our feeling.[1]

Veblen has made a subtle analysis of the way in which conduct is controlled by the individual's conception of his social rôle in his analysis of "invidious comparison" and "conspicuous expenditure."[2]

d) *Biological and social inheritance.*—The distinction between biological and social inheritance is sharply made by the noted biologist, J. Arthur Thomson, in the selection entitled "Nature and Nurture." The so-called "acquired characters" or modifications of original nature through experience, he points out, are transmitted not through the germ plasm but through communication.

Thorndike's "Inventory of Original Tendencies" offers a detailed classification of the traits transmitted biologically. Since there exists no corresponding specific analysis of acquired traits, the following brief inventory of types of social heritages is offered.

TYPES OF SOCIAL HERITAGES

(a) means of communication, as language, gesture, etc.;

(b) social attitudes, habits, wishes, etc.;

(c) character;

(d) social patterns, as folkways, mores, conventions, ideals, etc.;

(e) technique;

(f) culture (as distinguished from technique, formal organization, and machinery);

(g) social organization (primary group life, institutions, sects, secondary groups, etc.).

On the basis of the work of Mendel, biologists have made marked progress in determining the inheritance of specific traits of original nature. The selection from a foremost American student of heredity and eugenics, C. B. Davenport, entitled "Inheritance of Original Nature" indicates the precision and accuracy with which the prediction of the inheritance of individual innate traits is made.

---

[1] Charles H. Cooley, *Human Nature and the Social Order*, pp. 152–53.

[2] *The Theory of the Leisure Class* (New York, 1899).

The mechanism of the transmission of social heritages, while more open to observation than biological inheritance, has not been subjected to as intensive study. The transmission of the social heritage takes place by communication, as Keller points out, through the medium of the various senses. The various types of the social heritages are transmitted in two ways: (a) by tradition, as from generation to generation, and (b) by acculturation, as from group to group.

In the communication of the social heritages, either by tradition or by acculturation, two aspects of the process may be distinguished: (a) Because of temperament, interest, and run of attention of the members of the group, the heritage, whether a word, an act of skill, or a social attitude, may be selected, appropriated, and incorporated into its culture. This is communication by *imitation*. (b) On the other hand, the heritage may be imposed upon the members of the group through authority and routine, by tabu and repression. This is communication by *inculcation*. In any concrete situation the transmission of a social heritage may combine varying elements of both processes. Education, as the etymology of the term suggests, denotes culture of original tendencies; yet the routine of a school system is frequently organized about formal discipline rather than around interest, aptitude, and attention.

Historically, the scientific interest in the question of biological and social inheritance has concerned itself with the rather sterile problem of the weight to be attached on the one hand to physical heredity and on the other to social heritage. The selection,"Temperament, Tradition, and Nationality" suggests that a more important inquiry is to determine how the behavior patterns and the culture of a racial group or a social class are determined by the interaction of original nature and the social tradition. According to this conception, racial temperament is an active selective agency, determining interest and the direction of attention. The group heritages on the other hand represent a detached external social environment, a complex of stimuli, effective only in so far as they call forth responses. The culture of a group is the sum total and organization of the social heritages which have acquired a social meaning because of racial temperament and of the historical life of the group.

II. MATERIALS

A. THE ORIGINAL NATURE OF MAN

1. Original Nature Defined[1]

A man's nature and the changes that take place in it may be described in terms of the responses—of thought, feeling, action, and attitude—which he makes, and of the bonds by which these are connected with the situations which life offers. Any fact of intellect, character, or skill means a tendency to respond in a certain way to a certain situation—involves a *situation* or state of affairs influencing the man, a *response* or state of affairs in the man, and a *connection* or bond whereby the latter is the result of the former.

Any man possesses at the very start of his life—that is, at the moment when the ovum and spermatozoön which are to produce him have united—numerous well-defined tendencies to future behavior. Between the situations which he will meet and the responses which he will make to them, pre-formed bonds exist. It is already determined by the constitution of these two germs that under certain circumstances he will see and hear and feel and act in certain ways. His intellect and morals, as well as his bodily organs and movements, are in part the consequence of the nature of the embryo in the first moment of its life. What a man is and does throughout life is a result of whatever constitution he has at the start and of the forces that act upon it before and after birth. I shall use the term "original nature" for the former and "environment" for the latter. His original nature is thus a name for the nature of the combined germ-cells from which he springs, and his environment is a name for the rest of the universe, so far as it may, directly or indirectly, influence him.

Three terms, reflexes, instincts, and inborn capacities, divide the work of naming these unlearned tendencies. When the tendency concerns a very definite and uniform response to a very simple sensory situation, and when the connection between the situation and the response is very hard to modify and is also very strong so that it is almost inevitable, the connection or response to which it leads is called a reflex. Thus the knee-jerk is a very definite and uniform response to the simple sense-stimulus of sudden hard pressure against a certain spot.

[1] From Edward L. Thorndike, *The Original Nature of Man*, pp. 1–7. (Teachers College, Columbia University, 1913. Author's copyright.)

When the response is more indefinite, the situation more complex, and the connection more modifiable, instinct becomes the customary term. Thus one's misery at being scorned is too indefinite a response to too complex a situation and is too easily modifiable to be called a reflex. When the tendency is to an extremely indefinite response or set of responses to a very complex situation, as when the connection's final degree of strength is commonly due to very large contributions from training, it has seemed more appropriate to replace reflex and instinct by some term like capacity, or tendency, or potentiality. Thus an original tendency to respond to the circumstances of school education by achievement in learning the arts and sciences is called the capacity for scholarship.

There is, of course, no gap between reflexes and instincts, or between instincts and the still less easily describable original tendencies. The fact is that original tendencies range with respect to the nature of the responses from such as are single, simple, definite, uniform within the individual and only slightly variable amongst individuals, to responses that are highly compound, complex, vague, and variable within one individual's life and amongst individuals.

A typical reflex, or instinct, or capacity, as a whole, includes the ability to be sensitive to a certain situation, the ability to make a certain response, and the existence of a bond or connection whereby that response is made to that situation. For instance, the young chick is sensitive to the absence of other members of his species, is able to peep, and is so organized that the absence of other members of the species makes him peep. But the tendency to be sensitive to a certain situation may exist without the existence of a connection therewith of any further exclusive response, and the tendency to make a certain response may exist without the existence of a connection limiting that response exclusively to any single situation. The three-year-old child is by inborn nature markedly sensitive to the presence and acts of other human beings, but the exact nature of his response varies. The original tendency to cry is very strong, but there is no one situation to which it is exclusively bound. Original nature seems to decide that the individual will respond somehow to certain situations more often than it decides just what he will do, and to decide that he will make certain responses more often than it decides just when he will make them. So, for convenience in thinking about man's unlearned equipment, this appearance of *multiple response* to one same situation and *multiple causation* of one same response may be taken roughly as the fact.

2. No Separate Instincts[1]

It will be asserted that there are definite, independent, original instincts which manifest themselves in specific acts in a one-to-one correspondence. Fear, it will be said, is a reality, and so is anger, and rivalry, and love of mastery of others, and self-abasement, maternal love, sexual desire, gregariousness and envy, and each has its own appropriate deed as a result. Of course they are realities. So are suction, rusting of metals, thunder and lightning and lighter-than-air flying machines. But science and invention did not get on as long as men indulged in the notion of special forces to account for such phenomena. Men tried that road, and it only led them into learned ignorance. They spoke of nature's abhorrence of a vacuum; of a force of combustion; of intrinsic nisus toward this and that; of heaviness and levity as forces. It turned out that these "forces" were only the phenomena over again, translated from a specific and concrete form (in which they were at least actual) into a generalized form in which they were verbal. They converted a problem into a solution which afforded a simulated satisfaction.

Advance in insight and control came only when the mind turned squarely around. After it had dawned upon inquirers that their alleged causal forces were only names which condensed into a duplicate form a variety of complex occurrences, they set about breaking up phenomena into minute detail and searching for correlations, that is, for elements in other gross phenomena which also varied. Correspondence of variations of elements took the place of large and imposing forces. The psychology of behavior is only beginning to undergo similar treatment. But as yet we tend to regard sex, hunger, fear, and even much more complex active interests as if they were lump forces, like the combustion or gravity of old-fashioned physical science.

It is not hard to see how the notion of a single and separate tendency grew up in the case of simpler acts like hunger and sex. The paths of motor outlet or discharge are comparatively few and are

[1] Adapted from John Dewey, *Human Nature and Conduct*, pp. 149-57. (Henry Holt & Co., 1922.)

fairly well defined.   Specific bodily organs are conspicuously involved. Hence there is suggested the notion of a correspondingly separate psychic force or impulse.   There are two fallacies in this assumption. The first consists in ignoring the fact that no activity (even one that is limited by routine habit) is confined to the channel which is most flagrantly involved in its execution.   The whole organism is concerned in every act to some extent and in some fashion, internal organs as well as muscular, those of circulation, secretion, etc.   Since the total state of the organism is never exactly twice alike, in so far the phenomena of hunger and sex are never twice the same in fact.   The difference may be negligible for some purposes, and yet give the key for the purposes of a psychological analysis which shall terminate in a correct judgment of value.   Even physiologically the context of organic changes accompanying an act of hunger or sex makes the difference between a normal and a morbid phenomenon.

In the second place, the environment in which the act takes place is never twice alike.   Even when the overt organic discharge is substantially the same, the acts impinge upon a different environment and thus have different consequences.   It is impossible to regard these differences of objective result as indifferent to the quality of the acts.   They are immediately sensed if not clearly perceived; and they are the only *components of the meaning* of the act.   When feelings, dwelling antecedently in the soul, were supposed to be the causes of acts, it was natural to suppose that each psychic element had its own inherent quality which might be directly read off by introspection. But when we surrender this notion, it becomes evident that the only way of telling what an organic act is like is by the sensed or perceptible changes which it occasions.   Some of these will be intra-organic, and (as just indicated) they will vary with every act.   Others will be external to the organism, and these consequences are more important than the intra-organic ones for determining the quality of the act. For they are consequences in which others are concerned and which evoke reactions of favor and disfavor as well as co-operative and resisting activities of a more indirect sort.

A child gives way to what, grossly speaking, we call anger.   Its felt or appreciated quality depends in the first place upon the condition of his organism at the time, and this is never twice alike.   In the second place, the act is at once modified by the environment upon which it impinges so that different consequences are immediately reflected back to the doer. In one case, anger is directed say at older and stronger playmates who immediately avenge themselves upon the offender, perhaps cruelly. In another case, it takes effect upon weaker and impotent children, and the reflected appreciated consequence is one of achievement, victory, power and a knowledge of the means of having one's own way. The notion that anger still remains a single force is a lazy mythology. Even in the cases of hunger and sex, where the channels of action are fairly demarcated by antecedent conditions (or "nature"), the actual content and feel of hunger and sex are indefinitely varied according to their social contexts. Only when a man is starving, is hunger an unqualified natural impulse; as it approaches this limit, it tends to lose, moreover, its psychological distinctiveness and to become a raven of the entire organism.

The treatment of sex by psycho-analysts is most instructive, for it flagrantly exhibits both the consequences of artificial simplification and the transformation of social results into psychic causes. Writers, usually male, hold forth on the psychology of woman, as if they were dealing with a Platonic universal entity, although they habitually treat men as individuals, varying with structure and environment. They treat phenomena which are peculiarly symptoms of the civilization of the West at the present time as if they were the necessary effects of fixed native impulses of human nature. Romantic love as it exists today, with all the varying perturbations it occasions, is as definitely a sign of specific historic conditions as are big battle ships with turbines, internal-combustion engines, and electrically driven machines. It would be as sensible to treat the latter as effects of a single psychic cause as to attribute the phenomena of disturbance and conflict which accompany present sexual relations as manifestations of an original single psychic force or *Libido*. Upon this point at least a Marxian simplification is nearer the truth than that of Jung.

Again it is customary to suppose that there is a single instinct of fear, or at most a few well-defined sub-species of it. In reality, when one is afraid the whole being reacts, and this entire responding organism is never twice the same. In fact, also, every reaction takes place in a different environment, and its meaning is never twice alike, since the difference in environment makes a difference in consequences. There is no such thing as an environment in general; there are specific changing objects and events. Hence the kind of evasion or running away or shrinking up which takes place is directly correlated with specific surrounding conditions. There is no one fear having diverse manifestations; there are as many qualitatively different fears as there are objects responded to and different consequences sensed and observed.

Fear of the dark is different from fear of publicity, fear of the dentist from fear of ghosts, fear of conspicuous success from fear of humiliation, fear of a bat from fear of a bear. Cowardice, embarassment, caution and reverence may all be regarded as forms of fear. They all have certain physical organic acts in common—those of organic shrinkage, gestures of hesitation and retreat. But each is qualitatively unique. Each is what it is in virtue of its total interactions or correlations with other acts and with the environing medium, with consequences. High explosives and the aeroplane have brought into being something new in conduct. There is no error in calling it fear. But there is error, even from a limited clinical standpoint, in permitting the classifying name to blot from view the difference between fear of bombs dropped from the sky and the fears which previously existed. The new fear is just as much and just as little original and native as a child's fear of a stranger.

For any activity is original when it first occurs. As conditions are continually changing, new and *primitive* activities are continually occurring. The traditional psychology of instincts obscures recognition of this fact. It sets up a hard-and-fast preordained class under which specific acts are subsumed, so that their own quality and originality are lost from view. This is why the novelist and dramatist are so much more illuminating as well as more interesting commentators on conduct than is the schematizing psychologist.

The artist makes perceptible individual responses and thus displays a new phase of human nature evoked in new situations. In putting the case visibly and dramatically he reveals vital actualities. The scientific systematizer treats each art as merely another example of some old principle, or as a mechanical combination of elements drawn from a ready-made inventory.

When we recognize the diversity of native activities and the varied ways in which they are modified through interactions with one another in response to different conditions, we are able to understand moral phenomena otherwise baffling. In the career of any impulse activity there are speaking generally three possibilities. It may find a surging, explosive discharge—blind, unintelligent. It may be sublimated— that is, become a factor co-ordinated intelligently with others in a continuing course of action. Thus a gust of anger may, because of its dynamic incorporation into disposition, be converted into an abiding conviction of social injustice to be remedied, and furnish the dynamic to carry the conviction into execution. Or an excitation of sexual attraction may reappear in art or in tranquil domestic attachments and services. Such an outcome represents the normal or desirable functioning of impulse; in which, to use our previous language, the impulse operates as a pivot, or reorganization of habit. Or again a released impulsive activity may be neither immediately expressed in isolated spasmodic action, nor indirectly employed in an enduring interest. It may be "suppressed."

Suppression is not annihilation. "Psychic" energy is no more capable of being abolished than the forms we recognize as physical. If it is neither exploded nor converted, it is turned inwards, to lead a surreptitious, subterranean life. An isolated or spasmodic manifestation is a sign of immaturity, crudity, savagery; a suppressed activity is the cause of all kinds of intellectual and moral pathology. One form of the resulting pathology constitutes "reaction" in the sense in which the historian speaks of reactions. A conventionally familiar instance is Stuart license after Puritan restraint. A striking modern instance is the orgy of extravagance following upon the enforced economies and hardships of war, the moral let-down after its highstrung exalted idealisms, the deliberate carelessness after an attention too intense and too narrow. Outward manifestation of many normal activities had been suppressed. But activities were not suppressed. They were merely dammed up awaiting their chance.

3. Man Not Born Human[1]

Man is not born human. It is only slowly and laboriously, in fruitful contact, co-operation, and conflict with his fellows, that he attains the distinctive qualities of human nature. In the course of his prenatal life he has already passed roughly through, or, as the

[1] From Robert E. Park, *Principles of Human Behavior*, pp. 9–16. (The Zalaz Corporation, 1915.)

biologists say, "recapitulated," the whole history of his animal ancestors. He brings with him at birth a multitude of instincts and tendencies, many of which persist during life and many of which are only what G. Stanley Hall calls "vestigial traces" of his brute ancestry, as is shown by the fact that they are no longer useful and soon disappear.

These non-volitional movements of earliest infancy and of later childhood (such as licking things, clicking with the tongue, grinding the teeth, biting the nails, shrugging corrugations, pulling buttons, or twisting garments, strings, etc., twirling pencils, etc.) are relics of past forms of utilities now essentially obsolete. Ancient modes of locomotion, prehension, balancing, defense, attack, sensuality, etc., are all rehearsed, some quite fully and some only by the faintest mimetic suggestion, flitting spasmodic tensions, gestures, or facial expressions.

Human nature may therefore be regarded on the whole as a superstructure founded on instincts, dispositions, and tendencies, inherited from a long line of human and animal ancestors. It consists mainly in a higher organization of forces, a more subtle distillation of potencies latent in what Thorndike calls "the original nature of man."

The original nature of man is roughly what is common to all men minus all adaptations to tools, houses, clothes, furniture, words, beliefs, religions, laws, science, the arts, and to whatever in other men's behavior is due to adaptations to them. From human nature as we find it, take away, first, all that is in the European but not in the Chinaman, all that is in the Fiji Islander but not in the Esquimaux, all that is local or temporary. Then take away also the effects of all products of human art. What is left of human intellect and character is largely original—not wholly, for all those elements of knowledge which we call ideas and judgments must be subtracted from his responses. Man originally possesses only capacities which, after a given amount of education, will produce ideas and judgments.

Such, in general, is the nature of human beings before that nature has been modified by experience and formed by the education and the discipline of contact and intercourse with their fellows.

Several writers, among them William James, have attempted to make a rough inventory of the special instinctive tendencies with which human beings are equipped at birth. First of all there are the simpler reflexes such as "crying, sneezing, snoring, coughing, sighing, sobbing, gagging, vomiting, hiccuping, starting, moving the limb in response to its being tickled, touched or blown upon, spreading the toes in response to its being touched, tickled, or stroked on the sole of the foot, extending and raising the arms at any sudden sensory stimulus, or the quick pulsation of the eyelid."

Then there are the more complex original tendencies such as sucking, chewing, sitting up, and gurgling. Among the more general unlearned responses of children are fear, anger, pugnacity, envy, jealousy, curiosity, constructiveness, love of festivities, ceremonies and ordeals, sociability and shyness, secretiveness, etc. Thorndike, who quotes this list at length, has sought to give definiteness to its descriptions by clearly defining and distinguishing the character of the situation to which the behavior cited is a response. For example, to the situation, "strange man or animal, to solitude, black things, dark places, holes and corners, a human corpse," the native and unlearned response is fear. The original response of man to being alone is an experience of discomfort, to perceiving a crowd, "a tendency to join them and do what they are doing and an unwillingness to leave off and go home." It is part of man's original nature when he is in love to conceal his love affairs, and so forth.

It is evident from this list that what is meant by original nature is not confined to the behavior which manifests itself at birth, but includes man's spontaneous and unlearned responses to situations as they arise in the experience of the individual.

The widespread interest in the study of children has inspired in recent years a considerable literature bearing upon the original and inherited tendencies of human nature. The difficulty of distinguishing between what is original and what is acquired among the forms of behavior reported upon, and the further difficulty of obtaining accurate descriptions of the situations to which the behavior described was a response, has made much of this literature of doubtful value for scientific purposes. These studies have, nevertheless, contributed to a radical change in our conceptions of human nature. They have shown that the distinction between the mind of man and that of the lower animals is not so wide nor so profound as was once supposed. They have emphasized the fact that human nature rests on animal nature, and the transition from one to the other, in spite of the contrast in their separate achievements, has been made by imperceptible gradations. In the same way they have revealed, beneath differences in culture and individual achievement, the outlines of a pervasive and relatively unchanging human nature in which all races and individuals have a common share.

The study of human nature begins with description, but it goes on from that point to explanation. If the descriptions which we have thus far had of human nature are imperfect and lacking in precision, it is equally true that the explanations thus far invented have, on the whole, been inadequate. One reason for this has been the difficulty of the task. The mechanisms which control human behavior are, as might be expected, tremendously complicated, and the problem of analyzing them into their elementary forms and reducing their varied manifestations to precise and lucid formulas is both intricate and perplexing.

The foundation for the explanation of human nature has been laid, however, by the studies of behavior in animals and the comparative study of the physiology of the nervous system. Progress has been made, on the one hand, by seeking for the precise psychochemical process involved in the nervous reactions, and on the other, by reducing all higher mental processes to elementary forms represented by the tropisms and reflex actions.

In this, science has made a considerable advance upon common sense in its interpretations of human behavior, but has introduced no new principle; it has simply made its statements more detailed and exact. For example, common sense has observed that "the burnt child shuns the fire," that "the moth seeks the flame." These are both statements of truths of undoubted generality. In order to give them the validity of scientific truth, however, we need to know what there is in the nature of the processes involved that makes it inevitable that the child should shun the fire and the moth should seek the flame. It is not sufficient to say that the action in one case is instinctive and in the other intelligent, unless we are able to give precise and definite meanings to those terms; unless, in short, we are able to point out the precise mechanisms through which these reactions are carried out. The following illustration from Loeb's volume on the comparative physiology of the brain will illustrate the distinction between the common sense and the more precise scientific explanation of the behavior in man and the lower animals.

It is a well-known fact that if an ant be removed from a nest and afterward put back it will not be attacked, while almost invariably an ant belonging to another nest will be attacked. It has been customary to use the words memory, enmity, friendship, in describing this fact. Now Bethe made the following experiment: an ant was placed in the liquids (blood and lymph) squeezed out from the bodies of nest companions and was then put back into its nest; it was not attacked. It was then put in the juice taken from the inmates of a "hostile" nest and was at once attacked and killed. Bethe was able to prove by special experiments that these reactions of ants are not learned by experience, but are inherited. The "knowing" of "friend and foe" among ants is thus reduced to different reactions, depending upon the nature of the chemical stimulus and in no way depending upon memory.

Here, again, there is no essential difference between the common sense and the scientific explanation of the behavior of the ant except so far as the scientific explanation is more accurate, defining the precise mechanisms by which the recognition of "friend and foe" is effected, and the limitations to which it is subject.

Another result of the study of the comparative behavior of man and the lower animals has been to convince students that there is no fundamental difference between what was formerly called intelligent and instinctive behavior; that they may rather be reduced, as has been said, to the elementary form of reaction represented by the simple reflex in animals and the tropism in plants. Thus Loeb says:

A prominent psychologist has maintained that reflexes are to be considered as the mechanical effects of acts of volition of past generations. The ganglion-cell seems the only place where such mechanical effects could be stored up. It has therefore been considered the most essential element of the reflex mechanism, the nerve-fibers being regarded, and probably correctly, merely as conductors.

Both the authors who emphasize the purposefulness of the reflex act, and those who see in it only a physical process, have invariably looked upon the ganglion-cell as the principal bearer of the structures for the complex co-ordinated movements in reflex action.

I should have been as little inclined as any other physiologist to doubt the correctness of this conception had not the establishment of the identity of the reactions of animals and plants to light proved the untenability of this view and at the same time offered a different conception of reflexes.

The flight of the moth into the flame is a typical reflex process. The light stimulates the peripheral sense organs, the stimulus passes to the central nervous system, and from there to the muscles of the wings, and the moth is caused to fly into the flame. This reflex process agrees in every point with the heliotropic effects of light on plant organs. Since plants possess no nerves, this identity of animal with plant heliotropism can offer but one inference—these heliotropic effects must depend upon conditions which are common to both animals and plants.

On the other hand, Watson, in his *Introduction to Comparative Psychology*, defines the reflex as "a unit of analysis of instinct," and this means that instinctive actions in man and in animals may be regarded as combinations of simple reflex actions, that is to say of "fairly definite and generally predictable but unlearned responses of lower and higher organisms to stimuli." Many of these reflex responses are not fixed, as they were formerly supposed to be, but "highly unstable and indefinite." This fact makes possible the formation of habits, by combination and fixation of these inherited responses.

These views in the radical form in which they are expressed by Loeb and Watson have naturally enough been the subject of considerable controversy, both on scientific and sentimental grounds. They seem to reduce human behavior to a system of chemical and physical reactions, and rob life of all its spiritual values. On the other hand, it must be remembered that human beings, like other forms of nature, have this mechanical aspect and it is precisely the business of natural science to discover and lay them bare. It is only thus that we are able to gain control over ourselves and of others. It is a matter of common experience that we do form habits and that education and social control are largely dependent upon our ability to establish habits in ourselves and in others. Habit is, in fact, a characteristic example of just what is meant by "mechanism," in the sense in which it is here used. It is through the fixation of habit that we gain that control over our "original nature," which lifts us above the brutes and gives human nature its distinctive character as human. Character is nothing more than the sum and co-ordination of those mechanisms which we call habit and which are formed on the basis of the inherited and instinctive tendencies and dispositions which we share in so large a measure with the lower animals.

CHAPTER III

SOCIETY AND THE GROUP

I. INTRODUCTION

1. Society, the Community, and the Group

Human nature and the person are products of society. This is the sum and substance of the readings in the preceding chapter. But what, then, is society—this web in which the lives of individuals are so inextricably interwoven, and which seems at the same time so external and in a sense alien to them? From the point of view of common sense, "society" is sometimes conceived as the sum total of social institutions. The family, the church, industry, the state, all taken together, constitute society. In this use of the word, society is identified with social structure, something more or less external to individuals.

In accordance with another customary use of the term, "society" denotes a collection of persons. This is a vaguer notion but it at least identifies society with individuals instead of setting it apart from them. But this definition is manifestly superficial. Society is not a collection of persons in the sense that a brick pile is a collection of bricks. However we may conceive the relation of the parts of society to the whole, society is not a mere physical aggregation and not a mere mathematical or statistical unit.

Various explanations that strike deeper than surface observation have been proposed as solutions for this cardinal problem of the social one and the social many; of the relation of society to the individual. Society has been described as a tool, an instrument, as it were, an extension of the individual organism. The argument runs something like this: The human hand, though indeed a part of the physical organism, may be regarded as an instrument of the body as a whole. If as by accident it be lost, it is conceivable that a mechanical hand might be substituted for it, which, though not a part of the body, would function for all practical purposes as a hand of flesh and blood. A hoe may be regarded as a highly specialized hand, so also logically, if less figuratively, a plow. So the hand of another person if it does your bidding may be regarded as your instrument, your hand. Language is witness to the fact that employers speak of "the hands" which they "work." Social institutions may likewise be thought of as tools of individuals for accomplishing their purposes. Logically, therefore, society, either as a sum of institutions or as a collection of persons, may be conceived of as a sum total of instrumentalities, extensions of the functions of the human organism which enable individuals to carry on life-activities. From this standpoint society is an immense co-operative concern of mutual services.

This latter is an aspect of society which economists have sought to isolate and study. From this point of view the relations of individuals are conceived as purely external to one another, like that of the plants in a plant community. Co-operation, so far as it exists, is competitive and "free."

In contrast with the view of society which regards social institutions and the community itself as the mere instruments and tools of the individuals who compose it, is that which conceives society as resting upon biological adaptations, that is to say upon instincts, gregariousness, for example, imitation, or like-mindedness. The classic examples of societies based on instinct are the social insects, the well-known bee and the celebrated ant. In human society the family, with its characteristic differences and interdependences of the sexes and the age groups, husband and wife, children and parents, most nearly realizes this description of society. In so far as the organization of society is predetermined by inherited or constitutional differences, as is the case pre-eminently in the so-called animal societies, competition ceases and the relations of its component individuals become, so to speak, internal, and a permanent part of the structure of the group.

The social organization of human beings, on the other hand, the various types of social groups, and the changes which take place in them at different times under varying circumstances, are determined not merely by instincts and by competition but by custom, tradition, public opinion, and contract. In animal societies as herds, flocks, and packs, collective behavior seems obviously to be explained in terms of instinct and emotion. In the case of man, however, instincts are changed into habits; emotions, into sentiments. Furthermore, all these forms of behavior tend to become conventionalized and thus become relatively independent of individuals and of instincts. The behavior of the person is thus eventually controlled by the formal standards which, implicit in the mores, are explicit in the laws. Society now may be defined as the social heritage of *habit and sentiment, folkways and mores, technique and culture,* all of which are incident or necessary to collective human behavior.

Human society, then, unlike animal society, is mainly a social heritage, created in and transmitted by communication. The continuity and life of a society depend upon its success in transmitting from one generation to the next its folkways, mores, technique, and ideals. From the standpoint of collective behavior these cultural traits may all be reduced to the one term "consensus." Society viewed abstractly is an organization of individuals; considered concretely it is a complex of organized habits, sentiments, and social attitudes—in short, consensus.

The terms society, community, and social group are now used by students with a certain difference of emphasis but with very little difference in meaning. Society is the more abstract and inclusive term, and society is made up of social groups, each possessing its own specific type of organization but having at the same time all the general characteristics of society in the abstract. Community is the term which is applied to societies and social groups where they are considered from the point of view of the geographical distribution of the individuals and institutions of which they are composed. It follows that every community is a society, but not every society is a community. An individual may belong to many social groups but he will not ordinarily belong to more than one community, except in so far as a smaller community of which he is a member is included in a larger of which he is also a member. However, an individual is not, at least from a sociological point of view, a member of a community because he lives in it but rather because, and to the extent that, he participates in the common life of the community.

The term social group has come into use with the attempts of students to classify societies. Societies may be classified with reference to the rôle which they play in the organization and life of larger social groups or societies. The internal organization of any given social group will be determined by its external relation to other groups in the society of which it is a part as well as by the relations of individuals within the group to one another.   A boys' gang, a girls' clique, a college class, or a neighborhood conforms to this definition quite as much as a labor union, a business enterprise, a political party, or a nation.   One advantage of the term "group" lies in the fact that it may be applied to the smallest as well as to the largest forms of human association.

2.   Classification of the Materials

Society, in the most inclusive sense of that term, the Great Society, as Graham Wallas described it, turns out upon analysis to be a constellation of other smaller societies, that is to say races, peoples, parties, factions, cliques, clubs, etc.   The community, the world-community, on the other hand, which is merely the Great Society viewed from the standpoint of the territorial distribution of its members, presents a different series of social groupings and the Great Society in this aspect exhibits a totally different pattern.   From the point of view of the territorial distribution of the individuals that constitute it, the world-community is composed of nations, colonies, spheres of influence, cities, towns, local communities, neighborhoods, and families.

These represent in a rough way the subject-matter of sociological science.   Their organization, interrelation, constituent elements, and the characteristic changes (social processes) which take place in them are the phenomena of sociological science.

Human beings as we meet them are mobile entities, variously distributed through geographical space.   What is the nature of the connection between individuals which permits them at the same time to preserve their distances and act corporately and consentiently— with a common purpose, in short ?   These distances which separate individuals are not merely spatial, they are psychical.   Society exists where these distances have been *relatively* overcome.   Society exists, in short, not merely where there are people but where there is communication.

The materials in this chapter are intended to show (1) the fundamental character of the relations which have been established between individuals through communication; (2) the gradual evolution of these relations in animal and human societies. On the basis of the principle thus established it is possible to work out a rational classification of social groups.

Espinas defines society in terms of corporate action. Wherever separate individuals act together as a unit, where they co-operate as though they were parts of the same organism, there he finds society. Society from this standpoint is not confined to members of one species, but may be composed of different members of species where there is permanent joint activity. In the study of symbiosis among animals, it is significant to note the presence of structural adaptations in one or both species. In the taming and domestication of animals by man the effects of symbiosis are manifest. Domestication, by the selection in breeding of traits desired by man, changes the original nature of the animal. Taming is achieved by control of habits in transferring to man the filial and gregarious responses of the young naturally given to its parents and members of its kind. Man may be thought of as domesticated through natural social selection. Eugenics is a conscious program of further domestication by the elimination of defective physical and mental racial traits and by the improvement of the racial stock through the social selection of superior traits. Taming has always been a function of human society, but it is dignified by such denominations as "education," "social control," "punishment," and "reformation."

The plant community offers the simplest and least qualified example of the community. Plant life, in fact, offers an illustration of a *community* which is *not a society*. It is not a society because it is an organization of individuals whose relations, if not wholly external, are, at any rate, "unsocial" in so far as there is no consensus. The plant community is interesting, moreover, because it exhibits in the barest abstraction, the character of *competitive co-operation*, the aspect of social life which constitutes part of the special subject-matter of economic science.

This struggle for existence, in some form or other, is in fact essential to the existence of society. Competition, segregation, and accommodation serve to maintain the social distances, to fix the status, and preserve the independence of the individual in the social relation. A society in which all distances, physical as well as psychical, had been abolished, in which there was neither taboo, prejudice, nor reserve of any sort; a society in which the intimacies were absolute, would be a society in which there were neither persons nor freedom. The processes of competition, segregation, and accommodation brought out in the description of the plant community are quite comparable with the same processes in animal and human communities. A village, town, city, or nation may be studied from the standpoint of the adaptation, struggle for existence, and survival of its individual members in the environment created by the community as a whole.

Society, as Dewey points out, if based on instinct is an effect of communication. *Consensus* even more than *co-operation* or *corporate action* is the distinctive mark of human society. Dewey, however, seems to restrict the use of consensus to group decisions in which all the members consciously and rationally participate. Tradition and sentiment are, however, forms of consensus quite as much as constitutions, rules, and elections.

Le Bon's classification of social groups into heterogeneous and homogeneous crowds, while interesting and suggestive, is clearly inadequate. Many groups familiar to all of us, as the family, the play-group, the neighborhood, the public, find no place in his system.[1]

Concrete descriptions of group behavior indicate three aspects in the consensus of the members of the group. The first is the characteristic state of group feeling called *esprit de corps*. The enthusiasm of the two sides in a football contest, the ecstasy of religious ceremonial, the fellowship of members of a fraternity, the brotherhood of a monastic band are all different manifestations of group spirit.

The second aspect of consensus has become familiar through the term "morale." Morale may be defined as the collective will. Like the will of the individual it represents an organization of behavior tendencies. The discipline of the individual, his subordination to the group, lies in his participation and reglementation in social activities.

The third aspect of consensus which makes for unified behavior of the members of the group has been analyzed by Durkheim under the term "collective representations." Collective representations are the concepts which embody the objectives of group activity.

[1] See *supra*, chap. i, pp. 50–51.

The totem of primitive man, the flag of a nation, a religious creed, the number system, and Darwin's theory of the descent of man—all these are collective representations. Every society and every social group has, or tends to have, its own symbols and its own language. The language and other symbolic devices by which a society carries on its collective existence are collective representations. Animals do not possess them.

II. MATERIALS

A. SOCIETY AND SYMBIOSIS

1. Definition of Society [1]

The idea of society is that of a permanent co-operation in which separate living beings undertake to accomplish an identical act. These beings may find themselves brought by their conditions to a point where their co-operation forces them to group themselves in space in some definite form, but it is by no means necessary that they should be in juxtaposition for them to act together and thus to form a society. A customary reciprocation of services among more or less independent individualities is the characteristic feature of the social life, a feature that contact or remoteness does not essentially modify, nor the apparent disorder nor the regular disposition of the parties in space.

Two beings may then form what is to the eyes a single mass, and may live, not only in contact with each other, but even in a state of mutual penetration without constituting a society. It is enough in such a case that one looks at them as entirely distinct, that their activities tend to opposite or merely different ends. If their functions, instead of co-operating, diverge; if the good of one is the evil of the other, whatever the intimacy of their contact may be, no social bond unites them.

But the nature of the functions and the form of the organs are inseparable. If two beings are endowed with functions that necessarily combine, they are also endowed with organs, if not similar, at least corresponding. And these beings with like or corresponding organs are either of the same species or of very nearly the same species.

[1] Translated from Alfred Espinas, *Des sociétés animales* (1878), pp. 157–60.

However, circumstances may be met where two beings with quite different organs and belonging even to widely remote species may be accidentally and at a single point useful to each other. A habitual relation may be established between their activities, but only on this one point, and in the time limits in which the usefulness exists. Such a case gives the occasion, if not for a society, at least for an association; that is to say, a union less necessary, less strict, less durable, may find its origin in such a meeting. In other words, beside the normal societies formed of elements specifically alike, which cannot exist without each other, there will be room for more accidental groupings, formed of elements more or less specifically unlike, which convenience unites and not necessity. We will commence with a study of the latter.

To society the most alien relations of two living beings which can be produced are those of the predator and his prey. In general, the predator is bulkier than his prey, since he overcomes him and devours him. Yet smaller ones sometimes attack larger creatures, consuming them, however, by instalments, and letting them live that they themselves may live on them as long as possible. In such a case they are forced to remain for a longer or a shorter time attached to the body of their victim, carried about by it wherever the vicissitudes of its life lead them. Such animals have received the name of parasites. Parasitism forms the line inside of which our subject begins; for if one can imagine that the parasite, instead of feeding on the animal from whom he draws his subsistence, is content to live on the remains of the other's meals, one will find himself in the presence, not yet of an actual society, but of half the conditions of a society; that is to say, a relation between two beings such that, all antagonism ceasing, one of the two is useful to the other. Such is commensalism. However, this association does not yet offer the essential element of all society, co-operation. There is co-operation when the commensal is not less useful to his host than the latter is to the commensal himself, when the two are concerned in living in a reciprocal relation and in developing their double activity in corresponding ways toward a single and an identical goal. One has given to this mode of activity the name of mutualism. Domestication is only one form of it. Parasitism, commensalism, mutualism, exist with animals among the different species.

2. Symbiosis (literally "living together")[1]

In gaining their wide and intimate acquaintance with the vegetable world the ants have also become acquainted with a large number of insects that obtain their nutriment directly from plants, either by sucking up their juices or by feeding on their foliage. To the former group belong the phytophthorous Homoptera, the plant lice, scale insects, or mealy bugs, tree-hoppers, lantern flies, and jumping plant lice; to the latter belong the caterpillars of the lycaenid butterflies, the "blues," or "azures," as they are popularly called. All of these creatures excrete liquids which are eagerly sought by the ants and constitute the whole, or, at any rate, an important part of the food of certain species. In return the Homoptera and caterpillars receive certain services from the ants, so that the relations thus established between these widely different insects may be regarded as a kind of symbiosis. These relations are most apparent in the case of the aphids, and these insects have been more often and more closely studied in Europe and America.

The consociation of the ants with the aphids is greatly facilitated by the gregarious and rather sedentary habits of the latter, especially in their younger, wingless stages, for the ants are thus enabled to obtain a large amount of food without losing time and energy in ranging far afield from their nests. Then, too, the ants may establish their nests in the immediate vicinity of the aphid droves or actually keep them in their nests or in "sheds" carefully constructed for the purpose.

Some ants obtain the honey-dew merely by licking the surface of the leaves and stems on which it has fallen, but many species have learned to stroke the aphids and induce them to void the liquid gradually so that it can be imbibed directly. A drove of plant lice, especially when it is stationed on young and succulent leaves or twigs, may produce enough honey-dew to feed a whole colony of ants for a considerable period.

As the relations between ants and the various Homoptera have been regarded as mutualistic, it may be well to marshal the facts which seem to warrant this interpretation. The term "mutualism" as applied to these cases means, of course, that the aphids, coccids,

[1] Adapted from William M. Wheeler, *Ants, Their Structure, Development, Behavior*, pp. 339–424. (Columbia University Press, 1910.)

and membracids are of service to the ants and in turn profit by the companionship of these more active and aggressive insects. Among the modifications in structure and behavior which may be regarded as indicating on the part of aphids unmistakable evidence of adaptation to living with ants, the following may be cited:

1. The aphids do not attempt to escape from the ants or to defend themselves with their siphons, but accept the presence of these attendants as a matter of course.

2. The aphids respond to the solicitations of the ants by extruding the droplets of honey-dew gradually and not by throwing them off to a distance with a sudden jerk, as they do in the absence of ants.

3. Many species of Aphididae that live habitually with ants have developed a perianal circlet of stiff hairs which support the drop of honey-dew till it can be imbibed by the ants. This circlet is lacking in aphids that are rarely or never visited by ants.

4. Certain observations go to show that aphids, when visited by ants, extract more of the plant juices than when unattended.

The adaptations on the part of the ants are, with a single doubtful exception, all modifications in behavior and not in structure.

1. Ants do not seize and kill aphids as they do when they encounter other sedentary defenseless insects.

2. The ants stroke the aphids in a particular manner in order to make them excrete the honey-dew, and know exactly where to expect the evacuated liquid.

3. The ants protect the aphids. Several observers have seen the ants driving away predatory insects.

4. Many aphidicolous ants, when disturbed, at once seize and carry their charges in their mandibles to a place of safety, showing very plainly their sense of ownership and interest in these helpless creatures.

5. This is also exhibited by all ants that harbor root-aphids and root-coccids in their nests. Not only are these insects kept in confinement by the ants, but they are placed by them on the roots. In order to do this the ants remove the earth from the surfaces of the roots and construct galleries and chambers around them so that the Homoptera may have easy access to their food and even move about at will.

6. Many ants construct, often at some distance from their nests, little closed pavilions or sheds of earth, carton, or silk, as a protection for their cattle and for themselves. The singular habit may be merely a more recent development from the older and more general habit of excavating tunnels and chambers about roots and subterranean stems.

7. The solicitude of the ants not only envelops the adult aphids and coccids, but extends also to their eggs and young. Numerous observers have observed ants in the autumn collecting and storing aphid eggs in the chambers of their nests, caring for them through the winter and in the spring placing the recently hatched plant lice on the stems and roots of the plants.

In the foregoing I have discussed the ethological relations of ants to a variety of other organisms. This, however, did not include an account of some of the most interesting symbiotic relations, namely, those of the ants to other species of their own taxonomic group and to termites. This living together of colonies of different species may be properly designated as social symbiosis, to distinguish it from the simple symbiosis that obtains between individual organisms of different species and the intermediate form of symbiosis exhibited by individual organisms that live in ant or termite colonies.

The researches of the past forty years have brought to light a remarkable array of instances of social symbiosis, varying so much in intimacy and complexity that it is possible to construct a series ranging from mere simultaneous occupancy of a very narrow ethological station, or mere contiguity of domicile, to an actual fusion, involving the vital dependence or parasitism of a colony of one species on that of another. Such a series is, of course, purely conceptual and does not represent the actual course of development in nature, where, as in the animal and vegetable kingdoms in general, development has not followed a simple linear course, but has branched out repeatedly and terminated in the varied types at the present time.

It is convenient to follow the European writers, von Hagens, Forel, Wasmann, and others, in grouping all the cases of social symbiosis under two heads, the compound nests and the mixed colonies. Different species of ants or of ants and termites are said to form compound nests when their galleries are merely contiguous or actually interpenetrate and open into one another, although the colonies which inhabit them bring up their respective offspring in different apartments. In mixed colonies, on the other hand, which, in a state of nature, can be formed only by species of ants of close taxonomic affinities, the insects live together in a single nest and bring up their young in common. Although each of these categories comprises a number of dissimilar types of social symbiosis, and although it is possible, under certain circumstances, as will be shown in the sequel, to convert a compound nest into a mixed colony, the distinction is nevertheless fundamental. It must be admitted, however, that both types depend in last analysis on the dependent, adoption-seeking instincts of the queen ant and on the remarkable plasticity which enables allied species and genera to live in very close proximity to one another. By a strange paradox these peculiarities have been produced in the struggle for existence, although this struggle is severer among different species of ants than between ants and other organisms. As Forel says: "The greatest enemies of ants are other ants, just as the greatest enemies of men are other men."

3. The Taming and the Domestication of Animals[1]

Primitive man was a hunter almost before he had the intelligence to use weapons, and from the earliest times he must have learned something about the habits of the wild animals he pursued for food or for pleasure, or from which he had to escape. It was probably as a hunter that he first came to adopt young animals which he found in the woods or the plains, and made the surprising discovery that these were willing to remain under his protection and were pleasing and useful. He passed gradually from being a hunter to becoming a keeper of flocks and herds. From these early days to the present time, the human race has taken an interest in the lower animals, and yet extremely few have been really domesticated. The living world would seem to offer an almost unlimited range of creatures which might be turned to our profit and as domesticated animals minister to our comfort or convenience. And yet it seems as if there were some obstacle rooted in the nature of animals or in the powers of man, for the date of the adoption by man of the few domesticated species lies in remote, prehistoric antiquity. The surface of the earth has been explored, the physiology of breeding and feeding

[1] Adapted from P. Chalmers Mitchell, *The Childhood of Animals*, pp. 204-21. (Frederick A. Stokes & Co., 1912.)

has been studied, our knowledge of the animal kingdom has been vastly increased, and yet there is hardly a beast bred in the farm-yard today with which the men who made stone weapons were not acquainted and which they had not tamed. Most of the domestic animals of Europe, America, and Asia came originally from Central Asia, and have spread thence in charge of their masters, the primitive hunters who captured them.

No monkeys have been domesticated. Of the carnivores only the cat and the dog are truly domesticated. Of the ungulates there are horses and asses, pigs, cattle, sheep, goats, and reindeer. Among rodents there are rabbits and guinea-pigs, and possibly some of the fancy breeds of rats and mice should be included. Among birds there are pigeons, fowls, peacocks, and guinea-fowl, and aquatic birds such as swans, geese, and ducks, whilst the only really domes-ticated passerine bird is the canary. Goldfish are domesticated, and the invertebrate bees and silk-moths must not be forgotten. It is not very easy to draw a line between domesticated animals and animals that are often bred in partial or complete captivity. Such antelopes as elands, fallow-deer, roe-deer, and the ostriches of ostrich farms are on the border-line of being domesticated.

It is also difficult to be quite certain as to what is meant by a tame animal. Cockroaches usually scuttle away when they are disturbed and seem to have learnt that human beings have a just grievance against them. But many people have no horror of them. A pretty girl, clean and dainty in her ways, and devoted to all kinds of animals, used to like sitting in a kitchen that was infested with these repulsive creatures, and told me that when she was alone they would run over her dress and were not in the least startled when she took them up. I have heard of a butterfly which used to come and sip sugar from the hand of a lady; and those who have kept spiders and ants declare that these intelligent creatures learn to dis-tinguish their friends. So also fish, like the great carp in the garden of the palace of Fontainebleau, and many fishes in aquaria and private ponds, learn to come to be fed. I do not think, however, that these ought to be called tame animals. Most of the wild animals in menageries very quickly learn to distinguish one person from another, to obey the call of their keeper and to come to be fed, although certainly they would be dangerous even to the keeper if he were to enter their cages. To my mind, tameness is something more than merely coming to be fed, and, in fact, many tame animals are least tame when they are feeding. Young carnivores, for instance, which can be handled freely and are affectionate, very seldom can be touched whilst they are feeding. The real quality of tameness is that the tame animal is not merely tolerant of the presence of man, not merely has learned to associate him with food, but takes some kind of pleasure in human company and shows some kind of affection.

On the other hand, we must not take our idea of tameness merely from the domesticated animals. These have been bred for many generations, and those that were most wild and that showed any resistance to man were killed or allowed to escape. Dogs are always taken as the supreme example of tameness, and sentimentalists have almost exhausted the resources of language in praising them. Like most people, I am very fond of dogs, but it is an affection without respect. Dogs breed freely in captivity, and in the enormous period of time that has elapsed since the first hunters adopted wild puppies there has been a constant selection by man, and every dog that showed any independence of spirit has been killed off. Man has tried to produce a purely subservient creature, and has succeeded in his task. No doubt a dog is faithful and affectionate, but he would be shot or drowned or ordered to be destroyed by the local magistrate if he were otherwise. A small vestige of the original spirit has been left in him, merely from the ambition of his owners to possess an animal that will not bite them, but will bite anyone else. And even this watch-dog trait is mechanical, for the guardian of the house will worry the harmless, necessary postman, and welcome the bold burglar with fawning delight. The dog is a slave, and the crowning evidence of his docility, that he will fawn on the person who has beaten him, is the result of his character having been bred out of him. The dog is an engaging companion, an animated toy more diverting than the cleverest piece of clockwork, but it is only our colossal vanity that makes us take credit for the affection and faithfulness of our own particular animal. The poor beast cannot help it; all else has been bred out of him generations ago.

When wild animals become tame, they are really extending or transferring to human beings the confidence and affection they naturaliy give their mothers, and this view will be found to explain more facts about tameness than any other. Every creature that would naturally enjoy maternal, or it would be better to say parental, care, as the father sometimes shares in or takes upon himself the duty of guarding the young, is ready to transfer its devotion to other animals or to human beings, if the way be made easy for it, and if it be treated without too great violation of its natural instincts. The capacity to be tamed is greatest in those animals that remain longest with their parents and that are most intimately associated with them. The capacity to learn new habits is greatest in those animals which naturally learn most from their parents, and in which the period of youth is not merely a period of growing, a period of the awakening of instincts, but a time in which a real education takes place. These capacities of being tamed and of learning new habits are greater in the higher mammals than in the lower mammals, in mammals than in birds, and in birds than in reptiles. They are very much greater in very young animals, where dependence on the parents is greatest, than in older animals, and they gradually fade away as the animal grows up, and are least of all in fully grown and independent creatures of high intelligence.

Young animals born in captivity are no more easy to tame than those which have been taken from the mother in her native haunts. If they remain with the mother, they very often grow up even shyer and more intolerant of man than the mothers themselves. There is no inherited docility or tameness, and a general survey of the facts fully bears out my belief that the process of taming is almost entirely a transference to human beings of the confidence and affection that a young animal would naturally give its mother. The process of domestication is different, and requires breeding a race of animals in captivity for many generations and gradually weeding out those in which youthful tameness is replaced by the wild instinct of adult life, and so creating a strain with new and abnormal instincts.

B. PLANT COMMUNITIES AND ANIMAL SOCIETIES
1. Plant Communities[1]

Certain species group themselves into natural associations, that is to say, into communities which we meet with more or less frequently

[1] Adapted from Eugenius Warming, *Oecology of Plants*, pp. 12–13, 91–95. (Oxford University Press, 1909.)

and which exhibit the same combination of growth-forms and the same facies. As examples in northern Europe may be cited a meadow with its grasses and perennial herbs, or a beech forest with its beech trees and all the species usually accompanying these. Species that form a community must either practice the same economy, making approximately the same demands on its environment (as regards nourishment, light, moisture, and so forth), or one species present must be dependent for its existence upon another species, sometimes to such an extent that the latter provides it with what is necessary or even best suited to it (Oxalis Acetosella and saprophytes which profit from the shade of the beech and from its humus soil); a kind of symbiosis seems to prevail between such species. In fact, one often finds, as in beech forests, that the plants growing under the shade and protection of other species, and belonging to the most diverse families, assume growth-forms that are very similar to one another, but essentially different from those of the forest trees, which, in their turn, often agree with one another.

The ecological analysis of a plant-community leads to the recognition of the growth-forms composing it as its ultimate units. From what has just been said in regard to growth-forms it follows that species of very diverse physiognomy can very easily occur together in the same natural community. But beyond this, as already indicated, species differing widely, not only in physiognomy but also in their whole economy, may be associated. We may therefore expect to find both great variety of form and complexity of interrelations among the species composing a natural community; as an example we may cite the richest of all types of communities—the tropical rain-forest. It may also be noted that the physiognomy of a community is not necessarily the same at all times of the year, the distinction sometimes being caused by a rotation of species.

The different communities, it need hardly be stated, are scarcely ever sharply marked off from one another. Just as soil, moisture, and other external conditions are connected by the most gradual transitions, so likewise are the plant-communities, especially in cultivated lands. In addition, the same species often occur in several widely different communities; for example, Linnaea borealis grows not only in coniferous forests, but also in birch woods, and even high above the tree limit on the mountains of Norway and on the fell-fields of Greenland. It appears that different combinations of external factors can replace one another and bring into existence approximately the same community, or at least can satisfy equally well one and the same species, and that, for instance, a moist climate often completely replaces the forest shade of dry climates.

The term "community" implies a diversity but at the same time a certain organized uniformity in the units. The units are the many individual plants that occur in every community, whether this be a beech forest, a meadow, or a heath. Uniformity is established when certain atmospheric, terrestrial, and other factors are co-operative, and appears either because a certain defined economy makes its impress on the community as a whole, or because a number of different growth-forms are combined to form a single aggregate which has a definite and constant guise.

The analysis of a plant-community usually reveals one or more of the kinds of symbiosis as illustrated by parasites, saprophytes, epiphytes, and the like. There is scarce a forest or a bushland where examples of these forms of symbiosis are lacking; if, for instance, we investigate the tropical rain-forest we are certain to find in it all conceivable kinds of symbiosis. But the majority of individuals of a plant-community are linked by bonds other than those mentioned—bonds that are best described as *commensal*. The term *commensalism* is due to Van Beneden, who wrote, "Le commensal est simplement un compagnon de table"; but we employ it in a somewhat different sense to denote the relationship subsisting between species which share with one another the supply of food-material contained in soil and air, and thus feed at the same table.

More detailed analysis of the plant-community reveals very considerable distinctions among commensals. Some relationships are considered in the succeeding paragraphs.

Like commensals.—When a plant-community consists solely of individuals belonging to one species—for example, solely of beech, ling, or Aira flexuosa—then we have the purest example of like commensals. These all make the same demands as regards nutriment, soil, light, and other like conditions; as each species requires a certain amount of space and as there is scarcely ever sufficient nutriment for all the offspring, a struggle for food arises among the plants so soon as the space is occupied by the definite numbers of individuals which, according to the species, can develop thereon. The individuals lodged in unfavorable places and the weaklings are vanquished and exterminated. This competitive struggle takes place in all plant-communities, with perhaps the sole exceptions of sub-glacial communities and in deserts. In these *open communities* the soil is very often or always so open and so irregularly clothed that there is space for many more individuals than are actually present; the cause for this is obviously to be sought in the climatically unfavorable conditions of life, which either prevent plants from producing seed and other propagative bodies in sufficient numbers to clothe the ground or prevent the development of seedlings. On such soil one can scarcely speak of a competitive struggle for existence; in this case a struggle takes place between the plant and inanimate nature, but to little or no extent between plant and plant.

That a congregation of individuals belonging to one species into one community may be profitable to the species is evident; it may obviously in several ways aid in maintaining the existence of the species, for instance, by facilitating abundant and certain fertilization (especially in anemophilous plants) and maturation of seeds; in addition, the social mode of existence may confer other less-known advantages. But, on the other hand, it brings with it greater danger of serious damage and devastation wrought by parasites.

The bonds that hold like individuals to a like habitat are, as already indicated, identical demands as regards existence, and these demands are satisfied in their precise habitat to such an extent that the species can maintain itself here against rivals. Natural unmixed associations of forest trees are the result of struggles with other species. But there are differences as regards the ease with which a community can arise and establish itself. Some species are more social than others, that is to say, better fitted to form communities. The causes for this are biological, in that some species, like Phragmites, Scirpus lacustris, Psamma (Ammophila) arenaria, Tussilago, Farfara, and Asperula odorata, multiply very readily by means of stolons; or others, such as Cirsium arvense, and Sonchus arvensis, produce buds from their roots; or yet others produce numerous seeds which are easily dispersed and may remain for a long time capable of germinating, as is the case with Calluna, Picea excelsa, and Pinus; or still other species, such as beech and spruce, have the power of enduring shade or even suppressing other species by the shade they cast. A number of species, such as Pteris aquilina, Acorus Calamus, Lemna minor, and Hypnum Schreberi, which are social, and likewise very widely distributed, multiply nearly exclusively by vegetative means, rarely or never producing fruit. On the contrary, certain species, for example, many orchids and Umbelliferae, nearly always grow singly.

In the case of many species certain geological conditions have favored their grouping together into pure communities. The forests of northern Europe are composed of few species, and are not mixed in the same sense as are those in the tropics, or even those in Austria and other southern parts of Europe: the cause for this may be that the soil is geologically very recent, inasmuch as the time that has elapsed since the glacial epoch swept it clear has been too short to permit the immigration of many competitive species.

Unlike commensals.—The case of a community consisting of individuals belonging to one species is, strictly speaking, scarcely ever met with; but the dominant individuals of a community may belong to a single species, as in the case of a beech forest, spruce forest, or ling heath—and only thus far does the case proceed. In general, many species grow side by side, and many different growth-forms and types of symbiosis, in the extended sense, are found collected in a community. For even when one species occupies an area as completely as the nature of the soil will permit, other species can find room and can grow between its individuals; in fact, if the soil is to be completely covered the vegetation must necessarily always be heterogeneous. The greatest aggregate of existence arises where the greatest diversity prevails. The kind of communal life resulting will depend upon the nature of the demands made by the species in regard to conditions of life. As in human communities, so in this case, the *struggle between the like* is the *most severe*, that is, between the species making more or less the same demands and wanting the same dishes from the common table. In a tropical mixed forest there are hundreds of species of trees growing together in such profuse variety that the eye can scarce see at one time two individuals of the same species, yet all of them undoubtedly represent tolerable uniformity in the demands they make as regards conditions of life, and in so far they are alike. And among them a severe competition for food must be taking place. In those cases in which certain species readily grow in each other's company—and cases of this kind are familiar to florists—when, for instance, Isoetes, Lobelia Dortmanna, and Litorella lacustris occur together—the common demands made as regards external conditions obviously form the bond that unites them. Between such species a competitive struggle must take place. Which of the species shall be represented by the greatest number of individuals certainly often depends upon casual conditions, a slight change in one direction or the other doubtless often playing a decisive rôle; but apart from this it appears that morphological and biological features, for example, development at a different season, may change the nature of the competition.

Yet there are in every plant-community numerous species which *differ widely* in the demands they make for light, heat, nutriment, and so on. Between such species there is less competition, the greater the disparity in their wants; the case is quite conceivable in which the *one species should require exactly what the other would avoid;* the two species would then be complementary to one another in their occupation and utilization of the same soil.

There are also obvious cases in which different species are of service to each other. The carpet of moss in a pine forest, for example, protects the soil from desiccation and is thus useful to the pine; yet, on the other hand, it profits from the shade cast by the latter.

As a rule, limited numbers of definite species are the most potent, and, like absolute monarchs, can hold sway over the whole area; while other species, though possibly present in far greater numbers than these, are subordinate or even dependent on them. This is the case where subordinate species only flourish in the shade or among the fallen fragments of dominant species. Such is obviously the relationship between trees and many plants growing on the ground of high forest, such as mosses, fungi, and other saprophytes, ferns, Oxalis Acetosella, and their associates. In this case, then, there is a commensalism in which individuals feed at the same table but on different fare. An additional factor steps in when species do not absorb their nutriment at the same season of the year. Many spring plants—for instance, Galanthus nivalis, Corydalis solida, and C. cava—have withered before the summer plants commence properly to develop. Certain species of animals are likewise confined to certain plant-communities. But one and the same tall plant may, in different places or soils, have different species of lowly plants as companions; the companion plants of high beech forests depend, for instance, upon climate and upon the nature of the forest soil; Pinus nigra, according to von Beck, can maintain under it in the different parts of Europe a Pontic, a central European, or a Baltic vegetation.

There are certain points of resemblance between communities of plants and those of human beings or animals; one of these is the competition for food which takes place between similar individuals and causes the weaker to be more or less suppressed. But far greater are the distinctions. The plant-community is the lowest form; it is merely a congregation of units, among which there is no co operation for the common weal, but rather a ceaseless struggle of all against all. Only in a loose sense can we speak of certain individuals protecting others, as for example, when the outermost and most exposed individuals of scrub serve to shelter from the wind others, which consequently become taller and finer; for they do not afford protection from any special motive, such as is met with in some animal communities, nor are they in any way specially adapted to act as guardians against a common foe. In the plant-community egoism reigns supreme. The plant-community has no higher units or personages in the sense employed in connection with human communities, which have their own organizations and their members co-operating, as prescribed by law, for the common good. In plant-communities there is, it is true, often (or always) a certain natural dependence or reciprocal influence of many species upon one another; they give rise to definite organized units of a higher order; but there is no thorough or organized division of labor such as is met with in human and animal communities, where certain individuals or groups of individuals work as organs, in the wide sense of the term, for the benefit of the whole community.

Woodhead has suggested the term *complementary association* to denote a community of species that live together in harmony, because their rhizomes occupy different depths in the soil; for example, he described an "association" in which Holcus mollis is the "surface plant," Pteris aquilina has deeper-seated rhizomes, and Scilla festalis buries its bulbs at the greatest depth. The photophilous parts of these plants are "seasonably complementary." The opposite extreme is provided by *competitive associations,* composed of species that are battling with each other.

2. Ant Society[1]

There is certainly a striking parallelism between the development of human and ant societies. Some anthropologists, like Topinard, distinguish in the development of human societies six different types or stages, designated as the hunting, pastoral, agricultural, commercial, industrial, and intellectual. The ants show stages corresponding to the first three of these, as Lubbock has remarked.

Some species, such as *Formica fusca,* live principally on the produce of the chase; for though they feed partially on the honey-dew of aphids, they have not domesticated these insects. These ants probably retain the habits once common to all ants. They resemble the lower races of men, who subsist mainly by hunting. Like them they frequent woods and wilds, live in comparatively small communities, as the instincts of collective action are but little developed among them. They hunt singly, and their battles are single combats, like those of Homeric heroes. Such species as *Lasius flavus* represent a distinctly higher type of social life; they show more skill in architecture, may literally be said to have domesticated certain species of aphids, and may be compared to the pastoral stage of human progress—to the races which live on the products of their flocks and herds. Their communities are more numerous; they act much more in concert; their battles are not mere single combats, but they know how to act in combination. I am disposed to hazard the conjecture that they will gradually exterminate the mere hunting species, just as savages disappear before more advanced races. Lastly, the agricultural nations may be compared with the harvesting ants.

Granting the resemblances above mentioned between ant and human societies, there are nevertheless three far-reaching differences between insect and human organization and development to be constantly borne in mind:

a) Ant societies are societies of females. The males really take no part in the colonial activities, and in most species are present in the nest only for the brief period requisite to secure the impregnation

[1] Adapted from William M. Wheeler, *Ants, Their Structure, Development, and Behavior,* pp. 5–7. (Columbia University Press, 1910.)

of the young queens.   The males take no part in building, provision-
ing, or guarding the nest or in feeding the workers or the brood.   They
are in every sense the *sexus sequior*.   Hence the ants resemble certain mythical human societies like the Amazons, but unlike these,
all their activities center in the multiplication and care of the coming
generations.

b) In human society, apart from the functions depending on
sexual dimorphism, and barring individual differences and deficiencies
which can be partially or wholly suppressed, equalized, or augmented
by an elaborate system of education, all individuals have the same
natural endowment.   Each normal individual retains its various
physiological and psychological needs and powers intact, not necessarily sacrificing any of them for the good of the community.   In
ants, however, the female individuals, of which the society properly
consists, are not all alike but often very different, both in their structure (polymorphism) and in their activities (physiological division of
labor).   Each member is *visibly* predestined to certain social activities to the exclusion of others, not as a man through the education
of some endowment common to all the members of the society, but
through the exigencies of structure, fixed at the time of hatching, i.e.,
the moment the individual enters on its life as an active member of
the community.

c) Owing to this pre-established structure and the specialized
functions which it implies, ants are able to live in a condition of
anarchistic socialism, each individual instinctively fulfilling the
demands of social life without "guide, overseer, or ruler," as Solomon
correctly observed, but not without the imitation and suggestion
involved in an appreciation of the activities of its fellows.

An ant society, therefore, may be regarded as little more than an
expanded family, the members of which co-operate for the purpose of
still further expanding the family and detaching portions of itself to
found other families of the same kind.   There is thus a striking analogy,
which has not escaped the philosophical biologist, between the ant
colony and the cell colony which constitutes the body of a Metazoan
animal; and many of the laws that control the cellular origin, development, growth, reproduction, and decay of the individual Metazoan, are
seen to hold good also of the ant society regarded as an individual of a
higher order.   As in the case of the individual animal, no further purpose of the colony can be detected than that of maintaining itself in

the face of a constantly changing environment till it is able to reproduce other colonies of a like constitution.   The queen-mother of the ant colony displays the generalized potentialities of all the individuals, just as the Metazoan egg contains *in potentia* all the other cells of the body.   And, continuing the analogy, we may say that since the different castes of the ant colony are morphologically specialized for the performance of different functions, they are truly comparable with the differentiated tissues of the Metazoan body.

C.   HUMAN SOCIETY

1.   Social Life [1]

The most notable distinction between living and inanimate beings is that the former maintain themselves by renewal.   A stone when struck resists.   If its resistance is greater than the force of the blow struck, it remains outwardly unchanged.   Otherwise, it is shattered into smaller bits.   Never does the stone attempt to react in such a way that it may maintain itself against the blow, much less so as to render the blow a contributing factor to its own continued action. While the living thing may easily be crushed by superior force, it none the less tries to turn the energies which act upon it into means of its own further existence.   If it cannot do so, it does not just split into smaller pieces (at least in the higher forms of life), but loses its identity as a living thing.

As long as it endures, it struggles to use surrounding energies in its own behalf.   It uses light, air, moisture, and the material of soil. To say that it uses them is to say that it turns them into means of its own conservation.   As long as it is growing, the energy it expends in thus turning the environment to account is more than compensated for by the return it gets: it grows.   Understanding the word "control" in this sense, it may be said that a living being is one that subjugates and controls for its own continued activity the energies that would otherwise use it up.   Life is a self-renewing process through action upon the environment.   Continuity of life means continual readaptation of the environment to the needs of living organisms.

[1] From John Dewey, *Democracy and Education*, pp. 1–7.   (Published by The Macmillan Co., 1916.   Reprinted by permission.)

We have been speaking of life in its lowest terms—as a physical thing. But we use the word "life" to denote the whole range of experience, individual and racial. When we see a book called the *Life of Lincoln* we do not expect to find within its covers a treatise on physiology. We look for an account of social antecedents; a description of early surroundings, of the conditions and occupation of the family; of the chief episodes in the development of character; of signal struggles and achievements; of the individual's hopes, tastes, joys, and sufferings. In precisely similar fashion we speak of the life of a savage tribe, of the Athenian people, of the American nation. "Life" covers customs, institutions, beliefs, victories and defeats, recreations and occupations.

We employ the word "experience" in the same pregnant sense. And to it, as well as to life in tne bare physiological sense, the principle of continuity through renewal applies. With the renewal of physical existence goes, in the case of human beings, the re-creation of beliefs, ideals, hopes, happiness, misery, and practices. The continuity of any experience, through renewing of the social group, is a literal fact. Education, in its broadest sense, is the means of this social continuity of life. Every one of the constituent elements of a social group, in a modern city as in a savage tribe, is born immature, helpless, without language, beliefs, ideas, or social standards. Each individual, each unit who is the carrier of the life-experience of his group, in time passes away. Yet the life of the group goes on.

Society exists through a process of transmission, quite as much as biological life. This transmission occurs by means of communication of habits of doing, thinking, and feeling from the older to the younger. Without this communication of ideals, hopes, expectations, standards, opinions from those members of society who are passing out of the group life to those who are coming into it, social life could not survive.

Society not only continues to exist *by* transmission, *by* communication, but it may fairly be said to exist *in* transmission, *in* communication. There is more than a verbal tie between the words common, community, and communication. Men live in a community in virtue of the things which they have in common; and communication is the way in which they come to possess things in common. What they must have in common in order to form a community or society are aims, beliefs, aspirations, knowledge—a common understanding—like-mindedness, as the sociologists say. Such things cannot be passed physically from one to another, like bricks; they cannot be shared as persons would share a pie by dividing it into physical pieces. The communication which insures participation in a common under-standing is one which secures similar emotional and intellectual dis-positions—like ways of responding to expectations and requirements.

Persons do not become a society by living in physical proximity any more than a man ceases to be socially influenced by being so many feet or miles removed from others. A book or a letter may institute a more intimate association between human beings separated thousands of miles from each other than exists between dwellers under the same roof. Individuals do not even compose a social group because they all work for a common end. The parts of a machine work with a maximum of co-operativeness for a common result, but they do not form a community. If, however, they were all cognizant of the common end and all interested in it so that they regulated their specific activity in view of it, then they would form a community. But this would involve communication. Each would have to know what the other was about and would have to have some way of keeping the other informed as to his own purpose and progress. Consensus demands communications.

We are thus compelled to recognize that within even the most social group there are many relations which are not as yet social. A large number of human relationships in any social group are still upon the machine-like plane. Individuals use one another so as to get desired results, without reference to the emotional and intellectual disposition and consent of those used. Such uses express physical superiority, or superiority of position, skill, technical ability, and command of tools, mechanical or fiscal. So far as the relations of parent and child, teacher and pupil, employer and employee, gover-nor and governed, remain upon this level, they form no true social group, no matter how closely their respective activities touch one another. Giving and taking of orders modifies action and results, but does not of itself effect a sharing of purposes, a communication of interests.

Not only is social life identical with communication, but all communication (and hence all genuine social life) is educative. To be a recipient of a communication is to have an enlarged and changed experience. One shares in what another has thought and felt, and in so far, meagerly or amply, has his own attitude modified. Nor is the one who communicates left unaffected. Try the experiment of communicating, with fulness and accuracy, some experience to another, especially if it be somewhat complicated, and you will find your own attitude toward your experience changing; otherwise you resort to expletives and ejaculations. The experience has to be formulated in order to be communicated. To formulate requires getting outside of it, seeing it as another would see it, considering what points of contact it has with the life of another so that it may be got into such form that he can appreciate its meaning. Except in dealing with commonplaces and catch phrases one has to assimilate, imaginatively, something of another's experience in order to tell him intelligently of one's own experience. All communication is like art. It may fairly be said, therefore, that any social arrangement that remains vitally social, or vitally shared, is educative to those who participate in it. Only when it becomes cast in a mold and runs in a routine way does it lose its educative power.

In final account, then, not only does social life demand teaching and learning for its own permanence, but the very process of living together educates. It enlarges and enlightens experience; it stimulates and enriches imagination; it creates responsibility for accuracy and vividness of statement and thought. A man really living alone (alone mentally as well as physically) would have little or no occasion to reflect upon his past experience to extract its net meaning. The inequality of achievement between the mature and the immature not only necessitates teaching the young, but the necessity of this teaching gives an immense stimulus to reducing experience to that order and form which will render it most easily communicable and hence most usable.

2. Behavior and Conduct[1]

The word "behavior" is commonly used in an interesting variety of ways. We speak of the behavior of ships at sea, of soldiers in battle, and of little boys in Sunday school.

[1] From Robert E. Park, *Principles of Human Behavior*, pp. 1–9. (The Zalaz Corporation, 1915.)

"The geologist," as Lloyd Morgan remarks, "tells us that a glacier behaves in many respects like a river, and discusses how the crust of the earth behaves under the stresses to which it is subjected. Weatherwise people comment on the behavior of the mercury in the barometer as a storm approaches. When Mary, the nurse maid, returns with the little Miss Smiths from Master Brown's birthday party, she is narrowly questioned as to their behavior."

In short, the word is familiar both to science and to common sense, and is applied with equal propriety to the actions of physical objects and to the manners of men. The abstract sciences, quite as much as the concrete and descriptive, are equally concerned with behavior. "The chemist and the physicist often speak of the behavior of the atoms and the molecules, or of that of gas under changing conditions of temperature and pressure." The fact is that every science is everywhere seeking to describe and explain the movements, changes, and reactions, that is to say the behavior, of some portion of the world about us. Indeed, wherever we consciously set ourselves to observe and reflect upon the changes going on about us, it is always behavior that we are interested in. Science is simply a little more persistent in its curiosity and a little nicer and more exact in its observation than common sense. And this disposition to observe, to take a disinterested view of things, is, by the way, one of the characteristics of human nature which distinguishes it from the nature of all other animals.

Since every science has to do with some form of behavior, the first question that arises is this: What do we mean by behavior in human beings as distinguished from that in other animals? What is there distinctive about the actions of human beings that marks them off and distinguishes them from the actions of animals and plants with which human beings have so much in common?

The problem is the more difficult because, in some one or other of its aspects, human behavior involves processes which are characteristic of almost every form of nature. We sometimes speak, for example, of the human machine. Indeed, from one point of view human beings may be regarded as psycho-physical mechanisms for carrying on the vital processes of nutrition, reproduction, and movement. The human body is, in fact, an immensely complicated machine, whose operations involve an enormous number of chemical and physical reactions, all of which may be regarded as forms of human behavior.

Human beings are, however, not wholly or merely machines; they are living organisms and as such share with the plants and the lower animals certain forms of behavior which it has not thus far, at any rate, been possible to reduce to the exact and lucid formulas of either chemistry or physics.

Human beings are, however, not merely organisms: they are the home and the habitat of minuter organisms. The human body is, in a certain sense, an organization—a sort of social organization—of the minute and simple organisms of which it is composed, namely, the cells, each of which has its own characteristic mode of behavior. In fact, the life of human beings, just as the life of all other creatures above the simple unicellular organisms, may be said to consist of the corporate life of the smaller organisms of which it is composed. In human beings, as in some great city, the division of labor among the minuter organisms has been carried further, the interdependence of the individual parts is more complete, and the corporate life of the whole more complex.

It is not strange, therefore, that Lloyd Morgan begins his studies of animal behavior by a description of the behavior of the cells and Thorndike in his volume, *The Original Nature of Man*, is led to the conclusion that the original tendencies of man have their basis in the neurones, or nerve cells, and in the changes which these cells and their ancestors have undergone, as a result of the necessity of carrying on common and corporate existences as integral parts of the human organism. All acquired characteristics of men, everything that they learn, is due to mutual stimulations and associations of the neurones, just as sociologists are now disposed to explain civilization and progress as phenomena due to the interaction and association of human beings, rather than to any fundamental changes in human nature itself. In other words, the difference between a savage and a civilized man is not due to any fundamental differences in their brain cells but to the connections and mutual stimulations which are established by experience and education between those cells. In the savage those possibilities are not absent but latent. In the same way the difference between the civilization of Central Africa and that of Western Europe is due, not to the difference in native abilities of the individuals and the peoples who have created them, but rather to the form which the association and interaction between those individuals and groups of individuals has taken. We sometimes attribute the difference in culture which we meet among races to the climate and physical conditions generally, but, in the long run, the difference is determined by the way in which climate and physical condition determine the contacts and communications of individuals.

So, too, in the corporate life of the individual man it is the association of the nerve cells, their lines of connection and communication, that is responsible for the most of the differences between the ignorant and the educated, the savage and civilized man. The neurone, however, is a little unicellular animal, like the amoeba or the paramecium. Its life consists of: (1) eating, (2) excreting waste products, (3) growing, (4) being sensitive, and (5) movement, and, as Thorndike expresses it: "The safest provisional hypothesis about the action of the neurones singly is that they retain the modes of behavior common to unicellular animals, so far as consistent with the special conditions of their life as an element of man's nervous system."

In the widest sense of the term, behavior may be said to include all the chemical and physical changes that go on inside the organism, as well as every response to stimulus either from within or from without the organism. In recent studies of animal behavior, however, the word has acquired a special and technical meaning in which it is applied exclusively to those actions that have been, or may be, modified by conscious experience. What the animal does in its efforts to find food is behavior, but the processes of digestion are relegated to another field of observation, namely, physiology.

In all the forms of behavior thus far referred to, human and animal nature are not fundamentally distinguished. There are, however, ways of acting that are peculiar to human nature, forms of behavior that man does not share with the lower animals. One thing which seems to distinguish man from the brute is self-consciousness. One of the consequences of intercourse, as it exists among human beings, is that they are led to reflect upon their own impulses and motives for action, to set up standards by which they seek to govern themselves. The clock is such a standard. We all know from experience that time moves more slowly on dull days, when there is nothing doing, than in moments of excitement. On the other hand, when life is active and stirring, time flies. The clock standardizes our subjective tempos and we control ourselves by the clock. An animal never looks at the clock and this is typical of the different ways in which human beings and animals behave.

Human beings, so far as we have yet been able to learn, are the only creatures who habitually pass judgment upon their own actions, or who think of them as right or wrong. When these thoughts about our actions or the actions of others get themselves formulated and expressed they react back upon and control us. That is one reason we hang mottoes on the wall. That is why one sees on the desk of a busy man the legend "Do it now!" The brutes do not know these devices. They do not need them perhaps. They have no aim in life. They do not work.

What distinguishes the action of men from animals may best be expressed in the word "conduct." Conduct as it is ordinarily used is applied to actions which may be regarded as right or wrong, moral or immoral. As such it is hardly a descriptive term since there does not seem to be any distinctive mark about the actions which men have at different times and places called moral or immoral. I have used it here to distinguish the sort of behavior which may be regarded as distinctively and exclusively human, namely, that which is self-conscious and personal. In this sense blushing may be regarded as a form of conduct, quite as much as the manufacture of tools, trade and barter, conversation or prayer.

No doubt all these activities have their beginnings in, and are founded upon, forms of behavior of which we may find the rudiments in the lower animals. But there is in all distinctively human activities a conventional, one might almost say a contractual, element which is absent in action of other animals. Human actions are more often than not controlled by a sense or understanding of what they look like or appear to be to others. This sense and understanding gets itself embodied in some custom or ceremonial observance. In this form it is transmitted from generation to generation, becomes an object of sentimental respect, gets itself embodied in definite formulas, is an object not only of respect and reverence but of reflection and speculation as well. As such it constitutes the mores, or moral customs, of a group and is no longer to be regarded as an individual possession

3. Instinct and Character [1]

In no part of the world, and at no period of time, do we find the behavior of men left to unchartered freedom. Everywhere human life is in a measure organized and directed by customs, laws, beliefs, ideals, which shape its ends and guide its activities. As this guidance of life by rule is universal in human society, so upon the whole it is peculiar to humanity. There is no reason to think that any animal except man can enunciate or apply general rules of conduct. Nevertheless, there is not wanting something that we can call an organization of life in the animal world. How much of intelligence underlies the social life of the higher animals is indeed extremely hard to determine. In the aid which they often render to one another, in their combined hunting, in their play, in the use of warning cries, and the employment of "sentinels," which is so frequent among birds and mammals, it would appear at first sight that a considerable measure of *mutual understanding* is implied, that we find at least an analogue to human custom, to the assignment of functions, the division of labor, which mutual reliance renders possible. How far the analogy may be pressed, and whether terms like "custom" and "mutual understanding," drawn from human experience, are rightly applicable to animal societies, are questions on which we shall touch presently. Let us observe first that as we descend the animal scale the sphere of *intelligent activity* is gradually narrowed down, and yet behavior is still regulated. The lowest organisms have their definite methods of action under given conditions. The amoeba shrinks into itself at a touch, withdraws the pseudopodium that is roughly handled, or makes its way round the small object which will serve it as food. Given the conditions, it acts in the way best suited to avoid danger or to secure nourishment. We are a long way from the intelligent regulation of conduct by a general principle, but we still find action adapted to the requirements of organic life.

When we come to human society we find the basis for a social organization of life already laid in the animal nature of man. Like others of the higher animals, man is a gregarious beast. His interests lie in his relations to his fellows, in his love for wife and children, in his companionship, possibly in his rivalry and striving with his fellow-

[1] Adapted from L. T. Hobhouse, *Morals in Evolution*, pp. 1–2, 10–12. (Henry Holt & Co., 1915.)

men. His loves and hates, his joys and sorrows, his pride, his wrath,
his gentleness, his boldness, his timidity—all these permanent qualities, which run through humanity and vary only in degree, belong
to his inherited structure. Broadly speaking, they are of the nature
of instincts, but instincts which have become highly plastic in their
mode of operation and which need the stimulus of experience to call
them forth and give them definite shape.

The mechanical methods of reaction which are so prominent low
down in the animal scale fill quite a minor place in human life. The
ordinary operations of the body, indeed, go upon their way mechanically enough. In walking or in running, in saving ourselves from a
fall, in coughing, sneezing, or swallowing, we react as mechanically
as do the lower animals; but in the distinctly human modes of
behavior, the place taken by the inherited structure is very different.
Hunger and thirst no doubt are of the nature of instincts, but the
methods of satisfying hunger and thirst are acquired by experience or
by teaching. Love and the whole family life have an instinctive basis,
that is to say, they rest upon tendencies inherited with the brain and
nerve structure; but everything that has to do with the satisfaction of
these impulses is determined by the experience of the individual, the
laws and customs of the society in which he lives, the woman whom
he meets, the accidents of their intercourse, and so forth. Instinct,
already plastic and modifiable in the higher animals, becomes in man
a basis of character which determines how he will take his experience,
but without experience is a mere blank form upon which nothing is
yet written.

For example, it is an ingrained tendency of average human
nature to be moved by the opinion of our neighbors. This is a powerful motive in conduct, but the kind of conduct to which it will incite
clearly depends on the kind of thing that our neighbors approve.
In some parts of the world ambition for renown will prompt a man
to lie in wait for a woman or child in order to add a fresh skull to
his collection. In other parts he may be urged by similar motives
to pursue a science or paint a picture. In all these cases the same
hereditary or instinctive element is at work, that quality of character
which makes a man respond sensitively to the feelings which others
manifest toward him. But the kind of conduct which this sensitiveness may dictate depends wholly on the social environment in which

the man finds himself. Similarly it is, as the ordinary phrase quite justly puts it, "in human nature" to stand up for one's rights. A man will strive, that is, to secure that which he has counted on as his due. But as to what he counts upon, as to the actual treatment which he expects under given circumstances, his views are determined by the "custom of the country," by what he sees others insisting on and obtaining, by what has been promised him, and so forth. Even such an emotion as sexual jealousy, which seems deeply rooted in the animal nature, is largely limited in its exercise and determined in the form it takes by custom. A hospitable savage, who will lend his wife to a guest, would kill her for acting in the same way on her own motion. In the one case he exercises his rights of proprietorship; in the other, she transgresses them. It is the maintenance of a claim which jealousy concerns itself with, and the standard determining the claim is the custom of the country.

In human society, then, the conditions regulating conduct are from the first greatly modified. Instinct, becoming vague and more general, has evolved into "character," while the intelligence finds itself confronted with customs to which it has to accommodate conduct. But how does custom arise? Let us first consider what custom is. It is not merely a habit of action; but it implies also a judgment upon action, and a judgment stated in general and impersonal terms. It would seem to imply a bystander or third party. If A hits B, B probably hits back. It is his "habit" so to do. But if C, looking on, pronounces that it was or was not a fair blow, he will probably appeal to the "custom" of the country—the traditional rules of fighting, for instance—as the ground of his judgment. That is, he will lay down a rule which is general in the sense that it would apply to other individuals under similar conditions, and by it he will, as an impartial third person, appraise the conduct of the contending parties. The formation of such rules, resting as it does on the power of framing and applying general conceptions, is the prime differentia of human morality from animal behavior. The fact that they arise and are handed on from generation to generation makes social tradition at once the dominating factor in the regulation of human conduct. Without such rules we can scarcely conceive society to exist, since it is only through the general conformity to custom that men can understand each other, that each can know how the other will act under given circumstances, and without this amount of understanding the reciprocity, which is the vital principle of society, disappears.

4. Collective Representation and Intellectual Life[1]

Logical thought is made up of concepts. Seeking how society can have played a rôle in the genesis of logical thought thus reduces itself to seeking how it can have taken a part in the formation of concepts.

The concept is opposed to sensual representations of every order —sensations, perceptions, or images—by the following properties.

Sensual representations are in a perpetual flux; they come after each other like the waves of a river, and even during the time that they last they do not remain the same thing. Each of them is an integral part of the precise instant when it takes place. We are never sure of again finding a perception such as we experienced it the first time; for if the thing perceived has not changed, it is we who are no longer the same. On the contrary, the concept is, as it were, outside of time and change; it is in the depths below all this agitation; it might be said that it is in a different portion of the mind, which is serener and calmer. It does not move of itself, by an internal and spontaneous evolution, but, on the contrary, it resists change. It is a manner of thinking that, at every moment of time, is fixed and crystallized. In so far as it is what it ought to be, it is immutable. If it changes, it is not because it is its nature to do so, but because we have discovered some imperfection in it; it is because it had to be rectified. The system of concepts with which we think in everyday life is that expressed by the vocabulary of our mother-tongue; for every word translates a concept. Now language is something fixed; it changes but very slowly, and consequently it is the same with the conceptual system which it expresses. The scholar finds himself in the same situation in regard to the special terminology employed by the science to which he has consecrated himself, and hence in regard to the special scheme of concepts to which this terminology corresponds. It is true that he can make innovations, but these are always a sort of violence done to the established ways of thinking.

[1] Adapted from Émile Durkheim, *The Elementary Forms of Religious Life*, pp. 432–37. (Allen & Unwin, 1915.)

And at the same time that it is relatively immutable, the concept is universal, or at least capable of becoming so. A concept is not my concept; I hold it in common with other men, or, in any case, can communicate it to them. It is impossible for me to make a sensation pass from my consciousness into that of another; it holds closely to my organism and personality and cannot be detached from them. All that I can do is to invite others to place themselves before the same object as myself and to leave themselves to its action. On the other hand, conversation and all intellectual communication between men is an exchange of concepts. The concept is an essentially impersonal representation; it is through it that human intelligences communicate.

The nature of the concept, thus defined, bespeaks its origin. If it is common to all, it is the work of the community. Since it bears the mark of no particular mind, it is clear that it was elaborated by a unique intelligence, where all others meet each other, and after a fashion, come to nourish themselves. If it has more stability than sensations or images, it is because the collective representations are more stable than the individual ones; for while an individual is conscious even of the slight changes which take place in his environment, only events of a greater gravity can succeed in affecting the mental status of a society. Every time that we are in the presence of a *type* of thought or action which is imposed uniformly upon particular wills or intelligences, this pressure exercised over the individual betrays the intervention of the group. Also, as we have already said, the concepts with which we ordinarily think are those of our vocabulary. Now it is unquestionable that language, and consequently the system of concepts which it translates, is the product of collective elaboration. What it expresses is the manner in which society as a whole represents the facts of experience. The ideas which correspond to the diverse elements of language are thus collective representations.

Even their contents bear witness to the same fact. In fact, there are scarcely any words among those which we usually employ whose meaning does not pass, to a greater or less extent, the limits of our personal experience. Very frequently a term expresses things which we have never perceived or experiences which we have never had or of which we have never been the witnesses. Even when

we know some of the objects which it concerns, it is only as
particular examples that they serve to illustrate the idea which
they would never have been able to form by themselves.   Thus
there is a great deal of knowledge condensed in the word which I
never collected, and which is not individual; it even surpasses me
to such an extent that I cannot even completely appropriate all its
results.   Which of us knows all the words of the language he speaks
and the entire signification of each ?

This remark enables us to determine the sense in which we mean
to say that concepts are collective representations.   If they belong
to a whole social group, it is not because they represent the average
of the corresponding individual representations; for in that case
they would be poorer than the latter in intellectual content, while, as
a matter of fact, they contain much that surpasses the knowledge of
the average individual.   They are not abstractions which have a
reality only in particular consciousnesses, but they are as concrete
representations as an individual could form of his own personal
environment; they correspond to the way in which this very special
being, society, considers the things of its own proper experience.
If, as a matter of fact, the concepts are nearly always general ideas,
and if they express categories and classes rather than particular
objects, it is because the unique and variable characteristics of things
interest society but rarely; because of its very extent, it can scarcely
be affected by more than their general and permanent qualities.
Therefore it is to this aspect of affairs that it gives its attention:
it is a part of its nature to see things in large and under the aspect
which they ordinarily have.   But this generality is not necessary for
them, and, in any case, even when these representations have the
generic character which they ordinarily have, they are the work of
society and are enriched by its experience.

The collective consciousness is the highest form of the psychic
life, since it is the consciousness of the consciousnesses.   Being placed
outside of and above individual and local contingencies, it sees things
only in their permanent and essential aspects, which it crystallizes
into communicable ideas.   At the same time that it sees from above,
it sees farther; at every moment of time, it embraces all known
reality; that is why it alone can furnish the mind with the molds
which are applicable to the totality of things and which make it

possible to think of them.   It does not create these molds artificially; it finds them within itself;   it does nothing but become conscious of them.   They translate the ways of being which are found in all the stages of reality but which appear in their full clarity only at the summit, because the extreme complexity of the psychic life which passes there necessitates a greater development of consciousness.   Collective representations also contain subjective elements, and these must be progressively rooted out if we are to approach reality more closely. But howsoever crude these may have been at the beginning, the fact remains that with them the germ of a new mentality was given, to which the individual could never have raised himself by his own efforts;   by them the way was opened to a stable, impersonal and organized thought which then had nothing to do except to develop its nature.

D.   THE SOCIAL GROUP

1.   Definition of the Group[1]

The term "group" serves as a convenient sociological designation for any number of people, larger or smaller, between whom such relations are discovered that they must be thought of together. The "group" is the most general and colorless term used in sociology for combinations of persons.   A family, a mob, a picnic party, a trade union, a city precinct, a corporation, a state, a nation, the civilized or the uncivilized population of the world, may be treated as a group.   Thus a "group" for sociology is a number of persons whose relations to each other are sufficiently impressive to demand attention.   The term is merely a commonplace tool.   It contains no mystery.   It is only a handle with which to grasp the innumerable varieties of arrangements into which people are drawn by their variations of interest.   The universal condition of association may be expressed in the same commonplace way: people always live in groups, and the same persons are likely to be members of many groups.

Individuals nowhere live in utter isolation.   There is no such thing as a social vacuum.   The few Robinson Crusoes are not exceptions to the rule.   If they are, they are like the Irishman's horse.   The

[1] From Albion W. Small, *General Sociology*, pp. 495–97.   (The University of Chicago Press, 1905.)

moment they begin to get adjusted to the exceptional condition, they die. Actual persons always live and move and have their being in groups. These groups are more or less complex, more or less continuous, more or less rigid in character. The destinies of human beings are always bound up with the fate of the groups of which they are members. While the individuals are the real existences, and the groups are only relationships of individuals, yet to all intents and purposes the groups which people form are just as distinct and efficient molders of the lives of individuals as though they were entities that had existence entirely independent of the individuals.

The college fraternity or the college class, for instance, would be only a name, and presently not even that, if each of its members should withdraw. It is the members themselves, and not something outside of themselves. Yet to A, B, or C the fraternity or the class might as well be a river or a mountain by the side of which he stands, and which he is helpless to remove. He may modify it somewhat. He is surely modified by it somewhat; and the same is true of all the other groups in which A, B, or C belong. To a very considerable extent the question, Why does A, B, or C do so and so? is equivalent to the question, What are the peculiarities of the group to which A, B, or C belongs? It would never occur to A, B, or C to skulk from shadow to shadow of a night, with paint-pot and brush in hand, and to smear Arabic numerals of bill-poster size on sidewalk or buildings, if "class spirit" did not add stimulus to individual bent. Neither A, B, nor C would go out of his way to flatter and cajole a Freshman, if membership in a fraternity did not make a student something different from an individual. These are merely familiar cases which follow a universal law.

In effect, the groups to which we belong might be as separate and independent of us as the streets and buildings of a city are from the population. If the inhabitants should migrate in a body, the streets and buildings would remain. This is not true of human groups, but their reaction upon the persons who compose them is no less real and evident. We are in large part what our social set, our church, our political party, our business and professional circles are. This has always been the case from the beginning of the world, and will always be the case. To understand what society is, either in its larger or its smaller parts, and why it is so, and how far it is possible to make it different, we must invariably explain groups on the one hand, no less than individuals on the other. There is a striking illustration in Chicago at present (summer, 1905). Within a short time a certain man has made a complete change in his group-relations. He was one of the most influential trade-union leaders in the city. He has now become the executive officer of an association of employers. In the elements that are not determined by his group-relationships he is the same man that he was before. Those are precisely the elements, however, that may be canceled out of the social problem. All the elements in his personal equation that give him a distinct meaning in the life of the city are given to him by his membership in the one group or the other. Till yesterday he gave all his strength to organizing labor against capital. Now he gives all his strength to the service of capital against labor.

Whatever social problem we confront, whatever persons come into our field of view, the first questions involved will always be: To what groups do these persons belong? What are the interests of these groups? What sort of means do the groups use to promote their interests? How strong are these groups, as compared with groups that have conflicting interests? These questions go to one tap root of all social interpretation, whether in the case of historical events far in the past, or of the most practical problems of our own neighborhood.

2. The Unity of the Social Group [1]

It has long been a cardinal problem in sociology to determine just how to conceive in objective terms so very real and palpable a thing as the continuity and persistence of social groups. Looked at as a physical object society appears to be made up of mobile and independent units. The problem is to understand the nature of the bonds that bind these independent units together and how these connections are maintained and transmitted.

Conceived of in its lowest terms the unity of the social group may be compared to that of the plant communities. In these com-

[1] From R. E. Park, "Education in Its Relation to the Conflict and Fusion of Cultures," in the *Publications of the American Sociological Society*, VIII (1918), 38–40.

munities, the relation between the individual species which compose them seems at first wholly fortuitous and external. Co-operation and community, so far as it exists, consists merely in the fact that within a given geographical area, certain species come together merely because each happens to provide by its presence an environment in which the life of the other is easier, more secure, than if they lived in isolation. It seems to be a fact, however, that this communal life of the associated plants fulfils, as in other forms of life, a typical series of changes which correspond to growth, decay and death. The plant community comes into existence, matures, grows old, and eventually dies. In doing this, however, it provides by its own death an environment in which another form of community finds its natural habitat. Each community thus precedes and prepares the way for its successor. Under such circumstances the succession of the individual communities itself assumes the character of a life-process.

In the case of the animal and human societies we have all these conditions and forces and something more. The individuals associated in an animal community not only provide, each for the other, a physical environment in which all may live, but the members of the community are organically pre-adapted to one another in ways which are not characteristic of the members of a plant community. As a consequence, the relations between the members of the animal community assume a much more organic character. It is, in fact, a characteristic of animal society that the members of a social group are organically adapted to one another and therefore the organization of animal society is almost wholly transmitted by physical inheritance.

In the case of human societies we discover not merely organically inherited adaptation, which characterizes animal societies, but, in addition, a great body of habits and accommodations which are transmitted in the form of social inheritance. Something that corresponds to social tradition exists, to be sure, in animal societies. Animals learn by imitation from one another, and there is evidence that this social tradition varies with changes in environment. In man, however, association is based on something more than habits or instinct. In human society, largely as a result of language, there exists a conscious community of purpose. We have not merely folkways, which by an extension of that term might be attributed to animals, but we have mores and formal standards of conduct.

In a recent notable volume on education, John Dewey has formulated a definition of the educational process which he identifies with the process by which the social tradition of human society is transmitted. Education, he says in effect, is a self-renewing process, a process in which and through which the social organism lives.

With the renewal of physical existence goes, in the case of human beings, the re-creation of beliefs, ideals, hopes, happiness, misery and practices. The continuity of experience, through renewal of the social group, is a literal fact. Education, in its broadest sense, is the means of this social continuity of life.

Under ordinary circumstances the transmission of the social tradition is from the parents to the children. Children are born into the society and take over its customs, habits, and standards of life simply, naturally, and without conflict. But it will at once occur to anyone that the physical life of society is not always continued and maintained in this natural way, i.e., by the succession of parents and children. New societies are formed by conquest and by the imposition of one people upon another. In such cases there arises a conflict of cultures, and as a result the process of fusion takes place slowly and is frequently not complete. New societies are frequently formed by colonization, in which case new cultures are grafted on to older ones. The work of missionary societies is essentially one of colonization in this sense. Finally we have societies growing up, as in the United States, by immigration. These immigrants, coming as they do from all parts of the world, bring with them fragments of divergent cultures. Here again the process of assimilation is slow, often painful, not always complete.

CHAPTER IV

SOCIAL CONTACTS

I. INTRODUCTION

1. Preliminary Notions of Social Contact

The fundamental social process is that of interaction. This interaction is (*a*) of persons with persons, and (*b*) of groups with groups. The simplest aspect of interaction, or its primary phase, is contact. Contact may be considered as the initial stage of interaction, and preparatory to the later stages. The phenomena of social contact require analysis before proceeding to the more difficult study of the mechanism of social interaction.

"With whom am I in contact?" Common sense has in stock ready answers to this question.

There is, first of all, the immediate circle of contact through the senses. Touch is the most intimate kind of contact. Face-to-face relations include, in addition to touch, visual and auditory sensations. Speech and hearing by their very nature establish a bond of contact between persons.

Even in common usage, the expression "social contact" is employed beyond the limits fixed by the immediate responses of touch, sight, and hearing. Its area has expanded to include connection through all the forms of communication, i.e., language, letters, and the printed page; connection through the medium of the telephone, telegraph, radio, moving picture, etc. The evolution of the devices for communication has taken place in the fields of two senses alone, those of hearing and seeing. Touch remains limited to the field of primary association. But the newspaper with its elaborate mechanism of communication gives publicity to events in London, Moscow, and Tokio, and the motion picture unreels to our gaze scenes from distant lands and foreign peoples with all the illusion of reality.

The frontiers of social contact are farther extended to the widest horizons, by commerce. The economists, for example, include in their conception of society the intricate and complex maze of relations created by the competition and co-operation of individuals and societies within the limits of a world-wide economy. This inclusion of unconscious as well as conscious reciprocal influences in the concept of social relations brings into "contact" the members of a village missionary society with the savages of the equatorial regions of Africa; or the pale-faced drug addict, with the dark-skinned Hindu laborers upon the opium fields of Benares; or the man gulping down coffee at the breakfast table, with the Java planter; the crew of the Pacific freighter and its cargo of spices with the American whole-saler and retailer in food products. In short, everyone is in a real, though concealed and devious, way in contact with every other person in the world. Contacts of this type, remote from the familiar experiences of everyday life, have reality to the intellectual and the mystic and are appreciated by the masses only when co-operation breaks down, or competition becomes conscious and passes into conflict.

These three popular meanings of contacts emphasize (1) the intimacy of sensory responses, (2) the extension of contact through devices of communication based upon sight and hearing, and (3) the solidarity and interdependence created and maintained by the fabric of social life, woven as it is from the intricate and invisible strands of human interests in the process of a world-wide competition and co-operation.

2. The Sociological Concept of Contact

The use of the term "contact" in sociology is not a departure from, but a development of, its customary significance. In the preceding chapter the point was made that the distinction between isolation and contact is not absolute but relative. Members of a society spatially separate, but socially in contact through sense perception and through communication of ideas, may be thereby mobilized to collective behavior. Sociological interest in this situation lies in the fact that the various kinds of social contacts between persons and groups determine behavior. The student of problems of American society, for example, realizes the necessity of under-standing the mutual reactions involved in the contacts of the foreign and the native-born, of the white and the negro, and of employers and employees. In other words, contact, as the first stage of social interaction, conditions and controls the later stages of the process.

It is convenient, for certain purposes, to conceive of contact in terms of space. The contacts of persons and of groups may then be plotted in units of *social distance*. This permits graphic representation of relations of sequence and of coexistence in terms both of units of separation and of contact. This spatial conception may now be applied to the explanation of the readings in social contacts.

3. Classification of the Materials

In sociological literature there have grown up certain distinctions between types of social contacts. Physical contacts are distinguished from social contacts; relations within the "in-group" are perceived to be different from relations with the "out-group"; contacts of historical continuity are compared with contacts of mobility; primary contacts are set off from secondary contacts. How far and with what advantage may these distinctions be stated in spatial terms?

a) *Land as a basis for social contacts.*—The position of persons and peoples on the earth gives us a literal picture of the spatial conception of social contact. The cluster of homes in the Italian agricultural community suggests the difference in social life in comparison with the isolated homesteads of rural America. A gigantic spot map of the United States upon which every family would be indicated by a dot would represent schematically certain different conditions influencing group behavior in arid areas, the open country, hamlets, villages, towns, and cities. The movements of persons charted with detail sufficient to bring out variations in the daily, weekly, monthly, and yearly routine, would undoubtedly reveal interesting identities and differences in the intimacy and intensity of social contacts. It would be possible and profitable to classify people with reference to the routine of their daily lives.

b) *Touch as the physiological basis of social contact.*—According to the spatial conception the closest contacts possible are those of touch. The physical proximity involved in tactile sensations is, however, but the symbol of the intensity of the reactions to contact. Desire and aversion for contacts, as Crawley shows in his selection, arise in the most intimate relations of human life. Love and hate, longing and disgust, sympathy and hostility increase in intensity with intimacy of association. It is a current sociological fallacy that closeness of contact results only in the growth of good will. The fact is, that with increasing contact either attraction or repulsion may be the outcome, depending upon the situation and upon factors not yet fully analyzed. Peculiar conditions of contact, as its prolonged duration, its frequent repetition, just as in the case of isolation from normal association, may lead to the inversion of the original impulses and sentiments of affection and antipathy.[1]

c) *Contacts with the "in-group" and with the "out-group."*—The conception of the we-group in terms of distance is that of a group in which the solidarity of units is so complete that the movements and sentiments of all are completely regulated with reference to their interests and behavior as a group. This control by the in-group over its members makes for solidity and impenetrability in its relations with the out-group. Sumner in his *Folkways* indicates how internal sympathetic contacts and group egotism result in double standards of behavior: good-will and co-operation within the members of the in-group, hostility and suspicion toward the out-group and its members. The essential point is perhaps best brought out by Shaler in his distinction between sympathetic and categoric contacts. He describes the transition from contacts of the out-group to those of the in-group, or from remote to intimate relations. From a distance, a person has the characteristics of his group, upon close acquaintance he reveals his individuality.

d) *Historical continuity and mobility.*—Historical continuity, which maintains the identity of the present with the past, implies the existence of a body of tradition which is transmitted from the older to the younger generations. Through the medium of tradition, including in that term all the learning, science, literature, and practical arts, not to speak of the great body of oral tradition which is after all a larger part of life than we imagine, the historical and

---

[1] Alexander Pope, in smooth lines, and with apt phrases, has concretely described this process of perversion:

> "Vice is a monster of so frightful mien,
> As to be hated needs but to be seen;
> Yet seen too oft, familiar with her face,
> We first endure, then pity, then embrace."

cultural life is maintained. This is the meaning of the long period of childhood in man during which the younger generation is living under the care and protection of the older. When, for any reason, this contact of the younger with the older generation is interrupted— as is true in the case of immigrants—a very definite cultural deterioration frequently ensues.

Contacts of mobility are those of a changing present, and measure the number and variety of the stimulations which the social life and movements—the discovery of the hour, the book of the moment, the passing fads and fashions—afford. Contacts of mobility give us novelty and news. It is through contacts of this sort that change takes place.

Mobility, accordingly, measures not merely the social contacts that one gains from travel and exploration, but the stimulation and suggestions that come to us through the medium of communication, by which sentiments and ideas are put in social circulation. Through the newspaper, the common man of today participates in the social movements of his time. His illiterate forbear of yesterday, on the other hand, lived unmoved by the current of world-events outside his hamlet. The *tempo* of modern societies may be measured comparatively by the relative perfection of devices of communication and the rapidity of the circulation of sentiments, opinions, and facts. Indeed, the efficiency of any society or of any group is to be measured not alone in terms of numbers or of material resources, but also in terms of mobility and access through communication and publicity to the common fund of tradition and culture.

e) Primary and secondary contacts.—Primary contacts are those of "intimate face-to-face association"; secondary contacts are those of externality and greater distance. A study of primary association indicates that this sphere of contact falls into two areas: one of intimacy and the other of acquaintance. In the diagram which follows, the field of primary contacts has been subdivided so that it includes (x) a circle of greater intimacy, (y) a wider circle of acquaintanceship. The completed chart would appear as shown on page 285.

Primary contacts of the greatest intimacy are (a) those represented by the affections that ordinarily spring up within the family, particularly between parents and children, husband and wife; and (b) those of fellowship and affection outside the family as between lovers,

bosom friends, and boon companions.   These relations are all manifestations of a craving for response.   These personal relationships
are the nursery for the development of human nature and personality.
John Watson, who studied several hundred new-born infants in the
psychological laboratory, concludes that "the first few years are the
all-important ones, for shaping the emotional life of the child."[1]
The primary virtues and ideals of which Cooley writes so sympathetically are, for the most part, projections from family life.   Certainly
in these most intimate relations of life in the contacts of the family
circle, in the closest friendships, personality is most severely tried,
realizes its most characteristic expressions, or is most completely
disorganized.

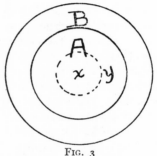

FIG. 3

A, primary contacts; *x*, greater intimacy; *y*, acquaintanceship;
B, secondary contacts

Just as the life of the family represents the contacts of touch and
response, the neighborhood or the village is the natural area of primary
contacts and the city the social environment of secondary contacts.
In primary association individuals are in contact with each other
at practically all points of their lives.   In the village "everyone
knows everything about everyone else."   Canons of conduct are
absolute, social control is omnipotent, the status of the family and
the individual is fixed.   In secondary association individuals are in
contact with each other at only one or two points in their lives.   In
the city, the individual becomes anonymous; at best he is generally
known in only one or two aspects of his life.   Standards of behavior

[1] H. S. Jennings, John B. Watson, Adolph Meyer, and W. I. Thomas, "Practical and Theoretical Problems in Instinct and Habit," *Suggestions of Modern
Science Concerning Education*, p. 174.

are relative; the old primary controls have disappeared; the new secondary instruments of discipline, necessarily formal, are for the most part crude and inefficient; the standing of the family and of the individual is uncertain and subject to abrupt changes upward or downward in the social scale.

Simmel has made a brilliant contribution in his analysis of the sociological significance of "the stranger." "The stranger" in the sociological sense is the individual who unites in his social relations primary and secondary contacts. Simmel himself employs the conception of social distance in his statement of the stranger as the combination of the near and the far. It is interesting and significant to determine the different types of the union of intimacy and externality in the relations of teacher and student, physician and patient, minister and layman, lawyer and client, social worker and applicant for relief.

A complete analysis of the bearing upon personal and cultural life of changes from a society based upon contacts of continuity and of primary relations to a society of increasing mobility organized around secondary contacts cannot be given here. Certain of the most obvious contrasts of the transition may, however, be stated. Increasing mobility of persons in society almost inevitably leads to change and therefore to loss of continuity. In primary groups, where social life moves slowly, there is a greater sense of continuity than in secondary groups where it moves rapidly.

There is a further contrast if not conflict between direct and intimate contacts and contacts based upon communication of ideas. All sense of values, as Windelband has pointed out, rests upon concrete experience, that is to say upon sense contacts. Society, to the extent that it is organized about secondary contacts, is based upon abstractions, upon science and technique. Secondary contacts of this type have only secondary values because they represent means rather than ends. Just as all behavior arises in sense impressions it must also terminate in sense impressions to realize its ends and attain its values. The effect of life in a society based on secondary contacts is to build up between the impulse and its end a world of means, to project values into the future, and to direct life toward the realization of distant hopes.

The ultimate effect upon the individual as he becomes accommodated to secondary society is to find a substitute expression for his primary response in the artificial physical environment of the city. The detachment of the person from intimate, direct, and spontaneous contacts with social reality is in large measure responsible for the intricate maze of problems of urban life.

The change from concrete and personal to abstract and impersonal relations in economic and social life began with the Industrial Revolution. The machine is the symbol of the monotonous routine of impersonal, unskilled, large-scale production just as the hand tool is the token of the interesting activity of personal, skilled, handicraft work. The so-called "instinct of workmanship" no longer finds expression in the anonymous standardized production of modern industry.[1]

It is not in industry alone that the natural impulses of the person for response, recognition, and self-expression are balked. In social work, politics, religion, art, and sport the individual is represented now by proxies where formerly he participated in person. All the forms of communal activity in which all persons formerly shared have been taken over by professionals. The great mass of men in most of the social activities of modern life are no longer actors, but spectators. The average man of the present time has been relegated by the influence of the professional politician to the rôle of taxpayer. In social work organized charity has come between the giver and the needy.

In these and other manifold ways the artificial conditions of city life have deprived the person of most of the natural outlets for the expression of his interests and his energies. To this fact is to be attributed in large part the restlessness, the thirst for novelty and excitement so characteristic of modern life. This emotional unrest has been capitalized by the newspapers, commercialized recreations, fashion, and agitation in their appeal to the sensations, the emotions, and the instincts loosened from the satisfying fixations of primary-group life. The *raison d'être* of social work, as well as the fundamental problem of all social institutions in city life must be understood in its relation to this background.

[1] Thorstein Veblen, *The Instinct of Workmanship, and the State of the Industrial Arts.* (New York, 1914.)

CHAPTER V

SOCIAL INTERACTION

I. INTRODUCTION

1. The Concept of Interaction

The idea of interaction is not a notion of common sense. It represents the culmination of long-continued reflection by human beings in their ceaseless effort to resolve the ancient paradox of unity in diversity, the "one" and the "many," to find law and order in the apparent chaos of physical changes and social events; and thus to find explanations for the behavior of the universe, of society, and of man.

The disposition to be curious and reflective about the physical and social universe is human enough. For men, in distinction from animals, live in a world of ideas as well as in a realm of immediate reality. This world of ideas is something more than the mirror that sense-perception offers us; something less than that ultimate reality to which it seems to be a prologue and invitation. Man, in his ambition to be master of himself and of nature, looks behind the mirror, to analyze phenomena and seek causes, in order to gain control. Science, natural science, is a research for causes, that is to say, for mechanisms, which in turn find application in technical devices, organization, and machinery, in which mankind asserts its control over physical nature and eventually over man himself. Education, in its technical aspects at least, is a device of social control, just as the printing press is an instrument that may be used for the same purpose.

Sociology, like other natural sciences, aims at prediction and control based on an investigation of the nature of man and society, and nature means here, as elsewhere in science, just those aspects of life that are determined and predictable. In order to describe man and society in terms which will reveal their nature, sociology is compelled to reduce the complexity and richness of life to the simplest terms, i.e., elements and forces. Once the concepts "elements" or "forces" have been accepted, the notion of interaction is an inevitable, logical development. In astronomy, for example, these elements are (*a*) the masses of the heavenly bodies, (*b*) their position, (*c*) the direction of their movement, and (*d*) their velocity. In sociology, these forces are institutions, tendencies, human beings, ideas, anything that embodies and expresses motives and wishes. In *principle*, and with reference to their logical character, the "forces" and "elements" in sociology may be compared with the forces and elements in any other natural science.

Ormond, in his *Foundations of Knowledge*,[1] gives an illuminating analysis of interaction as a concept which may be applied equally to the behavior of physical objects and persons.

The notion of interaction is not simple but very complex. The notion involves not simply the idea of bare collision and rebound, but something much more profound, namely, the internal modifiability of the colliding agents. Take for example the simplest possible case, that of one billiard ball striking against another. We say that the impact of one ball against another communicates motion, so that the stricken ball passes from a state of rest to one of motion, while the striking ball has experienced a change of an opposite character. But nothing is explained by this account, for if nothing happens but the communication of motion, why does it not pass through the stricken ball and leave its state unchanged? The phenomenon cannot be of this simple character, but there must be a point somewhere at which the recipient of the impulse gathers itself up, so to speak, into a knot and becomes the subject of the impulse which is thus translated into movement. We have thus movement, impact, impulse, which is translated again into activity, and outwardly the billiard ball changing from a state of rest to one of motion; or in the case of the impelling ball, from a state of motion to one of rest. Now the case of the billiard balls is one of the simpler examples of interaction. We have seen that the problem it supplies is not simple but very complex. The situation is not thinkable at all if we do not suppose the internal modifiability of the agents, and this means that these agents are able somehow to receive internally and to re-act upon impulses which are communicated externally in the form of motion or activity. The simplest form of interaction involves the supposition, therefore, of internal subject-points or their analogues from which impulsions are received and responded to.

[1] Pp. 70 and 72.

Simmel, among sociological writers, although he nowhere expressly defines the term, has employed the conception of interaction with a clear sense of its logical significance. Gumplowicz, on the other hand, has sought to define social interaction as a principle fundamental to all natural sciences, that is to say, sciences that seek to describe change in terms of a process, i.e., physics, chemistry, biology, psychology. The logical principle is the same in all these sciences; the *processes* and the *elements* are different.

2. Classification of the Materials

The material in this chapter will be considered here under three main heads: (*a*) society as interaction, (*b*) communication as the medium of interaction, and (*c*) imitation and suggestion as mechanisms of interaction.

a) *Society as interaction.*—Society stated in mechanistic terms reduces to interaction. A person is a member of society so long as he responds to social forces; when interaction ends, he is isolated and detached; he ceases to be a person and becomes a "lost soul." This is the reason that the limits of society are coterminous with the limits of interaction, that is, of the participation of persons in the life of society. One way of measuring the wholesome or the normal life of a person is by the sheer external fact of his membership in the social groups of the community in which his lot is cast.

Simmel has illustrated in a wide survey of concrete detail how interaction defines the group in time and space. Through contacts of historical continuity, the life of society extends backward to prehistoric eras. More potent over group behavior than contemporary discovery and invention is the control exerted by the "dead hand of the past" through the inertia of folkways and mores, through the revival of memories and sentiments and through the persistence of tradition and culture. Contacts of mobility, on the other hand, define the area of the interaction of the members of the group in space. The degree of departure from accepted ideas and modes of behavior and the extent of sympathetic approach to the strange and the novel largely depend upon the rate, the number, and the intensity of the contacts of mobility.

b) *Communication as the medium of social interaction.*—Each science postulates its own medium of interaction. Astronomy and physics assume a hypothetical substance, the ether. Physics has its principles of molar action and reaction; chemistry studies molecular interaction. Biology and medicine direct their research to the physiological interaction of organisms. Psychology is concerned with the behavior of the individual organism in terms of the interaction of stimuli and responses. Sociology, as collective psychology, deals with communication. Sociologists have referred to this process as intermental stimulation and response.

The readings on communication are so arranged as to make clear the three natural levels of interaction: (x) that of the senses; (y) that of the emotions; and (z) that of sentiments and ideas.

Interaction through sense-perceptions and emotional responses may be termed the natural forms of communication since they are common to man and to animals. Simmel's interpretation of interaction through the senses is suggestive of the subtle, unconscious, yet profound, way in which personal attitudes are formed. Not alone vision, but hearing, smell and touch exhibit in varying degrees the emotional responses of the type of appreciation. This means understanding other persons or objects on the perceptual basis.

The selections from Darwin and from Morgan upon emotional expression in animals indicate how natural expressive signs become a vehicle for communication. A prepossession for speech and ideas blinds man to the important rôle in human conduct still exerted by emotional communication, facial expression, and gesture. Blushing and laughter are peculiarly significant, because these forms of emotional response are distinctively human. To say that a person blushes when he is self-conscious, that he laughs when he is detached from, and superior to, and yet interested in, an occurrence means that blushing and laughter represent contrasted attitudes to a social situation. The relation of blushing and laughter to social control, as an evidence of the emotional dependence of the person upon the group, is at its apogee in adolescence.

Interaction through sensory impressions and emotional expression is restricted to the communication of attitudes and feelings. The selections under the heading "Language and the Communication of Ideas" bring out the uniquely human character of speech. Concepts, as Max Müller insists, are the common symbols wrought out in social experience. They are more or less conventionalized, objective, and intelligible symbols that have been defined in terms of a common experience or, as the logicians say, of a universe of discourse. Every group has its own universe of discourse. In short, to use Durkheim's phrase, concepts are "collective representations."

History has been variously conceived in terms of great events, epoch-making personalities, social movements, and cultural changes. From the point of view of sociology social evolution might profitably be studied in its relation to the development and perfection of the means and technique of communication. How revolutionary was the transition from word of mouth and memory to written records! The beginnings of ancient civilization with its five independent centers in Egypt, the Euphrates River Valley, China, Mexico, and Peru appear to be inextricably bound up with the change from pictographs to writing, that is to say from symbols representing words to symbols representing sounds. The modern period began with the invention of printing and the printing press. As books became the possession of the common man the foundation was laid for experiments in democracy. From the sociological standpoint the book is an organized objective mind whose thoughts are accessible to all. The rôle of the book in social life has long been recognized but not fully appreciated. The Christian church, to be sure, regards the Bible as the word of God. The army does not question the infallibility of the Manual of Arms. Our written Constitution has been termed "the ark of the covenant." The orthodox Socialist appeals in unquestioning faith to the ponderous tomes of Marx.

World-society of today, which depends upon the almost instantaneous communication of events and opinion around the world, rests upon the invention of telegraphy and the laying of the great ocean cables. Wireless telegraphy and radio have only perfected these earlier means and render impossible a monopoly or a censorship of inter-communication between peoples. The traditional cultures, the social inheritances of ages of isolation, are now in a world-process of interaction and modification as a result of the rapidity and the impact of these modern means of the circulation of ideas and sentiments. At the present time it is so popular to malign the newspaper that few recognize the extent to which news has freed mankind from the control of political parties, social institutions, and, it may be added, from the "tyranny" of books.

c) Imitation and suggestion the mechanistic forms of i·*teraction.* — In all forms of communication behavior changes occur, but in two cases the processes have been analyzed, defined, and reduced to simple terms, viz., in imitation and in suggestion.

Imitation, as the etymology of the term implies, is a process of copying or learning. But imitation is learning only so far as it has the character of an experiment, or trial and error. It is also obvious that so-called "instinctive" imitation is not learning at all. Since the results of experimental psychology have limited the field of instinctive imitation to a few simple activities, as the tendencies to run when others run, to laugh when others laugh, its place in human life becomes of slight importance as compared with imitation which involves persistent effort at reproducing standard patterns of behavior.

This human tendency, under social influences, to reproduce the copy Stout has explained in psychological terms of attention and interest. The interests determine the run of attention, and the direction of attention fixes the copies to be imitated. Without in any way discounting the psychological validity of this explanation, or its practical value in educational application, social factors controlling interest and attention should not be disregarded. In a primary group, social control narrowly restricts the selection of patterns and behavior. In an isolated group the individual may have no choice whatsoever. Then, again, attention may be determined, not by interests arising from individual capacity or aptitude, but rather from *rapport*, that is, from interest in the prestige or in the personal traits of the individual presenting the copy.

The relation of the somewhat complex process of imitation to the simple method of trial and error is of significance. Learning by imitation implies at once both identification of the person with the individual presenting the copy and yet differentiation from him. Through imitation we appreciate the other person. We are in sympathy or *en rapport* with him, while at the same time we appropriate his sentiment and his technique. Ribot and Adam Smith analyze this relation of imitation to sympathy and Hirn points out that in art this process of internal imitation is indispensable for aesthetic appreciation.

In this process of appreciation and learning the primitive method of trial and error comes into the service of imitation. In a real sense imitation is mechanical and conservative; it provides a basis for originality, but its function is to transmit, not to originate the new. On the other hand, the simple process of trial and error, a common possession of man and the animals, results in discovery and invention.

The most scientifically controlled situation for the play of suggestion is in hypnosis. An analysis of the observed facts of hypnotism will be helpful in arriving at an understanding of the mechanism of suggestion in everyday life. The essential facts of hypnotism may be briefly summarized as follows: (*a*) The establishment of a relation of *rapport* between the experimenter and the subject of such a nature that the latter carries out suggestions presented by the former. (*b*) The successful response by the subject to the suggestion is conditional upon its relation to his past experience. (*c*) The subject responds to his own idea of the suggestion, and not to the idea as conceived by the experimenter. A consideration of cases is sufficient to convince the student of a complete parallel between suggestion in social life with suggestion in hypnosis, so far, at least, as concerns the last two points. Wherever rapport develops between persons, as in the love of mother and son, the affection of lovers, the comradeship of intimate friends, there also arises the mechanism of the reciprocal influence of suggestion. But in normal social situations, unlike hypnotism, there may be the effect of suggestion where no rapport exists.

Herein lies the significance of the differentiation made by Bechterew between active perception and passive perception. In passive perception ideas and sentiments evading the "ego" enter the "subconscious mind" and, uncontrolled by the active perception, form organizations or complexes of "lost" memories. It thus comes about that in social situations, where no rapport exists between two persons, a suggestion may be made which, by striking the right chord of memory or by resurrecting a forgotten sentiment, may transform the life of the other, as in conversion. The area of suggestion in social life is indicated in a second paper selected from Bechterew. In later chapters upon "Social Control" and "Collective Behavior" the mechanism of suggestion in the determination of group behavior will be further considered.

Imitation and suggestion are both mechanisms of social interaction in which an individual or group is controlled by another individual or group. The distinction between the two processes is now clear. The characteristic mark of imitation is the tendency, under the influence of copies socially presented, to build up mechanisms of habits, sentiments, ideals, and patterns of life. The process of suggestion, as differentiated from imitation in social interaction, is to release under the appropriate social stimuli mechanisms already organized, whether instincts, habits, or sentiments. The other differences between imitation and suggestion grow out of this fundamental distinction. In imitation attention is alert, now on the copy and now on the response. In suggestion the attention is either absorbed in, or distracted from, the stimulus. In imitation the individual is self conscious; the subject in suggestion is unconscious of his behavior. In imitation the activity tends to reproduce the copy; in suggestion the response may be like or unlike the copy.

II. MATERIALS

A. SOCIETY AS INTERACTION

1. The Mechanistic Interpretation of Society[1]

In every natural process we may observe the two essential factors which constitute it, namely, heterogeneous elements and their reciprocal interaction which we ascribe to certain natural forces. We observe these factors in the natural process of the stars, by which the different heavenly bodies exert certain influences over each other, which we ascribe either to the force of attraction or to gravity.

"No material bond unites the planets to the sun. The direct activity of an elementary force, the general force of attraction, holds both in an invisible connection by the elasticity of its influence."

In the chemical natural process we observe the most varied elements related to each other in the most various ways. They attract or repulse each other. They enter into combinations or they withdraw from them. These are nothing but actions and interactions which we ascribe to certain forces inherent in these elements.

The vegetable and animal natural process begins, at any rate, with the contact of heterogeneous elements which we characterize as sexual cells (gametes). They exert upon each other a reciprocal influence which sets into activity the vegetable and animal process.

[1] Translated and adapted from Ludwig Gumplowicz, *Der Rassenkampf*, pp. 158–61. (Innsbruck: Wagnerische Univ. Buchhandlung, 1883.)

The extent to which science is permeated by the hypothesis that heterogeneous elements reacting upon each other are necessary to a natural process is best indicated by the atomic theory.

Obviously, it is conceded that the origins of all natural processes cannot better be explained than by the assumption of the existence in bodies of invisible particles, each of which has some sort of separate existence and reacts upon the others.

The entire hypothesis is only the consequence of the concept of a natural process which the observation of nature has produced in the human mind.

Even though we conceive the social process as characteristic and different from the four types of natural processes mentioned above, still there must be identified in it the two essential factors which constitute the generic conception of the natural process. And this is, in fact, what we find. The numberless human groups, which we assume as the earliest beginnings of human existence, constitute the great variety of heterogeneous ethnic elements. These have decreased with the decrease in the number of hordes and tribes. From the foregoing explanation we are bound to assume as certain that in this field we are concerned with ethnically different and heterogeneous elements.

The question now remains as to the second constitutive element of a natural process, namely, the definite interaction of these elements, and especially as to those interactions which are characterized by regularity and permanency. Of course, we must avoid analogy with the reciprocal interaction of heterogeneous elements in the domain of other natural processes. In strict conformity with the scientific method we take into consideration merely such interactions as the facts of common knowledge and actual experience offer us. Thus will we be able, happily, to formulate a principle of the reciprocal interaction of heterogeneous ethnic, or, if you will, social elements, the mathematical certainty and universality of which cannot be denied irrefutably, since it manifests itself ever and everywhere in the field of history and the living present.

This principle may be very simply stated: Every stronger ethnic or social group strives to subjugate and make serviceable to its purposes every weaker element which exists or may come within the field of its influence. This thesis of the relation of heterogeneous ethnic and social elements to each other, with all the consequences proceeding from it, contains within it the key to the solution of the entire riddle of the natural process of human history. We shall see this thesis illustrated ever and everywhere in the past and the present in the interrelations of heterogeneous ethnic and social elements and become convinced of its universal validity. In this latter relation it does not correspond at all to such natural laws, as, for example, attraction and gravitation or chemical affinity, or to the laws of vegetable and animal life. In order better to conceive of this social natural law in its general validity, we must study it in its different consequences and in the various forms which it assumes according to circumstances and conditions.

2. Social Interaction as the Definition of the Group in Time and Space[1]

Society exists wherever several individuals are in reciprocal relationship. This reciprocity arises always from specific impulses or by virtue of specific purposes. Erotic, religious, or merely associative impulses, purposes of defense or of attack, of play as well as of gain, of aid and instruction, and countless others bring it to pass that men enter into group relationships of acting for, with, against, one another; that is, men exercise an influence upon these conditions of association and are influenced by them. These reactions signify that out of the individual bearers of those occasioning impulses and purposes a unity, that is, a "society," comes into being.

An organic body is a unity because its organs are in a relationship of more intimate interchange of their energies than with any external being. A *state* is *one* because between its citizens the corresponding relationship of reciprocal influences exists. We could, indeed, not call the world *one* if each of its parts did not somehow influence every other, if anywhere the reciprocity of the influences, however mediated, were cut off. That unity, or socialization, may, according to the kind and degree of reciprocity, have very different gradations, from the ephemeral combination for a promenade to the family; from all relationships "at will" to membership in a state; from the temporary aggregation of the guests in a hotel to the intimate bond of a medieval guild.

[1] Translated from Georg Simmel, *Soziologie*, by Albion W. Small, *American Journal of Sociology*, XV (1909), 296–98; III (1898), 667–83.

Everything now which is present in the individuals—the immediate concrete locations of all historical actuality—in the nature of impulse, interest, purpose, inclination, psychical adaptability, and movement of such sort that thereupon or therefrom occurs influence upon others, or the reception of influence from them—all this I designate as the content or the material of socialization. In and of themselves, these materials with which life is filled, these motivations which impel it, are not social in their nature. Neither hunger nor love, neither labor nor religiosity, neither the technique nor the functions and results of intelligence, as they are given immediately and in their strict sense, signify socialization. On the contrary, they constitute it only when they shape the isolated side-by-sideness of the individuals into definite forms of with-and-for-one-another, which belong under the general concept of reciprocity. Socialization is thus the *form*, actualizing itself in countless various types, in which the individuals—on the basis of those interests, sensuous or ideal, momentary or permanent, conscious or unconscious, casually driving or purposefully leading—grow together into a unity, and within which these interests come to realization.

That which constitutes "society" is evidently types of reciprocal influencing. Any collection of human beings whatsoever becomes "society," not by virtue of the fact that in each of the number there is a life-content which actuates the individual as such, but only when the vitality of these contents attains the form of reciprocal influencing. Only when an influence is exerted, whether immediately or through a third party, from one upon another has society come into existence in place of a mere spatial juxtaposition or temporal contemporaneousness or succession of individuals. If, therefore, there is to be a science, the object of which is to be "society" and nothing else, it can investigate only these reciprocal influences, these kinds and forms of socialization. For everything else found within "society" and realized by means of it is not "society" itself, but merely a content which builds or is built by this form of coexistence, and which indeed only together with "society" brings into existence the real structure, "society," in the wider and usual sense.

The persistence of the group presents itself in the fact that, in spite of the departure and the change of members, the group remains identical. We say that it is the same state, the same association, the same army, which now exists that existed so and so many decades or centuries ago;

this, although no single member of the original organization remains. Here is one of the cases in which the temporal order of events presents a marked analogy with the spatial order. Out of individuals existing side by side, that is, apart from each other, a social unity is formed. The inevitable separation which space places between men is nevertheless overcome by the spiritual bond between them, so that there arises an appearance of unified interexistence. In like manner the temporal separation of individuals and of generations presents their union in our conceptions as a coherent, uninterrupted whole. In the case of persons spatially separated, this unity is effected by the reciprocity maintained between them across the dividing distance. The unity of complex being means nothing else than the cohesion of elements which is produced by the reciprocal exercise of forces. In the case of temporally separated persons, however, unity cannot be effected in this manner, because reciprocity is lacking. The earlier may influence the later, but the later cannot influence the earlier. Hence the persistence of the social unity in spite of shifting membership presents a peculiar problem which is not solved by explaining how the group came to exist at a given moment.

a) Continuity by continuance of locality.—The first and most obvious element of the continuity of group unity is the continuance of the locality, of the place and soil on which the group lives. The state, still more the city, and also countless other associations, owe their unity first of all to the territory which constitutes the abiding substratum for all change of their contents. To be sure, the continuance of the locality does not of itself alone mean the continuance of the social unity, since, for instance, if the whole population of a state is driven out or enslaved by a conquering group, we speak of a changed civic group in spite of the continuance of the territory. Moreover, the unity of whose character we are speaking is psychical, and it is this psychical factor itself which makes the territorial substratum a unity. After this has once taken place, however, the locality constitutes an essential point of attachment for the further persistence of the group. But it is only one such element, for there are groups that get along without a local substratum. On the one hand, there are the very small groups, like the family, which continue precisely the same after the residence is changed. On the other hand, there are the very large groups, like that ideal community of the "republic of letters," or the other international associations in the interest of culture, or the groups conducting international commerce.

Their peculiar character comes from entire independence of all attachment to a definite locality.

b) *Continuity through blood relationship.*—In contrast with this more formal condition for the maintenance of the group is the physiological connection of the generations. Community of stock is not always enough to insure unity of coherence for a long time. In many cases the local unity must be added. The social unity of the Jews has been weakened to a marked degree since the dispersion, in spite of their physiological and confessional unity. It has become more compact in cases where a group of Jews have lived for a time in the same territory, and the efforts of the modern "Zionism" to restore Jewish unity on a larger scale calculate upon concentration in one locality. On the other hand, when other bonds of union fail, the physiological is the last recourse to which the self-maintenance of the group resorts. The more the German guilds declined, the weaker their inherent power of cohesion became, the more energetically did each guild attempt to make itself exclusive, that is, it insisted that no persons should be admitted as guildmasters except sons or sons-in-law of masters or the husbands of masters' widows.

The physiological coherence of successive generations is of incomparable significance for the maintenance of the unitary self of the group, for the special reason that the displacement of one generation by the following *does not take place all at once.* By virtue of this fact it comes about that a continuity is maintained which conducts the vast majority of the individuals who live in a given moment into the life of the next moment. The change, the disappearance and entrance of persons, affects in two contiguous moments a number relatively small compared with the number of those who remain constant. Another element of influence in this connection is the fact that human beings are not bound to a definite mating season, but that children are begotten at any time. It can never properly be asserted of a group, therefore, that at any given moment a new generation begins. The departure of the older and the entrance of the younger elements proceed so gradually and continuously that the group seems as much like a unified self as an organic body in spite of the change of its atoms.

If the change were instantaneous, it is doubtful if we should be justified in calling the group "the same" after the critical moment as before. The circumstance alone that the transition affected in a given moment only a minimum of the total life of the group makes it possible for the group to retain its selfhood through the change. We may express this schematically as follows: If the totality of individuals or other conditions of the life of the group be represented by *a, b, c, d, e;* in a later moment by *m, n, o, p, q;* we may nevertheless speak of the persistence of identical selfhood if the development takes the following course: *a, b, c, d, e—m, b, c, d, e—m, n, c, d, e—m, n, o, d, e—m, n, o, p, e—m, n, o, p, q.* In this case each stage is differentiated from the contiguous stage by only one member, and at each moment it shares the same chief elements with its neighboring moments.

c) *Continuity through membership in the group.*—This continuity in change of the individuals who are the vehicles of the group unity is most immediately and thoroughly visible when it rests upon procreation. The same form is found, however, in cases where this physical agency is excluded, as, for example, within the Catholic clerus. Here the continuity is secured by provision that enough persons always remain in office to initiate the neophytes. This is an extremely important sociological fact. It makes bureaucracies tenacious, and causes their character and spirit to endure in spite of all shifting of individuals. The physiological basis of self-maintenance here gives place to a psychological one. To speak exactly, the preservation of group identity in this case depends, of course, upon the amount of invariability in the vehicles of this unity, but, at all events, the whole body of members belonging in the group at any given moment only separate from the group after they have been associated with their successors long enough to assimilate the latter fully to themselves, i.e., to the spirit, the form, the tendency of the group. The immortality of the group depends upon the fact that the change is sufficiently slow and gradual.

The fact referred to by the phrase "immortality of the group" is of the greatest importance. The preservation of the identical selfhood of the group through a practically unlimited period gives to the group a significance which, *ceteris paribus*, is far superior to that of the individual. The life of the individual, with its purposes, its valuations, its force, is destined to terminate within a limited time, and to a certain extent each individual must start at the beginning. Since the life of the group has no such a priori fixed time limit, and its forms are really arranged as though they were to last forever, the group accomplishes a summation of the achievements, powers, experiences, through which it makes itself far superior to the fragmentary individual lives. Since the early Middle Ages this has been the source of the power of municipal corporations in England. Each had from the beginning the right, as Stubbs expresses it, "of perpetuating its existence by filling up vacancies as they occur." The ancient privileges were given expressly only to the burghers and their heirs. As a matter of fact, they were exercised as a right to add new members so that, whatever fate befell the members and their physical descendants, the corporation, as such, was held intact. This had to be paid for, to be sure, by the disappearance of the individual importance of the units behind their rôle as vehicles of the maintenance of the group, for the group security must suffer, the closer it is bound up with the perishable individuality of the units. On the other hand, the more anonymous and unpersonal the unit is, the more fit is he to step into the place of another, and so to insure to the group uninterrupted self-maintenance. This was the enormous advantage through which during the Wars of the Roses the Commons repulsed the previously superior power of the upper house. A battle that destroyed half the nobility of the country took also from the House of Lords one-half its force, because this is attached to the personalities. The House of Commons is in principle assured against such weakening. That estate at last got predominance which, through the equalizing of its members, demonstrated the most persistent power of group existence. This circumstance gives every group an advantage in competition with an individual.

d) *Continuity through leadership.*—On this account special arrangements are necessary so soon as the life of the group is intimately bound up with that of a leading, commanding individual. What dangers to the integrity of the group are concealed in this sociological form may be learned from the history of all interregnums—dangers which, of course, increase in the same ratio in which the ruler actually forms the central point of the functions through which the group preserves its unity, or, more correctly, at each moment creates its unity anew. Consequently a break between rulers may be a matter of indifference where the prince only exercises a nominal sway—"reigns, but does not govern"—while, on the other hand, we observe even in the swarm of bees that anarchy results so soon as the queen is removed. Although it is entirely false to explain this latter phenomenon by analogy of a human ruler, since the queen bee gives no orders, yet the queen occupies the middle point of the activity of the hive. By means of her antennae she is in constant communication with the workers, and so all the signals coursing through the hive pass through her. By virtue of this very fact the hive feels itself a unity, and this unity dissolves with the disappearance of the functional center.

e) Continuity through the hereditary principle.—In political groups the attempt is made to guard against all the dangers of personality, particularly those of possible intervals between the important persons, by the principle: "The king never dies." While in the early Middle Ages the tradition prevailed that when the king dies his peace dies with him, this newer principle contains provision for the self-preservation of the group. It involves an extraordinarily significant sociological conception, viz., the king is no longer king as a person, but the reverse is the case, that is, his person is only the in itself irrelevant vehicle of the abstract kingship, which is as unalterable as the group itself, of which the kingship is the apex. The group reflects its immortality upon the kingship, and the sovereign in return brings that immortality to visible expression in his own person, and by so doing reciprocally strengthens the vitality of the group. That mighty factor of social coherence which consists of loyalty of sentiment toward the reigning power might appear in very small groups in the relation of fidelity toward the person of the ruler. For large groups the definition that Stubbs once gave must certainly apply, viz.: "Loyalty is a habit of strong and faithful attachment to a person, not so much by reason of his personal character as of his official position." By becoming objectified in the deathless office, the princely principle gains a new psychological power for concentration and cohesion within the group, while the old princely principle that rested on the mere personality of the prince necessarily lost power as the size of the group increased.

f) Continuity through a material symbol.—The objectification of the coherence of the group may also do away with the personal form to such an extent that it attaches itself to a material symbol. Thus in the German lands in the Middle Ages the imperial jewels were looked upon as the visible realization of the idea of the realm and of its continuity, so that the possession of them gave to a pretender a decided advantage over all other aspirants, and this was one of the influences which evidently assisted the heir of the body of the deceased emperor in securing the succession.

In view of the destructibility of a material object, since too this disadvantage cannot be offset, as in the case of a person, by the continuity of heredity, it is very dangerous for the group to seek such a support for its self-preservation. Many a regiment has lost its coherence with the loss of its standard. Many kinds of associations have dissolved after their palladium, their storehouse, their grail, was destroyed. When, however, the social coherence is lost in this way, it is safe to say that it must have suffered serious internal disorder before, and that in this case the loss of the external symbol representing the unity of the group is itself only the symbol that the social elements have lost their coherence. When this last is not the case, the loss of the group symbol not only has no disintegrating effect but it exerts a direct integrating influence. While the symbol loses its corporeal reality, it may, as mere thought, longing, ideal, work much more powerfully, profoundly, indestructibly. We may get a good view of these two opposite influences of the forms of destruction of the group symbol upon the solidity of the group by reference to the consequences of the destruction of the Jewish temple by Titus. The hierarchal Jewish state was a thorn in the flesh of the Roman statecraft that aimed at the unity of the empire. The purpose of dissolving this state was accomplished, so far as a certain number of the Jews were concerned, by the destruction of the temple. Such was the effect with those who cared little, anyway, about this centralization. Thus the alienation of the Pauline Christians from Judaism was powerfully promoted by this event. For the Palestinian Jews, on the other hand, the breach between Judaism and the rest of the world was deepened. By this destruction of its symbol their national religious exclusiveness was heightened to desperation.

g) Continuity through group honor.—The sociological significance of honor as a form of cohesion is extraordinarily great. Through the appeal to honor, society secures from its members the kind of conduct conducive to its own preservation, particularly within the spheres of conduct intermediate between the purview of the criminal code, on the one hand, and the field of purely personal morality, on the other. By the demands upon its members contained in the group standard of honor the group preserves its unified character and its distinctness from the other groups within the same inclusive association. The essential thing is the specific idea of honor in narrow groups—family honor, officers' honor, mercantile honor, yes, even the "honor among thieves." Since the individual belongs to various groups, the individual may, at the same time, be under the demands of several sorts of honor which are independent of each other. One may preserve his mercantile honor, or his scientific honor as an investigator, who has forfeited his family honor, and vice versa; the robber may strictly observe the requirements of thieves' honor after he has violated every other; a woman may have lost her womanly honor and in every other respect be most honorable, etc. Thus honor consists in the relation of the individual to a particular circle, which in this respect manifests its separateness, its sociological distinctness, from other groups.

h) *Continuity through specialized organs.*—From such recourse of social self-preservation to individual persons, to a material substance, to an ideal conception, we pass now to the cases in which social persistence takes advantage of an organ composed of a number of persons. Thus a religious community embodies its coherence and its life principle in its priesthood; a political community its inner principle of union in its administrative organization, its union against foreign power in its military system; this latter in its corps of officers; every permanent union in its official head; transitory associations in their committees; political parties in their parliamentary representatives.

B.   THE NATURAL FORMS OF COMMUNICATION

1.   Sociology of the Senses: Visual Interaction[1]

It is through the medium of the senses that we perceive our fellow-men. This fact has two aspects of fundamental sociological significance: (*a*) that of appreciation, and (*b*) that of comprehension.

a) *Appreciation.*—Sense-impressions may induce in us affective responses of pleasure or pain, of excitement or calm, of tension or

[1] Translated and adapted from Georg Simmel, *Soziologie*, pp. 646–51. (Leipzig: Duncker und Humblot, 1908.)

relaxation, produced by the features of a person, or by the tone of his voice, or by his mere physical presence in the same room. These affective responses, however, do not enable us to understand or to define the other person. Our emotional response to the sense-image of the other leaves his real self outside.

b) Comprehension.—The sense-impression of the other person may develop in the opposite direction when it becomes the medium for understanding the other. What I see, hear, feel of him is only the bridge over which I reach his real self. The sound of the voice and its meaning, perhaps, present the clearest illustration. The speech, quite as much as the appearance, of a person, may be immediately either attractive or repulsive. On the other hand, what he says enables us to understand not only his momentary thoughts but also his inner self. The same principle applies to all sense-impressions.

The sense-impressions of any object produce in us not only emotional and aesthetic attitudes toward it but also an understanding of it. In the case of reaction to non-human objects, these two responses are, in general, widely separated. We may appreciate the emotional value of any sense-impression of an object. The fragrance of a rose, the charm of a tone, the grace of a bough swaying in the wind, is experienced as a joy engendered within the soul. On the other hand, we may desire to understand and to comprehend the rose, or the tone, or the bough. In the latter case we respond in an entirely different way, often with conscious endeavor. These two diverse reactions which are independent of each other are with human beings generally integrated into a unified response. Theoretically, our sense-impressions of a person may be directed on the one hand to an appreciation of his emotional value, or on the other to an impulsive or deliberate understanding of him. Actually, these two reactions are coexistent and inextricably interwoven as the basis of our relation to him. Of course, appreciation and comprehension develop in quite different degrees. These two diverse responses— to the tone of voice and to the meaning of the utterance; to the appearance of a person and to his individuality; to the attraction or repulsion of his personality and to the impulsive judgment upon his character as well as many times upon his grade of culture—are present in any perception in very different degrees and combinations.

Of the special sense-organs, the eye has a uniquely sociological function. The union and interaction of individuals is based upon mutual glances. This is perhaps the most direct and purest reciprocity which exists anywhere. This highest psychic reaction, however, in which the glances of eye to eye unite men, crystallizes into no objective structure; the unity which momentarily arises between two persons is present in the occasion and is dissolved in the function. So tenacious and subtle is this union that it can only be maintained by the shortest and straightest line between the eyes, and the smallest deviation from it, the slightest glance aside, completely destroys the unique character of this union. No objective trace of this relationship is left behind, as is universally found, directly or indirectly, in all other types of associations between men, as, for example, in interchange of words. The interaction of eye and eye dies in the moment in which the directness of the function is lost. But the totality of social relations of human beings, their self-assertion and self-abnegation, their intimacies and estrangements, would be changed in unpredictable ways if there occurred no glance of eye to eye. This mutual glance between persons, in distinction from the simple sight or observation of the other, signifies a wholly new and unique union between them.

The limits of this relation are to be determined by the significant fact that the glance by which the one seeks to perceive the other is itself expressive. By the glance which reveals the other, one discloses himself. By the same act in which the observer seeks to know the observed, he surrenders himself to be understood by the observer. The eye cannot take unless at the same time it gives. The eye of a person discloses his own soul when he seeks to uncover that of another. What occurs in this direct mutual glance represents the most perfect reciprocity in the entire field of human relationships.

Shame causes a person to look at the ground to avoid the glance of the other. The reason for this is certainly not only because he is thus spared the visible evidence of the way in which the other regards his painful situation, but the deeper reason is that the lowering of his glance to a certain degree prevents the other from comprehending the extent of his confusion. The glance in the eye of the other serves not only for me to know the other but also enables him to know me. Upon the line which unites the two eyes, it conveys to the other the real personality, the real attitude, and the real impulse. The "ostrich policy" has in this explanation a real justification: who does not see the other actually conceals himself in part from the observer. A person is not at all completely present to another, when the latter sees him, but only when he also sees the other.

The sociological significance of the eye has special reference to the expression of the face as the first object of vision between man and man. It is seldom clearly understood to what an extent even our practical relations depend upon mutual recognition, not only in the sense of all external characteristics, as the momentary appearance and attitude of the other, but what we know or intuitively perceive of his life, of his inner nature, of the immutability of his being, all of which colors unavoidably both our transient and our permanent relations with him. The face is the geometric chart of all these experiences. It is the symbol of all that which the individual has brought with him as the pre-condition of his life. In the face is deposited what has been precipitated from past experience as the substratum of his life, which has become crystallized into the permanent features of his face. To the extent to which we thus perceive the face of a person, there enters into social relations, in so far as it serves practical purposes, a super-practical element. It follows that a man is first known by his countenance, not by his acts. The face as a medium of expression is entirely a theoretical organ; it does not act, as the hand, the foot, the whole body; it transacts none of the internal or practical relations of the man, it only tells about him. The peculiar and important sociological art of "knowing" transmitted by the eye is determined by the fact that the countenance is the essential object of the inter-individual sight. This knowing is still somewhat different from understanding. To a certain extent, and in a highly variable degree, we know at first glance with whom we have to do. Our unconsciousness of this knowledge and its fundamental significance lies in the fact that we direct our attention from this self-evident intuition to an understanding of special features which determine our practical relations to a particular individual. But if we become conscious of this self-evident fact, then we are amazed how much we know about a person in the first glance at him. We do not obtain meaning from his expression, susceptible to analysis into individual traits. We cannot unqualifiedly say whether he is clever or stupid, good- or ill-natured, temperamental or phlegmatic. All these traits are general characteristics which he shares with unnumbered others. But what this first glance at him transmits to us cannot be analyzed or appraised into any such conceptual and expressive elements. Yet our initial impression remains ever the keynote of all later knowledge of him; it is the direct perception of his individuality which his appearance, and especially his face, discloses to our glance.

The sociological attitude of the blind is entirely different from that of the deaf-mute. For the blind, the other person is actually present only in the alternating periods of his utterance. The expression of the anxiety and unrest, the traces of all past events, exposed to view in the faces of men, escape the blind, and that may be the reason for the peaceful and calm disposition, and the unconcern toward their surroundings, which is so often observed in the blind. Indeed, the majority of the stimuli which the face presents are often puzzling; in general, what we see of a man will be interpreted by what we hear from him, while the opposite is more unusual. Therefore the one who sees, without hearing, is much more perplexed, puzzled, and worried, than the one who hears without seeing. This principle is of great importance in understanding the sociology of the modern city.

Social life in the large city as compared with the towns shows a great preponderance of occasions to *see* rather than to *hear* people. One explanation lies in the fact that the person in the town is acquainted with nearly all the people he meets. With these he exchanges a word or a glance, and their countenance represents to him not merely the visible but indeed the entire personality. Another reason of especial significance is the development of public means of transportation. Before the appearance of omnibuses, railroads, and street cars in the nineteenth century, men were not in a situation where for periods of minutes or hours they could or must look at each other without talking to one another. Modern social life increases in ever growing degree the rôle of mere visual impression which always characterizes the preponderant part of all sense relationship between man and man, and must place social attitudes and feelings upon an entirely changed basis. The greater perplexity which characterizes the person who only sees, as contrasted with the one who only hears, brings us to the problems of the emotions of modern life: the lack of orientation in the collective life, the sense of utter lonesomeness, and the feeling that the individual is surrounded on all sides by closed doors.

2. The Expression of the Emotions[1]

Actions of all kinds, if regularly accompanying any state of the mind, are at once recognized as expressive. These may consist of movements of any part of the body, as the wagging of a dog's tail, the shrugging of a man's shoulders, the erection of the hair, the exudation of perspiration, the state of the capillary circulation, labored breathing, and the use of the vocal or other sound-producing instruments. Even insects express anger, terror, jealousy, and love by their stridulation. With man the respiratory organs are of especial importance in expression, not only in a direct, but to a still higher degree in an indirect, manner.

Few points are more interesting in our present subject than the extraordinarily complex chain of events which lead to certain expressive movements. Take, for instance, the oblique eyebrows of a man suffering from grief or anxiety. When infants scream loudly from hunger or pain, the circulation is affected, and the eyes tend to become gorged with blood; consequently the muscles surrounding the eyes are strongly contracted as a protection. This action, in the course of many generations, has become firmly fixed and inherited; but when, with advancing years and culture, the habit of screaming is partially repressed, the muscles round the eyes still tend to contract, whenever even slight distress is felt. Of these muscles, the pyramidals of the nose are less under the control of the will than are the others, and their contraction can be checked only by that of the central fasciae of the frontal muscle; these latter fasciae draw up the inner ends of the eyebrows and wrinkle the forehead in a peculiar manner, which we instantly recognize as the expression of grief or anxiety. Slight movements, such as these just described, or the scarcely perceptible drawing down of the corners of the mouth, are the last remnants or rudiments of strongly marked and intelligible movements. They are as full of significance to us in regard to

[1] Adapted from Charles Darwin, *The Expression of the Emotions*, pp. 350–67. (John Murray, 1873.)

expression as are ordinary rudiments to the naturalist in the classification and genealogy of organic beings.

That the chief expressive actions exhibited by man and by the lower animals are now innate or inherited—that is, have not been learned by the individual—is admitted by everyone. So little has learning or imitation to do with several of them that they are from the earliest days and throughout life quite beyond our control; for instance, the relaxation of the arteries of the skin in blushing, and the increased action of the heart in anger. We may see children only two or three years old, and even those born blind, blushing from shame; and the naked scalp of a very young infant reddens from passion. Infants scream from pain directly after birth, and all their features then assume the same form as during subsequent years. These facts alone suffice to show that many of our most important expressions have not been learned; but it is remarkable that some, which are certainly innate, require practice in the individual before they are performed in a full and perfect manner; for instance, weeping and laughing. The inheritance of most of our expressive actions explains the fact that those born blind display them, as I hear from the Rev. R. H. Blair, equally well with those gifted with eyesight. We can thus also understand the fact that the young and the old of widely different races, both with man and animals, express the same state of mind by the same movement.

We are so familiar with the fact of young and old animals displaying their feelings in the same manner that we hardly perceive how remarkable it is that a young puppy should wag its tail when pleased, depress its ears and uncover its canine teeth when pretending to be savage, just like an old dog; or that a kitten should arch its little back and erect its hair when frightened and angry, like an old cat. When, however, we turn to less common gestures in ourselves, which we are accustomed to look at as artificial or conventional— such as shrugging the shoulders as a sign of impotence, or the raising the arms with open hands and extended fingers as a sign of wonder— we feel perhaps too much surprise at finding that they are innate. That these and some other gestures are inherited we may infer from their being performed by very young children, by those born blind, and by the most widely distinct races of man. We should also bear in mind that new and highly peculiar tricks, in association with certain states of the mind, are known to have arisen in certain individuals and to have been afterward transmitted to their offspring, in some cases for more than one generation.

Certain other gestures, which seem to us so natural that we might easily imagine that they were innate, apparently have been learned like the words of a language. This seems to be the case with the joining of the uplifted hands and the turning up of the eyes in prayer. So it is with kissing as a mark of affection; but this is innate, in so far as it depends on the pleasure derived from contact with a beloved person. The evidence with respect to the inheritance of nodding and shaking the head as signs of affirmation and negation is doubtful, for they are not universal, yet seem too general to have been independently acquired by all the individuals of so many races.

We will now consider how far the will and consciousness have come into play in the development of the various movements of expression. As far as we can judge, only a few expressive movements, such as those just referred to, are learned by each individual; that is, were consciously and voluntarily performed during the early years of life for some definite object, or in imitation of others, and then became habitual. The far greater number of the movements of expression, and all the more important ones, are, as we have seen, innate or inherited; and such cannot be said to depend on the will of the individual. Nevertheless, all those included under our first principle were at first voluntarily performed for a definite object, namely, to escape some danger, to relieve some distress, or to gratify some desire. For instance, there can hardly be a doubt that the animals which fight with their teeth have acquired the habit of drawing back their ears closely to their heads when feeling savage from their progenitors having voluntarily acted in this manner in order to protect their ears from being torn by their antagonists; for those animals which do not fight with their teeth do not thus express a savage state of mind. We may infer as highly probable that we ourselves have acquired the habit of contracting the muscles round the eyes whilst crying gently, that is, without the utterance of any loud sound, from our progenitors, especially during infancy, having experienced during the act of screaming an uncomfortable sensation in their eyeballs. Again, some highly expressive movements result from the endeavor to check or prevent other expressive movements;

thus the obliquity of the eyebrows and the drawing down of the corners of the mouth follow from the endeavor to prevent a screaming-fit from coming on or to check it after it has come on. Here it is obvious that the consciousness and will must at first have come into play; not that we are conscious in these or in other such cases what muscles are brought into action, any more than when we perform the most ordinary voluntary movements.

The power of communication between the members of the same tribe by means of language has been of paramount importance in the development of man; and the force of language is much aided by the expressive movements of the face and body. We perceive this at once when we converse on an important subject with any person whose face is concealed. Nevertheless there are no grounds, as far as I can discover, for believing that any muscle has been developed or even modified exclusively for the sake of expression. The vocal and other sound-producing organs by which various expressive noises are produced seem to form a partial exception; but I have elsewhere attempted to show that these organs were first developed for sexual purposes, in order that one sex might call or charm the other. Nor can I discover grounds for believing that any inherited movement which now serves as a means of expression was at first voluntarily and consciously performed for this special purpose— like some of the gestures and the finger-language used by the deaf and dumb. On the contrary, every true or inherited movement of expression seems to have had some natural and independent origin. But when once acquired, such movements may be voluntarily and consciously employed as a means of communication. Even infants, if carefully attended to, find out at a very early age that their screaming brings relief, and they soon voluntarily practice it. We may frequently see a person voluntarily raising his eyebrows to express surprise, or smiling to express pretended satisfaction and acquiescence. A man often wishes to make certain gestures conspicuous or demonstrative, and will raise his extended arms with widely opened fingers above his head to show astonishment or lift his shoulders to his ears to show that he cannot or will not do something.

We have seen that the study of the theory of expression confirms to a certain limited extent the conclusion that man is derived from some lower animal form, and supports the belief of the specific or subspecific unity of the several races; but as far as my judgment serves, such confirmation was hardly needed. We have also seen that expression in itself, or the language of the emotions, as it has sometimes been called, is certainly of importance for the welfare of mankind. To understand, as far as is possible, the source or origin of the various expressions which may be hourly seen on the faces of the men around us, not to mention our domesticated animals, ought to possess much interest for us. From these several causes we may conclude that the philosophy of our subject has well deserved that attention which it has already received from several excellent observers, and that it deserves still further attention, especially from any able physiologist.

3. Blushing[1]

Blushing is the most peculiar and the most human of all expressions. Monkeys redden from passion, but it would require an overwhelming amount of evidence to make us believe that any animal could blush. The reddening of the face from a blush is due to the relaxation of the muscular coats of the small arteries, by which the capillaries become filled with blood; and this depends on the proper vasomotor center being affected. No doubt if there be at the same time much mental agitation, the general circulation will be affected; but it is not due to the action of the heart that the network of minute vessels covering the face becomes under a sense of shame gorged with blood. We can cause laughing by tickling the skin, weeping or frowning by a blow, trembling from the fear of pain, and so forth; but we cannot cause a blush by any physical means— that is, by any action on the body. It is the mind which must be affected. Blushing is not only involuntary, but the wish to restrain it, by leading to self-attention, actually increases the tendency.

The young blush much more freely than the old, but not during infancy, which is remarkable, as we know that infants at a very. early age redden from passion. I have received authentic accounts of two little girls blushing at the ages of between two and three years; and of another sensitive child, a year older, blushing when reproved for a fault. Many children at a somewhat more advanced

[1] Adapted from Charles Darwin, *The Expression of the Emotions*, pp. 310–37. (John Murray, 1873.)

age blush in a strongly marked manner. It appears that the mental powers of infants are not as yet sufficiently developed to allow of their blushing. Hence, also, it is that idiots rarely blush. Dr. Crichton Browne observed for me those under his care, but never saw a genuine blush, though he has seen their faces flush, apparently from joy, when food was placed before them, and from anger. Nevertheless some, if not utterly degraded, are capable of blushing. A microcephalous idiot, for instance, thirteen years old, whose eyes brightened a little when he was pleased or amused, has been described by Dr. Behn as blushing and turning to one side when undressed for medical examination.

Women blush much more than men. It is rare to see an old man, but not nearly so rare to see an old woman, blushing. The blind do not escape. Laura Bridgman, born in this condition, as well as completely deaf, blushes. The Rev. R. H. Blair, principal of the Worcester College, informs me that three children born blind, out of seven or eight then in the asylum, are great blushers. The blind are not at first conscious that they are observed, and it is a most important part of their education, as Mr. Blair informs me, to impress this knowledge on their minds; and the impression thus gained would greatly strengthen the tendency to blush, by increasing the habit of self-attention.

The tendency to blush is inherited. Dr. Burgess gives the case of a family consisting of a father, mother, and ten children, all of whom, without exception, were prone to blush to a most painful degree. The children were grown up; "and some of them were sent to travel in order to wear away this diseased sensibility, but nothing was of the slightest avail." Even peculiarities in blushing seem to be inherited. Sir James Paget, whilst examining the spine of a girl, was struck at her singular manner of blushing; a big splash of red appeared first on one cheek, and then other splashes, variously scattered over the face and neck. He subsequently asked the mother whether her daughter always blushed in this peculiar manner and was answered, "Yes, she takes after me." Sir J. Paget then perceived that by asking this question he had caused the mother to blush and she exhibited the same peculiarity as her daughter.

In most cases the face, ears, and neck are the sole parts which redden; but many persons, whilst blushing intensely, feel that their whole bodies grow hot and tingle; and this shows that the entire surface must be in some manner affected. Blushes are said sometimes to commence on the forehead, but more commonly on the cheeks, afterward spreading to the ears and neck. In two albinos examined by Dr. Burgess, the blushes commenced by a small circumscribed spot on the cheeks, over the parotidean plexus of nerves, and then increased into a circle; between this blushing circle and the blush on the neck there was an evident line of demarcation, although both arose simultaneously. The retina, which is naturally red in the albino, invariably increased at the same time in redness. Every one must have noticed how easily after one blush fresh blushes chase each other over the face. Blushing is preceded by a peculiar sensation in the skin. According to Dr. Burgess the reddening of the skin is generally succeeded by a slight pallor, which shows that the capillary vessels contract after dilating. In some rare cases paleness instead of redness is caused under conditions which would naturally induce a blush. For instance, a young lady told me that in a large and crowded party she caught her hair so firmly on the button of a passing servant that it took some time before she could be extricated; from her sensation she imagined that she had blushed crimson but was assured by a friend that she had turned extremely pale.

The mental states which induce blushing consist of shyness, shame, and modesty, the essential element in all being self-attention. Many reasons can be assigned for believing that originally self-attention directed to personal appearance, in relation to the opinion of others, was the exciting cause, the same effect being subsequently produced, through the force of association, by self-attention in relation to moral conduct. It is not the simple act of reflecting on our own appearance, but the thinking what others think of us, which excites a blush. In absolute solitude the most sensitive person would be quite indifferent about his appearance. We feel blame or disapprobation more acutely than approbation; and consequently depreciatory remarks or ridicule, whether of our appearance or conduct, cause us to blush much more readily than does praise. But undoubtedly praise and admiration are highly efficient: a pretty girl blushes when a man gazes intently at her, though she may know perfectly well that he is not depreciating her. Many children, as well as old and sensitive persons, blush when they are much praised. Hereafter the question will be discussed how it has arisen that the consciousness that others are attending to our personal appearance should have led to the capillaries, especially those of the face, instantly becoming filled with blood.

My reasons for believing that attention directed to personal appearance, and not to moral conduct, has been the fundamental element in the acquirement of the habit of blushing will now be given. They are separately light, but combined possess, as it appears to me, considerable weight. It is notorious that nothing makes a shy person blush so much as any remark, however slight, on his personal appearance. One cannot notice even the dress of a woman much given to blushing without causing her face to crimson. It is sufficient to stare hard at some persons to make them, as Coleridge remarks, blush—"account for that he who can."

With the two albinos observed by Dr. Burgess, "the slightest attempt to examine their peculiarities" invariably caused them to blush deeply. Women are much more sensitive about their personal appearance than men are, especially elderly women in comparison with elderly men, and they blush much more freely. The young of both sexes are much more sensitive on this same head than the old, and they also blush much more freely than the old. Children at a very early age do not blush; nor do they show those other signs of self-consciousness which generally accompany blushing; and it is one of their chief charms that they think nothing about what others think of them. At this early age they will stare at a stranger with a fixed gaze and unblinking eyes, as on an inanimate object, in a manner which we elders cannot imitate.

It is plain to everyone that young men and women are highly sensitive to the opinion of each other with reference to their personal appearance; and they blush incomparably more in the presence of the opposite sex than in that of their own. A young man, not very liable to blush, will blush intensely at any slight ridicule of his appearance from a girl whose judgment on any important subject he would disregard. No happy pair of young lovers, valuing each other's admiration and love more than anything else in the world, probably ever courted each other without many a blush. Even the barbarians of Tierra del Fuego, according to Mr. Bridges, blush "chiefly in regard to women, but certainly also at their own personal appearance."

Of all parts of the body, the face is most considered and regarded, as is natural from its being the chief seat of expression and the source of the voice. It is also the chief seat of beauty and of ugliness, and throughout the world is the most ornamented. The face, therefore, will have been subjected during many generations to much closer and more earnest self-attention than any other part of the body; and in accordance with the principle here advanced we can understand why it should be the most liable to blush. Although exposure to alternations of temperature, etc., has probably much increased the power of dilatation and contraction in the capillaries of the face and adjoining parts, yet this by itself will hardly account for these parts blushing much more than the rest of the body; for it does not explain the fact of the hands rarely blushing. With Europeans the whole body tingles slightly when the face blushes intensely; and with the races of men who habitually go nearly naked, the blushes extend over a much larger surface than with us. These facts are, to a certain extent, intelligible, as the self-attention of primeval man, as well as of the existing races which still go naked, will not have been so exclusively confined to their faces, as is the case with the people who now go clothed.

We have seen that in all parts of the world persons who feel shame for some moral delinquency are apt to avert, bend down, or hide their faces, independently of any thought about their personal appearance. The object can hardly be to conceal their blushes, for the face is thus averted or hidden under circumstances which exclude any desire to conceal shame, as when guilt is fully confessed and repented of. It is, however, probable that primeval man before he had acquired much moral sensitiveness would have been highly sensitive about his personal appearance, at least in reference to the other sex, and he would consequently have felt distress at any depreciatory remarks about his appearance; and this is one form of shame. And as the face is the part of the body which is most regarded, it is intelligible that any one ashamed of his personal appearance would desire to conceal this part of his body. The habit, having been thus acquired, would naturally be carried on when shame from strictly moral causes was felt; and it is not easy otherwise to see why under these circumstances there should be a desire to hide the face more than any other part of the body.

The habit, so general with everyone who feels ashamed, of turning away or lowering his eyes, or restlessly moving them from side to side, probably follows from each glance directed toward those present, bringing home the conviction that he is intently regarded; and he endeavors, by not looking at those present, and especially not at their eyes, momentarily to escape from this painful conviction.

4. Laughing[1]

Sympathy, when it is not the direct cause, is conditional to the existence of laughter. Sometimes it provokes it; always it spreads it, sustains and strengthens it.

First of all, it is so much the nature of laughter to communicate itself that when it no longer communicates itself it ceases to exist. One might say that outbursts of merriment need to be encouraged, that they are not self-sufficient. Not to share them is to blow upon them and extinguish them. When, in an animated and mirthful group, some one remains cold or gloomy, the laughter immediately stops or is checked. Yet those whom the common people call, in their picturesque language, wet blankets, spoil-sports, or kill-joys, are not necessarily hostile to the gaiety of the rest. They may only have, and, in fact, very often do have, nothing but the one fault of being out of tune with this gaiety. But even their calm appears an offense to the warmth and the high spirits of the others and kills by itself alone this merriment.

Not only is laughter maintained by sympathy but it is even born of sympathy. The world is composed of two kinds of people: those who make one laugh and those who are made to laugh, these latter being infinitely more numerous. How many there are, indeed, who have no sense of humor, and who, of themselves, would not think of laughing at things at which they do nevertheless laugh heartily because they see others laugh. As for those who have a ready wit and a sense of the comic, do they not enjoy the success of their jokes as much, if not more, than their jokes themselves? Their mirthfulness, then, at least, grows with the joy of spreading it. Very often it happens that many good humorists are temperamentally far from gay, and laugh at their jokes only on the rebound, echoing

[1] Translated and adapted from L. Dugas, *Psychologie du rire*, pp. 32–153. (Félix Alcan, 1902.)

the laughter which they provoke. To laugh, then, is to share the gaiety of others, whether this gaiety is communicated from them to us or from us to them. It seems that we can be moved to laughter only by the merriment of others, that we possess ours only indirectly when others send it to us. Human solidarity never appears more clearly than in the case of laughter.

Yet can one say that sympathy actually produces laughter? Is it not enough to say that it increases it, that it strengthens its effects? All our sentiments are without doubt in a sense revealed to us by others. How many, as Rochefoucald says, would be ignorant of love if they had never read novels! How many in the same way would never have discovered by themselves the laughable side of people and things. Yet even the feelings which one experiences by contagion one can experience only of one's own accord, in one's own way, and according to one's disposition. This fact alone of their contagion proves that from one's birth one carries the germ in himself. Sympathy would explain, then, contagion, but not the birth, of laughter. The fact is that our feelings exist for ourselves only when they acquire a communicative or social value; they have to be diffused in order to manifest themselves. Sympathy does not create them but it gives them their place in the world. It gives them just that access of intensity without which their nature cannot develop or even appear: thus it is that our laughter would be for us as if it did not exist, if it did not find outside itself an echo which increases it.

From the fact that sympathy is the law of laughter, does it follow that it is the cause? Not at all. It would be even contradictory to maintain this. A laugh being given, others are born out of sympathy. But the first laugh or one originally given, where does it get its origin? Communicated laughter implies spontaneous laughter as the echo implies a sound. If sympathy explains one, it is, it would seem, an antipathy or the absence of sympathy which produces the other. "The thing at which we laugh," says Aristotle, "is a defect or ugliness which is not great enough to cause suffering or injury. Thus, for example, a ridiculous face is an ugly or misshapen face, but one on which suffering has not marked." Bain says likewise, "The laughable is the deformed or ugly thing which is not pushed to the point where it is painful or injurious. An occasion for laughter is the degradation of a person of dignity in circumstances which do not arouse a strong emotion," like indignation, anger, or pity. Descartes puts still more limits upon laughter. Speaking of malice he says that laughter cannot be provoked except by misfortunes not only *light* but also *unforseen* and *deserved*. "Derision or mockery," he says, "is a kind of joy mixed with hate, which comes from one's perceiving some *little misfortune* in a person *who one thinks deserves it*. We hate this misfortune but are happy at seeing it in some one who merits it, and, *when this happens unexpectedly, surprise causes us to burst out laughing*. But this misfortune must be small, for if it is great we cannot believe that he who meets it deserves it, unless one has a very malicious or hateful nature."

This fact can be established directly by analyzing the most cruel laughter. If we enter into the feelings of the one who laughs and set aside the disagreeable sentiments, irritation, anger, and disgust, which at times they produce upon us, we come to understand even the savage sneer which appears to us as an insult to suffering; the laugh of the savage, trampling his conquered enemy under foot, or that of the child torturing unfortunate animals. This laugh is, in fact, inoffensive in its way, it is cruel in fact but not in intention. What it expresses is not a perverse, satanic joy but a *heartlessness*, as is so properly said. In the child and the savage sympathy has not been born, that is to say, the absence of imagination for the sufferings of others is complete. As a result we have a negative cruelty, a sort of altruistic or social anaesthesia.

When such an anaesthesia is not complete, when the altruistic sensibility of one who laughs is only dull, his egotism being very keen, his laughter might appear still less hatefully cruel. It would express then not properly the joy of seeing others suffer but that of not having to undergo their suffering and the power of seeing it only as a spectacle.

Analogous facts may be cited closer to us, easier to verify. Those who enjoy robust health often laugh at invalids: their imagination does not comprehend physical suffering, they are incapable of sympathizing with those who experience it. Likewise those who possess calm and even dispositions cannot witness without laughing an excess of mad anger or of impotent rage. In general we do not take seriously those feelings to which we ourselves are strangers; we consider them extravagant and amusing. "How can one be a

Persian?" To laugh is to detach one's self from others, to separate one's self and to take pleasure in this separation, to amuse one's self by contrasting the feelings, character, and temperament of others and one's own feelings, character, and temperament. *Insensibility* has been justly noted by M. Bergson as an essential characteristic of him who laughs. But this *insensibility*, this heartlessness, gives very much the effect of a positive and real ill nature, and M. Bergson had thus simply repeated and expressed in a new way, more precise and correct, the opinion of Aristotle: the cause of laughter is malice mitigated by insensibility or the absence of sympathy.

Thus defined, malice is after all essentially relative, and when one says that the object of our laughter is the misfortune of someone else, *known by us* to be endurable and slight, it must be understood that this misfortune may be *in itself* very serious as well as undeserved, and in this way laughter is often really cruel.

The coarser men are, the more destitute they are of sympathetic imagination, and the more they laugh at one another with an offensive and brutal laugh. There are those who are not even touched by contact with physical suffering; such ones have the heart to laugh at the shufflings of a bandy-legged man, at the ugliness of a hunchback, or the repulsive hideousness of an idiot. Others there are who are moved by physical suffering but who are not at all affected by moral suffering. These laugh at a self-love touched to the quick, at a wounded pride, at the tortured self-consciousness of one abashed or humiliated. These are, in their eyes, harmless, and slight pricks which they themselves, by a coarseness of nature, or a fine moral health, would endure perhaps with equanimity, which at any rate they do not feel in behalf of others, with whom they do not suffer in sympathy.

Castigat ridendo mores. According to M. A. Michiels, the author of a book upon the *World of Humor and of Laughter*, this maxim must be understood in its broadest sense. "Everything that is contrary to the absolute ideal of human perfection," in whatever order it be, whether physical, intellectual, moral, or social, arouses laughter. The fear of ridicule is the most dominant of our feelings, that which controls us in most things and with the most strength. Because of this fear one does "what one would not do for the sake of justice, scrupulousness, honor, or good will;" one submits to an infinite number of obligations which morality would not dare to prescribe and which are not included in the laws. "Conscience and the written laws," says A. Michiels, "form two lines of ramparts against evil, the ludicrous is the third line of defense, it stops, brands, and condemns the little misdeeds which the guards have allowed to pass."

Laughter is thus the great censor of vices, it spares none, it does not even grant indulgence to the slightest imperfections, of whatever nature they be. This mission, which M. Michiels attributes to laughter, granting that it is fulfilled, instead of taking its place in the natural or providential order of things, does it not answer simply to those demands, whether well founded or not, which society makes upon each of us? M. Bergson admits this, justly enough, it appears, when he defines laughter as a social bromide. But then it is no longer mere imperfection in general, it is not even immorality, properly speaking; it is merely unsociability, well or badly understood, which laughter corrects. More precisely, it is a special unsociability, one which escapes all other penalties, which it is the function of laughter to reach. What can this unsociability be? It is the self-love of each one of us in so far as it has anything disagreeable to others in it, an abstraction of every injurious or hateful element. It is the harmless self-love, slight, powerless, which one does not fear but one scorns, yet for all that does not pardon but on the contrary pitilessly pursues, wounds, and galls. Self-love thus defined is vanity, and what is called the moral correction administered by laughter is the wound to self-love. "The specific remedy for vanity," says M. Bergson, "is laughter, and the essentially ridiculous is vanity."

One sees in what sense laughter is a "correction." Whether one considers the jests uttered, the feelings of the jester, or of him at whom one jests, laughter appears from the point of view of morality as a correction most often undeserved, unjust—or at least disproportionate to the fault—pitiless, and cruel.

In fact, the self-love at which one laughs is, as we have said, harmless. Besides it is often a natural failing, a weakness, not a vice. Even if it were a vice, the jester would not be justified in laughing at it, for it does not appear that he himself is exempt. On the contrary, his vanity is magnified when that of others is upon the rack. Finally the humiliation caused by laughter is not a chastisement which one accepts but a torture to which one submits;

it is a feeling of resentment, of bitterness, not a wholesome sense of shame, nor one from which anyone is likely to profit. Laughter may then have a social use; but it is not an act of justice. It is a quick and summary police measure which will not stand too close a scrutiny but which it would be imprudent either to condemn or to approve without reserve. Society is established and organized according to natural laws which seem to be modeled on those of reason, but self-loves discipline themselves, they enter into conflict and hold each other in check.

C. LANGUAGE AND THE COMMUNICATION OF IDEAS

1. Intercommunication in the Lower Animals[1]

The foundations of intercommunication, like those of imitation, are laid in certain instinctive modes of response, which are stimulated by the acts of other animals of the same social group.

Some account has already been given of the sounds made by young birds, which seem to be instinctive and to afford an index of the emotional state at the time of utterance. That in many cases they serve to evoke a like emotional state and correlated expressive behavior in other birds of the same brood cannot be questioned. The alarm note of a chick will place its companions on the alert; and the harsh "krek" of a young moor-hen, uttered in a peculiar crouching attitude, will often throw others into this attitude, though the maker of the warning sound may be invisible. That the cries of her brood influence the conduct of the hen is a matter of familiar observation; and that her danger signal causes them at once to crouch or run to her for protection is not less familar. No one who has watched a cat with her kittens, or a sheep with her lambs, can doubt that such "dumb animals" are influenced in their behavior by suggestive sounds. The important questions are, how they originate, what is their value, and how far such intercommunication—if such we may call it—extends.

There can be but little question that in all cases of animals under natural conditions such behavior has an instinctive basis. Though the effect may be to establish a means of communication, such is not

[1] Adapted from C. Lloyd Morgan, *Animal Behaviour*, pp. 193–205. (Edward Arnold, 1908.)

their conscious purpose at the outset. They are presumably con-
genital and hereditary modes of emotional expression which serve
to evoke responsive behavior in another animal—the reciprocal
action being generally in its primary origin between mate and mate,
between parent and offspring, or between members of the same
family group. *And it is this reciprocal action which constitutes it
a factor in social evolution.* Its chief interest in connection with the
subject of behavior lies in the fact that it shows the instinctive foundations on which intelligent and eventually rational modes of intercommunication are built up. For instinctive as the sounds are at
the outset, by entering into the conscious situation and taking their
part in the association-complex of experience, they become factors
in the social life as modified and directed by intelligence. To their
original instinctive value as the outcome of stimuli, and as themselves
affording stimuli to responsive behavior, is added a value for consciousness in so far as they enter into those guiding situations by which
intelligent behavior is determined. And if they also serve to evoke,
in the reciprocating members of the social group, similar or allied
emotional states, there is thus added a further social bond, inasmuch
as there are thus laid the foundations of sympathy.

"What makes the old sow grunt and the piggies sing and whine?"
said a little girl to a portly, substantial farmer. "I suppose they
does it for company, my dear," was the simple and cautious reply.
So far as appearances went, that farmer looked as guiltless of theories
as man could be. And yet he gave terse expression to what may
perhaps be regarded as the most satisfactory hypothesis as to the
primary purpose of animal sounds. They are a means by which each
indicates to others the fact of his comforting presence; and they
still, to a large extent, retain their primary function. The chirping
of grasshoppers, the song of the cicada, the piping of frogs in the pool,
the bleating of lambs at the hour of dusk, the lowing of contented
cattle, the call-notes of the migrating host of birds—all these, whatever else they may be, are the reassuring social links of sound, the
grateful signs of kindred presence. Arising thus in close relation to
the primitive feelings of social sympathy, they would naturally be
called into play with special force and suggestiveness at times of strong
emotional excitement, and the earliest differentiations would, we
may well believe, be determined along lines of emotional expression.

Thus would originate mating cries, male and female after their kind; and parental cries more or less differentiated into those of mother and offspring, the deeper note of the ewe differing little save in pitch and timbre from the bleating of her lamb, while the cluck of the hen differs widely from the peeping note of the chick in down. Thus, too, would arise the notes of anger and combat, of fear and distress, of alarm and warning. If we call these the instinctive language of emotional expression, we must remember that such "language" differs markedly from the "language" of which the sentence is the recognized unit.

It is, however, not improbable that, through association in the conscious situation, sounds, having their origin in emotional expression and evoking in others like emotional states, may acquire a new value in suggesting, for example, the presence of particular enemies. An example will best serve to indicate my meaning. The following is from H. B. Medlicott:

> In the early dawn of a grey morning I was geologizing along the base of the Muhair Hills in South Behar, when all of a sudden there was a stampede of many pigs from the fringe of the jungle, with porcine shrieks of *sauve qui peut* significance. After a short run in the open they took to the jungle again, and in a few minutes there was another uproar, but different in sound and in action; there was a rush, presumably of the fighting members, to the spot where the row began, and after some seconds a large leopard sprang from the midst of the scuffle. In a few bounds he was in the open, and stood looking back, licking his chops. The pigs did not break cover, but continued on their way. They were returning to their lair after a night's feeding on the plain, several families having combined for mutual protection; while the beasts of prey were evidently waiting for the occasion. I was alone, and, though armed, I did not care to beat up the ground to see if in either case a kill had been effected. The numerous herd covered a considerable space, and the scrub was thick. The prompt concerted action must in each case have been started by the special cry. I imagine that the first assailant was a tiger, and the case was at once known to be hopeless, the cry prompting instant flight, while in the second case the cry was for defense. It can scarcely be doubted that in the first case each adult pig had a vision of a tiger, and in the second of a leopard or some minor foe.

If we accept Mr. Medlicott's interpretation as in the main correct, we have in this case: (1) common action in social behavior, (2) community of emotional state, and (3) the suggestion of natural enemies not unfamiliar in the experience of the herd. It is a not improbable hypothesis, therefore, that in the course of evolution the initial value of uttered sounds is emotional; but that on this may be grafted in further development the indication of particular enemies. If, for example, the cry which prompts instant flight among the pigs is called forth by a tiger, it is reasonable to suppose that this cry would give rise to a representative generic image of that animal having its influence on the conscious situation. But if the second cry, for defense, was prompted sometimes by a leopard and sometimes by some other minor foe, then this cry would not give rise to a representative image of the same definiteness. Whether animals have the power of intentionally differentiating the sounds they make to indicate different objects is extremely doubtful. Can a dog bark in different tones to indicate "cat" or "rat," as the case may be? Probably not. It may, however, be asked why, if a pig may squeak differently, and thus, perhaps, incidentally indicate on the one hand "tiger" and on the other hand "leopard," should not a dog bark differently and thus indicate appropriately "cat" or "rat"? Because it is assumed that the two different cries in the pig are the instinctive expression of two different emotional states, and Mr. Medlicott could distinguish them; whereas, in the case of the dog, we can distinguish no difference between his barking in the one case and the other, nor do the emotional states appear to be differentiated. Of course there may be differences which we have failed to detect. What may be regarded, however, as improbable is the *intentional* differentiation of sounds by barking in different tones with the *purpose* of indicating "cat" or "rat."

Such powers of intercommunication as animals possess are based on direct association and refer to the here and the now. A dog may be able to suggest to his companion the fact that he has descried a worriable cat; but can a dog tell his neighbor of the delightful worry he enjoyed the day before yesterday in the garden where the man with the biscuit tin lives? Probably not, bark he never so expressively.

From the many anecdotes of dogs calling others to their assistance or bringing others to those who feed them or treat them kindly, we may indeed infer the existence of a social tendency and of the suggestive effects of behavior, but we cannot derive conclusive evidence of anything like descriptive communication.

Such intentional communication as is to be found in animals, if indeed we may properly so call it, seems to arise by an association of the performance of some act in a conscious situation involving further behavior for its complete development. Thus the cat which touches the handle of the door when it wishes to leave the room has had experience in which the performance of this act has coalesced with a specific development of the conscious situation. The case is similar when your dog drops a ball or stick at your feet, wishing you to throw it for him to fetch. Still, it is clear that such an act would be the perceptual precursor of the deliberate conduct of the rational being by whom the sign is definitely realized as a sign, the intentional meaning of which is distinctly present to thought. This involves a judgment concerning the sign as an object of thought; and this is probably beyond the capacity of the dog. For, as Romanes himself says, "It is because the human mind is able, so to speak, to stand outside of itself and thus to constitute its own ideas the subject-matter of its own thought that it is capable of judgment, whether in the act of conception or in that of predication. We have no evidence to show that any animal is capable of objectifying its own ideas; and therefore we have no evidence that any animal is capable of judgment."

2. The Concept as the Medium of Human Communication[1]

There is a petrified philosophy in language, and if we examine the most ancient word for "name," we find it is *nâman* in Sanskrit, *nomen* in Latin, *namô* in Gothic. This *nâman* stands for *gnâman*, and is derived from the root *gnâ*, to know, and meant originally that by which we know a thing.

And how do we know things?

The first step toward the real knowledge, a step which, however small in appearance, separates man forever from all other animals, is *the naming of a thing*, or the making a thing knowable. All naming is classification, bringing the individual under the general; and

[1] Adapted from F. Max Müller, *The Science of Language*, I, 520–27. (Longmans, Green & Co., 1891.)

whatever we know, whether empirically or scientifically, we know it by means of our general ideas.

At the very point where man parts company with the brute world, at the first flash of reason as the manifestation of the light within us, there we see the true genesis of language. Analyze any word you like and you will find that it expresses a general idea peculiar to the individual to whom the name belongs. What is the meaning of moon? The measurer. What is the meaning of sun? The begetter. What is the meaning of earth? The ploughed.

If the serpent is called in Sankrit *sarpa*, it is because it was conceived under the general idea of creeping, an idea expressed by the root *srip*.

An ancient word for man was the Sanskrit *marta*, the Greek *brotos*, the Latin *mortalis*. *Marta* means "he who dies," and it is remarkable that, where everything else was changing, fading, and dying, this should have been chosen as the distinguishing name for man.

There were many more names for man, as there were many names for all things in ancient languages. Any feature that struck the observing mind as peculiarly characteristic could be made to furnish a new name. In common Sanskrit dictionaries we find 5 words for hand, 11 for light, 15 for cloud, 20 for moon, 26 for snake, 33 for slaughter, 35 for fire, 37 for sun. The sun might be called the bright, the warm, the golden, the preserver, the destroyer, the wolf, the lion, the heavenly eye, the father of light and life. Hence that superabundance of synonyms in ancient dialects, and hence that struggle for life carried on among these words, which led to the destruction of the less strong, the less fertile, the less happy words, and ended in the triumph of *one* as the recognized and proper name for every object in every language. On a very small scale this process of natural selection, or, as it would better be called, elimination, may still be watched even in modern languages, that is to say, even in languages so old and stricken in years as English and French. What it was at the first burst of dialects we can only gather from such isolated cases as when von Hammer counts 5,744 words all relating to the camel.

The fact that every word is originally a predicate—that names, though signs of individual conceptions, are all, without exception, derived from general ideas—is one of the most important discoveries in the science of language. It was known before that language is the distinguishing characteristic of man; it was known also that the having of general ideas is that which puts a perfect distinction betwixt man and brutes; but that these two were only different expressions of the same fact was not known till the theory of roots had been established as preferable to the theories both of onomato-poieia and of interjections. But, though our modern philosophy did not know it, the ancient poets and framers of language must have known it. For in Greek, language is *logos*, but *logos* means also reason, and *alogon* was chosen as the name and the most proper name, for brute. No animal, so far as we know, thinks and speaks except man. Language and thought are inseparable. Words without thought are dead sounds; thoughts without words are nothing. To think is to speak low; to speak is to think aloud. The word is the thought incarnate.

What are the two problems left unsettled at the end of the *Science of Language:* "How do mere cries become phonetic types?" and "How can sensations be changed into concepts?" What are these two, if taken together, but the highest problem of all philosophy, viz., "What is the origin of reason?"

3. Writing as a Form of Communication[1]

The earliest stages of writing were those in which pictographic forms were used; that is, a direct picture was drawn upon the writing surface, reproducing as nearly as possible the kind of impression made upon the observer by the object itself. To be sure, the drawing used to represent the object was not an exact reproduction or full copy of the object, but it was a fairly direct image. The visual memory image was thus aroused by a direct perceptual appeal to the eye. Anyone could read a document written in this pictograph form, if he had ever seen the objects to which the pictures referred. There was no special relation between the pictures or visual forms at this stage of development and the sounds used in articulate language. Concrete examples of such writing are seen in early monuments, where the moon is represented by the crescent, a king by the drawing of a man wearing a crown.

[1] Adapted from Charles H. Judd, *Psychology*, pp. 219–24. (Ginn & Co., 1917.)

The next stage of development in writing began when the pictographic forms were reduced in complexity to the simplest possible lines. The reduction of the picture to a few sketchy lines depended upon the growing ability of the reader to contribute the necessary interpretation. All that was needed in the figure was something which would suggest the full picture to the mind. Indeed, it is probably true that the full picture was not needed, even in the reader's consciousness. Memory images are usually much simplified reproductions of the perceptual facts. In writing we have a concrete expression of this tendency of memory to lose its full reproductive. form and to become reduced to the point of the most meager contents for conscious thought. The simplification of the written forms is attained very early, and is seen even in the figures which are used by savage tribes. Thus, to represent the number of an enemy's army, it is not necessary to draw full figures of the forms of the enemy; it is enough if single straight lines are drawn with some brief indication, perhaps at the beginning of the series of lines, to show that these stand each for an individual enemy. This simplification of the drawing leaves the written symbol with very much larger possibilities of entering into new relations in the mind of the reader. Instead, now, of being a specific drawing related to a specific object, it invites by its simple character a number of different interpretations. A straight line, for example, can represent not only the number of an enemy's army but it can represent also the number of sheep in a flock, or the number of tents in a village, or anything else which is capable of enumeration. The use of a straight line for these various purposes stimulates new mental developments. This is shown by the fact that the development of the idea of the number relation, as distinguished from the mass of possible relations in which an object may stand, is greatly facilitated by this general written symbol for numbers. The intimate relation between the development of ideas on the one hand and the development of language on the other is here very strikingly illustrated. The drawing becomes more useful because it is associated with more elaborate ideas, while the ideas develop because they find in the drawing a definite content which helps to mark and give separate character to the idea.

As soon as the drawing began to lose its significance as a direct perceptual reproduction of the object and took on new and broader meanings through the associations which attached to it, the written form became a symbol, rather than a direct appeal to visual memory. As a symbol it stood for something which, in itself, it was not. The way was thus opened for the written symbol to enter into relation with oral speech, which is also a form of symbolism. Articulate sounds are simplified forms of experience capable through association with ideas of expressing meanings not directly related to the sounds themselves. When the written symbol began to be related to the sound symbol, there was at first a loose and irregular relation between them. The Egyptians seem to have established such relations to some extent. They wrote at times with pictures standing for sounds, as we now write in rebus puzzles. In such puzzles the picture of an object is intended to call up in the mind of the reader, not the special group of ideas appropriate to the object represented in the picture, but rather the sound which serves as the name of this object. When the sound is once suggested to the reader, he is supposed to attend to that and to connect with it certain other associations appropriate to the sound. To take a modern illustration, we may, for example, use the picture of the eye to stand for the first personal pronoun. The relationship between the picture and the idea for which it is used is in this case through the sound of the name of the object depicted. That the early alphabets are of this type of rebus pictures appears in their names. The first three letters of the Hebrew alphabet, for example, are named, respectively, *aleph* which means ox, *beth* which means house, and *gimmel* which means camel.

The complete development of a sound alphabet from this type of rebus writing required, doubtless, much experimentation on the part of the nations which succeeded in establishing the association. The Phoenicians have generally been credited with the invention of the forms and relations which we now use. Their contribution to civilization cannot be overestimated. It consisted, not in the presentation of new material or content to conscious experience, but rather in the bringing together by association of groups of contents which, in their new relation, transformed the whole process of thought and expression. They associated visual and auditory content and gave to the visual factors a meaning through association which was of such unique importance as to justify us in describing the association as a new invention.

There are certain systems of writing which indicate that the type of relationship which we use is not the only possible type of relationship. The Chinese, for example, have continued to use simple symbols which are related to complex sounds, not to elementary sounds, as are our own letters. In Chinese writing the various symbols, though much corrupted in form, stand each for an object. It is true that the forms of Chinese writing have long since lost their direct relationship to the pictures in which they originated. The present forms are simplified and symbolical. So free has the symbolism become that the form has been arbitrarily modified to make it possible for the writer to use freely the crude tools with which the Chinaman does his writing. These practical considerations could not have become operative, if the direct pictographic character of the symbols had not long since given place to a symbolical character which renders the figure important, not because of what it shows in itself, but rather because of what it suggests to the mind of the reader. The relation of the symbol to elementary sounds has, however, never been established. This lack of association with elementary sounds keeps the Chinese writing at a level much lower and nearer to primitive pictographic forms than is our writing.

Whether we have a highly elaborated symbolical system, such as that which appears in Chinese writing, or a form of writing which is related to sound, the chief fact regarding writing, as regarding all language, is that it depends for its value very much more upon the ideational relations into which the symbols are brought in the individual's mind than upon the impressions which they arouse.

The ideational associations which appear in developed language could never have reached the elaborate form which they have at present if there had not been social co-operation. The tendency of the individual when left to himself is to drop back into the direct adjustments which are appropriate to his own life. He might possibly develop articulation to a certain extent for his own sake, but the chief impulse to the development of language comes through intercourse with others. As we have seen, the development of the simplest forms of communication, as in animals, is a matter of social imitation. Writing is also an outgrowth of social relations. It is extremely doubtful whether even the child of civilized parents would ever have any sufficient motive for the development of writing, if it were not for the social encouragement he receives.

4. The Extension of Communication by Human Invention[1]

No one who is asked to name the agencies that weave the great web of intellectual and material influences and counter-influences by which modern humanity is combined into the unity of society will need much reflection to give first rank to the newspaper, along with the post, railroad, and telegraph.

In fact, the newspaper forms a link in the chain of modern commercial machinery; it is one of those contrivances by which in society the exchange of intellectual and material goods is facilitated. Yet it is not an instrument of commercial intercourse in the sense of the post or the railway, both of which have to do with the transport of persons, goods, and news, but rather in the sense of the letter and circular. These make the news capable of transport only because they are enabled by the help of writing and printing to cut it adrift, as it were, from its originator and give it corporeal independence.

However great the difference between letter, circular, and news-paper may appear today, a little reflection shows that all three are essentially similar products, originating in the necessity of communicating news and in the employment of writing in its satisfaction. The sole difference consists in the letter being addressed to individuals, the circular to several specified persons, the newspaper to many unspecified persons. Or, in other words, while letter and circular are instruments for the private communication of news, the news-paper is an instrument for its publication.

Today we are, of course, accustomed to the regular printing of the newspaper and its periodical appearance at brief intervals. But neither of these is an essential characteristic of the newspaper as a means of news publication. On the contrary, it will become apparent directly that the primitive paper from which this mighty instrument of commercial intercourse is sprung appeared neither in printed form nor periodically, but that it closely resembled the letter from which, indeed, it can scarcely be distinguished. To be sure, repeated appearance at brief intervals is involved in the very nature of news publication. For news has value only so long as it is fresh; and to preserve for it the charm of novelty its publication must follow in the footsteps of the events. We shall, however, soon see that the

[1] Adapted from Carl Bücher, *Industrial Evolution*. Translated by S. Morley Wickett, pp. 216–43. (Henry Holt & Co., 1907.)

periodicity of these intervals, as far as it can be noticed in the infancy of journalism, depended upon the regular recurrence of opportunities to transport the news, and was in no way connected with the essential nature of the newspaper.

The regular collection and despatch of news presupposes a widespread interest in public affairs, or an extensive area of trade exhibiting numerous commercial connections and combinations of interest, or both at once. Such interest is not realized until people are united by some more or less extensive political organization into a certain community of life-interest. The city republics of ancient times required no newspaper; all their needs of publication could be met by the herald and by inscriptions, as occasion demanded. Only when Roman supremacy had embraced or subjected to its influence all the countries of the Mediterranean was there need of some means by which those members of the ruling class who had gone to the provinces as officials, tax-farmers, and in other occupations, might receive the current news of the capital. It is significant that Caesar, the creator of the military monarchy and of the administrative centralization of Rome, is regarded as the founder of the first contrivance resembling a newspaper.

Indeed, long before Caesar's consulate it had become customary for Romans in the provinces to keep one or more correspondents at the capital to send them written reports on the course of political movement and on other events of the day. Such a correspondent was generally an intelligent slave or freedman intimately acquainted with affairs at the capital, who, moreover, often made a business of reporting for several. He was thus a species of primitive reporter, differing from those of today only in writing, not for a newspaper, but directly for readers. On recommendation of their employers, these reporters enjoyed at times admission even to the senate discussions. Antony kept such a man, whose duty it was to report to him not merely on the senate's resolutions but also on the speeches and votes of the senators. Cicero, when proconsul, received through his friend, M. Caelius, the reports of a certain Chrestus, but seems not to have been particularly well satisfied with the latter's accounts of gladiatorial sports, law-court proceedings, and the various pieces of city gossip. As in this case, such correspondence never extended beyond a rude relation of facts that required supplementing through letters from party friends of the absent person. These friends, as we know from Cicero, supplied the real report on political feeling.

The innovation made by Caesar consisted in instituting the publication of a brief record of the transactions and resolutions of the senate, and in his causing to be published the transactions of the assemblies of the plebs, as well as other important matters of public concern.

The Germanic peoples who, after the Romans, assumed the lead in the history of Europe were neither in civilization nor in political organization fitted to maintain a similar constitution of the news service; nor did they require it. All through the Middle Ages the political and social life of men was bounded by a narrow horizon; culture retired to the cloisters and for centuries affected only the people of prominence. There were no trade interests beyond the narrow walls of their own town or manor to draw men together. It is only in the later centuries of the Middle Ages that extensive social combinations once more appear. It is first the church, embracing with her hierarchy all the countries of Germanic and Latin civilization, next the burgher class with its city confederacies and common trade interests, and, finally, as a counter-influence to these, the secular territorial powers, who succeed in gradually realizing some form of union. In the twelfth and thirteenth centuries we notice the first traces of an organized service for transmission of news and letters in the messengers of monasteries, the universities, and the various spiritual dignitaries; in the fourteenth and fifteenth centuries we have advanced to a comprehensive, almost postlike, organization of local messenger bureaus for the epistolary intercourse of traders and of municipal authorities. And now, for the first time, we meet with the word *Zeitung*, or newspaper. The word meant originally that which was happening at the time (*Zeit*="time"), a present occurrence; then information on such an event, a message, a report, news.

Venice was long regarded as the birthplace of the newspaper in the modern acceptation of the word. As the channel of trade between the East and the West, as the seat of a government that first organized the political news service and the consular system in the modern sense, the old city of lagoons formed a natural collecting center for important news items from all lands of the known world. Even early in the fifteenth century, as has been shown by the investigations of Valentinelli, the librarian of St. Mark's Library, collections of news had been made at the instance of the council of Venice regarding events that had either occurred within the republic or been reported by ambassadors, consuls, and officials, by ships' captains, merchants, and the like. These were sent as circular despatches to the Venetian representatives abroad to keep them posted on international affairs. Such collections of news were called *fogli d'avvisi.*

The further development of news publication in the field that it has occupied since the more general adoption of the printing-press has been peculiar. At the outset the publisher of a periodical printed newspaper differed in no wise from the publisher of any other printed work—for instance, of a pamphlet or a book. He was but the multiplier and seller of a literary product, over whose content he had no control. The newspaper publisher marketed the regular post-news in its printed form just as another publisher offered the public a herbal or an edition of an old writer.

But this soon changed. It was readily perceived that the contents of a newspaper number did not form an entity in the same sense as the contents of a book or pamphlet. The news items there brought together, taken from different sources, were of varying reliability. They needed to be used judicially and critically: in this a political or religious bias could find ready expression. In a still higher degree was this the case when men began to discuss contemporary political questions in the newspapers and to employ them as a medium for disseminating party opinions.

This took place first in England during the Long Parliament and the Revolution of 1640. The Netherlands and a part of the imperial free towns of Germany followed later. In France the change was not consummated before the era of the great Revolution: in most other countries it occurred in the nineteenth century. The newspaper, from being a mere vehicle for the publication of news, became an instrument for supporting and shaping public opinion and a weapon of party politics.

The effect of this upon the internal organization of the newspaper undertaking was to introduce a third department, the *editorship*, between news collecting and news publication. For the newspaper publisher, however, it signified that from a mere seller of news he had become a dealer in public opinion as well.

At first this meant nothing more than that the publisher was placed in a position to shift a portion of the risk of his undertaking upon a party organization, a circle of interested persons, or a government. If the leanings of the paper were distasteful to the readers, they ceased to buy the paper. Their wishes thus remained, in the final analysis, the determining factor for the contents of the newspapers.

The gradually expanding circulation of the printed newspapers nevertheless soon led to their employment by the authorities for making public announcements. With this came, in the first quarter of the last century, the extension of private announcements, which have now attained, through the so-called advertising bureaus, some such organization as political news-collecting possesses in the correspondence bureaus.

The modern newspaper is a capitalistic enterprise, a sort of news-factory in which a great number of people (correspondents, editors, typesetters, correctors, machine-tenders, collectors of advertisements, office clerks, messengers, etc.) are employed on wage, under a single administration, at very specialized work. This paper produces wares for an unknown circle of readers, from whom it is, furthermore, frequently separated by intermediaries, such as delivery agencies and postal institutions. The simple needs of the reader or of the circle of patrons no longer determine the quality of these wares; it is now the very complicated conditions of competition in the publication market. In this market, however, as generally in wholesale markets, the consumers of the goods, the newspaper readers, take no direct part; the determining factors are the wholesale dealers and the speculators in news: the governments, the telegraph bureaus dependent upon their special correspondents, the political parties, artistic and scientific cliques, men on 'change, and, last but not least, the advertising agencies and large individual advertisers.

Each number of a great journal which appears today is a marvel of economic division of labor, capitalistic organization, and mechanical technique; it is an instrument of intellectual and economic intercourse, in which the potencies of all other instruments of commerce—the railway, the post, the telegraph, and the telephone—are united as in a focus.

D. IMITATION

1. Definition of Imitation[1]

The term "imitation" is used in ordinary language to designate any repetition of any act or thought which has been noted by an observer. Thus one imitates the facial expression of another, or his mode of speech. The term has been brought into prominence in scientific discussions through the work of Gabriel Tarde, who in his *Les lois de l'imitation* points out that imitation is a fundamental fact underlying all social development. The customs of society are imitated from generation to generation. The fashions of the day are imitated by large groups of people without any consciousness of the social solidarity which is derived from this common mode of behavior. There is developed through these various forms of imitation a body of experiences which is common to all of the members of a given social group. In complex society the various imitations which tend to set themselves up are frequently found to be in conflict; thus the tendency toward elaborate fashions in dress is constantly limited by the counter-tendency toward simpler fashions. The conflict of tendencies leads to individual variations from the example offered at any given time, and, as a result, there are new examples to be followed. Complex social examples are thus products of conflict.

This general doctrine of Tarde has been elaborated by a number of recent writers. Royce calls attention to the fundamental importance of imitation as a means of social inheritance. The same doctrine is taken up by Baldwin in his *Mental Development in the Child and Race*, and in *Social and Ethical Interpretations*. With these later writers, imitation takes on a significance which is somewhat technical and broader than the significance which it has either with Tarde or in the ordinary use of the term. Baldwin uses the term to cover that case in which an individual repeats an act because he has himself gone through the act. In such a case one imitates himself and sets up what Baldwin terms a circular reaction. The principle of imitation is thus introduced into individual psychology as well as into general social psychology, and the relation between the individual's

[1] From Charles H. Judd, "Imitation," in *Monroe's Cyclopedia of Education*, III, 388–89. (Published by The Macmillan Co., 1912. Reprinted by permission.)

acts and his own imagery is brought under the same general principle as the individual's responses to his social environment. The term "imitation" in this broader sense is closely related to the processes of sympathy.

The term "social heredity" has very frequently been used in connection with all of the processes here under discussion. Society tends to perpetuate itself in the new individual in a fashion analogous to that in which the physical characteristics of the earlier generation tend to perpetuate themselves in the physical characteristics of the new generation. Since modes of behavior, such as acts of courtesy, cannot be transmitted through physical structure, they would tend to lapse if they were not maintained through imitation from generation to generation. Thus imitation gives uniformity to social practices and consequently is to be treated as a form of supplementary inheritance extending beyond physical inheritance and making effective the established forms of social practice.

2. Attention, Interest, and Imitation[1]

Imitation is a process of very great importance for the development of mental life in both men and animals. In its more complex forms it presupposes trains of ideas; but in its essential features it is present and operative at the perceptual level. It is largely through imitation that the results of the experience of one generation are transmitted to the next, so as to form the basis for further development. Where trains of ideas play a relatively unimportant part, as in the case of animals, imitation may be said to be the sole form of social tradition. In the case of human beings, the thought of past generations is embodied in language, institutions, machinery, and the like. This distinctively human tradition presupposes trains of ideas in past generations, which so mold the environment of a new generation that in apprehending and adapting itself to this environment it must re-think the old trains of thought. Tradition of this kind is not found in animal life, because the animal mind does not proceed by way of trains of ideas. None the less, the more intelligent animals depend largely on tradition. This tradition consists essentially in imitation by the young of the actions of their parents, or

[1] Adapted from G. F. Stout, *A Manual of Psychology*, pp. 390–91. (The University Tutorial Press, 1913.)

of other members of the community in which they are born.   The same directly imitative process, though it is very far from forming the whole of social tradition in human beings, forms a very important part of it.

a) The imitative impulse.—We must distinguish between ability to imitate and impulse to imitate.   We may be already fully able to perform an action, and the sight of it as performed by another may merely prompt us to reproduce it.   But the sight of an act performed by another may also have an educational influence; it may not only stimulate us to do what we are already able to do without its aid; it may also enable us to do what we could not do without having an example to follow.   When the cough of one man sets another coughing, it is evident that imitation here consists only in the impulse to follow suit.   The second man does not learn how to cough from the example of the first.   He is simply prompted to do on this particular occasion what he is otherwise quite capable of doing.   But if I am learning billiards and someone shows me by his own example how to make a particular stroke, the case is different.   It is not his example which in the first instance prompts me to the action.   He merely shows the way to do what I already desire to do.

We have then first to discuss the nature of the imitative impulse— the impulse to perform an action which arises from the perception of it as performed by another.

This impulse is an affair of attentive consciousness.   The perception of an action prompts us to reproduce it when and so far as it excites interest or is at least intimately connected with what does excite interest.   Further, the interest must be of such a nature that it is more fully gratified by partially or wholly repeating the interesting action.   Thus imitation is a special development of attention. Attention is always striving after a more vivid, more definite, and more complete apprehension of its object.   Imitation is a way in which this endeavor may gratify itself when the interest in the object is of a certain kind.   It is obvious that we do not try to imitate all manner of actions, without distinction, merely because they take place under our eyes.   What is familiar and commonplace or what for any other reason is unexciting or insipid fails to stir us to re-enact it.   It is otherwise with what is strikingly novel or in any way impressive, so that our attention dwells on it with relish or fascination. It is, of course, not true that whatever act fixes attention prompts to imitation. This is only the case where imitation helps attention, where it is, in fact, a special development of attention. This is so when interest is directly concentrated on the activity itself for its own sake rather than for the sake of its possible consequences and the like ulterior motives. But it is not necessary that the act in itself should be interesting; in a most important class of cases the interest centers, not directly in the external act imitated, but in something else with which this act is so intimately connected as virtually to form a part of it. Thus there is a tendency to imitate not only interesting acts but also the acts of interesting persons. Men are apt to imitate the gestures and modes of speech of those who excite their admiration or affection or some other personal interest. Children imitate their parents or their leaders in the playground. Even the mannerisms and tricks of a great man are often unconsciously copied by those who regard him as a hero. In such instances the primary interest is in the whole personality of the model; but this is more vividly and distinctly brought before consciousness by reproducing his external peculiarities. Our result, then, is that interest in an action prompts to imitation in proportion to its intensity, provided the interest is of a kind which will be gratified or sustained by imitative activity.

b) Learning by imitation.—Let us now turn to the other side of the question. Let us consider the case in which the power of performing an action is acquired in and by the process of imitation itself. Here there is a general rule which is obvious when once it is pointed out. It is part of the still more general rule that "to him that hath shall be given." Our power of imitating the activity of another is strictly proportioned to our pre-existing power of performing the same general kind of action independently. For instance, one devoid of musical faculty has practically no power of imitating the violin playing of Joachim. Imitation may develop and improve a power which already exists, but it cannot create it. Consider the child beginning for the first time to write in a copybook. He learns by imitation; but it is only because he has already some rudimentary ability to make such simple figures as pothooks that the imitative process can get a start. At the outset, his pothooks are very unlike the model set before him. Gradually he improves; increased power of independent production gives step by step increased power of imitation, until he approaches too closely the limits of his capacity in this direction to make any further progress of an appreciable kind.

But this is an incomplete account of the matter. The power of learning by imitation is part of the general power of learning by experience; it involves mental plasticity. An animal which starts life with congenital tendencies and aptitudes of a fixed and stereo- typed kind, so that they admit of but little modification in the course of individual development, has correspondingly little power of learning by imitation.

At higher levels of mental development the imitative impulse is far less conspicuous because impulsive activity in general is checked and overruled by activity organized in a unified system. Civilized men imitate not so much because of immediate interest in the action imitated as with a view to the attainment of desirable results.

CHAPTER VI

COMPETITION

I. INTRODUCTION

1. Popular Conception of Competition

Competition, as a universal phenomenon, was first clearly conceived and adequately described by the biologists. As defined in the evolutionary formula "the struggle for existence" the notion captured the popular imagination and became a commonplace of familiar discourse. Prior to that time competition had been regarded as an economic rather than a biological phenomenon.

It was in the eighteenth century and in England that we first find any general recognition of the new rôle that commerce and the middleman were to play in the modern world. "Competition is the life of trade" is a trader's maxim, and the sort of qualified approval that it gives to the conception of competition contains the germ of the whole philosophy of modern industrial society as that doctrine was formulated by Adam Smith and the physiocrats.

The economists of the eighteenth century were the first to attempt to rationalize and justify the social order that is based on competition and individual freedom. They taught that there was a natural harmony in the interests of men, which once liberated would inevitably bring about, in the best of all possible worlds, the greatest good to the greatest number.

The individual man, in seeking his own profit, will necessarily seek to produce and sell that which has most value for the community, and so "he is in this, as in many other cases," as Adam Smith puts it, "led by an invisible hand to promote an end which was no part of his intention."

The conception has been stated with even greater unction by the French writer, Frédéric Bastiat.

Since goods which seem at first to be the exclusive property of individuals become by the estimable decrees of a wise providence [competition] the common possession of all; since the natural advantages of situation, the fertility, temperature, mineral richness of the soil and even industrial skill do not accrue to the producers, because of competition among themselves, but contribute so much the more to the profit of the consumer; it follows that there is no country that is not interested in the advancement of all the others.[1]

The freedom which commerce sought and gained upon the principle of laissez faire has enormously extended the area of competition and in doing so has created a world-economy where previously there were only local markets. It has created at the same time a division of labor that includes all the nations and races of men and incidentally has raised the despised middleman to a position of affluence and power undreamed of by superior classes of any earlier age. And now there is a new demand for the control of competition in the interest, not merely of those who have not shared in the general prosperity, but in the interest of competition itself.

"Unfair competition" is an expression that is heard at the present time with increasing frequency. This suggests that there are rules governing competition by which, in its own interest, it can and should be controlled. The same notion has found expression in the demand for "freedom of competition" from those who would safeguard competition by controlling it. Other voices have been raised in denunciation of competition because "competition creates monopoly." In other words, competition, if carried to its logical conclusion, ends in the annihilation of competition. In this destruction of competition by competition we seem to have a loss of freedom by freedom, or, to state it in more general terms, unlimited liberty, without social control, ends in the negation of freedom and the slavery of the individual. But the limitation of competition by competition, it needs to be said, means simply that the process of competition tends invariably to establish an equilibrium.

The more fundamental objection is that in giving freedom to economic competition society has sacrificed other fundamental interests that are not directly involved in the economic process. In any case economic freedom exists in an order that has been created and maintained by society. Economic competition, as we know it, pre-

[1] Bastiat, Frédéric, Œuvres complètes, tome VI, "Harmonies économiques," 9ᵉ édition, p. 381. (Paris, 1884.)

supposes the existence of the right of private property, which is a creation of the state. It is upon this premise that the more radical social doctrines, communism and socialism, seek to abolish competition altogether.

2. Competition a Process of Interaction

Of the four great types of interaction—competition, conflict, accommodation, and assimilation—competition is the elementary, universal and fundamental form. Social contact, as we have seen, initiates interaction. But competition, strictly speaking, is *interaction without social contact*. If this seems, in view of what has already been said, something of a paradox, it is because in human society competition is always complicated with other processes, that is to say, with conflict, assimilation, and accommodation.

It is only in the plant community that we can observe the process of competition in isolation, uncomplicated with other social processes. The members of a plant community live together in a relation of mutual interdependence which we call social probably because, while it is close and vital, it is not biological. It is not biological because the relation is a merely external one and the plants that compose it are not even of the same species. They do not interbreed. The members of a plant community adapt themselves to one another as all living things adapt themselves to their environment, but there is no conflict between them because they are not conscious. Competition takes the form of conflict or rivalry only when it becomes conscious, when competitors identify one another as rivals or as enemies.

This suggests what is meant by the statement that competition is interaction *without social contact*. It is only when minds meet, only when the meaning that is in one mind is communicated to another mind so that these minds mutually influence one another, that social contact, properly speaking, may be said to exist.

On the other hand, social contacts are not limited to contacts of touch or sense or speech, and they are likely to be more intimate and more pervasive than we imagine. Some years ago the Japanese, who are brown, defeated the Russians, who are white. In the course of the next few months the news of this remarkable event penetrated, as we afterward learned, uttermost ends of the earth. It sent a thrill through all Asia and it was known in the darkest corners of Central Africa. Everywhere it awakened strange and fantastic dreams. This is what is meant by social contact.

a) *Competition and competitive co-operation.*—Social contact, which inevitably initiates conflict, accommodation, or assimilation, invariably creates also sympathies, prejudices, personal and moral relations which modify, complicate, and control competition. On the other hand, within the limits which the cultural process creates, and custom, law, and tradition impose, competition invariably tends to create an impersonal social order in which each individual, being free to pursue his own profit, and, in a sense, compelled to do so, makes every other individual a means to that end. In doing so, however, he inevitably contributes through the mutual exchange of services so established to the common welfare. It is just the nature of the trading transaction to isolate the motive of profit and make it the basis of business organization, and so far as this motive becomes dominant and exclusive, business relations inevitably assume the impersonal character so generally ascribed to them.

"Competition," says Walker, "is opposed to sentiment. Whenever any economic agent does or forbears anything under the influence of any sentiment other than the desire of giving the least and gaining the most he can in exchange, be that sentiment patriotism, or gratitude, or charity, or vanity, leading him to do otherwise than as self interest would prompt, in that case also, the rule of competition is departed from. Another rule is for the time substituted."[1]

This is the significance of the familiar sayings to the effect that one "must not mix business with sentiment," that "business is business," "corporations are heartless," etc. It is just because corporations are "heartless," that is to say impersonal, that they represent the most advanced, efficient, and responsible form of business organization. But it is for this same reason that they can and need to be regulated in behalf of those interests of the community that cannot be translated immediately into terms of profit and loss to the individual.

The plant community is the best illustration of the type of social organization that is created by competitive co-operation because in the plant community competition is unrestricted.

[1] Walker, Francis A., *Political Economy*, p. 92. (New York, 1887.)

b) Competition and freedom.—The economic organization of society, so far as it is an effect of free competition, is an ecological organization. There is a human as well as a plant and an animal ecology.

If we are to assume that the economic order is fundamentally ecological, that is, created by the struggle for existence, an organization like that of the plant community in which the relations between individuals are conceivably at least wholly external, the question may be very properly raised why the competition and the organization it has created should be regarded as social at all. As a matter of fact sociologists have generally identified the social with the moral order, and Dewey, in his *Democracy and Education,* makes statements which suggest that the purely economic order, in which man becomes a means rather than an end to other men, is unsocial, if not antisocial.

The fact is, however, that this character of *externality* in human relations is a fundamental aspect of society and social life. It is merely another manifestation of what has been referred to as the distributive aspect of society. Society is made up of individuals spatially separated, territorially distributed, and capable of independent locomotion. This capacity of independent locomotion is the basis and the symbol of every other form of independence. Freedom is fundamentally freedom to move and individuality is inconceivable without the capacity and the opportunity to gain an individual experience as a result of independent action.

On the other hand, it is quite as true that society may be said to exist only so far as this independent activity of the individual is *controlled* in the interest of the group as a whole. That is the reason why the problem of control, using that term in its evident significance, inevitably becomes the central problem of sociology.

c) Competition and control.—Conflict, assimilation and accommodation as distinguished from competition are all intimately related to control. Competition is the process through which the distributive and ecological organization of society is created. Competition determines the distribution of population territorially and vocationally. The division of labor and all the vast organized economic interdependence of individuals and groups of individuals characteristic of modern life are a product of competition. On the other hand, the moral and political order, which imposes itself upon this competitive organization, is a product of conflict, accommodation and assimilation.

Competition is universal in the world of living things. Under ordinary circumstances it goes on unobserved even by the individuals who are most concerned. It is only in periods of crisis, when men are making new and conscious efforts to control the conditions of their common life, that the forces with which they are competing get identified with persons, and competition is converted into conflict. It is in what has been described as the *political process* that society consciously deals with its crises.[1] War is the political process par excellence. It is in war that the great decisions are made. Political organizations exist for the purpose of dealing with conflict situations. Parties, parliaments and courts, public discussion and voting are to be considered simply as substitutes for war.

d) Accommodation, assimilation, and competition.—Accommodation, on the other hand, is the process by which the individuals and groups make the necessary internal adjustments to social situations which have been created by competition and conflict. War and elections change situations. When changes thus effected are decisive and are accepted, conflict subsides and the tensions it created are resolved in the process of accommodation into profound modifications of the competing units, i.e., individuals and groups. A man once thoroughly defeated is, as has often been noted, "never the same again." Conquest, subjugation, and defeat are psychological as well as social processes. They establish a new order by changing, not merely the status, but the attitudes of the parties involved. Eventually the new order gets itself fixed in habit and custom and is then transmitted as part of the established social order to succeeding generations. Neither the physical nor the social world is made to satisfy at once all the wishes of the natural man. The rights of property, vested interests of every sort, the family organization, slavery, caste and class, the whole social organization, in fact, represent accommodations, that is to say, limitations of the natural wishes of the individual. These socially inherited accommodations have presumably grown up in the pains and struggles of previous generations, but they have been transmitted to and accepted by succeeding generations as part of the natural, inevitable social order. All of these are forms of control in which competition is limited by status.

[1] See chap. i, pp. 51–54.

Conflict is then to be identified with the political order and with conscious control. Accommodation, on the other hand, is associated with the social order that is fixed and established in custom and the mores.

Assimilation, as distinguished from accommodation, implies a more thoroughgoing transformation of the personality—a transformation which takes place gradually under the influence of social. contacts of the most concrete and intimate sort.

Accommodation may be regarded, like religious conversion, as a kind of mutation. The wishes are the same but their organization is different. Assimilation takes place not so much as a result of changes in the organization as in the content, i.e., the memories, of the personality. The individual units, as a result of intimate association, interpenetrate, so to speak, and come in this way into possession of a common experience and a common tradition. The permanence and solidarity of the group rest finally upon this body of common experience and tradition. It is the rôle of history to preserve this body of common experience and tradition, to criticise and reinterpret it in the light of new experience and changing conditions, and in this way to preserve the continuity of the social and political life.

The relation of social structures to the processes of competition, conflict, accommodation, and assimilation may be represented schematically as follows:

SOCIAL PROCESS	SOCIAL ORDER
Competition	The economic equilibrium
Conflict	The political order
Accommodation	Social organization
Assimilation	Personality and the cultural heritage

3. Classification of the Materials

The materials in this chapter have been selected to exhibit (1) the rôle which competition plays in social life and all life, and (2) the types of organization that competition has everywhere created as a result of the division of labor it has everywhere enforced. These materials fall naturally under the following heads: (a) the struggle for existence; (b) competition and segregation; and (c) economic competition.

This order of the materials serves the purpose of indicating the stages in the growth and extension of man's control over nature and over man himself. The evolution of society has been the progressive extension of control over nature and the substitution of a moral for the natural order.

Competition has its setting in the struggle for existence. This struggle is ordinarily represented as a chaos of contending individuals in which the unfit perish in order that the fit may survive. This conception of the natural order as one of anarchy, "the war of each against all," familiar since Hobbes to the students of society, is recent in biology. Before Darwin, students of plant and animal life saw in nature, not disorder, but order; not selection, but design. The difference between the older and the newer interpretation is not so much a difference of fact as of point of view. Looking at the plant and animal species with reference to their classification they present a series of relatively fixed and stable types. The same thing may be said of the plant and animal communities. Under ordinary circumstances the adjustment between the members of the plant and animal communities and the environment is so complete that the observer interprets it as an order of co-operation rather than a condition of competitive anarchy.

Upon investigation it turns out, however, that the plant and animal communities are in a state of unstable equilibrium, such that any change in the environment may destroy them. Communities of this type are not organized to resist or adapt themselves as communities to changes in the environment. The plant community, for example, is a mere product of segregation, an aggregate without nerves or means of communication that would permit the individuals to be controlled in the interest of the community as a whole.[1]

The situation is different in the so-called animal societies. Animals are adapted in part to the situation of competition, but in part also to the situation of co-operation. With the animal, maternal instinct, gregariousness, sex attraction restrict competition to a greater or less extent among individuals of the same family, herd, or

[1] The introduction of the rabbit into Australia, where predatory competitors are absent, has resulted in so great a multiplication of the members of this species that their numbers have become an economic menace. The appearance of the boll weevil, an insect which attacks the cotton boll, has materially changed the character of agriculture in areas of cotton culture in the South. Scientists are now looking for some insect enemy of the boll weevil that will restore the equilibrium.

species. In the case of the ant community competition is at a minimum and co-operation at a maximum.

With man the free play of competition is restrained by sentiment, custom, and moral standards, not to speak of the more conscious control through law.

It is a characteristic of competition, when unrestricted, that it is invariably more severe among organisms of the same than of different species. Man's greatest competitor is man. On the other hand, man's control over the plant and animal world is now well-nigh complete, so that, generally speaking, only such plants and animals are permitted to exist as serve man's purpose.

Competition among men, on the other hand, has been very largely converted into rivalry and conflict. The effect of conflict has been to extend progressively the area of control and to modify and limit the struggle for existence within these areas. The effect of war has been, on the whole, to extend the area over which there is peace. Competition has been restricted by custom, tradition, and law, and the struggle for existence has assumed the form of struggle for a livelihood and for status.

Absolute free play of competition is neither desirable nor even possible. On the other hand, from the standpoint of the individual, competition means mobility, freedom, and, from the point of view of society, pragmatic or experimental change. Restriction of competition is synonymous with limitation of movement, aquiescence in control, and telesis, Ward's term for changes ordained by society in distinction from the natural process of change.

The political problem of every society is the practical one: how to secure the maximum values of competition, that is, personal freedom, initiative, and originality, and at the same time to control the energies which competition has released in the interest of the community.

II. MATERIALS

A. THE STRUGGLE FOR EXISTENCE

1. Different Forms of the Struggle for Existence[1]

The formula "struggle for existence," familiar in human affairs, was used by Darwin in his interpretation of organic life, and he

[1] Adapted from J. Arthur Thomson, *Darwinism and Human Life*, pp. 72-75. (Henry Holt & Co., 1910.)

showed that we gain clearness in our outlook on animate nature if we recognize there, in continual process, a struggle for existence not merely analogous to, but fundamantally the same as, that which goes on in human life. He projected on organic life a sociological idea, and showed that it fitted. But while he thus vindicated the relevancy and utility of the sociological idea within the biological realm, he declared explicitly that the phrase "struggle for existence" was meant to be a shorthand formula, summing up a vast variety of strife and endeavor, of thrust and parry, of action and reaction.

Some of Darwin's successors have taken pains to distinguish a great many different forms of the struggle for existence, and this kind of analysis is useful in keeping us aware of the complexities of the process. Darwin himself does not seem to have cared much for this logical mapping out and defining; it was enough for him to insist that the phrase was used "in a large and metaphorical sense," and to give full illustrations of its various modes. For our present purpose it is enough for us to follow his example.

a) *Struggle between fellows.*—When the locusts of a huge swarm have eaten up every green thing, they sometimes turn on one another. This cannibalism among fellows of the same species—illustrated, for instance, among many fishes—is the most intense form of the struggle for existence. The struggle does not need to be direct to be real; the essential point is that the competitors seek after the same desiderata, of which there is a limited supply.

As an instance of keen struggle between nearly related species, Darwin referred to the combats of rats. The black rat was in possession of many European towns before the brown rat crossed the Volga in 1727; whenever the brown rat arrived, the black rat had to go to the wall. Thus at the present day there are practically no black rats in Great Britain. Here the struggle for existence is again directly competitive. It is difficult to separate the struggle for food and foothold from the struggle for mates, and it seems clearest to include here the battles of the stags and the capercailzies, or the extraordinary lek of the blackcock, showing off their beauty at sunrise on the hills.

b) *Struggle between foes.*—In the locust swarm and in the rats' combats there is competition between fellows of the same or nearly

related species, but the struggle for existence includes much wider
antipathies. We see it between foes of entirely different nature,
between carnivores and herbivores, between birds of prey and small
mammals. In both these cases there may be a stand-up fight, for
instance between wolf and stag, or between hawk and ermine; but
neither the logic nor the biology of the process is different when all
the fight is on one side. As the lemmings, which have overpopulated
the Scandinavian valleys, go on the march they are followed by
birds and beasts of prey, which thin their ranks. Moreover, the
competition between species need not be direct; it will come to the
same result if both types seek after the same things. The victory
will be with the more effective and the more prolific.

   c) *Struggle with fate.*—Our sweep widens still further, and we
pass beyond the idea of competition altogether to cases where the
struggle for existence is between the living organism and the inanimate conditions of its life—for instance, between birds and the
winter's cold, between aquatic animals and changes in the water,
between plants and drought, between plants and frost—in a wide
sense, between Life and Fate.

   We cannot here pursue the suggestive idea that, besides struggle
between individuals, there is struggle between groups of individuals—the latter most noticeably developed in mankind. Similarly,
working in the other direction, there is struggle between parts or
tissues in the body, between cells in the body, between equivalent
germ-cells, and, perhaps, as Weismann pictures, between the various
multiplicate items that make up our inheritance.

2.   Competition and Natural Selection[1]

   The term "struggle for existence" is used in a large and metaphorical sense, including dependence of one being on another, and
including (which is more important) not only the life of the individual
but success in leaving progeny. Two canine animals in a time of
dearth may be truly said to struggle with each other which shall get
food and live. But a plant on the edge of a desert is said to struggle
for life against the drought, though more properly it should be said

   [1] Adapted from Charles Darwin, *The Origin of Species*, pp. 50-61.   (D. Appleton & Co., 1878.)

to be dependent on the moisture. A plant which annually produces a thousand seeds, of which only one of an average comes to maturity, may be more truly said to struggle with the plants of the same and other kinds which already clothe the ground. The mistletoe is dependent on the apple and a few other trees, but can only in a far-fetched sense be said to struggle with these trees, for, if too many of these parasites grow on the same tree, it languishes and dies. But several seedling mistletoes growing close together on the same branch may more truly be said to struggle with each other. As the mistletoe is disseminated by birds, its existence depends on them; and it may metaphorically be said to struggle with other fruit-bearing plants in tempting the birds to devour and thus disseminate its seeds. In these several senses which pass into each other, I use for convenience' sake the general term of "struggle for existence."

A struggle for existence inevitably follows from the high rate at which all organic beings tend to increase. Every being which during its natural lifetime produces several eggs or seeds must suffer destruction during some period of its life, and during some season or occasional year, otherwise, on the principle of geometrical increase, its numbers would quickly become so inordinately great that no country could support the product. Hence, as more individuals are produced than can possibly survive, there must in every case be a struggle for existence, either one individual with another of the same species, or with the individuals of distinct species, or with the physical conditions of life. It is the doctrine of Malthus applied with manifold force to the whole animal and vegetable kingdoms; for in this case there can be no artificial increase of food, and no prudential restraint from marriage. Although some species may be now increasing more or less rapidly in numbers, all cannot do so, for the world would not hold them.

There is no exception to the rule that every organic being naturally increases at so high a rate that, if not destroyed, the earth would soon be covered by the progeny of a single pair. Even slow-breeding man has doubled in twenty-five years, and at this rate in less than a thousand years there would literally not be standing-room for his progeny. Linnaeus has calculated that if an annual plant produced only two seeds—and there is no plant so unproductive as this—and their seedlings next year produced two, and so on, then in twenty years there would be a million plants. The elephant is reckoned the slowest breeder of all known animals, and I have taken some pains to estimate its probable minimum rate of natural increase; it will be safest to assume that it begins breeding when thirty years old and goes on breeding till ninety years old, bringing forth six young in the interval and surviving till one hundred years old; if this be so, after a period of from 740 to 750 years there would be nearly nineteen million elephants alive, descended from the first pair.

The struggle for life is most severe between individuals and varieties of the same species. As the species of the same genus usually have, though by no means invariably, much similarity in habits and constitution, and always similarity in structure, the struggle will generally be more severe between them if they come into competition with each other than between the species of distinct genera. We see this in the recent extension over parts of the United States of one species of swallow having caused the decrease of another species. The recent increase of the missel-thrush in parts of Scotland has caused the decrease of the song-thrush. How frequently we hear of one species of rat taking the place of another species under the most different climates! In Russia the small Asiatic cockroach has everywhere driven before it its great congener. In Australia the imported hive-bee is rapidly exterminating the small, stingless native bee. We can dimly see why the competition should be most severe between allied forms which fill nearly the same place in the economy of nature; but probably in no one case could we precisely say why one species has been victorious over another in the great battle of life.

A corollary of the highest importance may be deduced from the foregoing remarks, namely, that the structure of every organic being is related, in the most essential yet often hidden manner, to that of all the other organic beings with which it comes into competition for food or residence or from which it has to escape or on which it preys. This is obvious in the structure of the teeth and talons of the tiger; and in that of the legs and claws of the parasite which clings to the hair on the tiger's body. But in the beautifully plumed seed of the dandelion, and in the flattened and fringed legs of the water-beetle, the relation seems at first confined to the elements of air and water. Yet the advantage of plumed seeds no doubt stands in the closest relations to the land being already thickly clothed with other plants; so that the seeds may be widely distributed and fall on unoccupied ground.   In the water beetle, the structure of its legs, so well adapted for diving, allows it to compete with other aquatic insects, to hunt for its own prey, and to escape serving as prey to other animals.

The store of nutriment laid up within the seeds of many plants seems at first sight to have no sort of relation to other plants.   But from the strong growth of young plants produced from such seeds, as peas and beans, when sown in the midst of long grass, it may be suspected that the chief use of the nutriment in the seed is to favor the growth of seedlings whilst struggling with other plants growing vigorously all around.

Look at a plant in the midst of its range; why does it not double or quadruple its numbers?   We know that it can perfectly well withstand a little more heat or cold, dampness or dryness, for elsewhere it ranges into slightly hotter or colder, damper or drier, districts.   In this case we can clearly see that if we wish in imagination to give the plant the power of increasing in number, we should have to give it some advantage over its competitors, or over the animals which prey upon it.   On the confines of its geographical range, a change of constitution with respect to climate would clearly be an advantage to our plant; but we have reason to believe that only a few plants or animals range so far, that they are destroyed exclusively by the rigor of the climate.   Not until we reach the extreme confines of life, in the Arctic regions or on the borders of an utter desert, will competition cease.   The land may be extremely cold or dry, yet there will be competition between some few species, or between the individuals of the same species, for the warmest or dampest spots.

Hence we can see that when a plant or an animal is placed in a new country amongst new competitors, the conditions of its life will generally be changed in an essential manner, although the climate may be exactly the same as in its former home.   If its average numbers are to increase in its new home, we should have to modify it in a different way to what we should have had to do in its native country; for we should have to give it some advantage over a different set of competitors or enemies.

It is good thus to try in imagination to give to any one species an advantage over another.   Probably in no single instance should we know what to do. This ought to convince us of our ignorance on the mutual relations of all organic beings, a conviction as necessary as it is difficult to acquire. All that we can do is to keep steadily in mind that each organic being is striving to increase in a geometrical ratio; that each at some period of its life, during some season of the year, during each generation or at intervals, has to struggle for life and to suffer great destruction. When we reflect on this struggle, we may console ourselves with the full belief that the war of nature is not incessant, that no fear is felt, that death is generally prompt, and that the vigorous, the healthy, and the happy survive and multiply.

3. Competition, Specialization, and Organization[1]

Natural selection acts exclusively by the preservation and accumulation of variations, which are beneficial under the organic and inorganic conditions to which each creature is exposed at all periods of life. The ultimate result is that each creature tends to become more and more improved in relation to its conditions. This improvement inevitably leads to the gradual advancement of the organization of the greater number of living beings throughout the world.

But here we enter on a very intricate subject, for naturalists have not defined to each other's satisfaction what is meant by an advance in organization. Amongst the vertebrata the degree of intellect and an approach in structure to man clearly come into play. It might be thought that the amount of change which the various parts and organs pass through in their development from the embryo to maturity would suffice as a standard of comparison; but there are cases, as with certain parasitic crustaceans, in which several parts of the structure become less perfect, so that the mature animal cannot be called higher than its larva. Von Baer's standard seems the most widely applicable and the best, namely, the amount of differentiation of the parts of the same organic being, in the adult state, as I should be inclined to add, and their specialization for different functions; or, as Milne Edwards would express it, the completeness of the division of physiological labor. But we shall see how obscure this subject is if we look, for instance, to fishes, amongst which some naturalists rank those as highest which, like the sharks, approach nearest to

[1] Adapted from Charles Darwin, *The Origin of Species*, pp. 97-100. (D. Appleton & Co., 1878.)

amphibians; whilst other naturalists rank the common bony or teleostean fishes as the highest, inasmuch as they are most strictly fishlike and differ most from the other vertebrate classes. We see still more plainly the obscurity of the subject by turning to plants, amongst which the standard of intellect is, of course, quite excluded; and here some botanists rank those plants as highest which have every organ, as sepals, petals, stamens, and pistils, fully developed in each flower; whereas other botanists, probably with more truth, look at the plants which have their several organs much modified and reduced in number as the highest.

If we take as the standard of high organization the amount of differentiation and specialization of the several organs in each being when adult (and this will include the advancement of the brain for intellectual purposes), natural selection clearly leads toward this standard; for all physiologists admit that the specialization of organs, inasmuch as in this state they perform their functions better, is an advantage to each being; and hence the accumulation of variations tending toward specialization is within the scope of natural selection. On the other hand, we can see, bearing in mind that all organic beings are striving to increase at a high ratio and to seize on every unoccupied or less well-occupied place in the economy of nature, that it is quite possible for natural selection gradually to fit a being to a situation in which several organs would be superfluous or useless: in such cases there would be retrogression in the scale of organization.

But it may be objected that if all organic beings thus tend to rise in the scale, how is it that throughout the world a multitude of the lowest forms still exist; and how is it that in each great class some forms are far more highly developed than others? Why have not the more highly developed forms everywhere supplanted and exterminated the lower? On our theory the continued existence of lowly organisms offers no difficulty for natural selection, or the survival of the fittest does not necessarily include progressive development— it only takes advantage of such variations as arise and are beneficial to each creature under its complex relations of life. And it may be asked what advantage, as far as we can see, would it be to an infusorian animalcule—to an intestinal worm, or even to an earthworm— to be highly organized. If it were no advantage, these forms would be left, by natural selection, unimproved or but little improved, and might remain for indefinite ages in their present lowly condition. And geology tells us that some of the lowest forms, as the infusoria and rhizopods, have remained for an enormous period in nearly their present state. But to suppose that most of the many low forms now existing have not in the least advanced since the first dawn of life would be extremely rash; for every naturalist who has dissected some of the beings now ranked as very low in the scale must have been struck with their really wondrous and beautiful organization.

Nearly the same remarks are applicable if we look to the different grades of organization within the same great group; for instance, in the vertebrata to the coexistence of mammals and fish; amongst mammalia to the coexistence of man and the ornithorhynchus; amongst fishes to the coexistence of the shark and the lancelet (Amphioxus), which later fish in the extreme simplicity of its structure approaches the invertebrate classes. But mammals and fish hardly come into competition with each other; the advancement of the whole class of mammals, or of certain members in this class, to the highest grade would not lead to their taking the place of fishes. Physiologists believe that the brain must be bathed by warm blood to be highly active, and this requires aerial respiration; so that warm-blooded mammals when inhabiting the water lie under a disadvantage in having to come continually to the surface to breathe. With fishes, members of the shark family would not tend to supplant the lancelet; for the lancelet, as I hear from Fritz Müller, has as sole companion and competitor on the barren sandy shore of South Brazil an anomalous annelid. The three lowest orders of mammals, namely, marsupials, edentata, and rodents, coexist in South America in the same region with numerous monkeys, and probably interfere little with each other.

Although organization, on the whole, may have advanced and may be still advancing throughout the world, yet the scale will always present many degrees of perfection; for the high advancement of certain whole classes, or of certain members of each class, does not at all necessarily lead to the extinction of those groups with which they do not enter into close competition. In some cases, lowly organized forms appear to have been preserved to the present day from inhabiting confined or peculiar stations, where they have been subjected to less severe competition and where their scanty numbers have retarded the chance of favorable variations arising.

Finally, I believe that many lowly organized forms now exist throughout the world from various causes. In some cases variations or individual differences of a favorable nature may never have arisen for natural selection to act on and accumulate. In no case, probably, has time sufficed for the utmost possible amount of development. In some few cases there has been what we must call retrogression of organization. But the main cause lies in the fact that under very simple conditions of life a high organization would be of no service— possibly would be of actual disservice, as being of a more delicate nature and more liable to be put out of order and injured.

4. Man: An Adaptive Mechanism[1]

Everything in nature, living or not living, exists and develops at the expense of some other thing, living or not living. The plant borrows from the soil; the soil from the rocks and the atmosphere; men and animals take from the plants and from each other the elements which they in death return to the soil, the atmosphere, and the plants. Year after year, century after century, eon after eon, the mighty, immeasurable, ceaseless round of elements goes on, in the stupendous process of chemical change, which marks the eternal life of matter.

To the superficial observer, nature in all her parts seems imbued with a spirit of profound peace and harmony; to the scientist it is obvious that every infinitesimal particle of the immense concourse is in a state of desperate and ceaseless struggle to obtain such share of the available supply of matter and energy as will suffice to maintain its present ephemeral form in a state of equilibrium with its surroundings. Not only is this struggle manifest among living forms, among birds and beasts and insects in their competition for food and habitat, but—if we may believe the revelations of the science of radio-activity—a process of transmutation, of disintegration of the atoms of one element with simultaneous formation of another element, is taking place in every fragment of inanimate matter, a process which parallels in character the more transitory processes

[1] Adapted from George W. Crile, *Man: An Adaptive Mechanism*, pp. 17-39. (Published by The Macmillan Co.. 1916. Reprinted by permission.)

of life and death in organisms and is probably a representation of the primary steps in that great process of evolution by which all terrestrial forms, organic and inorganic, have been evolved from the original ether by an action inconceivably slow, continuous, and admitting of no break in the series from inanimate to animate forms.

From colloidal slime to man is a long road, the conception of which taxes our imaginations to the utmost, but it is an ascent which is now fairly well demonstrated. Indeed, the problems of the missing links are not so difficult as is the problem of the origin of the organs and functions which man has acquired as products of adaptation. For whether we look upon the component parts of our present bodies as useful or useless mechanisms, we must regard them as the result of age-long conflicts between environmental forces and organisms.

Everywhere something is pursuing and something is escaping another creature. It is a constant drama of getting food and of seeking to escape being made food, evolving in the conflict structures fitted to accomplish both reactions. Everywhere the strong prey upon the weak, the swift upon the slow, the clever upon the stupid; and the weak, the slow, the stupid, retaliate by evolving mechanisms of defense, which more or less adequately repel or render futile the oppressor's attack. For each must live, and those already living have proved their right to existence by a more or less complete adaptation to their environment. The result of this twofold conflict between living beings is to evolve the manifold structures and functions— teeth, claws, skin, color, fur, feathers, horns, tusks, wily instincts, strength, stealth, deceit, and humility—which make up character in the animal world. According to the nature and number of each being's enemies has its own special mechanism been evolved, distinguishing it from its fellows and enabling it to get a living in its particular environment.

In every case the fate of each creature seems to have been staked upon one mechanism. The tiger by its teeth and claws, the elephant and the rhinoceros by their strength, the bird by its wings, the deer by its fleetness, the turtle by its carapace—all are enabled to counter the attacks of enemies and to procreate. Where there is a negative defense, such as a shell or quills, there is little need and no evidence of intelligence; where a rank odor, no need and no presence of claws or carapace; where sting or venom, no need and no possession of odor, claws, shell, extraordinary strength, or sagacity. Where the struggle is most bitter, there exist the most complex and most numerous contrivances for living.

Throughout its whole course the process of evolution, where it is visible in the struggle of organisms, has been marked by a progressive victory of brain over brawn. And this, in turn, may be regarded as but a manifestation of the process of survival by *lability* rather than by *stability*. Everywhere the organism that exhibits the qualities of quick response, of extreme sensibility to stimuli, of capacity to change, is the individual that survives, "conquers," "advances." The quality most useful in nature, from the point of view of the domination of a wider environment, is the quality of *changeableness, plasticity, mobility*, or *versatility*. Man's particular means of adaptation to his environment is this quality of versatility. By means of this quality expressed through the manifold reactions of his highly organized central nervous system, man has been able to dominate the beasts and to maintain himself in an environment many times more extensive than theirs. Like the defensive mechanisms of shells, poisons, and odors, man's particular defensive mechanism—his versatility of nervous response (mind)—was acquired automatically as a result of a particular combination of circumstances in his environment.

In the Tertiary era—some twenty millions of years ago—the earth, basking in the warmth of a tropical climate, had produced a luxuriant vegetation and a swarming progeny of gigantic small-brained animals for which the exuberant vegetation provided abundant and easily acquired sustenance. They were a breed of huge, clumsy, and grotesque monsters, vast in bulk and strength, but of little intelligence, that wandered heavily on the land and gorged lazily on the abundant food at hand. With the advance of the carnivora, the primitive forerunners of our tigers, wolves, hyenas, and foxes, came a period of stress, comparable to a seven years of famine following a seven years of plenty, which subjected the stolid herbivorous monsters to a severe selective struggle.

Before the active onslaught of lighter, lither, more intelligent foes, the clumsy, inelastic types succumbed, those only surviving which, through the fortunate possession of more varied reactions, were able to evolve modes of defense equal to the modes of attack possessed by their enemies. Many, unable to evolve the acute senses and the fleet limbs necessary for the combat on the ground, shrank from the fray and acquired more negative and passive means of defense. Some, like the bat, escaped into the air. Others, such as the squirrel and the ape, took refuge in the trees.

It was in this concourse of weak creatures which fled to the trees because they lacked adequate means of offense, defense, or escape on the ground that the lineaments of man's ancient ancestor might have been discerned. One can imagine what must have been the pressure from the carnivora that forced a selective transformation of the feet of the progenitor of the anthropoids into grasping hands. Coincidentally with the tree life, man's special line of adaptation—*versatility*—was undoubtedly rapidly evolved. Increased versatility and the evolution of hands enabled man to come down from the trees millions of years thereafter, to conquer the world by the further evolution and exercise of his organ of strategy—the brain. Thus we may suppose have arisen the intricate reactions we now call mind, reason, foresight, invention, etc.

Man's claim to a superior place among animals depends less upon *different* reactions than upon a *greater number* of reactions as compared with the reactions of "lower" animals. Ability to respond adaptively to more elements in the environment gives a larger dominion, that is all.

The same measure applies within the human species—the number of nervous reactions of the artist, the financier, the statesman, the scientist, being invariably greater than the reactions of the stolid savage. That man alone of all animals should have achieved the degree of versatility sufficient for such advance is no more remarkable than that the elephant should have evolved a larger trunk and tusks than the boar; that the legs of the deer should be fleeter than those of the ox; that the wings of the swallow should outfly those of the bat. Each organism, in evolving the combination of characters commensurate with safety in its particular environment, has touched the limit of both its necessity and its power to "advance." There exists abundant and reliable evidence of the fact that wherever man has been subjected to the stunting influences of an unchanging environment fairly favorable to life, he has shown no more disposition to progress than the most stolid animals. Indeed, he has usually retrograded. The need to fight for food and home has been the spur that has ever driven man forward to establish the manifold forms of physical and mental life which make up human existence today. Like the simple adaptive mechanisms of the plant by which it gets air, and of the animal by which it overcomes its rivals in battle, the supremely differentiated functions of thought and human relations are the outcome of the necessity of the organism to become adapted to entities in its environment.

B.   COMPETITION AND SEGREGATION

1.   Plant Migration, Competition, and Segregation[1]

Invasion is the complete or complex process of which migration, ecesis (the adjustment of a plant to a new home), and competition are the essential parts. It embraces the whole movement of a plant or group of plants from one area into another and their colonization in the latter. From the very nature of migration, invasion is going on at all times and in all directions.

Effective invasion is predominantly local. It operates in mass only between bare areas and adjacent communities which contain species capable of pioneering, or between contiguous communities which offer somewhat similar conditions or contain species of wide range of adjustment. Invasion into a remote region rarely has any successional effect (effect tending to transform the character of a plant community), as the invaders are too few to make headway against the plants in possession or against those much nearer a new area. Invasion into a new area or a plant community begins with migration when this is followed by ecesis. In new areas, ecesis produces reaction (the effect which a plant or a community exerts upon its habitat) at once, and this is followed by aggregation and competition, with increasing reaction. In an area already occupied by plants, ecesis and competition are concomitant and quickly produce reactions. Throughout the development migrants are entering and leaving, and the interactions of the various processes come to be complex in the highest degree.

[1] Adapted from F. E. Clements, *Plant Succession*. An analysis of the development of vegetation, pp. 75–79. (Carnegie Institution of Washington, 1916.)

Local invasion in force is essentially *continuous* or *recurrent*. Between contiguous communities it is *mutual*, unless they are too dissimilar. The result is a transition area or ecotone which epitomizes the next stage in development. By far the greater amount of invasion into existing vegetation is of this sort. The movement into a bare area is likewise continuous, though it is necessarily not mutual, and hence there is no ecotone during the earlier stages. The significant feature of continuous invasion is that an outpost may be repeatedly reinforced, permitting rapid aggregation and ecesis, and the production of new centers from which the species may be extended over a wide area. Contrasted with continuous invasion is intermittent or periodic movement into distant regions, but this is rarely concerned in succession. When the movement of invaders into a community is so great that the original occupants are driven out, the invasion is *complete*.

A topographic feature or a physical or a biological agency that restricts or prevents invasions is a barrier. Topographic features are usually permanent and produce permanent barriers. Biological ones are often temporary and exist for a few years or even a single season. Temporary barriers are often recurrent, however. Barriers are complete or incomplete with respect to the thoroughness of their action. They may affect invasion either by limiting migration or by preventing ecesis.

Biological barriers comprise plant communities, man and animals, and parasitic plants. The limiting effect of a plant community is exhibited in two ways. In the first place, an association acts as a barrier to the ecesis of species invading it from associations of another type, on account of the physical differences of the habitats. Whether such a barrier be complete or partial will depend upon the relative unlikeness of the two areas. Shade plants are unable to invade a prairie, though the species of open thickets or woodland may do so to a certain degree. Closed communities (one in which all the soil is occupied) likewise exert a marked influence in decreasing invasion by reason of the intense and successful competition which all invaders must meet. Closed associations usually act as complete barriers, while more open ones restrict invasion in direct proportion to the degree of occupation. To this fact may be traced the fundamental law of succession (the law by which one type of community or formation is succeeded by another) that the number of stages is determined largely by the increasing difficulty of invasion as the area becomes stabilized.   Man and animals affect invasion by the destruction of germules.   Both in bare areas and in seral stages the action of rodents and birds is often decisive to the extent of altering the whole course of development.   Man and animals operate as marked barriers to ecesis wherever they alter conditions unfavorably to invaders or where they turn the scale in competition by cultivating, grazing, camping, parasitism, etc.   The absence of pollinating insects is sometimes a curious barrier to the complete ecesis of species far out of their usual habitat or region.   Parasitic fungi decrease migration in so far as they affect seed production.   They restrict or prevent ecesis either by the destruction of invaders or by placing them at a disadvantage with respect to the occupants.

By the term *reaction* is understood the effect which a plant or a community exerts upon its habitat.   In connection with succession, the term is restricted to this special sense alone.   It is entirely distinct from the response of the plant or group, i.e., its adjustment and adaptation to the habitat.   In short, the habitat causes the plant to function and grow, and the plant then reacts upon the habitat, changing one or more of its factors in decisive or appreciable degree.   The two processes are mutually complementary and often interact in most complex fashion.

The reaction of a community is usually more than the sum of the reactions of the component species and individuals.   It is the individual plant which produces the reaction, though the latter usually becomes recognizable through the combined action of the group.   In most cases the action of the group accumulates or emphasizes an effect which would otherwise be insignificant or temporary. A community of trees casts less shade than the same number of isolated individuals, but the shade is constant and continuous, and hence controlling.   The significance of the community reaction is especially well shown in the case of leaf mold and duff.   The leaf litter is again only the total of the fallen leaves of all the individuals but its formation is completely dependent upon the community.   The reaction of plants upon wind-borne sand and silt-laden waters illustrates the same fact.

2. Migration and Segregation[1]

All prehistoric investigation, as far as it relates to the phenomena of the animate world, necessarily rests upon the hypothesis of migration. The distribution of plants, of the lower animals, and of men over the surface of the earth; the relationships existing between the different languages, religious conceptions, myths and legends, customs and social institutions—all these seem in this one assumption to find their common explanation.

Each fresh advance in culture commences, so to speak, with a new period of wandering. The most primitive agriculture is nomadic, with a yearly abandonment of the cultivated area; the earliest trade is migratory trade; the first industries that free themselves from the household husbandry and become the special occupations of separate individuals are carried on itinerantly. The great founders of religion, the earliest poets and philosophers, the musicians and actors of past epochs, are all great wanderers. Even today, do not the inventor, the preacher of a new doctrine, and the virtuoso travel from place to place in search of adherents and admirers—notwithstanding the immense recent development in the means of communicating information?

As civilization grows older, settlement becomes more permanent. The Greek was more settled than the Phoenician, the Roman than the Greek, because one was always the inheritor of the culture of the other. Conditions have not changed. The German is more migratory than the Latin, the Slav than the German. The Frenchman cleaves to his native soil; the Russian leaves it with a light heart to seek in other parts of his broad fatherland more favorable conditions of living. Even the factory workman is but a periodically wandering peasant.

To all that can be adduced from experience in support of the statement that in the course of history mankind has been ever growing more settled, there comes a general consideration of a twofold nature. In the first place, the extent of fixed capital grows with advancing culture; the producer becomes stationary with his means of production.

[1] Adapted from Carl Bücher, *Industrial Evolution*, pp. 345–69. (Henry Holt & Co., 1907.)

The itinerant smith of the southern Slav countries and the West-phalian iron works, the pack-horses of the Middle Ages and the great warehouses of our cities, the Thespian carts and the resident theater mark the starting and the terminal points of this evolution. In the second place, the modern machinery of transportation has in a far higher degree facilitated the transport of goods than of persons. The distribution of labor determined by locality thereby attains greater importance than the natural distribution of the means of production; the latter in many cases draws the former after it, where previously the reverse occurred.

The migrations occurring at the opening of the history of European peoples are migrations of whole tribes, a pushing and pressing of collective units from east to west, which lasted for centuries. The migrations of the Middle Ages ever affect individual classes alone; the knights in the crusades, the merchants, the wage-craftsmen, the journeymen hand-workers, the jugglers and minstrels, the villeins seeking protection within the walls of a town. Modern migrations, on the contrary, are generally a matter of private concern, the individuals being led by the most varied motives. They are almost invariably without organization. The process repeating itself daily a thousand times is united only through the one characteristic, that it is everywhere a question of change of locality by persons seeking more favorable conditions of life.

Among all the phenomena of masses in social life suited to statistical treatment, there is without doubt scarcely one that appears to fall of itself so completely under the general law of causality as migrations; and likewise hardly one concerning whose real cause such misty conceptions prevail.

The whole department of migrations has never yet undergone systematic statistical observation; exclusive attention has hitherto been centered upon remarkable individual occurrences of such phenomena. Even a rational classification of migrations in accord with the demand of social science is at the present moment lacking.

Such a classification would have to take as its starting-point the result of migrations from the point of view of population. On this basis they would fall into these groups: (1) migrations with continuous change of locality; (2) migrations with temporary change of settlement; (3) migrations with permanent settlement.

To the *first* group belong gypsy life, peddling, the carrying on of itinerant trades, tramp life; to the *second*, the wandering of journeymen craftsmen, domestic servants, tradesmen seeking the most favorable spots for temporary undertakings, officials to whom a definite office is for a time entrusted, scholars attending foreign institutions of learning; to the *third*, migration from place to place within the same country or province and to foreign parts, especially across the ocean.

An intermediate stage between the first and second group is found in the *periodical migrations*. To this stage belong the migrations of farm laborers at harvest-time, of the sugar laborers at the time of the *campagne*, of the masons of Upper Italy and the Ticino district, common day-laborers, potters, chimney-sweeps, chestnut-roasters, etc., which occur at definite seasons.

In this division the influence of the natural and political insulation of the different countries is, it is true, neglected. It must not, however, be overlooked that in the era of nationalism and protection of national labor political allegiance has a certain importance in connection with the objective point of the migrations. It would, therefore, in our opinion, be more just to make another division, taking as a basis the politico-geographical extent of the migrations. From this point of view migrations would fall into *internal* and *foreign* types.

Internal migrations are those whose points of departure and destination lie within the same national limits; foreign, those extending beyond these. The foreign may again be divided into *continental* and *extra-European* (generally transmaritime) emigration. One can, however, in a larger sense designate all migrations that do not leave the limits of the Continent as internal, and contrast with them real emigration, or transfer of domicile to other parts of the globe.

Of all these manifold kinds of migration, the transmaritime alone has regularly been the subject of official statistics; and even it has been but imperfectly treated, as every student of this subject knows. The periodic emigrations of labor and the peddling trade have occasionally been also subjected to statistical investigation—mostly with the secondary aim of legislative restriction. Yet these migrations from place to place within the same country are vastly more numerous and in their consequences vastly more important than all other kinds of migration put together.

Of the total population of the kingdom of Belgium there were, according to the results of the census of December 31, 1880, not less than 32.8 per cent who were born outside the municipality in which they had their temporary domicile; of the population of Austria (1890), 34.8 per cent.   In Prussia, of 27,279,111 persons, 11,552,033, or 42.4 per cent, were born outside the municipality where they were domiciled.   More than two-fifths of the population had changed their municipality at least once.

If we call the total population born in a given place and domiciled anywhere within the borders of the country that locality's *native* population, then according to the conditions of interchange of population just presented the native population of the country places is greater than their actual population; that of the cities, smaller.

A balancing of the account of the internal migrations in the grand duchy of Oldenburg gives the cities a surplus, and country municipalities a deficit, of 15,162 persons.   In the economy of population one is the complement of the other, just as in the case of two brothers of different temperament, one of whom regularly spends what the other has laboriously saved.   To this extent, then, we are quite justified from the point of view of population in designating the cities man-consuming and the country municipalities man-producing social organisms.

There is a very natural explanation for this condition of affairs in the country.   Where the peasant, on account of the small population of his place of residence, is much restricted in his local choice of help, adjoining communities must supplement one another.   In like manner the inhabitants of small places will intermarry more frequently than the inhabitants of larger places where there is a greater choice among the native population.   Here we have the occasion for very numerous migrations to places not far removed.   Such migrations, however, only mean a local exchange of socially allied elements.

This absorption of the surplus of emigration over immigration is the characteristic of modern cities.   If in our consideration of this problem we pay particular attention to this urban characteristic and to a like feature of the factory districts—where the conditions as to internal migrations are almost similar—we shall be amply repaid bv the discovery that in such settlements the result of internal shiftings of population receives its clearest expression. Here, where the immigrant elements are most numerous, there develops between them and the native population a social struggle—a struggle for the best conditions of earning a livelihood or, if you will, for existence, which ends with the adaptation of one part to the other, or perhaps with the final subjugation of the one by the other. Thus, according to Schliemann, the city of Smyrna had in the year 1846 a population of 80,000 Turks and 8,000 Greeks; in the year 1881, on the contrary, there were 23,000 Turks and 76,000 Greeks. The Turkish portion of the population had thus in thirty-five years decreased by 71 per cent, while the Greeks had increased ninefold.

Not everywhere, to be sure, do those struggles take the form of such a general process of displacement; but in individual cases it will occur with endless frequency within a country that the stronger and better-equipped element will overcome the weaker and less well-equipped.

Thus we have here a case similar to that occurring so frequently in nature: on the same terrain where a more highly organized plant or animal has no longer room for subsistence, others less exacting in their demands take up their position and flourish. The coming of the new is in fact not infrequently the cause of the disappearance of those already there and of their withdrawal to more favorable surroundings.

If these considerations show that by no means the majority of internal migrations find their objective point in the cities, they at the same time prove that the trend toward the great centers of population can in itself be looked upon as having an extensive social and economic importance. It produces an alteration in the distribution of population throughout the state; and at its originating and objective points it gives rise to difficulties which legislative and executive authority has hitherto labored, usually with but very moderate success, to overcome. It transfers large numbers of persons almost directly from a sphere of life where barter predominates into one where money and credit exchange prevail, thereby affecting the social conditions of life and the social customs of the manual laboring classes in a manner to fill the philanthropist with grave anxiety.

3.   Demographic Segregation and Social Selection[1]

There are two ways in which demographic crystallization may have taken place. A people may have become rigid horizontally, divided into castes, or social strata; or it may be geographically segregated into localized communities, varying in size all the way from the isolated hamlet to the highly individualized nation. Both of these forms of crystallization are breaking down today under the pressure of modern industrialism and democracy, in Europe as well as in America.

The sudden growth of great cities is the first result of the phenomenon of migration which we have to note. We think of this as essentially an American problem. We comfort ourselves in our failures of municipal administration with that thought. This is a grievous deception.   Most of the European cities have increased in population more rapidly than in America. This is particularly true of great German urban centers. Berlin has outgrown our own metropolis, New York, in less than a generation, having in twenty-five years added as many actual new residents as Chicago, and twice as many as Philadelphia. Hamburg has gained twice as many in population since 1875 as Boston; Leipzig has distanced St. Louis. The same demographic outburst has occurred in the smaller German cities as well. Beyond the confines of the German Empire, from Norway to Italy, the same is true.

Contemporaneously with this marvellous growth of urban centers we observe a progressive depopulation of the rural districts. What is going on in our New England states, especially in Massachusetts, is entirely characteristic of large areas in Europe. Take France, for example. The towns are absorbing even more than the natural increment of country population; they are drawing off the middle-aged as well as the young. Thus great areas are being actually depopulated.

A process of selection is at work on a grand scale. The great majority today who are pouring into the cities are those who, like the emigrants to the United States in the old days of natural migration, come because they have the physical equipment and the mental

[1] From William Z. Ripley, *The Races of Europe*, pp. 537–59. (D. Appleton & Co., 1899.)

disposition to seek a betterment of their fortunes away from home. Of course, an appreciable contingent of such migrant types is composed of the merely discontented, of the restless, and the adventurous; but, in the main, the best blood of the land it is which feeds into the arteries of city life.

Another more certain mode of proof is possible for demonstrating that the population of cities is largely made up either of direct immigrants from the country or of their immediate descendants. In German cities, Hansen found that nearly one-half their residents were of direct country descent. In London it has been shown that over one-third of its population are immigrants; and in Paris the same is true. For thirty of the principal cities of Europe it has been calculated that only about one-fifth of their increase is from the loins of their own people, the overwhelming majority being of country birth.

The first physical characteristic of urban populations, as compared with those of country districts, which we have to note, is their tendency toward that shape of head characteristic of two of our racial types, Teutonic and Mediterranean respectively. It seems as if for some reason the broad-headed Alpine race was a distinctly rural type. Thirty years ago an observer in the ethnically Alpine district of south central France noted an appreciable difference between town and country in the head form of the people. In a half-dozen of the smaller cities his observations pointed to a greater prevalence of the long-headed type than in the country roundabout. Dr. Ammon of Carlsruhe, working upon measurements of thousands of conscripts of the Grand Duchy of Baden, discovered radical differences here between the head form in city and country, and between the upper and lower classes in the larger towns. Several explanations for this were possible. The direct influence of urban life might conceivably have brought it about, acting through superior education, habits of life, and the like. There was no psychological basis for this assumption. Another tenable hypothesis was that in these cities, situated, as we have endeavored to show, in a land where two racial types of population were existing side by side, the city for some reason exerted superior powers of attraction upon the long-headed race. If this were true, then by a combined process of social and racial selection, the towns would be continually drawing unto themselves that tall and blond Teutonic type of population which, as history teaches us, has dominated social and political affairs in Europe for centuries. This suggested itself as the probable solution of the question; and investigations all over Europe during the last five years have been directed to the further analysis of the matter.

Is this phenomenon, the segregation of a long-headed physical type in city populations, merely the manifestation of a restless tendency on the part of the Teutonic race to reassert itself in the new phases of nineteenth-century competition? All through history this type has been characteristic of the dominant classes, especially in military and political, perhaps rather than purely intellectual, affairs. All the leading dynasties of Europe have long been recruited from its ranks. The contrast of this type, whose energy has carried it all over Europe, with the persistently sedentary Alpine race is very marked. A certain passivity, or patience, is characteristic of the Alpine peasantry. As a rule, not characterized by the domineering spirit of the Teuton, this Alpine type makes a comfortable and contented neighbor, a resigned and peaceful subject. Whether this rather negative character of the Alpine race is entirely innate, or whether it is in part, like many of its social phenomena, merely a reflection from the almost invariably inhospitable habitat in which it has long been isolated, we may not pretend to decide.

Let us now for a moment take up the consideration of a second physical characteristic of city populations—viz., stature. If there be a law at all in respect of average statures, it demonstrates rather the depressing effects of city life than the reverse. For example, Hamburg is far below the average for Germany. All over Britain there are indications of this law, that town populations are, on the average, comparatively short of stature. Dr. Beddoe, the great authority upon this subject, concludes his investigation of the population of Great Britain thus: "It may therefore be taken as *proved* that the stature of men in the large towns of Britain is lowered considerably below the standard of the nation, and as *probable* that such degradation is hereditary and progressive."

A most important point in this connection is the great variability of city populations in size. All observers comment upon this. It is of profound significance. The people of the west and east ends in each city differ widely. The population of the aristocratic quarters is often found to exceed in stature the people of the tenement districts. We should expect this, of course, as a direct result of the depressing influence of unfavorable environment. Yet there is apparently another factor underlying that—viz., social selection. While cities contain so large a proportion of degenerate physical types as on the average to fall below the surrounding country in stature, nevertheless they also are found to include an inordinately large number of very tall and well-developed individuals. In other words, compared with the rural districts, where all men are subject to the same conditions of life, we discover in the city that the population has differentiated into the very tall and the very short.

The explanation for this phenomenon is simple. Yet it is not direct, as in Topinard's suggestion that it is a matter of race or that a change of environment operates to stimulate growth. Rather does it appear that it is the growth which suggests the change. The tall men are in the main those vigorous, mettlesome, presumably healthy individuals who have themselves, or in the person of their fathers, come to the city in search of the prizes which urban life has to offer to the successful. On the other hand, the degenerate, the stunted, those who entirely outnumber the others so far as to drag the average for the city as a whole below the normal, are the grist turned out by the city mill. They are the product of the tenement, the sweat shop, vice, and crime. Of course, normally developed men, as ever, constitute the main bulk of the population, but these two widely divergent classes attain a very considerable representation.

We have seen thus far that evidence seems to point to an aggregation of the Teutonic long-headed population in the urban centers of Europe. Perhaps a part of the tall stature in some cities may be due to such racial causes. A curious anomaly now remains, however, to be noted. City populations appear to manifest a distinct tendency toward brunetness—that is to say, they seem to comprise an abnormal proportion of brunet traits, as compared with the neighboring rural districts. This tendency was strikingly shown to characterize the entire German Empire when its six million school children were examined under Virchow's direction. In twenty-five out of thirty-three of the larger cities were the brunet traits more frequent than in the country.

Austria offers confirmation of the same tendency toward brunetness in twenty-four out of its thirty-three principal cities. Farther south, in Italy, it was noted much earlier that cities contained fewer blonds than were common in the rural districts roundabout. In conclusion let us add, not as additional testimony, for the data are too defective, that among five hundred American students at the Institute of Technology in Boston, roughly classified, there were 9 per cent of pure brunet type among those of country birth and training, while among those of urban birth and parentage the percentage of such brunet type rose as high as 15.

It is not improbable that there is in brunetness, in the dark hair and eye, some indication of vital superiority. If this were so, it would serve as a partial explanation for the social phenomena which we have been at so much pains to describe. If in the same community there were a slight vital advantage in brunetness, we should expect to find that type slowly aggregating in the cities; for it requires energy and courage, physical as well as mental, not only to break the ties of home and migrate, but also to maintain one's self afterward under the stress of urban life.

From the preceding formidable array of testimony it appears that the tendency of urban populations is certainly not toward the pure blond, long-headed, and tall Teutonic type. The phenomenon of urban selection is something more complex than a mere migration of a single racial element in the population toward the cities. The physical characteristics of townsmen are too contradictory for ethnic explanations alone. To be sure, the tendencies are slight; we are not even certain of their universal existence at all. We are merely watching for their verification or disproof. There is, however, nothing improbable in the phenomena we have noted. Naturalists have always turned to the environment for the final solution of many of the great problems of nature. In this case we have to do with one of the most sudden and radical changes of environment known to man. Every condition of city life, mental as well as physical, is at the polar extreme from those which prevail in the country. To deny that great modifications in human structure and functions may be effected by a change from one to the other is to gainsay all the facts of natural history.

4. Inter-racial Competition and Race Suicide[1]

I have thus far spoken of the foreign arrivals at our ports, as estimated. Beginning with 1820, however, we have custom-house statistics of the numbers of persons annually landing upon our shores. Some of these, indeed, did not remain here; yet, rudely speaking, we may call them all immigrants. Between 1820 and 1830, population grew to 12,866,020. The number of foreigners arriving in the ten years was 151,000. Here, then, we have for forty years an increase, substantially all out of the loins of the four millions of our own people living in 1790, amounting to almost nine millions, or 227 per cent. Such a rate of increase was never known before or since, among any considerable population over any extensive region.

About this time, however, we reach a turning-point in the history of our population. In the decade 1830–40 the number of foreign arrivals greatly increased. Immigration had not, indeed, reached the enormous dimensions of these later days. Yet, during the decade in question, the foreigners coming to the United States were almost exactly fourfold those coming in the decade preceding, or 599,000. The question now of vital importance is this: Was the population of the country correspondingly increased? I answer, No! The population of 1840 was almost exactly what, by computation, it would have been had no increase in foreign arrivals taken place. Again, between 1840 and 1850, a still further access of foreigners occurred, this time of enormous dimensions, the arrivals of the decade amounting to not less than 1,713,000. Of this gigantic total, 1,048,000 were from the British Isles, the Irish famine of 1846–47 having driven hundreds of thousands of miserable peasants to seek food upon our shores. Again we ask, Did this excess constitute a net gain to the population of the country? Again the answer is, No! Population showed no increase over the proportions established before immigration set in like a flood. In other words, as the foreigners began to come in larger numbers, the native population more and more withheld their own increase.

Now this correspondence might be accounted for in three different ways: (1) It might be said that it was a mere coincidence, no relation

[1] Adapted from Francis A. Walker, *Economics and Statistics*, II, 421–26. (Henry Holt & Co., 1899.)

of cause and effect existing between the two phenomena. (2) It might he said that the foreigners came because the native population was relatively declining, that is, failing to keep up its pristine rate of increase. (3) It might be said that the growth of the native population was checked by the incoming of the foreign elements in such large numbers.

The view that the correspondence referred to was a mere coincidence, purely accidental in origin, is perhaps that most commonly taken. If this be the true explanation, the coincidence is a most remarkable one. In the June number of this magazine, I cited the predictions as to the future population of the country made by Elkanah Watson, on the basis of the censuses of 1790, 1800, and 1810, while immigration still remained at a minimum. Now let us place together the actual census figures for 1840 and 1850, Watson's estimates for those years, and the foreign arrivals during the preceding decade:

	1840	1850
The census	17,069,453	23,191,876
Watson's estimates	17,116,526	23,185,368
The difference	−47,073	+6,508
Foreign arrivals during the preceding decade	599,000	1,713,000

Here we see that, in spite of the arrival of 500,000 foreigners during the period 1830–40, four times as many as had arrived during any preceding decade, the figures of the census coincided closely with the estimate of Watson, based on the growth of population in the pre-immigration era, falling short of it by only 47,073 in a total of 17,000,000; while in 1850 the actual population, in spite of the arrival of 1,713,000 more immigrants, exceeded Watson's estimates by only 6,508 in a total of 23,000,000. Surely, if this correspondence between the increase of the foreign element and the relative decline of the native element is a mere coincidence, it is one of the most astonishing in human history. The actuarial degree of improbability as to a coincidence so close, over a range so vast, I will not undertake to compute.

If, on the other hand, it be alleged that the relation of cause and effect existed between the two phenomena, this might be put in two widely different ways: either that the foreigners came in increasing numbers because the native element was relatively declining, or that the native element failed to maintain its previous rate of increase because the foreigners came in such swarms. What shall we say of the former of these explanations? Does anything more need to be said than that it is too fine to be the real explanation of a big human fact like this we are considering? To assume that at such a distance in space, in the then state of news-communication and ocean-transportation, and in spite of the ignorance and extreme poverty of the peasantries of Europe from which the immigrants were then generally drawn, there was so exact a degree of knowledge not only of the fact that the native element here was not keeping up its rate of increase but also of the precise ratio of that decline as to enable those peasantries, with or without a mutual understanding, to supply just the numbers necessary to bring our population up to its due proportions, would be little less than laughable. Today, with quick passages, cheap freights, and ocean transportation there is not a single wholesale trade in the world carried on with this degree of knowledge, or attaining anything like this point of precision in results.

The true explanation of the remarkable fact we are considering I believe to be the last of the three suggested. The access of foreigners, at the time and under the circumstances, constituted a shock to the principle of population among the native element. That principle is always acutely sensitive alike to sentimental and to economic conditions. And it is to be noted, in passing, that not only did the decline in the native element, as a whole, take place in singular correspondence with the excess of foreign arrivals, but it occurred chiefly in just those regions to which the newcomers most freely resorted.

But what possible reason can be suggested why the incoming of the foreigner should have checked the disposition of the native toward the increase of population at the traditional rate? I answer that the best of good reasons can be assigned. Throughout the northeastern and northern middle states, into which, during the period under consideration, the newcomers poured in such numbers, the standard of material living, of general intelligence, of social decency, had been singularly high. Life, even at its hardest, had always had its luxuries; the babe had been a thing of beauty, to be delicately nurtured and proudly exhibited; the growing child had been decently dressed, at least for school and church; the house had been kept in order, at whatever cost, the gate hung, the shutters in place, while the front yard had been made to bloom with simple flowers; the village church, the public schoolhouse, had been the best which the community, with great exertions and sacrifices, could erect and maintain. Then came the foreigner, making his way into the little village, bringing—small blame to him!—not only a vastly lower standard of living, but too often an actual present incapacity even to understand the refinements of life and thought in the community in which he sought a home. Our people had to look upon houses that were mere shells for human habitations, the gate unhung, the shutters flapping or falling, green pools in the yard, babes and young children rolling about half naked or worse, neglected, dirty, unkempt. Was there not in this a sentimental reason strong enough to give a shock to the principle of population? But there was, besides, an economic reason for a check to the native increase. The American shrank from the industrial competition thus thrust upon him. He was unwilling himself to engage in the lowest kind of day labor with these new elements of the population; he was even more unwilling to bring sons and daughters into the world to enter into that competition. For the first time in our history, the people of the free states became divided into classes. Those classes were natives and foreigners. Politically, the distinction had only a certain force, which yielded more or less readily under partisan pressure; but socially and industrially that distinction has been a tremendous power, and its chief effects have been wrought upon population. Neither the social companionship nor the industrial competition of the foreigner has, broadly speaking, been welcome to the native.

It hardly needs to be said that the foregoing descriptions are not intended to apply to all of the vast body of immigrants during this period. Thousands came over from good homes; many had all the advantages of education and culture; some possessed the highest qualities of manhood and citizenship.

But let us proceed with the census. By 1860 the causes operating to reduce the growth of the native element—to which had then manifestly been added the force of important changes in the manner of living, the introduction of more luxurious habits, the influence of city life, and the custom of "boarding"—had reached such a height as, in spite of a still-increasing immigration, to leave the population of the country 310,503 below the estimate. The fearful losses of the Civil War and the rapid extension of habits unfavorable to increase of numbers make any further use of Watson's computations uninstructive; yet still the great fact protrudes through all the subsequent history of our population that the more rapidly foreigners came into the United States, the smaller was the rate of increase, not merely among the native population separately, but throughout the population of the country, as a whole, including the foreigners. The climax of this movement was reached when, during the decade 1880–90, the foreign arrivals rose to the monstrous total of five and a quarter millions (twice what had ever before been known), while the population, even including this enormous re-enforcement, increased more slowly than in any other period of our history except, possibly, that of the great Civil War.

If the foregoing views are true, or contain any considerable degree of truth, foreign immigration into this country has, from the time it first assumed large proportions, amounted, not to a reinforcement of our population, but to a replacement of native by foreign stock. That if the foreigners had not come the native element would long have filled the places the foreigners usurped, I entertain not a doubt. The competency of the American stock to do this it would be absurd to question, in the face of such a record as that for 1790 to 1830. During the period from 1830 to 1860 the material conditions of existence in this country were continually becoming more and more favorable to the increase of population from domestic sources. The old man-slaughtering medicine was being driven out of civilized communities; houses were becoming larger; the food and clothing of the people were becoming ampler and better. Nor was the cause which, about 1840 or 1850, began to retard the growth of population here to be found in the climate which Mr. Clibborn stigmatizes so severely. The climate of the United States has been benign enough to enable us to take the English shorthorn and greatly to improve it, as the re-exportation of that animal to England at monstrous prices abundantly proves; to take the English race-horse and to improve him to a degree of which the startling victories of Parole, Iroquois, and Foxhall afford but a suggestion; to take the Englishman and to improve him, too, adding agility to his strength, making his eye keener and his hand steadier, so that in rowing, in riding, in shooting, and in boxing, the American of pure English stock is today the better animal. No! Whatever were the causes which checked the growth of the native population, they were neither physiological nor climatic. They were mainly social and economic; and chief among them was the access of vast hordes of foreign immigrants, bringing with them a standard of living at which our own people revolted.

5. Competition, Commercial Organization, and the Metropolitan Economy[1]

If we cast our thought no farther back than the permanent settlement of clans and tribes, we see that there are three general stages which sum up much of the economic life of the times: village economy, town economy, and metropolitan economy. Each is a unit of production. Each has a center of trade, though the importance of trade is, of course, not so great at first as later. . . . . In the progression from one stage to another we see not only a greater specialization, but a greater general division of labor, a larger surplus and store of goods, and more immunity from distress and famine.

Just as the tribal and later the feudal state reflected the village, as the early national state reflected the town, so does the state today reflect the metropolis. The village mobilized labor, the town mobilized skill in trade and manufacture, and now the metropolis mobilizes capital and management in support of the state.

By metropolitan economy is meant the concentration of the trade of a wide area in one great city. While the radius of the area dominated commercially by the medieval town had rarely been more than a score of miles, the radius of the area dominated by a metropolis is roughly a hundred miles or more in length.

The structure of the metropolitan economic unit is made up, firstly, of the metropolis itself with its merchants, bankers, warehousemen, transport officials, and other specialized men of business; and secondly, of the district or hinterland with its towns and villages, its countryside of farms, forests, streams, and mines. The metropolis

[1] From N. S. B. Gras, "The Development of Metropolitan Economy in Europe and America," *American Historical Review*, XXVII (1921–22), 698–705.

and its hinterland are integral parts of the metropolitan unit, but they are not constant in the areas which they occupy. While the metropolis itself widens its confines with general economic development, the hinterland decreases in size. The area occupied by greater London increases year by year, while the hinterland diminishes as Manchester-Liverpool grows in strength and influence. Greater Chicago grows while its hinterland is being nibbled away by Cleveland, St. Louis, Kansas City, and the Twin Cities.

The essential part of the metropolitan economy is not size or structure but function. The metropolis concentrates the trade of a wide district. It is the gathering-place for the products of that district. It is also the place from which wares already concentrated from many lands and sections radiate to the whole hinterland. Moreover, it is the point through which the hinterland normally trades with other metropolitan units. It is more economical for a few dealers in a metropolis to specialize in the inter-metropolitan trade, which is usually wholesale, than for traders located in small towns in the hinterland to maintain connections and credits with distant parts. If we wish to visualize the whole metropolitan mechanism we have only to think of a web with the master spider in the center. The concentration and radiation of such a pattern are in marked contrast to the duplication and parallelism of the alternative checkerboard. The saving in materials, labor, and management is enormous; otherwise the spider would not have so constructed its net. Metropolitan economy likewise exists because of its efficiency as a unit in production. Public policy, national administration, even socialism would hardly long continue an attempt to alter so economical an organization.

If we wish to visualize metropolitan growth we have only to examine the metropolis itself. The retail section may represent the old town economy. The wholesale district is the prosaic memorial of the first phase of metropolitan economy. The industrial suburb contains most of what is left of metropolitan manufacture after the period of decentralization. The wharves and the railroad terminals show where extended and hinterland trade meet within the metropolis. And the financial district with its mint, stock exchange, banks, insurance offices, and brokers constitutes the most sensitive spot in the metropolitan nerve-center.

Such is the fully developed metropolitan organization in the sense that it has a constitution, or that there is an agreement whereby transactions are made. It is just a unit of public economy that has grown up gradually to perform cheaply and efficiently the business of managing production. Goods enter the metropolis and leave it. The metropolis performs one set of tasks, the hinterland another. Both are industrial, financial, and commercial, but the metropolis is pre-eminently commercial and financial.

C. ECONOMIC COMPETITION

1. Changing Forms of Economic Competition[1]

There is a sense in which much of the orthodox system of political economy is eternally true. Conclusions reached by valid reasoning are always as true as the hypotheses from which they are deduced. It will remain forever true that if unlimited competition existed, most of the traditional laws would be realized in the practical world. It will also be true that in those corners of the industrial field which still show an approximation to Ricardian competition there will be seen as much of correspondence between theory and fact as candid reasoners claim. If political economy will but content itself with this kind of truth, it need never be disturbed by industrial revolutions. The science need not trouble itself to progress.

This hypothetical truth, or science of what would take place if society were fashioned after an ideal pattern, is not what Ricardo believed that he had discovered. His system was positive; actual life suggested it by developing tendencies for which the scientific formulas which at that time were traditional could not account. It was a new industrial world which called for a modernized system of economic doctrine. Ricardo was the first to understand the situation, to trace the new tendencies to their consummation, and to create a scientific system by insight and foresight. He outran history in the process, and mentally created a world more relentlessly competitive than any which has existed; and yet it was fact and not imagination that lay at the basis of the whole system. Steam had been utilized, machines were supplanting hand labor, workmen were migrating

[1] Adapted from John B. Clark, "The Limits of Competition," in Clark and Giddings, *The Modern Distributive Process*, pp. 2-8. (Ginn & Co., 1888.)

to new centers of production, guild regulations were giving way, and competition of a type unheard of before was beginning to prevail.

A struggle for existence had commenced between parties of unequal strength. In manufacturing industries the balance of power had been disturbed by steam, and the little shops of former times were disappearing. The science adapted to such conditions was an economic Darwinism; it embodied the laws of a struggle for existence between competitors of the new and predatory type and those of the peaceable type which formerly possessed the field. Though the process was savage, the outlook which it afforded was not wholly evil. The survival of crude strength was, in the long run, desirable. Machines and factories meant, to every social class, cheapened goods and more comfortable living. Efficient working establishments were developing; the social organism was perfecting itself for its contest with crude nature. It was a fuller and speedier dominion over the earth which was to result from the concentration of human energy now termed centralization.

The error unavoidable to the theorists of the time lay in basing a scientific system on the facts afforded by a state of revolution. This was attempting to derive permanent principles from transient phenomena. Some of these principles must become obsolete; and the work demanded of modern economists consists in separating the transient from the permanent in the Ricardian system. How much of the doctrine holds true when the struggle between unequal competitors is over, and when a few of the very strongest have possession of the field?

In most branches of manufacturing, and in other than local transportation, the contest between the strong and the weak is either settled or in process of rapid settlement. The survivors are becoming so few, so powerful, and so nearly equal that if the strife were to continue, it would bid fair to involve them all in a common ruin. What has actually developed is not such a battle of giants but a system of armed neutralities and federations of giants. The new era is distinctly one of consolidated forces; rival establishments are forming combinations, and the principle of union is extending itself to the labor and the capital in each of them. Laborers who once competed with each other are now making their bargains collectively with their employers.

Employers who under the old régime would have worked independently are merging their capital in corporations and allowing it to be managed as by a single hand.

Predatory competition between unequal parties was the basis of the Ricardian system. This process was vaguely conceived and never fully analyzed; what was prominent in the thought of men in connection with it was the single element of struggle. Mere effort to survive, the Darwinian feature of the process, was all that, in some uses, the term "competition" was made to designate. Yet the competitive action of an organized society is systematic; each part of it is limited to a specific field, and tends, within these limits, to self-annihilation.

An effort to attain a conception of competition that should remove some of the confusion was made by Professor Cairnes. His system of "non-competing groups" is a feature of his value theory, which is a noteworthy contribution to economic thought. Mr. Mill had followed Ricardo in teaching that the natural price of commodities is governed by the cost of producing them. Professor Cairnes accepts this statement, but attaches to it a meaning altogether new. He says, in effect:

Commodities do indeed exchange according to their cost of production; but cost is something quite different from what currently passes by that name. That is merely the outlay incurred by the capitalist-employer for raw materials, labor, etc. The real cost is the personal sacrifice made by the producing parties, workmen as well as employers. It is not a mercantile but a psychological phenomenon, a reaction upon the men themselves occasioned by the effort of the laborer and the abstinence of the capitalist. These personal sacrifices gauge the market value of commodities within the fields in which, in the terms of the theory, competition is free. The adjustment takes place through the spontaneous movement of capital and labor from employments that yield small returns to those that give larger ones. Capital migrates freely from place to place and from occupation to occupation. If one industry is abnormally profitable, capital seeks it, increases and cheapens its product, and reduces its profits to the prevailing level. Profits tend to a general uniformity.

Wages are said to tend to equality only within limits. The transfer of labor from one employment to another is checked by barriers.

What we find, in effect [continues Professor Cairnes], is not a whole population competing indiscriminately for all occupations, but a series of industrial layers, superimposed on one another, within each of which the various candidates for employment possess a real and effective power of selection, while those occupying the several strata are, for all purposes of effective competition, practically isolated from each other. We may perhaps venture to arrange them in some such order as this: first, at the bottom of the scale there would be the large group of unskilled or nearly unskilled laborers, comprising agricultural laborers, laborers engaged in miscellaneous occupations in towns, or acting in attendance on skilled labor. Secondly, there would be the artisan group, comprising skilled laborers of the secondary order—carpenters, joiners, smiths, masons, shoemakers, tailors, hatters, etc., etc.—with whom might be included the very large class of small retail dealers, whose means and position place them within the reach of the same industrial opportunities as the class of artisans. The third layer would contain producers and dealers of a higher order, whose work would demand qualifications only obtainable by persons of substantial means and fair educational opportunities; for example, civil and mechanical engineers, chemists, opticians, watchmakers, and others of the same industrial grade, in which might also find a place the superior class of retail tradesmen; while above these there would be a fourth, comprising persons still more favorably circumstanced, whose ampler means would give them a still wider choice. This last group would contain members of the learned professions, as well as persons engaged in the various careers of science and art, and in the higher branches of mercantile business.

It is essential to the theory that not only workmen but their children should be confined to a producing group. The equalizing process may take place even though men do not actually abandon one occupation and enter another; for there exists, in the generation of young men not yet committed to any occupation, a disposable fund of labor which will gravitate naturally to the occupations that pay the largest wages. It is not necessary that blacksmiths should ever become shoemakers, or vice versa, but only that the children of both classes of artisans should be free to enter the trade that is best rewarded.

Professor Cairnes does not claim that his classification is exhaustive, nor that the demarcation is absolute:

No doubt the various ranks and classes fade into each other by imperceptible gradations, and individuals from all classes are constantly passing up or dropping down; but while this is so, it is nevertheless true that the average workman, from whatever rank he be taken, finds his power of competition limited for practical purposes to a certain range of occupations, so that, however high the rates of remuneration in those which lie beyond may rise, he is excluded from sharing them. We are thus compelled to recognize the existence of non-competing industrial groups as a feature of our social economy.

It will be seen that the competition which is here under discussion is of an extraordinary kind; and the fact that the general term is applied to it without explanation is a proof of the vagueness of the conceptions of competition with which acute writers have contented themselves. Actual competition consists invariably in an effort to undersell a rival producer. A carpenter competes with a carpenter because he creates a similar utility and offers it in the market. In the theory of Professor Cairnes the carpenter is the competitor of the blacksmith, because his children may enter the blacksmith's calling. In the actual practice of his own trade, the one artisan in no wise affects the other. It is potential competition rather than actual that is here under discussion; and even this depends for its effectiveness on the action of the rising generation.

Modern methods of production have obliterated Professor Cairnes's dividing lines. Potential competition extends to every part of the industrial field in which men work in organized companies. Throwing out of account the professions, a few trades of the highest sort, and the class of labor which is performed by employers themselves and their salaried assistants, it is practically true that labor is in a universal ebb and flow; it passes freely to occupations which are, for the time being, highly paid, and reduces their rewards to the general level.

This objection to the proposed grouping is not theoretical. The question is one of fact; it is the development of actual industry that has invalidated the theory which, in the seventies, expressed an important truth concerning economic relations in England. Moreover, the author of the theory anticipated one change which would somewhat lessen its applicability to future conditions. He recorded his belief that education would prove a leveler, and that it would merge to some extent the strata of industrial society. The children of hod-carriers might become machinists, accountants, or lawyers when they could acquire the needed education. He admitted also that new countries afford conditions in which the lines of demarcation are faint. He was not in a position to appreciate the chief leveling agency, namely, the machine method of production as now extended and perfected. Education makes the laborer capable of things relatively difficult, and machines render the processes which he needs to master relatively easy. The so-called unskilled workmen stand on a higher personal level than those of former times; and the new methods of manufacturing are reducing class after class to that level. Mechanical labor is resolving itself into processes so simple that anyone may learn them. An old-time shoemaker could not become a watchmaker, and even his children would have found difficulties in their way had they attempted to master the higher trade; but a laster in a Lynn shoe factory can, if he will, learn one of the minute trades that are involved in the making of a Waltham watch. His children may do so without difficulty; and this is all that is necessary for maintaining the normal balance between the trades.

The largest surviving differences between workmen are moral. Bodily strength still counts for something, and mental strength for more; but the consideration which chiefly determines the value of a workman to the employer who intrusts to him costly materials and a delicate machine is the question of fidelity. Character is not monopolized by any social class; it is of universal growth, and tends by the prominent part which it plays in modern industry, to reduce to their lowest terms the class differences of the former era.

The rewards of professional life are gauged primarily by character and native endowment, and are, to this extent, open to the children of workmen. New barriers, however, arise here in the ampler education which, as time advances, is demanded of persons in these pursuits; and these barriers give to a part of the fourth and highest class in the scheme that we are criticising a permanent basis of existence. Another variety of labor retains a pre-eminence based on native adaptations and special opportunities. It is the work of the employer himself. It is an organizing and directing function, and in large industries is performed only in part by the owners. A portion of this work is committed to hired assistants. Strictly speaking, the entrepreneur, or employer, of a great establishment is not one man, but many, who work in a collective capacity, and who receive a reward that, taken in the aggregate, constitutes the "wages of superintendence." To some members of this administrative body the returns come in the form of salaries, while to others they come partly in the form of dividends; but if we regard their work in its entirety, and consider their wages in a single sum, we must class it with entrepreneur's profits rather than with ordinary wages. It is a different part of the product from the sum distributed among day laborers; and this fact separates the administrative group from the class considered in our present inquiry. Positions of the higher sort are usually gained either through the possession of capital or through relations to persons who possess it. Though clerkships of the lower grade demand no attainments which the children of workmen cannot gain, and though promotion to the higher grades is still open, the tendency of the time is to make the transition from the ranks of labor to those of administration more and more difficult. The true laboring class is merging its subdivisions, while it is separating more sharply from the class whose interests, in test questions, place them on the side of capital.

2.   Competition and the Natural Harmony of Individual Interests[1]

The general industry of the society never can exceed what the capital of the society can employ. As the number of workmen that can be kept in employment by any particular person must bear a certain proportion to his capital, so the number of those that can be continually employed by all the members of a great society must bear a certain proportion to the whole capital of that society and never can exceed that proportion. No regulation of commerce can increase the quantity of industry in any society beyond what its capital can maintain. It can only divert a part of it into a direction into which it might not otherwise have gone; and it is by no means certain that this artificial direction is likely to be more advantageous to the society than that into which it would have gone of its own accord.

Every individual is continually exerting himself to find out the most advantageous employment for whatever capital he can command. It is his own advantage, indeed, and not that of the society,

[1] Adapted from Adam Smith, *An Inquiry into the Nature and Causes of the Wealth of Nations*, I (1904), 419, 421. (By kind permission of Messrs. Methuen & Co.. Ltd.)

which he has in view. But the study of his own advantage naturally, or rather necessarily, leads him to prefer that employment which is most advantageous to the society.

As every individual, therefore, endeavors as much as he can both to employ his capital in the support of domestic industry and so to direct that industry that its product may be of the greatest value; every individual necessarily labors to render the annual revenue of the society as great as he can. He generally, indeed, neither intends to promote the public interest nor knows how much he is promoting it. By preferring the support of domestic to that of foreign industry, he intends only his own security; and by directing that industry in such a manner that its product may be of the greatest value, he intends only his own gain, and he is in this, as in many other cases, led by an invisible hand to promote an end which was no part of his intention. Nor is it always worse for the society that it was no part of it. By pursuing his own interest he frequently promotes that of the society more effectually than when he really intends to promote it. I have never known much good done by those who affected to trade for the public good. It is an affectation, indeed, not very common among merchants, and very few words need be employed in dissuading them from it.

What is the species of domestic industry which his capital can employ, and of which the product is likely to be of the greatest value, every individual, it is evident, can, in his local situation, judge much better than any statesman or lawgiver can do for him. The statesman who should attempt to direct private people in what manner they ought to employ their capitals would not only load himself with a most unnecessary attention but assume an authority which could safely be trusted, not only to no single person, but to no council or senate whatever, and which would nowhere be so dangerous as in the hands of a man who had folly and presumption enough to fancy himself fit to exercise it.

3. Competition and Freedom[1]

What, after all, is competition? Is it something that exists and acts of itself, like the cholera? No, competition is simply the absence of oppression. In reference to the matters that interest me, I *prefer*

---

[1] Translated from Frédéric Bastiat. *Œuvres complètes*, tome VI, "Harmonies economiques," 9° édition, p. 350. (Paris, 1884.)

to choose for myself and I do not want anyone else to choose for me against my will; that's all. And if anyone undertakes to substitute his judgment for mine in matters that concern me I shall demand the privilege of substituting my wishes for his in matters which concern him. What guaranty is there that this arrangement will improve matters? It is evident that competition is liberty. To destroy liberty of action is to destroy the possibility and consequently the faculty of choosing, judging, comparing; it is to kill intelligence, to kill thought, to kill man himself. Whatever the point of departure, there is where modern reforms always end; in order to improve society it is necessary to annihilate the individual, upon the assumption that the individual is the source of all evil, and as if the individual was not likewise the source of all good.

4. Money and Freedom[1]

Money not only makes the relation of individuals to the group a more independent one, but the content of the special forms of associations and the relations of the participants to these associations is subject to an entirely new process of differentiation.

The medieval corporations included in themselves all the human interests. A guild of cloth-makers was not an association of individuals which cultivated the interests of cloth-making exclusively. It was a community in a vocational, personal, religious, political sense and in many other respects. And however technical the interests that might be grouped together in such an association, they had an immediate and lively interest for all members. Members were wholly bound up in the association.

In contrast to this form of organization the capitalistic system has made possible innumerable associations which either require from their members merely money contributions or are directed toward mere money interests. In the case of the business corporation, especially, the basis of organization of members is exclusively an interest in the dividends, so exclusively that it is a matter of entire indifference to the individual what the society (enterprise) actually produces.

The independence of the person of the concrete objects, in which he has a mere money interest, is reflected, likewise, in his independence,

[1] Translated from Georg Simmel, *Philosophie des Geldes*, pp. 351–52. (Duncker und Humblot, 1900.)

in his personal relations, of the other individuals with whom he is connected by an exclusive money interest. This has produced one of the most effective cultural formations—one which makes it possible for individuals to take part in an association whose objective aim it will promote, use, and enjoy without this association bringing with it any further personal connection or imposing any further obligation. Money has brought it about that one individual may unite himself with others without being compelled to surrender any of his personal freedom or reserve. That is the fundamental and unspeakably significant difference between the medieval form of organization which made no difference between the association of men as men and the association of men as members of an organization. The medieval form or organization united equally in one circle the entire business, religious, political, and friendly interests of the individuals who composed it.

CHAPTER VII

CONFLICT

I. INTRODUCTION

1. The Concept of Conflict

The distinction between competition and conflict has already been indicated. Both are forms of interaction, but competition is a struggle between individuals, or groups of individuals, who are not necessarily in contact and communication; while conflict is a contest in which contact is an indispensable condition. Competition, unqualified and uncontrolled as with plants, and in the great impersonal life-struggle of man with his kind and with all animate nature, is unconscious. Conflict is always conscious, indeed, it evokes the deepest emotions and strongest passions and enlists the greatest concentration of attention and of effort. Both competition and conflict are forms of struggle. Competition, however, is continuous and impersonal, conflict is intermittent and personal.

Competition is a struggle for position in an economic order. The distribution of populations in the world-economy, the industrial organization in the national economy, and the vocation of the individual in the division of labor—all these are determined, in the long run, by competition. The status of the individual, or a group of individuals, in the social order, on the other hand, is determined by rivalry, by war, or by subtler forms of conflict.

"Two is company, three is a crowd" suggests how easily the social equilibrium is disturbed by the entrance of a new factor in a social situation. The delicate nuances and grades of attention given to different individuals moving in the same social circle are the superficial reflections of rivalries and conflicts beneath the smooth and decorous surfaces of polite society.

In general, we may say that competition determines the position of the individual in the community; conflict fixes his place in society. Location, position, ecological interdependence—these are the characteristics of the community. Status, subordination and super-ordination, control—these are the distinctive marks of a society.

The notion of conflict, like the fact, has its roots deep in human interest. Mars has always held a high rank in the hierarchy of the gods. Whenever and wherever struggle has taken the form of con-flict, whether of races, of nations, or of individual men, it has invari-ably captured and held the attention of spectators. And these spectators, when they did not take part in the fight, always took sides. It was this conflict of the non-combatants that made public opinion, and public opinion has always played an important rôle in the struggles of men. It is this that has raised war from a mere play of physical forces and given it the tragic significance of a moral struggle, a conflict of good and evil.

The result is that war tends to assume the character of litigation, a judicial procedure, in which custom determines the method of procedure, and the issue of the struggle is accepted as a judgment in the case.

The duello, as distinguished from the wager of battle, although it never had the character of a judicial procedure, developed a strict code which made it morally binding upon the individual to seek redress for wrongs, and determined in advance the methods of pro-cedure by which such redress could and should be obtained. The penalty was a loss of status in the particular group of which the individual was a member.

It was the presence of the public, the ceremonial character of the proceedings, and the conviction that the invisible powers were on the side of truth and justice that gave the trial by ordeal and the trial by battle a significance that neither the duello nor any other form of private vengeance ever had.

It is interesting in this connection, also, that political and judicial forms of procedure are conducted on a conflict pattern. An election is a contest in which we count noses when we do not break heads. A trial by jury is a contest in which the parties are represented by champions, as in the judicial duels of an earlier time.

In general, then, one may say competition becomes conscious and personal in conflict. In the process of transition competitors are transformed into rivals and enemies. In its higher forms, however, conflict becomes impersonal—a struggle to establish and maintain rules of justice and a moral order. In this case the welfare not merely of individual men but of the community is involved. Such are the struggles of political parties and religious sects. Here the issues are not determined by the force and weight of the contestants immediately involved, but to a greater or less extent, by the force and weight of public opinion of the community, and eventually by the judgment of mankind.

2. Classification of the Materials

The materials on conflict have been organized in the readings under four heads: (a) conflict as conscious competition; (b) war, instincts, and ideals; (c) rivalry, cultural conflicts, and social organization; and (d) race conflicts.

a) *Conscious competition.*—Self-consciousness in the individual arises in the contacts and conflicts of the person with other persons. It manifests itself variously in pride and in humility, vanity and self-respect, modesty and arrogance, pity and disdain, as well as in race prejudice, chauvinism, class and caste distinctions, and in every other social device by which the social distances are maintained.

It is in these various responses called forth by social contacts and intercourse that the personality of the individual is developed and his status defined. It is in the effort to maintain this status or improve it; to defend this personality, enlarge its possessions, extend its privileges, and maintain its prestige that conflicts arise. This applies to all conflicts, whether they are personal and party squabbles, sectarian differences, or national and patriotic wars, for the personality of the individual is invariably so bound up with the interests and order of his group and clan, that, in a struggle, he makes the group cause his own.

Much has been said and written about the economic causes of war, but whatever may be the ultimate sources of our sentiments, it is probably true that men never go to war for economic reasons merely. It is because wealth and possessions are bound up with prestige, honor, and position in the world, that men and nations fight about them.

b) *War, instincts, and ideals.*—War is the outstanding and the typical example of conflict. In war, where hostility prevails over every interest of sentiment or utility which would otherwise unite the contending parties or groups, the motives and the rôle of conflict in social life present themselves in their clearest outline. There is, moreover, a practical reason for fixing upon war as an illustration of conflict. The tremendous interest in all times manifested in war, the amazing energies and resources released in peoples organized for military aggression or defense, the colossal losses and sacrifices endured for the glory, the honor, or the security of the fatherland have made wars memorable. Of no other of the larger aspects of collective life have we such adequate records.

The problem of the relation of war to human instincts, on the one hand, and to human ideals, on the other, is the issue about which most recent observation and discussion has centered. It seems idle to assert that hostility has no roots in man's original nature. The concrete materials given in this chapter show beyond question how readily the wishes and the instincts of the person may take the form of the fighting pattern. On the other hand, the notion that tradition, culture, and collective representations have no part in determining the attitudes of nations toward war seems equally untenable. The significant sociological inquiry is to determine just in what ways a conjunction of the tendencies in original nature, the forces of tradition and culture, and the exigencies of the situation determine the organization of the fighting pattern. We have historical examples of warlike peoples becoming peaceful and of pacific nations militaristic. An understanding of the mechanism of the process is a first condition to any exercise of control.

c) Rivalry, cultural conflicts, and social organization.—Rivalry is a sublimated form of conflict where the struggle of individuals is subordinated to the welfare of the group. In the rivalry of groups, likewise, conflict or competition is subordinated to the interests of an inclusive group. Rivalry may then be defined as conflict controlled by the group in its interest. A survey of the phenomena of rivalry brings out its rôle as an organizing force in group life.

In the study of conflict groups it is not always easy to apply with certainty the distinction between rivalry and conflict made here. The sect is a conflict group. In its struggle for survival and success with other groups, its aim is the highest welfare of the inclusive society. Actually, however, sectarian warfare may be against the moral, social, and religious interests of the community. The denomination, which is an accommodation group, strives through rivalry and competition, not only to promote the welfare of the inclusive society, but also of its other component groups.

In cultural and political conflict the function of conflict in social life becomes understandable and reasonable. The rôle of mental conflicts in the life of the individual is for the purpose of making adjustments to changing situations and of assimilating new experiences. It is through this process of conflict of divergent impulses to act that the individual arrives at decisions—as we say, "makes up his mind." Only where there is conflict is behavior conscious and self-conscious; only here are the conditions for rational conduct.

d) Race conflicts.—Nowhere do social contacts so readily provoke conflicts as in the relations between the races, particularly when racial differences are re-enforced, not merely by differences of culture, but of color. Nowhere, it might be added, are the responses to social contact so obvious and, at the same time, so difficult to analyze and define.

Race prejudice, as we call the sentiments that support the racial taboos, is not, in America at least, an obscure phenomenon. But no one has yet succeeded in making it wholly intelligible. It is evident that there is in race prejudice, as distinguished from class and caste prejudice, an instinctive factor based on the fear of the unfamiliar and the uncomprehended. Color, or any other racial mark that emphasizes physical differences, becomes the symbol of moral divergences which perhaps do not exist. We at once fear and are fascinated by the stranger, and an individual of a different race always seems more of a stranger to us than one of our own. This naïve prejudice, unless it is re-enforced by other factors, is easily modified, as the intimate relations of the Negroes and white man in slavery show.

A more positive factor in racial antagonism is the conflict of cultures: the unwillingness of one race to enter into personal competition with a race of a different or inferior culture. This turns out, in the long run, to be the unwillingness of a people or a class occupying a superior status to compete on equal terms with a people of a lower status. Race conflicts like wars are fundamentally the struggles of racial groups for status. In this sense and from this point of view the struggles of the European nationalities and the so-called "subject peoples" for independence and self-determination are actually struggles for status in the family of nations.

Under the conditions of this struggle, racial or national consciousness as it manifests itself, for example, in Irish nationalism, Jewish Zionism, and Negro race consciousness, is the natural and obvious response to a conflict situation. The nationalistic movements in Europe, in India, and in Egypt are, like war, rivalry and more personal forms of conflict, mainly struggles for recognition— that is, honor, glory, and prestige.

II. MATERIALS

A. CONFLICT AS CONSCIOUS COMPETITION

1. The Natural History of Conflict[1]

All classes of society, and the two sexes to about the same degree, are deeply interested in all forms of contest involving skill and chance, especially where the danger or risk is great. Everybody will stop to watch a street fight, and the same persons would show an equal interest in a prize fight or a bull fight, if certain scruples did not stand in the way of their looking on. Our socially developed sympathy and pity may recoil from witnessing a scene where physical hurt is the object of the game, but the depth of our interest in the conflict type of activity is attested by the fascination which such a game as football has for the masses, where our instinctive emotional reaction to a conflict situation is gratified to an intense degree by a scene of the conflict pattern.

If we examine, in fact, our pleasures and pains, our moments of elation and depression, we find that they go back for the most part to instincts developed in the struggle for food and rivalry for mates. The structure of the organism has been built up gradually through the survival of the most efficient structures. Corresponding with a structure mechanically adapted to successful movements, there is developed on the psychic side an interest in the conflict situation as complete and perfect as is the structure itself. The emotional states are, indeed, organic preparations for action, corresponding broadly with

[1] Adapted from William I. Thomas, "The Gaming Instinct," in the *American Journal of Sociology*, VI (1900–1901), 750–63.

a tendency to advance or retreat; and a connection has even been made out between pleasurable states and the extensor muscles, and painful states and the flexor muscles. We can have no adequate idea of the time consumed and the experiments made in nature before the development of these types of structure and interest of the conflict pattern, but we know from the geological records that the time and experiments were long and many, and the competition so sharp that finally, not in man alone, but in all the higher classes of animals, body and mind, structure and interest, were working perfectly in motor actions of the violent type involved in a life of conflict, competition, and rivalry. There could not have been developed an organism depending on offensive and defensive movements for food and life without an interest in what we call a dangerous or precarious situation. A type without this interest would have been defective, and would have dropped out in the course of development.

The fact that our interests and enthusiasms are called out in situations of the conflict type is shown by a glance at the situations which arouse them most readily. War is simply an organized form of fight, and as such is most attractive, or, to say the least, arouses the interests powerfully. With the accumulation of property and the growth of sensibility and intelligence it becomes apparent that war is a wasteful and unsafe process, and public and personal interests lead us to avoid it as much as possible. But, however genuinely war may be deprecated, it is certainly an exciting game. The Rough Riders in this country recently, and more recently the young men of the aristocracy of England, went to war from motives of patriotism, no doubt, but there are unmistakable evidences that they also regarded it as the greatest sport they were likely to have a chance at in a lifetime. And there is evidence in plenty that the emotional attitude of women toward war is no less intense. Grey relates that half a dozen old women among the Australians will drive the men to war with a neighboring tribe over a fancied injury. The Jewish maidens went out with music and dancing and sang that Saul had slain his thousands, but David his ten thousands. The young women of Havana are alleged, during the late Spanish War, to have sent pieces of their wardrobe to young men of their acquaintance who hesitated to join the rebellion, with the suggestion that they wear these until they went to the war.

The feud is another mode of reaction of the violent, instinctive, and attractive type. The feud was originally of defensive value to the individual and to the tribe, since in the absence of criminal law the feeling that retaliation would follow was a deterrent from acts of aggression. But it was an expensive method of obtaining order in early society, since response to stimulus reinstated the stimulus, and every death called for another death; so, finally, after many experiments and devices, the state has forbidden the individual to take justice into his own hands. In out-of-the-way places, however, where governmental control is weak, men still settle their disputes personally, and one who is familiar with the course of a feud cannot avoid the conclusion that this practice is kept up, not because there is no law to resort to, but because the older mode is more immediate and fascinating. I mean simply that the emotional possibilities and actual emotional reactions in the feud are far more powerful than in due legal process.

Gladiatorial shows, bear baiting, bull fighting, dog and cock fighting, and prize fighting afford an opportunity to gratify the interest in conflict. The spectator has by suggestion emotional reactions analogous to those of the combatant, but without personal danger; and vicarious contests between slaves, captives, and animals, whose blood and life are cheap, are a pleasure which the race allowed itself until a higher stage of morality was reached. Pugilism is the modification of the fight in a slightly different way. The combatants are members of society, not slaves or captives, but the conflict is so qualified as to safeguard their lives, though injury is possible and is actually planned. The intention to do hurt is the point to which society and the law object. But the prize fight is a fight as far as it goes, and the difficulties which men will surmount to "pull off" and to witness these contests are sufficient proof of their fascination. A football game is also a fight, with the additional qualification that no injury is planned, and with an advantage over the prize fight in the fact that it is not a single-handed conflict, but an organized mêlée—a battle where the action is more massive and complex and the strategic opportunities are multiplied. It is a fact of interest in this connection that, unless appearances are deceptive, altogether the larger number of visitors to a university during the year are visitors to the football field. It is the only phase of university life which appeals directly and powerfully to the instincts, and it is consequently the only phase of university life which appeals equally to the man of culture, the artist, the business man, the man about town, the all-round sport, and, in fact, to all the world.

The instincts of man are congenital; the arts and industries are acquired by the race and must be learned by the individual after birth. We have seen why the instinctive activities are pleasurable and the acquired habits irksome. The gambler represents a class of men who have not been weaned from their instincts. There are in every species biological "sports" and reversions, and there are individuals of this kind among sporting men who are not reached by ordinary social suggestion and stimuli. But granting that what we may call the instinctive interests are disproportionately strong in the sporting class, as compared with, say, the merchant class, yet these instincts are also strongly marked in what may roughly be called the artist class and in spite of a marked psychic disposition for stimuli of the emotional type; and precisely because of this disposition, the artist class has a very high social value. Art products are, indeed, perhaps more highly esteemed than any other products whatever. The artist class is not, therefore, socially unmanageable because of its instinctive interest, though perhaps we may say that some of its members are saved from social vagabondage only because their emotional predisposition has found an expression in emotional activities to which some social value can be attached.

2. Conflict as a Type of Social Interaction[1]

That conflict has sociological significance inasmuch as it either produces or modifies communities of interest, unifications, organizations, is in principle never contested. On the other hand, it must appear paradoxical to the ordinary mode of thinking to ask whether conflict itself, without reference to its consequences or its accompaniments, is not a form of socialization. This seems, at first glance, to be merely a verbal question. If every reaction among men is a socialization, of course conflict must count as such, since it is one of the most intense reactions and is logically impossible if restricted to a

[1] Adapted from a translation of Georg Simmel, *Soziologie*, by Albion W. Small, "The Sociology of Conflict," in the *American Journal of Sociology*, IX (1903–4), 490–501.

single element. The actually dissociating elements are the causes of the conflict—hatred and envy, want and desire. If, however, from these impulses conflict has once broken out, it is in reality the way to remove the dualism and to arrive at some form of unity, even if through annihilation of one of the parties. The case is, in a way, illustrated by the most violent symptoms of disease. They frequently represent the efforts of the organism to free itself from disorders and injuries. This is by no means equivalent merely to the triviality, *si vis pacem para bellum*, but it is the wide generalization of which that special case is a particular. Conflict itself is the resolution of the tension between the contraries. That it eventuates in peace is only a single, specially obvious and evident, expression of the fact that it is a conjunction of elements.

As the individual achieves the unity of his personality, not in such fashion that its contents invariably harmonize according to logical or material, religious or ethical, standards, but rather as contradiction and strife not merely precede that unity but are operative in it at every moment of life; so it is hardly to be expected that there should be any social unity in which the converging tendencies of the elements are not incessantly shot through with elements of divergence. A group which was entirely centripetal and harmonious—that is, "unification" merely—is not only impossible empirically, but it would also display no essential life-process and no stable structure. As the cosmos requires *Liebe und Hass*, attraction and repulsion, in order to have a form, society likewise requires some quantitative relation of harmony and disharmony, association and dissociation, liking and disliking, in order to attain to a definite formation. Society, as it is given in fact, is the result of both categories of reactions, and in so far both act in a completely positive way. The misconception that the one factor tears down what the other builds up, and that what at last remains is the result of subtracting the one from the other (while in reality it is much rather to be regarded as the addition of one to the other), doubtless springs from the equivocal sense of the concept of unity.

We describe as unity the agreement and the conjunction of social elements in contrast with their disjunctions, separations, disharmonies. We also use the term unity, however, for the total synthesis of the persons, energies, and forms in a group, in which the final wholeness is made up, not merely of those factors which are unifying in the narrower sense, but also of those which are, in the narrower sense, dualistic. We associate a corresponding double meaning with disunity or opposition. Since the latter displays its nullifying or destructive sense *between the individual elements*, the conclusion is hastily drawn that it must work in the same manner upon the *total relationship*. In reality, however, it by no means follows that the factor which is something negative and diminutive in its action between individuals, considered in a given direction and separately, has the same working throughout the totality of its relationships. In this larger circle of relationships the perspective may be quite different. That which was negative and dualistic may, after deduction of its destructive action in particular relationships, on the whole, play an entirely positive rôle. This visibly appears especially in those instances where the social structure is characterized by exactness and carefully conserved purity of social divisions and gradations.

The social system of India rests not only upon the hierarchy of the castes but also directly upon the reciprocal repulsion. Enmities not merely prevent gradual disappearance of the boundaries within the society—and for this reason these enmities may be consciously promoted, as guaranty of the existing social constitution—but more than this, the enmities are directly productive sociologically. They give classes and personalities their position toward each other, which they would not have found if these objective causes of hostility had been present and effective in precisely the same way but had not been accompanied by the feeling of enmity. It is by no means certain that a secure and complete community life would always result if these energies should disappear which, looked at in detail, seem repulsive and destructive, just as a qualitatively unchanged and richer property results when unproductive elements disappear; but there would ensue rather a condition as changed, and often as unrealizable, as after the elimination of the forces of co-operation—sympathy, assistance, harmony of interests.

The opposition of one individual element to another in the same association is by no means merely a negative social factor, but it is in many ways the only means through which coexistence with individuals intolerable in themselves could be possible. If we had not power and right to oppose tyranny and obstinacy, caprice and tactlessness, we could not endure relations with people who betray such characteristics. We should be driven to deeds of desperation which would put the relationships to an end. This follows not alone for the self-evident reason—which, however, is not here essential—that such disagreeable circumstances tend to become intensified if they are endured quietly and without protest; but, more than this, opposition affords us a subjective satisfaction, diversion, relief, just as under other psychological conditions, whose variations need not here be discussed, the same results are brought about by humility and patience. Our opposition gives us the feeling that we are not completely crushed in the relationship. It permits us to preserve a consciousness of energy, and thus lends a vitality and a reciprocity to relationships from which, without this corrective, we should have extricated ourselves at any price. In case the relationships are purely external, and consequently do not reach deeply into the practical, the latent form of conflict discharges this service, i.e., aversion, the feeling of reciprocal alienation and repulsion, which in the moment of a more intimate contact of any sort is at once transformed into positive hatred and conflict. Without this aversion life in a great city, which daily brings each into contact with countless others, would have no thinkable form. The activity of our minds responds to almost every impression received from other people in some sort of a definite feeling, all the unconsciousness, transience, and variability of which seem to remain only in the form of a certain indifference. In fact, this latter would be as unnatural for us as it would be intolerable to be swamped under a multitude of suggestions among which we have no choice. Antipathy protects us against these two typical dangers of the great city. It is the initial stage of practical antagonism. It produces the distances and the buffers without which this kind of life could not be led at all. The mass and the mixtures of this life, the forms in which it is carried on, the rhythm of its rise and fall—these unite with the unifying motives, in the narrower sense, to give to a great city the character of an indissoluble whole. Whatever in this whole seems to be an element of division is thus in reality only one of its elementary forms of socialization.

A struggle for struggle's sake seems to have its natural basis in a certain formal impulse of hostility, which forces itself sometimes upon psychological observation, and in various forms. In the first place, it appears as that natural enmity between man and man which is often emphasized by skeptical moralists. The argument is: Since there is something not wholly displeasing to us in the misfortune of our best friends, and, since the presupposition excludes, in this instance, conflict of material interests, the phenomenon must be traced back to an a priori hostility, to that *homo homini lupus*, as the frequently veiled, but perhaps never inoperative, basis of all our relationships.

3. Types of Conflict Situations[1]

a) War.—The reciprocal relationship of primitive groups is notoriously, and for reasons frequently discussed almost invariably, one of hostility. The decisive illustration is furnished perhaps by the American Indians, among whom every tribe on general principles was supposed to be on a war footing' toward every other tribe with which it had no express treaty of peace. It is, however, not to be forgotten that in early stages of culture war constitutes almost the only form in which contact with an alien group occurs. So long as inter-territorial trade was undeveloped, individual tourneys unknown, and intellectual community did not extend beyond the group boundaries, there was, outside of war, no sociological relationship whatever between the various groups. In this case the relationship of the elements of the group to each other and that of the primitive groups to each other present completely contrasted forms. Within the closed circle hostility signifies, as a rule, the severing of relationships, voluntary isolation, and the avoidance of contact. Along with these negative phenomena there will also appear the phenomena of the passionate reaction of open struggle. On the other hand, the group as a whole remains indifferently side by side with similar groups so long as peace exists. The consequence is that these groups become significant for each other only when war breaks out. That the attitude of hostility, considered likewise from this point of view, may arise independently in the soul is the less to be doubted since it represents here, as in many another easily observable situation, the

[1] Adapted from a translation of Georg Simmel, *Soziologie*, by Albion W. Small, "The Sociology of Conflict," in the *American Journal of Sociology*, IX (1903–4), 505–8.

embodiment of an impulse which is in the first place quite general, but which also occurs in quite peculiar forms, namely, *the impulse to act in relationships with others.*

In spite of this spontaneity and independence, which we may thus attribute to the antagonistic impulse, there still remains the question whether it suffices to account for the total phenomena of hostility. This question must be answered in the negative. In the first place, the spontaneous impulse does not exercise itself upon every object but only upon those that are in some way promising. Hunger, for example, springs from the subject. It does not have its origin in the object. Nevertheless, it will not attempt to satisfy itself with wood or stone but it will select only edible objects. In the same way, love and hatred, however little their impulses may depend upon external stimuli, will yet need some sort of opposing object, and only with such co-operation will the complete phenomena appear. On the other hand, it seems to me probable that the hostile impulse, on account of its formal character, in general intervenes, only as a reinforcement of conflicts stimulated by material interest, and at the same time furnishes a foundation for the conflict. And where a struggle springs up from sheer formal love of fighting, which is also entirely impersonal and indifferent both to the material at issue and to the personal opponent, hatred and fury against the opponent as a person unavoidably increase in the course of the conflict, and probably also the interest in the stake at issue, because these affections stimulate and feed the psychical energy of the struggle. It is advantageous to hate the opponent with whom one is for any reason struggling, as it is useful to love him with whom one's lot is united and with whom one must co-operate. The reciprocal attitude of men is often intelligible only on the basis of the perception that actual adaptation to a situation teaches us those feelings which are appropriate to it; feelings which are the most appropriate to the employment or the overcoming of the circumstances of the situation; feelings which bring us, through psychical association, the energies necessary for discharging the momentary task and for defeating the opposing impulses.

Accordingly, no serious struggle can long continue without being supported by a complex of psychic impulses. These may, to be sure, gradually develop into effectiveness in the course of the struggle.

The purity of conflict merely for conflict's sake, accordingly, undergoes adulteration, partly through the admixture of objective interests, partly by the introduction of impulses which may be satisfied otherwise than by struggle, and which, in practice, form a bridge between struggle and other forms of reciprocal relationship.   I know in fact only a single case in which the stimulus of struggle and of victory in itself constitutes the exclusive motive, namely, the war game, and only in the case that no further gain is to arise than is included in the outcome of the game itself.   In this case the pure sociological attraction of self-assertion and predominance over another in a struggle of skill is combined with purely individual pleasure in the exercise of purposeful and successful activity, together with the excitement of taking risks with the hazard of fortune which stimulates us with a sense of mystic harmony of relationship to powers beyond the individual, as well as the social occurrences.   At all events, the war game, *in its sociological motivation,* contains absolutely nothing but struggle itself.   The worthless markers, for the sake of which men often play with the same earnestness with which they play for gold pieces, indicate the formalism of this impulse which, even in the play for gold pieces, often far outweighs the material interest.   The thing to be noticed, however, is that, in order that the foregoing situations may occur, certain sociological forms—in the narrower sense, unifications—are presupposed.   There must be agreement in order to struggle, and the struggle occurs under reciprocal recognition of norms and rules.   In the motivation of the whole procedure these unifications, as said above, do not appear, but the whole transaction shapes itself under the forms which these explicit or implicit agreements furnish.   They create the technique.   Without this, such a conflict, excluding all heterogeneous or objective factors, would not be possible.   Indeed, the conduct of the war game is often so rigorous, so impersonal, and observed on both sides with such nice sense of honor that unities of a corporate order can seldom in these respects compare with it.

b) Feud and faction.—The occasion for separate discussion of the feud is that here, instead of the consciousness of difference, an entirely new motive emerges—the peculiar phenomenon of social hatred, that is, of hatred toward a member of a group, not from personal motives, but because he threatens the existence of the group.

In so far as such a danger threatens through feud within the group, the one party hates the other, not alone on the material ground which instigated the quarrel, but also on the sociological ground, namely, that we hate the enemy of the group as such; that is, the one from whom danger to its unity threatens. Inasmuch as this is a reciprocal matter, and each attributes the fault of endangering the whole to the other, the antagonism acquires a severity which does not occur when membership in a group-unity is not a factor in the situation. Most characteristic in this connection are the cases in which an actual dismemberment of the group has not yet occurred. If this dismemberment has already taken place, it signifies a certain termination of the conflict. The individual difference has found its sociological termination, and the stimulus to constantly renewed friction is removed. To this result the tension between antagonism and still persisting unity must directly work. As it is fearful to be at enmity with a person to whom one is nevertheless bound, from whom one cannot be freed, whether externally or subjectively, even if one will, so there is increased bitterness if one will not detach himself from the community because he is not willing to give up the value of membership in the containing unity, or because he feels this unity as an objective good, the threatening of which deserves conflict and hatred. From such a correlation as this springs the embittering with which, for example, quarrels are fought out within a political faction or a trade union or a family.

The individual soul offers an analogy. The feeling that a conflict between sensuous and ascetic feelings, or selfish and moral impulses, or practical and intellectual ambitions, within us not merely lowers the claims of one or both parties and permits neither to come to quite free self-realization but also threatens the unity, the equilibrium, and the total energy of the soul as a whole—this feeling may in many cases repress conflict from the beginning. In case the feeling cannot avail to that extent, it, on the contrary, impresses upon the conflict a character of bitterness and desperation, an emphasis as though a struggle were really taking place for something much more essential than the immediate issue of the controversy. The energy with which each of these tendencies seeks to subdue the others is nourished not only by their egoistic interest but by the interest which goes much farther than that and attaches itself to the unity of the

ego, for which this struggle means dismemberment and destruction
if it does not end with a victory for unity. Accordingly, struggle
within a closely integrated group often enough grows beyond the
measure which its object and its immediate interest for the parties
could justify. The feeling accumulates that this struggle is an affair
not merely of the party but of the group as a whole; that each party
must hate in its opponent, not an opponent merely, but at the
same time the enemy of its higher sociological unity.

c) *Litigation.*—Moreover, what we are accustomed to call the
joy and passion of conflict in the case of a legal process is probably,
in most cases, something quite different, namely, the energetic sense
of justice, the impossibility of tolerating an actual or supposed invasion
of the sphere of right with which the ego feels a sense of solidarity.
The whole obstinacy and uncompromising persistence with which
parties in such struggles often maintain the controversy to their
own hurt has, even in the case of the aggressive party, scarcely the
character of an attack in the proper sense, but rather of a defense in
a deeper significance. The point at issue is the self-preservation of
the personality which so identifies itself with its possessions and its
rights that any invasion of them seems to be a destruction of the
personality; and the struggle to protect them at the risk of the
whole existence is thoroughly consistent. This individualistic
impulse, and not the sociological motive of struggle, will consequently
characterize such cases.

With respect to the form of the struggle itself, however, judicial
conflict is, to be sure, of an absolute sort; that is, the reciprocal
claims are asserted with a relentless objectivity and with employment
of all available means, without being diverted or modified by personal
or other extraneous considerations. The judicial conflict is, therefore, absolute conflict in so far as nothing enters the whole action
which does not properly belong in the conflict and which does not
serve the ends of conflict; whereas, otherwise, even in the most
savage struggles, something subjective, some pure freak of fortune,
some sort of interposition from a third side, is at least possible. In
the legal struggle everything of the kind is excluded by the matter-
of-factness with which the contention, and absolutely nothing outside the contention, is kept in view. This exclusion from the judicial
controversy of everything which is not material to the conflict may

to be sure, lead to a formalism of the struggle which may come to
have an independent character in contrast with the content itself.
This occurs, on the one hand, when real elements are not weighed
against each other at all but only quite abstract notions maintain
controversy with each other. On the other hand, the controversy is
often shifted to elements which have no relation whatever to the
subject which is to be decided by the struggle. Where legal controversies, accordingly, in higher civilizations are fought out by
attorneys, the device serves to abstract the controversy from all
personal associations which are essentially irrelevant. If, on the other
hand, Otto the Great ordains that a legal controversy shall be settled
by judicial duel between professional fighters, there remains of the
whole struggle of interests only the bare form, namely, that there
shall be struggle and victory.

This latter case portrays, in the exaggeration of caricature, the
reduction of the judicial conflict to the mere struggle element. But
precisely through its pure objectivity because it stands quite beyond
the subjective antitheses of pity and cruelty, this unpitying type of
struggle, as a whole, rests on the presupposition of a unity and a
community of the parties never elsewhere so severely and constantly
maintained. The common subordination to the law, the reciprocal
recognition that the decision can be made only according to the
objective weight of the evidence, the observance of forms which are
held to be inviolable by both parties, the consciousness throughout
the whole procedure of being encompassed by a social power and order
which are the means of giving to the procedure its significance and
security—all this makes the legal controversy rest upon a broad
basis of community and consensus between the opponents. It is
really a unity of a lesser degree which is constituted by the parties
to a compact or to a commercial transaction, a presupposition of
which is the recognition, along with the antithesis of interests, that
they are subject to certain common, constraining, and obligatory
rules. The common presuppositions, which exclude everything that
is merely personal from the legal controversy, have that character of
pure objectivity to which, on its side, the sharpness, the inexorableness,
and the absoluteness of the species of struggle correspond. The
reciprocity between the dualism and the unity of the sociological
relationship is accordingly shown by the judicial struggle not less

than by the war game. Precisely the most extreme and unlimited phases of struggle occur in both cases, since the struggle is surrounded and maintained by the severe unity of common norms and limitations.

d) *The conflict of impersonal ideals.*—Finally, there is the situation in which the parties are moved by an objective interest; that is, where the interest of the struggle, and consequently the struggle itself, is differentiated from the personality. The consciousness of being merely the representative of superindividual claims—that is, of fighting not for self but only for the thing itself—may lend to the struggle a radicalism and mercilessness which have their analogy in the total conduct of many very unselfish and high-minded men. Because they grant themselves no consideration, they likewise have none for others and hold themselves entirely justified in sacrificing everybody else to the idea to which they are themselves a sacrifice. Such a struggle, into which all the powers of the person are thrown, while victory accrues only to the cause, carries the character of respectability, for the reputable man is the wholly personal, who, however, understands how to hold his personality entirely in check. Hence objectivity operates as *noblesse*. When, however, this differentiation is accomplished, and struggle is objectified, it is not subjected to a further reserve, which would be quite inconsistent; indeed, that would be a sin against the content of the interest itself upon which the struggle had been localized. On the basis of this common element between the parties—namely, that each defends merely the issue and its right, and excludes from consideration everything selfishly personal—the struggle is fought out without the sharpness, but also without the mollifyings, which come from intermingling of the personal element. Merely the immanent logic of the situation is obeyed with absolute precision. This form of antithesis between unity and antagonism intensifies conflict perhaps most perceptibly in cases where both parties actually pursue one and the same purpose; for example, in the case of scientific controversies, in which the issue is the establishment of the truth. In such a case, every concession, every polite consent to stop short of exposing the errors of the opponent in the most unpitying fashion, every conclusion of peace previous to decisive victory, would be treason against that reality for the sake of which the personal element is excluded from the conflict.

With endless varieties otherwise, the social struggles since Marx have developed themselves in the above form. Since it is recognized that the situation of laborers is determined by the objective organization and formulas of the productive system, independent of the will and power of individual persons, the personal embitterment incident to the struggle in general and to local conflicts exemplifying the general conflict necessarily diminishes. The entrepreneur is no longer, as such, a blood-sucker and damnable egotist; the laborer is no longer universally assumed to act from sinful greed; both parties begin, at least, to abandon the program of charging the other with demands and tactics inspired by personal malevolence. This literalizing of the conflict has come about in Germany rather along the lines of theory; in England, through the operation of the trade unions, in the course of which the individually personal element of the antagonism has been overcome. In Germany this was effected largely through the more abstract generalization of the historical and class movement. In England it came about through the severe superindividual unity in the actions of the unions and of the combinations of employers. The intensity of the struggle, however, has not on that account diminished. On the contrary, it has become much more conscious of its purpose, more concentrated, and at the same time more aggressive, through the consciousness of the individual that he is struggling not merely, and often not at all, for himself but rather for a vast superpersonal end.

A most interesting symptom of this correlation was presented by the boycotting of the Berlin breweries by the labor body in the year 1894. This was one of the most intense local struggles of the last decade. It was carried on by both sides with extraordinary energy, yet without any personal offensiveness on either side toward the other, although the stimulus was close at hand. Indeed, two of the party leaders, in the midst of the struggle, published their opinions about it in the same journal. They agreed in their formulation of the objective facts, and disagreed in a partisan spirit only in the practical conclusions drawn from the facts. Inasmuch as the struggle eliminated everything irrelevantly personal, and thereby restricted antagonism quantitatively, facilitating an understanding about everything personal, producing a recognition of being impelled on both sides by historical necessities, this common basis did not reduce but rather increased, the intensity, the irreconcilability, and the obstinate consistency of the struggle.

B.   WAR, INSTINCTS, AND IDEALS

1. War and Human Nature[1]

What can be said of the causes of war—not its political and economic causes, nor yet the causes that are put forth by the nations engaged in the conflict, but its psychological causes?

The fact that war to no small extent removes cultural repressions and allows the instincts to come to expression in full force is undoubtedly a considerable factor.   In his unconscious man really takes pleasure in throwing aside restraints and permitting himself the luxury of the untrammeled expression of his primitive animal tendencies.   The social conventions, the customs, the forms, and institutions which he has built up in the path of his cultural progress represent so much energy in the service of repression. Repression represents continuous effort, while a state of war permits a relaxation of this effort and therefore relief.

We are familiar, in other fields, with the phenomena of the unconscious, instinctive tendencies breaking through the bounds imposed upon them by repression.   The phenomena of crime and of so-called "insanity" represent such examples, while drunkenness is one instance familiar to all.   *In vino veritas* expresses the state of the drunken man when his real, that is, his primitive, self frees itself from restraint and runs riot.   The psychology of the crowd shows this mechanism at work, particularly in such sinister instances as lynching, while every crowd of college students marching yelling and howling down the main street of the town after a successful cane rush exhibits the joy of unbottling the emotions in ways that no individual would for a moment think of availing himself.

In addition to these active demonstrations of the unconscious there are those of a more passive sort.   Not a few men are only too glad to step aside from the burden of responsibilities which they are forced to carry and seek refuge in a situation in which they no longer have to take the initiative but must only do as they are directed by a superior authority.   The government in some of its agencies takes

[1] Adapted from William A. White, *Thoughts of a Psychiatrist on the War and After*, pp. 75–87.   (Paul B. Hoeber, 1919.)

over certain of their obligations, such as the support of wife and children, and they clear out, free from the whole sordid problem of poverty, into a situation filled with dramatic interest. Then, too, if anything goes wrong at home they are not to blame, they have done their best, and what they have done meets with public approval. Is it any wonder that an inhabitant of the slums should be glad to exchange poverty and dirt, a sick wife and half-starved children, for glorious freedom, especially when he is urged by every sort of appeal to patriotism and duty to do so?

But all these are individual factors that enter into the causes of war. They represent some of the reasons why men like to fight, for it is difficult not to believe that if no one wanted to fight war would be possible at all. They too represent the darker side of the picture. War as already indicated offers, on the positive side, the greatest opportunities for the altruistic tendencies; it offers the most glorious occasion for service and returns for such acts the greatest possible premium in social esteem. But it seems to me that the causes of war lie much deeper, that they involve primarily the problems of the herd rather than the individual, and I think there are good biological analogies which make this highly probable.

The mechanism of integration explains how the development of the group was dependent upon the subordination of the parts to the whole. This process of integration tends to solve more and more effectively the problems of adjustment, particularly in some aspects, in the direction of ever-increasing stability. It is the process of the structuralization of function. This increase in stability, however, while it has the advantage of greater certainty of reaction, has the disadvantage of a lessened capacity for variation, and so is dependent for its efficiency upon a stable environment. As long as nothing unusual is asked of such a mechanism it works admirably, but as soon as the unusual arises it tends to break down completely. Life, however, is not stable; it is fluid, in a continuous state of flux, so, while the development of structure to meet certain demands of adaptation is highly desirable and necessary, it of necessity has limits which must sooner or later be reached in every instance. The most typical example of this is the process of growing old. The child is highly adjustable and for that reason not to be depended upon; the adult is more dependable but less adjustable; the old man has become stereotyped in his reactions. Nature's solution of this *impasse* is death. Death insures the continual removal of the no longer adjustable, and the places of those who die are filled by new material capable of the new demands. But it is the means that nature takes to secure the renewal of material still capable of adjustment that is of significance. From each adult sometime during the course of his life nature provides that a small bit shall be detached which, in the higher animals, in union with a similar detached bit of another individual will develop into a child and ultimately be ready to replace the adult when he becomes senile and dies. Life is thus maintained by a continuous stream of germ plasm and is not periodically interrupted in its course, as it seems to be, by death.

The characteristics of this detached bit of germ plasm are interesting. It does not manifest any of that complicated structure which we meet with in the other parts of the body. The several parts of the body are highly differentiated, each for a specific function. Gland cells are developed to secrete, muscle cells to contract, bone cells to withstand mechanical stresses, etc. Manifestly development along any one of these lines would not produce an individual possessing, in its several parts, all of these qualities. Development has to go back of the point of origin of these several variations in order to include them all. In other words, regeneration has to start with relatively undifferentiated material. This is excellently illustrated by many of the lower, particularly the unicellular, animals, in which reproduction is not yet sexual, but by the simple method of division. A cell comes to rest, divides into two, and each half then leads an independent existence. Before such a division and while the cell is quiescent— in the resting stage, as it is called—the differentiations of structure which it had acquired in its lifetime disappear; it becomes undifferentiated, relatively simple in structure. This process has been called dedifferentiation. When all the differentiations which had been acquired have been eliminated, then division—rejuvenescence— takes place.

From this point of view we may see in war the preliminary process of rejuvenescence. International adjustments and compromises are made until they can be made no longer; a condition is brought about which in Europe has been termed the balance of power, until the situation becomes so complicated that each new adjustment has such wide ramifications that it threatens the whole structure. Finally, as the result of the accumulated structure of diplomatic relations and precedents, a situation arises to which adjustment, with the machinery that has been developed, is impossible and the whole house of cards collapses. The collapse is a process of dedifferentiation during which the old structures are destroyed, precedents are disavowed, new situations occur with bewildering rapidity, for dealing with which there is no recognized machinery available. Society reverts from a state in which a high grade of individual initiative and development was possible to a relatively communistic and paternalistic state, the slate is wiped clear, and a start can be made anew along lines of progress mapped out by the new conditions—rejuvenescence is possible.

War, from this point of view, is a precondition for development along new lines of necessity, and the dedifferentiation is the first stage of a constructive process. Old institutions have to be torn down before the bricks with which they were built can be made available for new structures. This accounts for the periodicity of war, which thus is the outward and evident aspect of the progress of the life-force which in human societies, as elsewhere, advances in cycles. It is only by such means that an *impasse* can be overcome.

War is an example of ambivalency on the grandest scale. That is, it is at once potent for the greatest good and the greatest evil: in the very midst of death it calls for the most intense living; in the face of the greatest renunciation it offers the greatest premium; for the maximum of freedom it demands the utmost giving of one's self; in order to live at one's best it demands the giving of life itself. "No man has reached his ethical majority who would not die if the real interests of the community could thus be furthered. What would the world be without the values that have been bought at the price of death?" In this sense the great creative force, love, and the supreme negation, death, become one. That the larger life of the race should go forward to greater things, the smaller life of the individual must perish. In order that man shall be born again, he must first die.

Does all this necessarily mean that war, from time to time, in the process of readjustment, is essential? I think no one can doubt that it has been necessary in the past. Whether it will be in the future depends upon whether some sublimated form of procedure can adequately be substituted. We have succeeded to a large extent in dealing with our combative instincts by developing sports and the competition of business, and we have largely sublimated our hate instinct in dealing with various forms of anti-social conduct as exhibited in the so-called "criminal." It remains to be seen whether nations can unite to a similar end and perhaps, by the establishment of an international court, and by other means, deal in a similar way with infractions of international law.

2. War as a Form of Relaxation[1]

The fact is that it does not take a very careful reader of the human mind to see that all the utopias and all the socialistic schemes are based on a mistaken notion of the nature of this mind.

It is by no means sure that what man wants is peace and quiet and tranquillity. That is too close to ennui, which is his greatest dread. What man wants is not peace but a battle. He must pit his force against someone or something. Every language is most rich in synonyms for battle, war, contest, conflict, quarrel, combat, fight. German children play all day long with their toy soldiers. Our sports take the form of contests in football, baseball, and hundreds of others. Prize fights, dog fights, cock fights, have pleased in all ages. When Rome for a season was not engaged in real war, Claudius staged a sea fight for the delectation of an immense concourse, in which 19,000 gladiators were compelled to take a tragic part, so that the ships were broken to pieces and the waters of the lake were red with blood.

You may perhaps recall Professor James's astonishing picture of his visit to a Chautauqua. Here he found modern culture at its best, no poverty, no drunkenness, no zymotic diseases, no crime, no police, only polite and refined and harmless people. Here was a middle-class paradise, kindergarten and model schools, lectures and classes and music, bicycling and swimming, and culture and kindness

[1] From G. T. W. Patrick, "The Psychology of War," in the *Popular Science Monthly*, LXXXVII (1915), 166–68.

and elysian peace. But at the end of a week he came out into the real world, and he said:

Ouf! What a relief! Now for something primordial and savage, even though it were as bad as an Armenian massacre, to set the balance straight again. This order is too tame, this culture too second-rate, this goodness too uninspiring. This human drama, without a villain or a pang; this community so refined that ice-cream soda-water is the utmost offering it can make to the brute animal in man; this city simmering in the tepid lakeside sun; this atrocious harmlessness of all things—I cannot abide with them.

What men want, he says, is something more precipitous, something with more zest in it, with more adventure. Nearly all the utopias paint the life of the future as a kind of giant Chautauqua, in which every man and woman is at work, all are well fed, satisfied, and cultivated. But as man is now constituted he would probably find such a life flat, stale, and unprofitable.

Man is not originally a working animal. Civilization has imposed work upon man, and if you work him too hard he will quit work and go to war. Nietzsche says man wants two things—danger and play. War represents danger.

It follows that all our social utopias are wrongly conceived. They are all based on a theory of pleasure economy. But history and evolution show that man has come up from the lower animals through a pain economy. He has struggled up—fought his way up through never-ceasing pain and effort and struggle and battle. The utopias picture a society in which man has ceased to struggle. He works his eight hours a day—everybody works—and he sleeps and enjoys himself the other hours. But man is not a working animal, he is a fighting animal. The utopias are ideal—but they are not psychological. The citizens for such an ideal social order are lacking. Human beings will not serve.

Our present society tends more and more in its outward form in time of peace toward the Chautauqua plan, but meanwhile striving and passion burn in the brain of the human units, till the time comes when they find this insipid life unendurable. They resort to amusement crazes, to narcotic drugs. to political strife, to epidemics of crime, and finally to war. The alcohol question well illustrates the tendencies we are pointing out. Science and hygiene have at last shown beyond all question that alcohol, whether in large or smaller doses, exerts a damaging effect upon both mind and body. It lessens physical and mental efficiency, shortens life, and encourages social disorder. In spite of this fact and, what is still more amazing, in spite of the colossal effort now being put forth to suppress by legislative means the traffic in liquor, the per capita consumption of alcoholic drinks in the United States increases from year to year. From a per capita consumption of four gallons in 1850, it has steadily risen to nearly twenty-five gallons in 1913.

Narcotic drugs, such as alcohol and tobacco, relieve in an artificial way the tension upon the brain by slightly paralyzing temporarily the higher and more recently developed brain centers. The increase in the use of these drugs is therefore both an index of the tension of modern life and at the same time a means of relieving it to some extent. Were the use of these drugs suddenly checked, no student of psychology or of history could doubt that there would be an immediate increase of social irritability, tending to social instability and social upheavals.

Psychology, therefore, forces upon us this conclusion. Neither war nor alcohol can be banished from the world by summary means nor direct suppressions. The mind of man must be made over. As the mind of man is constituted, he will never be content to be a mere laborer, a producer and a consumer. He loves adventure, self-sacrifice, heroism, relaxation.

These things must somehow be provided. And then there must be a system of education of our young differing widely from our present system. The new education will not look to efficiency merely and ever more efficiency, but to the production of a harmonized and balanced personality. We must cease our worship of American efficiency and German *Streberthum* and go back to Aristotle and his teaching of "the mean."

3. The Fighting Animal and the Great Society[1]

We must agree that man as he has existed, so far as we can read the story of his development, has been, and as he exists today still is, a fighting animal—that is to say that he has in the past answered,

[1] Adapted from Henry Rutgers Marshall, *War and the Ideal of Peace*, pp. 96–110. (Duffield & Co., 1915.)

and still answers, certain stimuli by the immediate reactions which constitute fighting.

We find evidence of the existence of this fighting instinct in the ordinary men around us. Remove but for a moment the restraints given in our civilized lands and this tendency is likely to become prominent upon the slightest stimulation. We see this exemplified in the lives of the pioneer and adventurer the world over: in that of the cowboy of the far West, in that of the rubber collector on the Amazon, in that of the ivory trader on the Congo.

Then, too, the prize fighter is still a prominent person in our community, taken as a whole, and even in our sports, as engaged in by "gentlemen amateurs," we find it necessary to make rigid rules to prevent the friendly contest from developing into a fierce struggle for individual physical dominance.

But man gained his pre-eminent position among the animals mainly through his ability to form co-operative groups working to common ends; and long before the times of which anthropological research give us any clear knowledge, man had turned his individualistic fighting instincts to the service of his group or clan. That is to say, he had become a warrior, giving his best strength to co-operative aggression in behalf of satisfactions that could not be won by him as an individual acting for himself.

Our earlier studies have taught us also that if man's instinctive tendencies could in any manner be inhibited or modified, so that he came to display other characteristics than those observed in the present expression of these inborn instincts, then the law of his nature would in that very fact be changed. We are thus led to ask whether the biologist finds evidence that an animal's instincts can be thus changed in mode of expression.

The biologist speaks to us somewhat as follows. Although new racial characteristics have very rarely, if ever, been gained by the obliteration of instincts, changes in racial characteristics have not unfrequently occurred as the result of the control, rather than the loss, of these inherited instincts.

This control may become effective in either one of two ways: first, by the thwarting or inhibition of the expression of the instincts; or secondly, by the turning of its expression to other uses than that which originally resulted in its fixation.

As an example of the thwarting of the expression of an instinct we may take the functioning of the sexual instinct, which, as we see it in animals in general, has been inhibited in the human animal by the habits acquired by man as he has risen in the scale.

This mode of change—that of the mere chaining of the instinctive tendency—is subject to one great difficulty. The chain may by chance be broken; the inhibition may be removed; then the natural instinctive tendency at once shows itself. Remove the restraints of civilized society but a little, and manifestations of the sexual instinct of our race appear in forms that are not far removed from those observed in the animal. Place a man under conditions of starvation and he shows himself as greedy as the dog.

The second mode of change—that of the transference of functioning of the instincts into new channels—meets this special difficulty, for it does not depend upon the chaining of the instinct. It actually makes use of the instinct. And the more important to the race the newer reference of the instinct's functioning turns out to be, the more certain is it to replace the original reference. If the new mode of functioning brings marked advantage that is lost by reversion to the earlier manifestation of the instinct, so that such a reversion to this earlier manifestation is a detriment to the race, then the change is likely to become a permanent one.

No better example of this second mode of change of an instinct's functioning can be found than in the very existence of war itself. The basic instinct is one that led the savage man to fight to protect himself or to gain something for himself by aggressive attack. War has come into being as the result of a transfer of the functioning of this instinct, which at first had only an individualistic reference, so that it has come to have a clan or national reference. The early man found he could not have success as an individual unless he joined with his fellow-men in defense and aggression; and that meant war.

And note that this transfer of reference of the expression of this fighting instinct soon became so important to the race that reversion to its primal individualistic reference had to be inhibited. Aggressive attack by an individual upon another of his own clan or nation necessarily tended to weaken the social unit and to reduce its strength in its protective and aggressive wars; and thus such attacks by individuals came to be discountenanced and finally in large measure repressed.

Here, it will be observed, the fighting instinct of the individual has not been obliterated; it has not even been bound with chains; but its modes of expression have been altered to have racial significance, and to have so great a significance in this new relation that reversion to its primary form of expression has become a serious obstacle to racial advance.

So it appears after all that, although instincts can rarely if ever be obliterated, their manifestations may be so altered as to give the animal quite new characteristics. And this means that if the characteristics which we describe as the expressions of man's fighting instincts could be so changed that these expressions were inhibited or turned into quite new channels, the man would no longer be describable as a fighting animal.

The first indication in our conscious life of any tendency to inhibit or modify the functioning of any instinct or habit must appear in the form of a dislike of, a revulsion from, the resultants of this functioning; and in the creation of an ideal of functioning that shall avoid the discomforts attendant upon this revulsion. And when such an ideal has once been gained, it is possible, as we have seen, that the characteristics of nature may be changed by our creative efficiency through the devising of means looking to the realization of the ideal.

We have the clearest evidence that this process is developing in connection with these special instincts that make for war; for we men and women in these later times are repelled by the results of the functioning of these fighting instincts, and we have created the ideal of peace, the conception of a condition that is not now realized in nature, but which we think of as possible of realization.

But the very existence of an ideal is indicative of a tendency, on the part of the man who entertains it, to modify his characteristic activities. Thus it appears that we have in the very existence of this ideal of peace the evidence that we may look for a change in man's nature, the result of which will be that we shall no longer be warranted in describing him as a fighting animal.

C. RIVALRY, CULTURAL CONFLICTS, AND SOCIAL ORGANIZATION

1. Animal Rivalry[1]

Among mammals the instinct of one and all is to lord it over the others, with the result that the one more powerful or domineering gets the mastery, to keep it thereafter as long as he can. The lower animals are, in this respect, very much like us; and in all kinds that are at all fierce-tempered the mastery of one over all, and of a few under him over the others, is most salutary; indeed, it is inconceivable that they should be able to exist together under any other system.

On cattle-breeding establishments on the pampas, where it is usual to keep a large number of fierce-tempered dogs, I have observed these animals a great deal and presume they are much like feral dogs and wolves in their habits. Their quarrels are incessant; but when a fight begins, the head of the pack as a rule rushes to the spot, whereupon the fighters separate and march off in different directions or else cast themselves down and deprecate their tyrant's wrath with abject gestures and whines. If the combatants are both strong and have worked themselves into a mad rage before their head puts in an appearance, it may go hard with him; they know him no longer and all he can do is to join in the fray; then if the fighters turn on him he may be so injured that his power is gone and the next best dog in the pack takes his place. The hottest contests are always between dogs that are well matched; neither will give place to the other and so they fight it out; but from the foremost in power down to the weakest there is a gradation of authority; each one knows just how far he can go, which companion he can bully when he is in a bad temper or wishes to assert himself, and to which he must humbly yield in his turn. In such a state the weakest one must yield to all the others and cast himself down, seeming to call himself a slave and worshiper of any other member of the pack that chances to snarl at him or command him to give up his bone with good grace.

This masterful or domineering temper, so common among social mammals, is the cause of the persecution of the sick and weakly. When an animal begins to ail he can no longer hold his own; he ceases to resent the occasional ill-natured attacks made on him; his non-

[1] Adapted from William H. Hudson, "The Strange Instincts of Cattle," *Longman's Magazine*, XVIII (1891), 393–94.

combative condition is quickly discovered, and he at once drops down to a place below the lowest; it is common knowledge in the herd that he may be buffeted with impunity by all, even by those that have hitherto suffered buffets but have given none. But judging from my own observation, this persecution is not, as a rule, severe, and is seldom fatal.

2. The Rivalry of Social Groups[1]

Conflict, competition, and rivalry are the chief causes which force human beings into groups and largely determine what goes on within them. Conflicts, like wars, revolutions, riots, still persist, but possibly they may be thought of as gradually yielding to competitions which are chiefly economic. Many of these strivings seem almost wholly individual, but most of them on careful analysis turn out to be intimately related to group competition. A third form, rivalry, describes struggle for status, for social prestige, for the approval of inclusive publics which form the spectators for such contests. The nation is an arena of competition and rivalry.

Much of this emulation is of a concealed sort. Beneath the union services of churches there is an element, for the most part unconscious, of rivalry to secure the approval of a public which in these days demands brotherliness and good will rather than proselyting and polemics. Many public subscriptions for a common cause are based upon group rivalry or upon individual competition which is group-determined. The Rhodes scholarships are in one sense a means of furthering imperial interest. Christmas presents lavished upon children often have a bearing upon the ambition of the family to make an impression upon rival domestic groups. In the liberal policy of universities which by adding to the list of admission subjects desire to come into closer relations with the public schools, there is some trace of competition for students and popular applause. The interest which nations manifest in the Hague Tribunal is tinged with a desire to gain the good will of the international, peace-praising public. The professed eagerness of one or both parties in a labor dispute to have the differences settled by arbitration is a form of competition for the favor of the onlooking community. Thus in

[1] Adapted from George E. Vincent, "The Rivalry of Social Groups," in the *American Journal of Sociology*, XVI (1910-11), 471-84.

international relationships and in the life-process of each nation countless groups are in conflict, competition, or rivalry.

This idea of the group seeking survival, mastery, aggrandizement, prestige, in its struggles with other groups is a valuable means of interpretation. Let us survey rapidly the conditions of success as a group carries on its life of strife and emulation. In order to survive or to succeed the group must organize, cozen, discipline, and stimulate its members. Fortunately it finds human nature in a great measure fashioned for control.

Collective pride or group egotism is an essential source of strength in conflict. Every efficient group cultivates this sense of honor, importance, superiority, by many devices of symbol, phrase, and legend, as well as by scorn and ridicule of rivals. The college fraternity's sublime self-esteem gives it strength in its competition for members and prestige. There is a chauvinism of "boom" towns and religious sects, as well as of nations. What pride and self-confidence are to the individual, ethnocentrism, patriotism, local loyalty are to social unities. Diffidence, humility, self-distrust, tolerance, are as dangerous to militant groups as to fighting men.

Then too the group works out types of personality, hero types to be emulated, traitor types to be execrated. These personality types merge into abstract ideals and standards. "Booster" and "knocker" bring up pictures of a struggling community which must preserve its hopefulness and self-esteem at all hazards. "Statesman" and "demagogue" recall the problem of selection which every self-governing community must face. "Defender of the faith" and "heretic" are eloquent of the Church's dilemma between rigid orthodoxy and flexible accommodation to a changing order.

With a shifting in the conflict or rivalry crises, types change in value or emphasis, or new types are created in adjustment to the new needs. The United States at war with Spain sought martial heroes. The economic and political ideals of personality, the captains of industry, the fascinating financiers, the party idols, were for the time retired to make way for generals and admirals, soldiers and sailors, the heroes of camp and battleship. The war once over, the displaced types reappeared along with others which are being created to meet new administrative, economic, and ethical problems. The competing church retires its militant and disputatious leaders in an age which gives its applause to apostles of concord, fraternal feeling, and co-operation. At a given time the heroes and traitors of a group reflect its competitions and rivalries with other groups.

Struggle forces upon the group the necessity of cozening, beguiling, managing its members. The vast majority of these fall into a broad zone of mediocrity which embodies group character and represents a general adjustment to life-conditions. From this medial area individuals vary, some in ways which aid the group in its competition, others in a fashion which imperils group success. It is the task of the group both to preserve the solidarity of the medial zone and to discriminate between the serviceable and the menacing variants. The latter must be coerced or suppressed, the former encouraged and given opportunity. In Plato's *Republic* the guardians did this work of selection which in modern groups is cared for by processes which seem only slightly conscious and purposeful.

The competing group in seeking to insure acquiescence and loyalty elaborates a protective philosophy by which it creates within its members the belief that their lot is much to be preferred to that of other comradeships and associations. Western Americans take satisfaction in living in a free, progressive, hospitable way in "God's country." They try not to be pharisaical about the narrowness of the East, but they achieve a sincere scorn for the hidebound conventions of an effete society. Easterners in turn count themselves fortunate in having a highly developed civilization, and they usually attain real pity for those who seem to live upon a psychic, if not a geographic, frontier. The middle class have a philosophy with which they protect themselves against the insidious suggestions that come from the life of the conspicuous rich. These, on the other hand, half suspecting that simplicity and domesticity may have some virtue, speak superciliously of middle-class smugness and the bourgeois "home." The less prosperous of the professional classes are prone to lay a good deal of stress upon their intellectual resources as compared with the presumptive spiritual poverty of the affluent. Country folk encourage themselves by asserting their fundamental value to society and by extolling their own simple straightforward virtues, which present so marked a contrast to the devious machinations of city-dwellers. Booker Washington's reiterated assertion that if he were to be born again he would choose to be a Negro because the Negro race is the only one which has a great problem contains a suggestion of this protective philosophy. This tendency of a group to fortify itself by a satisfying theory of its lot is obviously related to group egotism and is immediately connected with group rivalry.

The competing group derides many a dissenter into conformity. This derision may be spontaneous, or reflective and concerted. The loud guffaw which greets one who varies in dress or speech or idea may come instantly or there may be a planned and co-operative ridicule systematically applied to the recalcitrant. Derision is one of the most effective devices by which the group sifts and tests the variants.

Upon the small number of rebels who turn a deaf ear to epithets, ostracism is brought to bear. This may vary from the "cold shoulder" to the complete "boycott." Losing the friendship and approval of comrades, being cut off from social sympathy, is a familiar form of group pressure. Ridicule and derision are a kind of evanescent ostracism, a temporary exclusion from the comradeship. There are many degrees in the lowering of the social temperature: coolness, formality of intercourse, averted looks, "cutting dead," "sending to Coventry," form a progressive series. Economic pressure is more and more a resort of modern groups. Loss of employment, trade, or professional practice brings many a rebel to time. All coercion obviously increases as the group is hard pressed in its conflicts, competitions, and rivalries.

These crises and conflicts of a competing group present problems which must be solved—problems of organization, of inventions of many kinds, of new ideas and philosophies, of methods of adjustment. The conditions of competition or rivalry upset an equilibrium of habit and custom, and a process of problem-solving ensues. A typhoid epidemic forces the village to protect itself against the competition of a more healthful rival. The resourceful labor union facing a corporation which offers profit-sharing and retiring allowances must formulate a protective theory and practice. A society clique too closely imitated by a lower stratum must regain its distinction and supremacy. A nation must be constantly alert to adjust itself to the changing conditions of international trade and to the war equipment and training of its rivals.

The theory of group rivalry throws light upon the individual. The person has as many selves as there are groups to which he belongs. He is simple or complex as his groups are few and harmonious or many and conflicting. What skilful management is required to keep business and moral selves from looking each other in the eye, to prevent scientific and theological selves from falling into discussion! Most men of many groups learn, like tactful hosts, to invite at a given time only congenial companies of selves. A few brave souls resolve to set their house in order and to entertain only such selves as can live together with good will and mutual respect. With these earnest folk their groups have to reckon. The conflicts of conscience are group conflicts.

Tolerance is a sign that once vital issues within the group are losing their significance, or that the group feels secure, or that it is slowly, even unconsciously, merging into a wider grouping. Theological liberality affords a case in point. In the earlier days of sectarian struggle tolerance was a danger both to group loyalty and to the militant spirit. Cynicism for other reasons is also a menace. It means loss of faith in the collective ego, in the traditions, shibboleths, symbols, and destiny of the group. Fighting groups cannot be tolerant; nor can they harbor cynics. Tolerance and cynicism are at once causes and results of group decay. They portend dissolution or they foreshadow new groupings for struggle over other issues on another plane. Evangelical churches are drawing together with mutual tolerance to present a united front against modern skepticism and cynicism which are directed against the older faiths and moralities.

The subjective side of group rivalry offers an important study. The reflection of the process of control in personal consciousness is full of interest. The means by which the rebellious variant protects himself against the coercion of his comrades have been already suggested in the description of ridicule and epithet. These protective methods resolve themselves into setting one group against another in the mind of the derided or stigmatized individual.

A national group is to be thought of as an inclusive unity with a fundamental character, upon the basis of which a multitude of groups compete with and rival each other. It is the task of the nation to control and to utilize this group struggle, to keep it on as high a plane as possible, to turn it to the common account. Government gets its chief meaning from the rivalry of groups to grasp political power in their own interests. Aristocracy and democracy may be interpreted in terms of group antagonism, the specialized few versus the undifferentiated many. The ideal merges the two elements of efficiency and solidarity in one larger group within which mutual confidence and emulation take the place of conflict. Just as persons must be disciplined into serving their groups, groups must be subordinated to the welfare of the nation. It is in conflict or competition with other nations that a country becomes a vivid unity to the members of constituent groups. It is rivalry which brings out the sense of team work, the social consciousness.

3. The Gang and Political Organization[1]

The importance of the gang as a social factor which the politician manipulates has never been fully appreciated except by the politician. It is a sufficiently commonplace trait of human nature for people to associate themselves together in groups and cliques, according to the attractions of congeniality. This force, however, seems to work with great intensity in the tenement-house districts. Without pausing to inquire the reasons, I shall describe the structure of the gang, and later show its relation to ward politics.

The tendency begins among the children. Almost every boy in the tenement-house quarters of the district is member of a gang. The boy who does not belong to one is not only the exception, but the very rare exception. There are certain characteristics in the make-up and life of all gangs. To begin with, every gang has a "corner" where its members meet. This "hang out," as it is sometimes called, may be in the centre of a block, but still the gang speak of it as the "corner." The size of a gang varies: it may number five or forty. As a rule, all the boys composing it come from the immediate vicinity of the corner. . . . .

Nightly after supper the boys drift to their "corner," not by appointment, but naturally. Then ensue idle talk, "jawing matches," as one boy expressed it, rough jokes, and horse-play. No eccentric

[1] From "The Roots of Political Power" in *The City Wilderness, a Settlement Study* edited by Robert A. Woods, pp. 114-23. (Houghton, Mifflin & Company, Boston, 1898. Author's copyright.)

individual gets by the gang without insult. Nearly every gang has
"talent": one or two members who can sing, perhaps a quartette;
also a buck-dancer, one or two who can play on the jew's-harp, and a
"funny man." I am referring now more particularly to boys over
fourteen years old. As a rule, the boys stay around their corner,
finding amusement in these ways. The songs are always new ones;
old ones are scorned. Not infrequently the singing, the horse-play,
or the dancing is interrupted by the roundsman. At the sight of the
brass buttons, there is an excited call of "cheese it," and singing or
talking, as it may be, is suddenly stopped; the gang disbands, dissolves,
and the boys flee down alleyways, into doorsteps and curious hiding-
places, and reappear only when the "cop" is well down the street.

It sometimes happens that members of the gang are arrested, for
standing on the corners, for insulting passers-by, or for some other
offense. As a rule, the other fellows raise the money to pay the fine
To reimburse themselves or the one who loaned the money, a dance
is "run" or a raffle is held. To show still further the *tenaciousness
of gang life:* the influx of Jews has caused many of the Irish to move
away from the South End to other parts of the city, but the boys on
Sunday may be found with the gang at their corner. About thirty
young men belonging to one of the gangs I know meet every Sunday
afternoon at their corner. Of this number, fully half are fellows
who live in the Highlands, at the edge of Roxbury. I know a boy
in the High School—he will graduate next year—who moved to
Dorchester, but comes regularly to the old corner on Sunday afternoon.
No new friends can supplant the gang. It is little wonder. The life
of the gang is exciting, melodramatic; the corner is full of associations,
of jokes and songs and good times, of escapades planned and carried
out. In comparison with this, the life of the suburb is tame.

It is interesting to know what becomes of these various gangs
when the boys get to be seventeen or eighteen years old. The more
respectable gangs, as a rule, club together and hire a room. The more
vicious gangs prefer to use what little money they have in carousing.
If by any chance they get a room, their rowdyism will cause their
ejection either by the landlord or by the police. Consequently they
have to fall back on the corner or some saloon, as their meeting-place.
They nearly always seek a back street or the wharves, unfrequented
by the police. . . . . .

At this point, it is necessary to give some account of the *young men's clubs*, in order that the important part that these clubs play in ward politics may be seen; for all this network of social life is taken in hand by the politician. As I said before, the gangs which coalesce and form these clubs are the most respectable ones. They are led to do this partly through a desire to have a warm room, and partly because they are tired of standing on the corner and meeting the rebuffs of the policeman. Then such a club opens up the freedom of the district, socially, to them. . . . .

Nearly all of the clubs have a common programme. In the first place, *each club*, without any exception, *gives a ball* each winter in some large hall. The tickets invariably sell for fifty cents. These balls are important social functions in the district. As a rule, they are well managed financially, one club clearing $165 last winter. Then besides this annual ball, each club has a "social" once a week. This is a dance of a lower type than the balls, being interspersed with comic songs, humorous recitations, and buck-dancing. About the same class of girls attend all the socials; they go from one club to the other. Almost without exception they are factory girls, and nearly all of them are bold and vulgar. It is a curious fact that the members do not want their sisters to attend these dances; and their custom is to leave the girls with whom they have danced before they reach the street. . . . .

Another feature of these clubs is the smoke talks. They are always held on holidays, and sometimes on Sundays. Several barrels of beer are on tap; and tonic is ordered for abstainers, but they are few. The smoke talk usually begins in the afternoon, and lasts as long as the beer does. When the end comes, those who are sober are in the minority. For entertainment there are comic songs and buck-dances, but the principal feature is the story-telling. . . . .

The worst *dance halls* are very nearly allied to the clubs, for all the halls have their special clientage. This clientage, like the club, is made up, though not so distinctly, of gangs. Consequently at nearly all the halls, the dancers are known to one another, and have more or less loyalty for the hall. . . . .

In addition to these social groups which taken on a political character at election time, there are usually in the tenement-house sections several distinctly political clubs. Standing at the head of these clubs is the "*machine club*." It is now quite the custom of those in control of the party, and known as the "machine," to have such an organization. All the men in the ward having good political jobs are members. In one local club it is estimated that the City employees belonging to it draw salaries to the amount of $30,000 per year; in another club, outside the district, $80,000. It is natural that all the men in these clubs are anxious to maintain the machine. It is a question of bread and butter with them. In addition to City employees the various machine workers are enrolled. The room of the club is ordinarily very pleasant. There are, of course, in these clubs the usual social attractions, among other things poker and drinking. At the head of the club stands the boss of the ward.

4. Cultural Conflicts and the Organization of Sects[1]

It is assumed, I suppose, that contradictions among ideas and beliefs are of various degrees and of various modes besides that specific one which we call logical incompatibility. A perception, for example, may be pictorially inconsistent or tonically discordant with another perception; a mere faith unsupported by objective evidence may be emotionally antagonistic to another mere faith, as truly as a judgment may be logically irreconcilable with another judgment. And this wide possibility of contradiction is particularly to be recognized when the differing ideas or beliefs have arisen not within the same individual mind but in different minds, and are therefore colored by personal or partisan interest and warped by idiosyncrasy of mental constitution. The contradictions of, or rather *among*, ideas and beliefs, with which we are now concerned, are more extensive and more varied than mere logical duels; they are also less definite, less precise. In reality they are culture conflicts in which the opposing forces, so far from being specific ideas only or pristine beliefs only, are in fact more or less bewildering complexes of ideas, beliefs, prejudices, sympathies, antipathies, and personal interests.

It is assumed also, I suppose, that any idea or group of ideas, any belief or group of beliefs, may happen to be or may become a common interest, shared by a small or a large number of individuals.

[1] Adapted from Franklin H. Giddings, "Are Contradictions of Ideas and Beliefs Likely to Play an Important Group-making Rôle in the Future?" in the *American Journal of Sociology*, XIII (1907-8), 784-91.

It may draw and hold them together in bonds of acquaintance, of association, even of co-operation. It thus may play a group-making rôle. Contradictory ideas or beliefs, therefore, may play a group-making rôle in a double sense. Each draws into association the individual minds that entertain it or find it attractive. Each also repels those minds to whom it is repugnant, and drives them toward the group which is being formed about the contradictory idea or belief. Contradictions among ideas and beliefs, then, it may be assumed, tend on the whole to sharpen the lines of demarcation between group and group.

These assumptions are, I suppose, so fully justified by the everyday observation of mankind and so confirmed by history that it is unnecessary now to discuss them or in any way to dwell upon them. The question before us therefore becomes specific: "Are contradictions among ideas and beliefs likely to play an *important* group-making rôle in the future?" I shall interpret the word important as connoting quality as well as quantity. I shall, in fact, attempt to answer the question set for me by translating it into this inquiry, namely: What kind or type of groups are the inevitable contradictions among ideas and beliefs most likely to create and to maintain within the progressive populations of the world from this time forth?

Somewhat more than three hundred years ago, Protestantism and geographical discovery had combined to create conditions extraordinarily favorable to the formation of groups or associations about various conflicting ideas and beliefs functioning as nuclei; and for nearly three hundred years the world has been observing a remarkable multiplication of culture groups of two fundamentally different types. One type is a sect, or denomination, having no restricted local habitation but winning adherents here and there in various communes, provinces, or nations, and having, therefore, a membership either locally concentrated or more or less widely dispersed; either regularly or most irregularly distributed. The culture group of the other type, or kind, is a self-sufficing community. It may be a village, a colony, a state, or a nation. Its membership is concentrated, its habitat is defined.

To a very great extent, as everybody knows, American colonization proceeded through the formation of religious communities. Such were the Pilgrim and the Puritan commonwealths. Such were the Quaker groups of Rhode Island and Pennsylvania. Such were the localized societies of the Dunkards, the Moravians, and the Mennonites.

As late as the middle of the nineteenth century the American people witnessed the birth and growth of one of the most remarkable religious communities known in history. The Mormon community of Utah, which, originating in 1830 as a band of relatives and acquaintances, clustered by an idea that quickly became a dogma, had become in fifty years a commonwealth *de facto*, defying the authority *de jure* of the United States.

We are not likely, however, again to witness a phenomenon of this kind in the civilized world. Recently we have seen the rise and the astonishingly rapid spread of another American religion, namely, the Christian Science faith. But it has created no community group. It has created only a dispersed sect. It is obvious to any intelligent observer, however untrained in sociological discrimination he may be, that the forces of Protestantism, still dividing and differentiating as they are, no longer to any great extent create new self-sufficing communities. They create only associations of irregular geographical dispersion, of more or less unstable or shifting membership. In a word, the conflicting-idea forces, which in our colonial days tended to create community groups as well as sects, tend now to create sectarian bodies only—mere denominational or partisan associations.

A similar contrast between an earlier and a later stage of culture group-making may be observed if we go back to centuries before the Protestant Reformation, there to survey a wider field and a longer series of historical periods.

It is a commonplace of historical knowledge that in all of the earliest civilizations there was an approximate identification of religion with ethnic consciousness and of political consciousness with both religious and race feeling. Each people had its own tribal or national gods, who were inventoried as national assets at valuations quite as high as those attached to tribal or national territory.

When, however, Roman imperial rule had been extended over the civilized world, the culture conflicts that then arose expended their group-creating force in simply bringing together like believers in sectarian association. Christianity, appealing to all bloods, in some measure to all economic classes, and spreading into all sections of the eastern Mediterranean region, did not to any great extent create communities. And what was true of Christianity was in like manner true of the Mithras cult, widely diffused in the second Christian century. Even Mohammedanism, a faith seemingly well calculated to create autonomous states, in contact with a world prepared by Roman organization could not completely identify itself with definite political boundaries.

The proximate causes of these contrasts are not obscure. We must suppose that a self-sufficing community might at one time, as well as at another, be drawn together by formative beliefs. But that it may take root somewhere and, by protecting itself against destructive external influences, succeed for a relatively long time in maintaining its integrity and its solidarity, it must enjoy a relative isolation. In a literal sense it must be beyond easy reach of those antagonistic forces which constitute for it the outer world of unbelief and darkness.

Such isolation is easily and often possible, however, only in the early stages of political integration. It is always difficult and unusual in those advanced stages wherein nations are combined in world-empires. It is becoming well-nigh impossible, now that all the continents have been brought under the sovereignty of the so-called civilized peoples, while these peoples themselves, freely communicating and intermingling, maintain with one another that good understanding which constitutes them, in a certain broad sense of the term, a world-society. The proximate effects also of the contrast that has been sketched are generally recognized.

So long as blood sympathy, religious faith, and political consciousness are approximately coterminous, the groups that they form, whether local communities or nations, must necessarily be rather sharply delimited. They must be characterized also by internal solidarity. Their membership is stable because to break the bond of blood is not only to make one's self an outcast but is also to be unfaithful to the ancestral gods; to change one's religion is not only to be impious but is also to commit treason; to expatriate one's self is not only to commit treason but is also to blaspheme against high heaven.

But when associations of believers or of persons holding in common any philosophy or doctrine whatsoever are no longer self-sufficing communities, and when nations composite in blood have become compound in structure, all social groups, clusters, or organizations, not only the cultural ones drawn together by formative ideas, but also the economic and the political ones, become in some degree plastic. Their membership then becomes to some extent shifting and renewable. Under these circumstances any given association of men, let it be a village, a religious group, a trade union, a corporation, or a political party, not only takes into itself new members from time to time; it also permits old members to depart. Men come and men go, yet the association or the group itself persists. As group or as organization it remains unimpaired.

The economic advantage secured by this plasticity and renewableness is beyond calculation enormous. It permits and facilitates the drafting of men at any moment from points where they are least needed, for concentration upon points where they are needed most. The spiritual or idealistic advantage is not less great. The concentration of attention and of enthusiasm upon strategic points gives ever-increasing impetus to progressive movements.

Let us turn now from these merely proximate causes and effects of group formation to take note of certain developmental processes which lie farther back in the evolutionary sequence and which also have significance for our inquiry, since, when we understand them, they may aid us in our attempt to answer the question, What kind of group-making is likely to be accomplished by cultural conflicts from this time forth?

The most readily perceived, because the most pictorial, of the conflicts arising between one belief and another are those that are waged between beliefs that have been localized and then through geographical expansion have come into competition throughout wide frontier areas. Of all such conflicts, that upon which the world has now fully entered between occidental and oriental ideas is not merely the most extensive; it is also by far the most interesting and picturesque.

Less picturesque but often more dramatic are the conflicts that arise within each geographical region, within each nation, between old beliefs and new—the conflicts of sequent, in distinction from coexistent, ideas; the conflicts in time, in distinction from the conflicts in space. A new knowledge is attained which compels us to question old dogmas.   A new faith arises which would displace the ancient traditions.   As the new waxes strong in some region favorable to it, it begins there, within local limits, to supersede the old. Only then, when the conflict between the old as old and the new as new is practically over, does the triumphant new begin to go forth spatially as a conquering influence from the home of its youth into regions outlying and remote.

Whatever the form, however, that the culture conflict assumes, whether serial and dramatic or geographical and picturesque, its antecedent psychological conditions are in certain great essentials the same.   Men array themselves in hostile camps on questions of theory and belief, not merely because they are variously and conflictingly informed, but far more because they are mentally unlike, their minds having been prepared by structural differentiation to seize upon different views and to cherish opposing convictions.   That is to say, some minds have become rational, critical, plastic, open, outlooking, above all, intuitive of objective facts and relations.   Others in their fundamental constitution have remained dogmatic, intuitive only of personal attitudes or of subjective moods, temperamentally conservative and instinctive.   Minds of the one kind welcome the new and wider knowledge; they go forth to embrace it.   Minds of the other kind resist it.

In the segregation thus arising, there is usually discoverable a certain tendency toward grouping by sex.

Whether the mental and moral traits of women are inherent and therefore permanent, or whether they are but passing effects of circumscribed experience and therefore possibly destined to be modified, is immaterial for my present purpose.   It is not certain that either the biologist or the psychologist is prepared to answer the question. It is certain that the sociologist is not.   It is enough for the analysis that I am making now if we can say that, as a merely descriptive fact, women thus far in the history of the race have generally been more instinctive, more intuitive of subjective states, more emotional, more conservative than men; and that men, more generally than women, have been intuitive of objective relations, inclined therefore to break with instinct and to rely on the later-developed reasoning processes of the brain, and willing, consequently, to take chances, to experiment, and to innovate.

If so much be granted, we may perhaps say that it is because of these mental differences that in conflicts between new and old ideas, between new knowledge and old traditions, it usually happens that a large majority of all women are found in the camp of the old, and that the camp of the new is composed mainly of men.

In the camp of the new, however, are always to be found women of alert intelligence, who happen also to be temperamentally radical; women in whom the reasoning habit has asserted sway over instinct, and in whom intuition has become the true scientific power to discern objective relations. And in the camp of the old, together with a majority of all women, are to be found most of the men of conservative instinct, and most of those also whose intuitive and reasoning powers are unequal to the effort of thinking about the world or anything in it in terms of impersonal causation. Associated with all of these elements, both male and female, may usually be discovered, finally, a contingent of priestly personalities; not necessarily religious priests, but men who love to assert spiritual dominion, to wield authority, to be reverenced and obeyed, and who naturally look for a following among the non-skeptical and easily impressed.

Such, very broadly and rudely sketched, is the psychological background of culture conflict. It is, however, a background only, a certain persistent grouping of forces and conditions; it is not the cause from which culture conflicts proceed.

D. RACIAL CONFLICTS

1. Social Contacts and Race Conflict[1]

There is a conviction, widespread in America at the present time, that among the most fruitful sources of international wars are racial prejudice and national egotism. This conviction is the nerve of much present-day pacifism. It has been the inspiration of such unofficial diplomacy, for example, as that of the Federal Council of the Churches of Christ in its effort to bring about a better understanding between the Japanese and America. This book, *The Japanese Invasion*, by Jesse F. Steiner, is an attempt to study this phenomenon of race prejudice and national egotism, so far as it reveals itself in the relations of the Japanese and the Americans in this country, and to esti-

[1] From Robert E. Park, Introduction to Jesse F. Steiner, *The Japanese Invasion*. (A. C. McClurg & Co., 1917.)

mate the rôle it is likely to play in the future relations of the two countries.

So far as I know, an investigation of precisely this nature has not hitherto been made. One reason for this is, perhaps, that not until very recent times did the problem present itself in precisely this form. So long as the nations lived in practical isolation, carrying on their intercourse through the medium of professional diplomats, and knowing each other mainly through the products they exchanged, census reports, and the discreet observations of polite travelers, racial prejudice did not disturb international relations. With the extension of international commerce, the increase of immigration, and the interpenetration of peoples, the scene changes. The railway, the steamship, and the telegraph are rapidly mobilizing the peoples of the earth. The nations are coming out of their isolation, and distances which separated the different races are rapidly giving way before the extension of communication.

The same human motives which have led men to spread a network of trade-communication over the whole earth in order to bring about an exchange of commodities are now bringing about a new distribution of populations. When these populations become as mobile as the commodities of commerce, there will be practically no limits— except those artificial barriers, like the customs and immigration restrictions, maintained by individual states—to a world-wide economic and personal competition. Furthermore when the natural barriers are broken down, artificial barriers will be maintained with increasing difficulty.

Some conception of the extent of the changes which are taking place in the world under the influence of these forces may be gathered from the fact that in 1870 the cost of transporting a bushel of grain in Europe was so great as to prohibit its sale beyond a radius of two hundred miles from a primary market. By 1883 the importation of grains from the virgin soil of the western prairies in the United States had brought about an agricultural crisis in every country in western Europe.

One may illustrate, but it is scarcely possible to estimate, the economic changes which have been brought about by the enormous increase in ocean transportation. In 1840 the first Cunard liner, of 740 horse-power with a speed of 8.5 knots per hour, was launched.

In 1907, when the Lusitania was built, ocean-going vessels had attained a speed of 25 knots an hour and were drawn by engines of 70,000 horse-power.

It is difficult to estimate the economic changes which have been brought about by the changes in ocean transportation represented by these figures. It is still less possible to predict the political effects of the steadily increasing mobility of the peoples of the earth. At the present time this mobility has already reached a point at which it is often easier and cheaper to transport the world's population to the source of raw materials than to carry the world's manufactures to the established seats of population.

With the progressive rapidity, ease, and security of transportation, and the increase in communication, there follows an increasing detachment of the population from the soil and a concurrent concentration in great cities. These cities in time become the centers of vast numbers of uprooted individuals, casual and seasonal laborers, tenement and apartment-house dwellers, sophisticated and emancipated urbanites, who are bound together neither by local attachment nor by ties of family, clan, religion, or nationality. Under such conditions it is reasonable to expect that the same economic motive which leads every trader to sell in the highest market and to buy in the lowest will steadily increase and intensify the tendency, which has already reached enormous proportions of the population in overcrowded regions with diminished resources, to seek their fortunes, either permanently or temporarily, in the new countries of undeveloped resources.

Already the extension of commerce and the increase of immigration have brought about an international and inter-racial situation that has strained the inherited political order of the United States. It is this same expansive movement of population and of commerce, together with the racial and national rivalries that have sprung from them, which first destroyed the traditional balance of power in Europe and then broke up the scheme of international control which rested on it. Whatever may have been the immediate causes of the world-war, the more remote sources of the conflict must undoubtedly be sought in the great cosmic forces which have broken down the barriers which formerly separated the races and nationalities of the world, and forced them into new intimacies and new forms of competition, rivalry, and conflict.

Since 1870 the conditions which I have attempted to sketch have steadily forced upon America and the nations of Europe the problem of assimilating their heterogeneous populations. What we call the race problem is at once an incident of this process of assimilation and an evidence of its failure.

The present volume, *The Japanese Invasion: A Study in the Psychology of Inter-racial Contact*, touches but does not deal with the general situation which I have briefly sketched. It is, as its title suggests, a study in "racial contacts," and is an attempt to distinguish and trace to their sources the attitudes and the sentiments—that is to say, mutual prejudices—which have been and still are a source of mutual irritation and misunderstanding between the Japanese and American peoples.

Fundamentally, prejudice against the Japanese in the United States is merely the prejudice which attaches to every alien and immigrant people. The immigrant from Europe, like the immigrant from Asia, comes to this country because he finds here a freedom of individual action and an economic opportunity which he did not find at home. It is an instance of the general tendency of populations to move from an area of relatively closed, to one of relatively open, resources. The movement is as inevitable and, in the long run, as resistless as that which draws water from its mountain sources to the sea. It is one way of redressing the economic balance and bringing about an economic equilibrium.

The very circumstances under which this modern movement of population has arisen implies then that the standard of living, if not the cultural level, of the immigrant is lower than that of the native population. The consequence is that immigration brings with it a new and disturbing form of competition, the competition, namely, of peoples of a lower and of a higher standard of living. The effect of this competition, where it is free and unrestricted, is either to lower the living standards of the native population; to expel them from the vocations in which the immigrants are able or permitted to compete; or what may, perhaps, be regarded as a more sinister consequence, to induce such a restriction of the birth rate of the native population as to insure its ultimate extinction. The latter is, in fact, what seems to be happening in the New England manufacturing towns where the birth rate in the native population for some years past has fallen below the death rate, so that the native stock has long since ceased to reproduce itself. The foreign peoples, on the other hand, are rapidly replacing the native stocks, not merely by the influence of new immigration, but because of a relatively high excess of births over deaths.

It has been assumed that the prejudice which blinds the people of one race to the virtues of another and leads them to exaggerate that other's faults is in the nature of a misunderstanding which further knowledge will dispel. This is so far from true that it would be more exact to say that our racial misunderstandings are merely the expression of our racial antipathies. Behind these antipathies are deep-seated, vital, and instinctive impulses. Racial antipathies represent the collision of invisible forces, the clash of interests, dimly felt but not yet clearly perceived. They are present in every situation where the fundamental interests of races and peoples are not yet regulated by some law, custom, or any other *modus vivendi* which commands the assent and the mutual support of both parties. We hate people because we fear them, because our interests, as we understand them at any rate, run counter to theirs. On the other hand, good will is founded in the long run upon co-operation. The extension of our so-called altruistic sentiments is made possible only by the organization of our otherwise conflicting interests and by the extension of the mach nery of co-operation and social control.

Race prejudice may be regarded as a spontaneous, more or less instinctive, defense-reaction, the practical effect of which is to restrict free competition between races. Its importance as a social function is due to the fact that free competition, particularly between people with different standards of living, seems to be, if not the original source, at least the stimulus to which race prejudice is the response.

From this point of view we may regard caste, or even slavery, as one of those accommodations through which the race problem found a natural solution. Caste, by relegating the subject race to an inferior status, gives to each race at any rate a monopoly of its own tasks. When this status is accepted by the subject people, as is the case where the caste or slavery systems become fully established, racial competition ceases and racial animosity tends to disappear. That is the explanation of the intimate and friendly relations which so often existed in slavery between master and servant. It is for this reason that we hear it said today that the Negro is all right in his place. In his place he is a convenience and not a competitor. Each race being in its place, no obstacle to racial co-operation exists.

The fact that race prejudice is due to, or is in some sense dependent upon, race competition is further manifest by a fact that Mr. Steiner has emphasized, namely, that prejudice against the Japanese is nowhere uniform throughout the United States. It is only where the Japanese are present in sufficient numbers to actually disturb the economic status of the white population that prejudice has manifested itself to such a degree as to demand serious consideration. It is an interesting fact also that prejudice against the Japanese is now more intense than it is against any other oriental people. The reason for this, as Mr. Steiner has pointed out, is that the Japanese are more aggressive, more disposed to test the sincerity of that statement of the Declaration of Independence which declares that all men are equally entitled to "life, liberty, and the pursuit of happiness"—a statement, by the way, which was merely a forensic assertion of the laissez faire doctrine of free and unrestricted competition as applied to the relations of individual men.

The Japanese, the Chinese, they too would be all right in their place, no doubt. That place, if they find it, will be one in which they do not greatly intensify and so embitter the struggle for existence of the white man. The difficulty is that the Japanese is still less disposed than the Negro or the Chinese to submit to the regulations of a caste system and to stay in his place. The Japanese are an organized and morally efficient nation. They have the national pride and the national egotism which rests on the consciousness of this efficiency. In fact, it is not too much to say that national egotism, if one pleases to call it such, is essential to national efficiency, just as a certain irascibility of temper seems to be essential to a good fighter.

Another difficulty is that caste and the limitation of free competition is economically unsound, even though it be politically desirable. A national policy of national efficiency demands that every individual have not merely the opportunity but the preparation necessary to perform that particular service for the community for which his natural disposition and aptitude fit him, irrespective of race or "previous condition."

Finally, caste and the limitation of economic opportunity is contrary, if not to our traditions, at least to our political principles. That means that there will always be an active minority opposed to any settlement based on the caste system as applied to either the black or the brown races, on grounds of political sentiment. This minority will be small in parts of the country immediately adversely affected by the competition of the invading race. It will be larger in regions which are not greatly affected. It will be increased if immigration is so rapid as to make the competition more acute. We must look to other measures for the solution of the Japanese problem, if it should prove true, as seems probable, that we are not able or, for various reasons, do not care permanently to hold back the rising tide of the oriental invasion.

I have said that fundamentally and in principle prejudice against the Japanese in America today was identical with the prejudice which attaches to any immigrant people. There is, as Mr. Steiner has pointed out, a difference. This is due to the existence in the human mind of a mechanism by which we inevitably and automatically classify every individual human being we meet. When a race bears an external mark by which every individual member of it can infallibly be identified, that race is by that fact set apart and segregated. Japanese, Chinese, and Negroes cannot move among us with the same freedom as the members of other races because they bear marks which identify them as members of their race. This fact isolates them. In the end the effect of this isolation, both in its effects upon the Japanese themselves and upon the human environment in which they live, is profound. Isolation is at once a cause and an effect of race prejudice. It is a vicious circle—isolation, prejudice; prejudice, isolation. Were there no other reasons which urge us to consider the case of the Japanese and the oriental peoples in a category different from that of the European immigrant, this fact, that they are bound to live in the American community a more or less isolated life, would impel us to do so.

In conclusion, I may perhaps say in a word what seems to me the practical bearing of Mr. Steiner's book. Race prejudice is a mechanism of the group mind which acts reflexly and automatically in response to its proper stimulus. That stimulus seems to be, in the cases where I have met it, unrestricted competition of peoples with different standards of living. Racial animosities and the so-called racial misunderstandings that grow out of them cannot be explained or argued away. They can only be affected when there has been a readjustment of relations and an organization of interests in such a way as to bring about a larger measure of co-operation and a lesser amount of friction and conflict. This demands something more than a diplomacy of kind words. It demands a national policy based on an unflinching examination of the facts.

2.   Conflict and Race Consciousness[1]

The Civil War weakened but did not fully destroy the *modus vivendi* which slavery had established between the slave and his master. With emancipation the authority which had formerly been exercised by the master was transferred to the state, and Washington, D.C., began to assume in the mind of the freedman the position that formerly had been occupied by the "big house" on the plantation. The masses of the Negro people still maintained their habit of dependence, however, and after the first confusion of the change had passed, life went on, for most of them, much as it had before the war. As one old farmer explained, the only difference he could see was that in slavery he "was working for old Marster and now he was working for himself."

There was one difference between slavery and freedom, nevertheless, which was very real to the freedman. And this was the liberty to move. To move from one plantation to another in case he was discontented was one of the ways in which a freedman was able to realize his freedom and to make sure that he possessed it. This liberty to move meant a good deal more to the plantation Negro than one not acquainted with the situation in the South is likely to understand.

If there had been an abundance of labor in the South; if the situation had been such that the Negro laborer was seeking the opportunity to work, or such that the Negro tenant farmers were

[1] From Robert E. Park, "Racial Assimilation in Secondary Groups," in *Publications of the American Sociological Society*, VIII (1913), 75–82.

competing for the opportunity to get a place on the land, as is so
frequently the case in Europe, the situation would have been fundamentally different from what it actually was.   But the South was,
and is today, what Nieboer called a country of "open," in contra-
distinction to a country of "closed" resources.   In other words, there
is more land in the South than there is labor to till it.   Land owners
are driven to competing for laborers and tenants to work their
plantations.

Owing to his ignorance of business matters and to a long-
established habit of submission, the Negro after emancipation was
placed at a great disadvantage in his dealings with the white man.
His right to move from one plantation to another became, therefore,
the Negro tenant's method of enforcing consideration from the
planter.   He might not dispute the planter's accounts, because he
was not capable of doing so, and it was unprofitable to attempt it,
but if he felt aggrieved he could move.

This was the significance of the exodus in some of the southern
states which took place about 1879, when 40,000 people left the
plantations in the Black Belts of Louisiana and Mississippi and
went to Kansas.   The masses of the colored people were dissatisfied
with the treatment they were receiving from the planters and made
up their minds to move to "a free country," as they described it.
At the same time it was the attempt of the planter to bind the Negro
tenant who was in debt to him to his place on the plantation that
gave rise to the system of peonage that still exists in a mitigated
form in the South today.

When the Negro moved off the plantation upon which he was
reared he severed the personal relations which bound him to his
master's people.   It was just at this point that the two races began
to lose touch with each other.   From this time on the relations of
the black man and white, which in slavery had been direct and
personal, became every year, as the old associations were broken,
more and more indirect and secondary.   There lingers still the disposition on the part of the white man to treat every Negro familiarly,
and the disposition on the part of every Negro to treat every white
man respectfully.   But these are habits which are gradually disappearing.   The breaking down of the instincts and habits of servitude and the acquisition by the masses of the Negro people of the

instincts and habits of freedom have proceeded slowly but steadily. The reason the change seems to have gone on more rapidly in some cases than others is explained by the fact that at the time of emancipation 10 per cent of the Negroes in the United States were already free, and others, those who had worked in trades, many of whom had hired their own time from their masters, had become more or less adapted to the competitive conditions of free society.

One of the effects of the mobilization of the Negro has been to bring him into closer and more intimate contact with his own people. Common interests have drawn the blacks together, and caste sentiment has kept the black and white apart. The segregation of the races, which began as a spontaneous movement on the part of both, has been fostered by the policy of the dominant race. The agitation of the Reconstruction period made the division between the races in politics absolute. Segregation and separation in other matters have gone on steadily ever since. The Negro at the present time has separate churches, schools, libraries, hospitals, Y.M.C.A. associations, and even separate towns. There are, perhaps, a half-dozen communities in the United States, every inhabitant of which is a Negro. Most of these so-called Negro towns are suburban villages; two of them, at any rate, are the centers of a considerable Negro farming population. In general it may be said that where the Negro schools, churches, and Y.M.C.A. associations are not separate they do not exist.

It is hard to estimate the ultimate effect of this isolation of the black man. One of the most important effects has been to establish a common interest among all the different colors and classes of the race. This sense of solidarity has grown up gradually with the organization of the Negro people. It is stronger in the South, where segregation is more complete, than it is in the North where, twenty years ago, it would have been safe to say it did not exist. Gradually, imperceptibly, within the larger world of the white man, a smaller world, the world of the black man, is silently taking form and shape.

Every advance in education and intelligence puts the Negro in possession of the technique of communication and organization of the white man, and so contributes to the extension and consolidation of the Negro world within the white.

The motive for this increasing solidarity is furnished by the increasing pressure, or perhaps I should say by the increasing sensibility of Negroes to the pressure and the prejudice without. The sentiment of racial loyalty, which is a comparatively recent manifestation of the growing self-consciousness of the race, must be regarded as a response and "accommodation" to changing internal and external relations of the race. The sentiment which Negroes are beginning to call "race pride" does not exist to the same extent in the North as in the South, but an increasing disposition to enforce racial distinctions in the North, as in the South, is bringing it into existence.

One or two incidents in this connection are significant. A few years ago a man who is the head of the largest Negro publishing business in this country sent to Germany and had a number of Negro dolls manufactured according to specifications of his own. At the time this company was started, Negro children were in the habit of playing with white dolls. There were already Negro dolls on the market, but they were for white children and represented the white man's conception of the Negro and not the Negro's ideal of himself. The new Negro doll was a mulatto with regular features slightly modified in favor of the conventional Negro type. It was a neat, prim, well-dressed, well-behaved, self-respecting doll. Later on, as I understand, there were other dolls, equally tidy and respectable in appearance, but in darker shades, with Negro features a little more pronounced. The man who designed these dolls was perfectly clear in regard to the significance of the substitution that he was making. He said that he thought it was a good thing to let Negro girls become accustomed to dolls of their own color. He thought it important, as long as the races were to be segregated, that the dolls, which, like other forms of art, are patterns and represent ideals, should be segregated also.

This substitution of the Negro model for the white is a very interesting and a very significant fact. It means that the Negro has begun to fashion his own ideals and in his own image rather than in that of the white man. It is also interesting to know that the Negro doll company has been a success and that these dolls are now widely sold in every part of the United States. Nothing exhibits more clearly the extent to which the Negro had become assimilated in slavery or the extent to which he has broken with the past in recent years than this episode of the Negro doll.

The incident is typical. It is an indication of the nature of tendencies and of forces that are stirring in the background of the Negro's mind, although they have not succeeded in forcing themselves, except in special instances, into clear consciousness.

In this same category must be reckoned the poetry of Paul Lawrence Dunbar, in whom, as William Dean Howells has said, the Negro "attained civilization." Before Paul Lawrence Dunbar, Negro literature had been either apologetic or self-assertive, but Dunbar "studied the Negro objectively." He represented him as he found him, not only without apology, but with an affectionate understanding and sympathy which one can have only for what is one's own. In Dunbar, Negro literature attained an ethnocentric point of view. Through the medium of his verses the ordinary shapes and forms of the Negro's life have taken on the color of his affections and sentiments, and we see the black man, not as he looks, but as he feels and is.

It is a significant fact that a certain number of educated—or rather the so-called educated—Negroes were not at first disposed to accept at their full value either Dunbar's dialect verse or the familiar pictures of Negro life which are the symbols in which his poetry usually found expression. The explanation sometimes offered for the dialect poems was that "they were made to please white folk." The assumption seems to have been that if they had been written for Negroes it would have been impossible in his poetry to distinguish black people from white. This was a sentiment which was never shared by the masses of the people, who, upon the occasions when Dunbar recited to them, were fairly bowled over with amusement and delight because of the authenticity of the portraits he offered them. At the present time Dunbar is so far accepted as to have hundreds of imitators.

Literature and art have played a similar and perhaps more important rôle in the racial struggles of Europe than of America. One reason seems to be that racial conflicts, as they occur in secondary groups, are primarily sentimental and secondarily economic. Literature and art, when they are employed to give expression to racial sentiment and form to racial ideals, serve, along with other agencies, to mobilize the group and put the masses *en rapport* with their leaders and with each other. In such cases art and literature are like silent drummers which summon into action the latent instincts and energies of the race.

These struggles, I might add, in which a submerged people seek to rise and make for themselves a place in a world occupied by superior and privileged races, are not less vital or less important because they are bloodless. They serve to stimulate ambitions and inspire ideals which years, perhaps, of subjection and subordination have suppressed. In fact, it seems as if it were through conflicts of this kind, rather than through war, that the minor peoples were destined to gain the moral concentration and discipline that fit them to share, on anything like equal terms, in the conscious life of the civilized world.

Until the beginning of the last century the European peasant, like the Negro slave, bound as he was to the soil, lived in the little world of direct and personal relations, under what we may call a domestic régime. It was military necessity that first turned the attention of statesmen like Frederick the Great of Prussia to the welfare of the peasant. It was the overthrow of Prussia by Napoleon in 1807 that brought about his final emancipation in that country. In recent years it has been the international struggle for economic efficiency which has contributed most to mobilize the peasant and laboring classes in Europe.

As the peasant slowly emerged from serfdom he found himself a member of a depressed class, without education, political privileges, or capital. It was the struggle of this class for wider opportunity and better conditions of life that made most of the history of the previous century. Among the peoples in the racial borderland the effect of this struggle has been, on the whole, to substitute for a horizontal organization of society—in which the upper strata, that is to say, the wealthy or privileged class, was mainly of one race and the poorer and subject class was mainly of another—a vertical organization in which all classes of each racial group were united under the title of their respective nationalities. Thus organized, the nationalities represent, on the one hand, intractable minorities engaged in a ruthless partisan struggle for political privilege or economic advantage and, on the other, they represent cultural groups, each struggling to maintain a sentiment of loyalty to the distinctive traditions, language, and institutions of the race they represent.

This sketch of the racial situation in Europe is, of course, the barest abstraction and should not be accepted realistically. It is intended merely as an indication of similarities, in the broader outlines, of the motives that have produced nationalities in Europe and are making the Negro in America, as Booker Washington says, "a nation within a nation."

It may be said that there is one profound difference between the Negro and the European nationalities, namely, that the Negro has had his separateness and consequent race consciousness thrust upon him because of his exclusion and forcible isolation from white society. The Slavic nationalities, on the contrary, have segregated themselves in order to escape assimilation and escape racial extinction in the larger cosmopolitan states.

The difference is, however, not so great as it seems. With the exception of the Poles, nationalistic sentiment may be said hardly to have existed fifty years ago. Forty years ago when German was the language of the educated classes, educated Bohemians were a little ashamed to speak their own language in public. Now nationalist sentiment is so strong that, where the Czech nationality has gained control, it has sought to wipe out every vestige of the German language. It has changed the names of streets, buildings, and public places. In the city of Prag, for example, all that formerly held German associations now fairly reeks with the sentiment of Bohemian nationality.

On the other hand, the masses of the Polish people cherished very little nationalist sentiment until after the Franco-Prussian War. The fact is that nationalist sentiment among the Slavs, like racial sentiment among the Negroes, has sprung up as the result of a struggle against privilege and discrimination based upon racial distinctions. The movement is not so far advanced among Negroes; sentiment is not so intense, and for several reasons probably never will be.

From what has been said it seems fair to draw one conclusion, namely: under conditions of secondary contact, that is to say, conditions of individual liberty and individual competition, characteristic of modern civilization, depressed racial groups tend to assume the form of nationalities.   A nationality, in this narrower sense, may be defined as the racial group which has attained self-consciousness, no matter whether it has at the same time gained political independence or not.

In societies organized along horizontal lines the disposition of individuals in the lower strata is to seek their models in the strata above them.   Loyalty attaches to individuals, particularly to the upper classes, who furnish, in their persons and in their lives, the models for the masses of the people below them.   Long after the nobility has lost every other social function connected with its vocation the ideals of the nobility have survived in our conception of the gentleman, genteel manners and bearing—gentility.

The sentiment of the Negro slave was, in a certain sense, not merely loyalty to his master but to the white race.   Negroes of the older generations speak very frequently, with a sense of proprietorship, of "our white folks."   This sentiment was not always confined to the ignorant masses.   An educated colored man once explained to me "that we colored people always want our white folks to be superior."   He was shocked when I showed no particular enthusiasm for that form of sentiment.

The fundamental significance of the nationalist movement must be sought in the effort of subject races, sometimes consciously, sometimes unconsciously, to substitute, for those supplied them by aliens, models based on their own racial individuality and embodying sentiments and ideals which spring naturally out of their own lives.

After a race has achieved in this way its moral independence, assimilation, in the sense of copying, will still continue.   Nations and races borrow from those whom they fear as well as from those whom they admire.   Materials taken over in this way, however, are inevitably stamped with the individuality of the nationalities that appropriate them.   These materials will contribute to the dignity, to the prestige, and to the solidarity of the nationality which borrows them, but they will no longer inspire loyalty to the race from which they are borrowed.   A race which has attained the character of a nationality may still retain its loyalty to the state of which it is a part, but only in so far as that state incorporates, as an integral part of its organization, the practical interests, the aspirations and ideals of that nationality.

The aim of the contending nationalities in Austria-Hungary at the present time seems to be a federation, like that of Switzerland, based upon the autonomy of the different races composing the empire. In the South, similarly, the races seem to be tending in the direction of a bi-racial organization of society, in which the Negro is gradually gaining a limited autonomy. What the ultimate outcome of this movement may be it is not safe to predict.

3. Conflict and Accommodation[1]

In the first place, what is race friction? To answer this elementary question it is necessary to define the abstract mental quality upon which race friction finally rests. This is racial "antipathy," popularly spoken of as "race prejudice." Whereas prejudice means mere predilection, either for or against, antipathy means "natural contrariety," "incompatibility," or "repugnance of qualities." To quote the Century Dictionary, antipathy "expresses most of constitutional feeling and least of volition"; "it is a dislike that seems constitutional toward persons, things, conduct, etc.; hence it involves a dislike for which sometimes no good reason can be given." I would define racial antipathy, then, as a natural contrariety, repugnancy of qualities, or incompatibility between individuals or groups which are sufficiently differentiated to constitute what, for want of a more exact term, we call races. What is most important is that it involves an instinctive feeling of dislike, distaste, or repugnance, for which sometimes no good reason can be given. Friction is defined primarily as a "lack of harmony," or a "mutual irritation." In the case of races it is accentuated by antipathy. We do not have to depend on race riots or other acts of violence as a measure of the growth of race friction. Its existence may be manifested by a look or a gesture as well as by a word or an act.

A verbal cause of much useless and unnecessary controversy is found in the use of the word "race." When we speak of "race problems" or "racial antipathies," what do we mean by "race"? Clearly nothing scientifically definite, since ethnologists themselves are not agreed upon any classification of the human family along racial lines.

[1] Adapted from Alfred H. Stone, "Is Race Friction between Blacks and Whites in the United States Growing and Inevitable?" in the *American Journal of Sociology*, XIII (1907-8), 677-96.

Nor would this so-called race prejudice have the slightest regard for such classification, if one were agreed upon. It is something which is not bounded by the confines of a philological or ethnological definition. The British scientist may tell the British soldier in India that the native is in reality his brother, and that it is wholly absurd and illogical and unscientific for such a thing as "race prejudice" to exist between them. Tommy Atkins simply replies with a shrug that to him and his messmates the native is a "nigger"; and in so far as their attitude is concerned, that is the end of the matter. The same suggestion, regardless of the scientific accuracy of the parallel, if made to the American soldier in the Philippines, meets with the same reply. We have wasted an infinite amount of time in interminable controversies over the relative superiority and inferiority of different races. Such discussions have a certain value when conducted by scientific men in a purely scientific spirit. But for the purpose of explaining or establishing any fixed principle of race relations they are little better than worthless. The Japanese is doubtless quite well satisfied of the superiority of his people over the mushroom growths of western civilization, and finds no difficulty in borrowing from the latter whatever is worth reproducing, and improving on it in adapting it to his own racial needs. The Chinese do not waste their time in idle chatter over the relative status of their race as compared with the white barbarians who have intruded themselves upon them with their grotesque customs, their heathenish ideas, and their childishly new religion. The Hindu regards with veiled contempt the racial pretensions of his conqueror, and, while biding the time when the darker races of the earth shall once more come into their own, does not bother himself with such an idle question as whether his temporary overlord is his racial equal. Only the white man writes volumes to establish on paper the fact of a superiority which is either self-evident and not in need of demonstration, on the one hand, or is not a fact and is not demonstrable, on the other. The really important matter is one about which there need be little dispute—the fact of racial differences. It is the practical question of differences—the fundamental differences of physical appearance, of mental habit and thought, of social customs and religious beliefs, of the thousand and one things keenly and clearly appreciable, yet sometimes elusive and undefinable—these are the things which at once create and find expression in what we call race problems and race prejudices, for want of better terms. In just so far as these differences are fixed and permanently associated characteristics of two groups of people will the antipathies and problems between the two be permanent.

Probably the closest approach we shall ever make to a satisfactory classification of races as a basis of antipathy will be that of grouping men according to color, along certain broad lines, the color being accompanied by various and often widely different, but always fairly persistent, differentiating physical and mental characteristics. This would give us substantially the white—not Caucasian, the yellow—not Chinese or Japanese, and the dark—not Negro, races. The antipathies between these general groups and between certain of their subdivisions will be found to be essentially fundamental, but they will also be found to present almost endless differences of degrees of actual and potential acuteness. Here elementary psychology also plays its part. One of the subdivisions of the Negro race is composed of persons of mixed blood. In many instances these are more white than black, yet the association of ideas has through several generations identified them with the Negro—and in this country friction between this class and white people is on some lines even greater than between whites and blacks.

Race conflicts are merely the more pronounced concrete expressions of such friction. They are the visible phenomena of the abstract quality of racial antipathy—the tangible evidence of the existence of racial problems. The form of such expressions of antipathy varies with the nature of the racial contact in each instance. Their different and widely varying aspects are the confusing and often contradictory phenomena of race relations. They are dependent upon diverse conditions, and are no more susceptible of rigid and permanent classification than are the whims and moods of human nature. It is more than a truism to say that a condition precedent to race friction or race conflict is contact between sufficient numbers of two diverse racial groups. There is a definite and positive difference between contact between individuals and contact between masses. The association between two isolated individual members of two races may be wholly different from contact between masses of the same race groups. The factor of numbers embraces, indeed, the very crux of the problems arising from contact between different races.

A primary cause of race friction is the vague, rather intangible, but wholly real, feeling of "pressure" which comes to the white man almost instinctively in the presence of a mass of people of a different race. In a certain important sense all racial problems are distinctly problems of racial distribution. Certainly the definite action of the controlling race, particularly as expressed in laws, is determined by the factor of the numerical difference between its population and that of the inferior group. This fact stands out prominently in the history of our colonial legislation for the control of Negro slaves. These laws increased in severity up to a certain point as the slave population increased in numbers. The same condition is disclosed in the history of the ante-bellum legislation of the southern, eastern, New England, and middle western states for the control of the free Negro population. So today no state in the Union would have separate car laws where the Negro constituted only 10 or 15 per cent of its total population. No state would burden itself with the maintenance of two separate school systems with a negro element of less than 10 per cent. Means of local separation might be found but there would be no expression of law on the subject.

Just as a heavy increase of Negro population makes for an increase of friction, direct legislation, the protection of drastic social customs, and a general feeling of unrest or uneasiness on the part of the white population, so a decrease of such population, or a relatively small increase as compared with the whites, makes for less friction, greater racial tolerance, and a lessening of the feeling of necessity for severely discriminating laws or customs. And this quite aside from the fact of a difference of increase or decrease of actual points of contact, varying with differences of numbers. The statement will scarcely be questioned that the general attitude of the white race, as a whole, toward the Negro would become much less uncompromising if we were to discover that through two census periods the race had shown a positive decrease in numbers. Racial antipathy would not decrease, but the conditions which provoke its outward expression would undergo a change for the better. There is a direct relation between the mollified attitude of the people of the Pacific coast toward the Chinese population and the fact that the Chinese population decreased between 1890 and 1900. There would in time be a difference of feeling toward the Japanese now there if the immigration of more were prohibited by treaty stipulation. There is the same immediate relation between the tolerant attitude of whites toward the natives in the Hawaiian Islands and the feeling that the native is a decadent and dying race. Aside from the influence of the Indian's warlike qualities and of his refusal to submit to slavery, the attitude and disposition of the white race toward him have been influenced by considerations similar to those which today operate in Hawaii. And the same influence has been a factor in determining the attitude of the English toward the slowly dying Maoris of New Zealand.

At no time in the history of the English-speaking people and at no place of which we have any record where large numbers of them have been brought into contact with an approximately equal number of Negroes have the former granted to the latter absolute equality, either political, social, or economic. With the exception of five New England states, with a total Negro population of only 16,084 in 1860, every state in the Union discriminated against the Negro politically before the Civil War. The white people continued to do so— North as well as South—as long as they retained control of the suffrage regulations of their states. The determination to do so renders one whole section of the country practically a political unit to this day. In South Africa we see the same determination of the white man to rule, regardless of the numerical superiority of the black. The same determination made Jamaica surrender the right of self-government and renders her satisfied with a hybrid political arrangement today. The presence of practically 100,000 Negroes in the District of Columbia makes 200,000 white people content to live under an anomaly in a self-governing country. The proposition is too elementary for discussion that the white man when confronted with a sufficient number of Negroes to create in his mind a sense of political unrest or danger either alters his form of government in order to be rid of the incubus or destroys the political strength of the Negro by force, by evasion, or by direct action.

In the main, the millions in the South live at peace with their white neighbors. The masses, just one generation out of slavery and thousands of them still largely controlled by its influences, accept the superiority of the white race as a race, whatever may be their private opinion of some of its members. And, furthermore, they accept this relation of superior and inferior as a mere matter of course—as part of their lives—as something neither to be questioned, wondered at, or worried over. Despite apparent impressions to the contrary, the average southern white man gives no more thought to the matter than does the Negro. As I tried to make clear at the outset, the status of superior and inferior is simply an inherited part of his instinctive mental equipment—a concept which he does not have to reason out. The respective attitudes are complementary, and under the mutual acceptance and understanding there still exist unnumbered thousands of instances of kindly and affectionate relations—relations of which the outside world knows nothing and understands nothing. In the mass, the southern Negro has not bothered himself about the ballot for more than twenty years, not since his so-called political leaders let him alone; he is not disturbed over the matter of separate schools and cars, and he neither knows nor cares anything about "social equality."

But what of the other class? The "masses" is at best an unsatisfactory and indefinite term. It is very far from embracing even the southern Negro, and we need not forget that seven years ago there were 900,000 members of the race living outside of the South. What of the class, mainly urban and large in number, who have lost the typical habit and attitude of the Negro of the mass, and who, more and more, are becoming restless and chafing under existing conditions? There is an intimate and very natural relation between the social and intellectual advance of the so-called Negro and the matter of friction along social lines. It is, in fact, only as we touch the higher groups that we can appreciate the potential results of contact upon a different plane from that common to the masses in the South. There is a large and steadily increasing group of men, more or less related to the Negro by blood and wholly identified with him by American social usage, who refuse to accept quietly the white man's attitude toward the race. I appreciate the mistake of laying too great stress upon the utterances of any one man or group of men, but the mistakes in this case lie the other way. The American white man knows little or nothing about the thought and opinion of the colored men and women who today largely mold and direct Negro public opinion in this country. Even the white man who considers himself a student of "the race question" rarely exhibits anything more than profound ignorance of the Negro's side of the problem. He does not know what the other man is thinking and saying on the subject. This composite type which we poetically call "black," but which in reality is every shade from black to white, is slowly developing a consciousness of its own racial solidarity. It is finding its own distinctive voice, and through its own books and papers and magazines, and through its own social organizations, is at once giving utterance to its discontent and making known its demands.

And with this dawning consciousness of race there is likewise coming an appreciation of the limitations and restrictions which hem in its unfolding and development. One of the best indices to the possibilities of increased racial friction is the Negro's own recognition of the universality of the white man's racial antipathy toward him. This is the one clear note above the storm of protest against the things that are, that in his highest aspirations everywhere the white man's "prejudice" blocks the colored man's path. And the white man may with possible profit pause long enough to ask the deeper significance of the Negro's finding of himself. May it not be only part of a general awakening of the darker races of the earth? Captain H. A. Wilson, of the English army, says that through all Africa there has penetrated in some way a vague confused report that far off somewhere, in the unknown, outside world, a great war has been fought between a white and a yellow race, and won by the yellow man. And even before the Japanese-Russian conflict, "Ethiopianism" and the cry of "Africa for the Africans" had begun to disturb the English in South Africa. It is said time and again that the dissatisfaction and unrest in India are accentuated by the results of this same war. There can be no doubt in the mind of any man who carefully reads American Negro journals that their rejoicing over the Japanese victory sounded a very different note from that of the white American. It was far from being a mere expression of sympathy with a people fighting for national existence against a power which had made itself odious to the civilized world by its treatment of its subjects. It was, instead, a quite clear cry of exultation over the defeat of a white race by a dark one. The white man is no wiser than the ostrich if he refuses to see the truth that in the possibilities of race friction the Negro's increasing consciousness of race is to play a part scarcely less important than the white man's racial antipathies, prejudices, or whatever we may elect to call them.

CHAPTER VIII

ACCOMMODATION

I. INTRODUCTION

1. Adaptation and Accommodation

The term *adaptation* came into vogue with Darwin's theory of the origin of the species by natural selection. This theory was based upon the observation that no two members of a biological species or of a family are ever exactly alike. Everywhere there is variation and individuality. Darwin's theory assumed this variation and explained the species as the result of natural selection. The individuals best fitted to live under the conditions of life which the environment offered, survived and produced the existing species. The others perished and the species which they represented disappeared. The differences in the species were explained as the result of the accumulation and per-petuation of the individual variations which had "survival value." Adaptations were the variations which had been in this way selected and transmitted.

The term *accommodation* is a kindred concept with a slightly different meaning. The distinction is that adaptation is applied to organic modifications which are transmitted biologically; while accommodation is used with reference to changes in habit, which are transmitted, or may be transmitted, sociologically, that is, in the form of social tradition. The term first used in this sense by Baldwin is defined in the *Dictionary of Philosophy and Psychology*.

In view of modern biological theory and discussion, two modes of adaptation should be distinguished: (*a*) adaptation through variation [hereditary]; (*b*) adaptation through modification [acquired]. For the functional adjustment of the individual to its environment [(*b*) above] J. Mark Baldwin has suggested the term "accommodation," recommending that adaptation be confined to the structural adjustments which are con-genital and heredity [(*a*) above]. The term "accommodation" applies to any acquired alteration of function resulting in better adjustment to environment and to the functional changes which are thus effected.[1]

The term accommodation, while it has a limited field of application in biology, has a wide and varied use in sociology. All the social heritages, traditions, sentiments, culture, technique, are accommodations—that is, acquired adjustments that are socially and not biologically transmitted. They are not a part of the racial inheritance of the individual, but are acquired by the person in social experience. The two conceptions are further distinguished in this, that adaptation is an effect of competition, while accommodation, or more properly social accommodation, is the result of conflict.

The outcome of the adaptations and accommodations, which the struggle for existence enforces, is a state of relative equilibrium among the competing species and individual members of these species. The equilibrium which is established by adaptation is biological, which means that, in so far as it is permanent and fixed in the race or the species, it will be transmitted by biological inheritance.

The equilibrium based on accommodation, however, is not biological; it is economic and social and is transmitted, if at all, by tradition. The nature of the economic equilibrium which results from competition has been fully described in chapter viii. The plant community is this equilibrium in its absolute form.

In animal and human societies the community has, so to speak, become incorporated in the individual members of the group. The individuals are adapted to a specific type of communal life, and these adaptations, in animal as distinguished from human societies, are represented in the division of labor between the sexes, in the instincts which secure the protection and welfare of the young, in the so-called gregarious instinct, and all these represent traits that are transmitted biologically. But human societies, although providing for the expression of original tendencies, are organized about tradition, mores, collective representations, in short, *consensus*. And consensus represents, not biological adaptations, but social accommodations.

Social organization, with the exception of the order based on competition and adaptation, is essentially an accommodation of differences through conflicts. This fact explains why diversemindedness rather than like-mindedness is characteristic of human as

[1] *Dictionary of Philosophy and Psychology*, I, 15, 8.

distinguished from animal society. Professor Cooley's statement of this point is clear:

> The unity of the social mind consists not in agreement but in organization, in the fact of reciprocal influence or causation among its parts, by virtue of which everything that takes place in it is connected with everything else, and so is an outcome of the whole.[1]

The distinction between accommodation and adaptation is illustrated in the difference between domestication and taming. Through domestication and breeding man has modified the original inheritable traits of plants and animals. He has changed the character of the species. Through taming, individuals of species naturally in conflict with man have become accommodated to him. Eugenics may be regarded as a program of biological adaptation of the human race in conscious realization of social ideals. Education, on the other hand, represents a program of accommodation or an organization, modification, and culture of original traits.

Every society represents an organization of elements more or less antagonistic to each other but united for the moment, at least, by an arrangement which defines the reciprocal relations and respective spheres of action of each. This accommodation, this *modus vivendi*, may be relatively permanent as in a society constituted by castes, or quite transitory as in societies made up of open classes. In either case, the accommodation, while it is maintained, secures for the individual or for the group a recognized status.

Accommodation is the natural issue of conflicts. In an accommodation the antagonism of the hostile elements is, for the time being, regulated, and conflict disappears as overt action, although it remains latent as a potential force. With a change in the situation, the adjustment that had hitherto successfully held in control the antagonistic forces fails. There is confusion and unrest which may issue in open conflict. Conflict, whether a war or a strike or a mere exchange of polite innuendoes, invariably issues in a new accommodation or social order, which in general involves a changed status in the relations among the participants. It is only with assimilation that this antagonism, latent in the organization of individuals or groups, is likely to be wholly dissolved.

[1] *Social Organization*, p. 4.

2. Classification of the Materials

The selections on accommodation in the materials are organized under the following heads: (*a*) forms of accommodation; (*b*) subordination and superordination; (*c*) conflict and accommodation; and (*d*) competition, status, and social solidarity.

a) *Forms of accommodation.*—There are many forms of accommodation. One of the most subtle is that which in human geography is called acclimatization, "accommodation to new climatic conditions." Recent studies like those of Huntington in his "Climate and Civilization" have emphasized the effects of climate upon human behavior. The selection upon acclimatization by Brinton states the problems involved in the adjustment of racial groups to different climatic environments. The answers which he gives to the questions raised are not to be regarded as conclusive but only as representative of one school of investigators and as contested by other authorities in this field.

Naturalization, which in its original sense means the process by which a person is made "natural," that is, familiar and at home in a strange social milieu, is a term used in America to describe the legal process by which a foreigner acquires the rights of citizenship. Naturalization, as a social process, is naturally something more fundamental than the legal ceremony of naturalization. It includes accommodation to the folkways, the mores, the conventions, and the social ritual (*Sittlichkeit*). It assumes also participation, to a certain extent at least, in the memories, the tradition, and the culture of a new social group. The proverb "In Rome do as the Romans do" is a basic principle of naturalization. The cosmopolitan is the person who readily accommodates himself to the codes of conduct of new social milieus.[1]

[1] A teacher in the public schools of Chicago came in possession of the following letter written to a friend in Mississippi by a Negro boy who had come to the city from the South two months previously. It illustrates his rapid accommodation to the situation including the hostile Irish group (the Wentworth Avenue "Mickeys").

Dear leon I write to you—to let you hear from me—Boy you dont know the time we have with Sled. it Snow up here Regular. We Play foot Ball. But Now we have So much Snow we dont Play foot Ball any More. We Ride on Sled. Boy I have a Sled call The king of The hill and She king to. tell Mrs. Sara that Coln Roscoe Conklin Simon Spoke at St Mark the church we Belong to.

Gus I havnt got chance to Beat But to Boy. Sack we show Runs them Mickeys. Boy them scoundle is bad on Wentworth Avenue.

Add ₃123a Breton St Chi ill.

The difficulty of social accommodation to a new social milieu is not always fully appreciated. The literature on homesickness and nostalgia indicates the emotional dependence of the person upon familiar associations and upon early intimate personal relations. Leaving home for the first time, the intense lonesomeness of the rural lad in the crowds of the city, the perplexity of the immigrant in the confusing maze of strange, and to him inexplicable, customs are common enough instances of the personal and social barriers to naturalization. But the obstacles to most social adjustments for a person in a new social world are even more baffling because of their subtle and intangible nature.

Just as in biology balance represents "a state of relatively good adjustment due to structural adaptation of the organism as a whole" so accommodation, when applied to groups rather than individuals, signifies their satisfactory co-ordination from the standpoint of the inclusive social organization.

Historically, the organization of the more inclusive society—i.e., states, confederations, empires, social and political units composed of groups accommodated but not fully assimilated—presents four typical constellations of the component group. Primitive society was an organization of kinship groups. Ancient society was composed of masters and slaves, with some special form of accommodation for the freeman and the stranger, who was not a citizen, to be sure, but was not a slave either.

Medieval society rested upon a system of class, approaching castes in the distances it enforced. In all these different situations competition took place only between individuals of the same status.

In contrast with this, modern society is made up of economic and social classes with freedom of economic competition and freedom in passage, therefore, from one class to the other.

b) *Subordination and superordination.*—Accommodation, in the area of personal relations, tends to take the form of subordination and superordination. Even where accommodation has been imposed, as in the case of slavery, by force, the personal relations of master and slave are invariably supported by appropriate attitudes and sentiments. The selection "Excerpts from the Journal of a West India Slave Owner" is a convincing exhibit of the way in which attitudes of superordination and subordination may find expression in the sentiments of a conscientious and self-complacent paternalism on the part of the master and of an ingratiating and reverential loyalty on the part of the slave. In a like manner the selection from the "Memories of an Old Servant" indicates the natural way in which sentiments of subordination which have grown up in conformity with an accepted situation eventually become the basis of a life-philosophy of the person.

Slavery and caste are manifestly forms of accommodation. The facts of subordination are quite as real, though not as obvious, in other phases of social life. The peculiar intimacy which exists, for example, between lovers, between husband and wife, or between physician and patient, involves relations of subordination and superordination, though not recognized as such. The personal domination which a coach exercises over the members of a ball team, a minister over his congregation, the political leader over his party followers are instances of the same phenomena.

Simmel in his interesting discussion of the subject points out the fact that the relations of subordination and superordination are reciprocal. In order to impose his will upon his slaves it was necessary for the master to retain their respect. No one had a keener appreciation of the aristocracy nor a greater scorn for the "poor white" than the Negro slaves in the South before the war.

The leader of the gang, although he seems to have decisions absolutely in his hand, has a sense of the attitudes of his followers. So the successful political leader, who sometimes appears to be taking risks in his advocacy of new issues, keeps "his ear close to the grass roots of public opinion."

In the selection upon "The Psychology of Subordination and Superordination" Münsterberg interprets suggestion, imitation, and sympathy in terms of domination and submission. Personal influence, prestige, and authority, in whatever form they find expression, are based, to a greater or less extent, on the subtle influences of suggestion.

The natural affections are social bonds which not infrequently assume the form of bondage. Many a mother has been reduced to a condition of abject subjection through her affection for a son or a daughter. The same thing is notoriously true of the relations between the sexes. It is in social complexes of this sort, rather than in the formal procedures of governments, that we must look for the fundamental mechanism of social control.

The conflicts and accommodations of persons with persons and of groups with groups have their prototypes in the conflicts and accommodations of the wishes of the person. The conflicts and accommodations in the mental life of the person have received the name in psychoanalysis of *sublimation*. The sublimation of a wish means its expression in a form which represents an accommodation with another conflicting wish which had repressed the original response of the first wish. The progressive organization of personality depends upon the successful functioning of this process of sublimation. The wishes of the person at birth are inchoate; with mental development these wishes come into conflict with each other and with the enveloping social milieu. Adolescence is peculiarly the period of "storm and stress." Youth lives in a maze of mental conflicts, of insurgent and aspiring wishes. Conversion is the sudden mutation of life-attitudes through a reorganization or transformation of the wishes.

c) Conflict and accommodation—The intrinsic relation between conflict and accommodation is stated in the materials by Simmel in his analysis of war and peace and the problems of compromise. "The situations existing in time of peace are precisely the conditions out of which war emerges." War, on the other hand, brings about the adjustments in the relations of competing and conflict groups which make peace possible. The problem, therefore, must find a solution in some method by which the conflicts which are latent in, or develop out of, the conditions of peace may be adjusted without a resort to war. In so far as war is an effect of the mere inhibitions which the conditions of peace impose, substitutes for war must provide, as William James has suggested, for the expression of the expanding energies of individuals and nations in ways that will contribute to the welfare of the community and eventually of mankind as a whole. The intention is to make life more interesting and at the same time more secure.

The difficulty is that the devices which render life more secure frequently make it less interesting and harder to bear. Competition, the struggle for existence and for, what is often more important than mere existence, namely, status, may become so bitter that peace is unendurable.

More than that, under the condition of peace, peoples whose life-habits and traditions have been formed upon a basis of war frequently multiply under conditions of peace to such an extent as to make an ultimate war inevitable. The natives of South Africa, since the tribal wars have ceased, have so increased in numbers as to be an increasing menace to the white population. Any amelioration of the condition of mankind that tends to disturb the racial equilibrium is likely to disturb the peace of nations. When representatives of the Rockefeller Medical Foundation proposed to introduce a rational system of medicine in China, certain of the wise men of that country, it is reported, shook their heads dubiously over the consequences that were likely to follow any large decrease in the death-rate, seeing that China was already overpopulated.

In the same way education, which is now in a way to become a heritage of all mankind, rather than the privilege of so-called superior peoples, undoubtedly has had the effect of greatly increasing the mobility and restlessness of the world's population. In so far as this is true, it has made the problem of maintaining peace more difficult and dangerous.

On the other hand, education and the extension of intelligence undoubtedly increase the possibility of compromise and conciliation which, as Simmel points out, represent ways in which peace may be restored and maintained other than by complete victory and subjugation of the conquered people. It is considerations of this kind that have led men like von Moltke to say that "universal peace is a dream and not even a happy one," and have led other men like Carnegie to build peace palaces in which the nations of the world might settle their differences by compromise and according to law.

d) *Competition, status, and social solidarity.*—Under the title "Competition, Status, and Social Solidarity" selections are introduced in the materials which emphasize the relation of competition to accommodation. Up to this point in the materials only the relations of conflict to accommodation have been considered. Status has been described as an effect of conflict. But it is clear that economic competition frequently becomes conscious and so passes over into some of the milder forms of conflict. Aside from this it is evident that competition in so far as it determines the vocation of the individual, determines indirectly also his status, since it determines the class of which he is destined to be a member. In the same way competition is indirectly responsible for the organization of society in so far as it determines the character of the accommodations and understandings which are likely to exist between conflict groups. Social types as well as status are indirectly determined by competition, since most of them are vocational. The social types of the modern city, as indicated by the selection on "Personal Competition and the Evolution of Individual Types," are an outcome of the division of labor. Durkheim points out that the division of labor in multiplying the vocations has increased and not diminished the unity of society. The interdependence of differentiated individuals and groups has made possible a social solidarity that otherwise would not exist.

II. MATERIALS

A. FORMS OF ACCOMMODATION

1. Acclimatization[1]

The most important ethnic question in connection with climate is that of the possibility of a race adapting itself to climatic conditions widely different from those to which it has been accustomed. This is the question of acclimatization.

Its bearings on ethnic psychology can be made at once evident by posing a few practical inquiries: Can the English people flourish in India? Will the French colonize successfully the Sudan? Have the Europeans lost or gained in power by their migration to the United States? Can the white or any other race ultimately become the sole residents of the globe?

It will be seen that on the answers to such questions depends the destiny of races and the consequences to the species of the facilities of transportation offered by modern inventions. The subject has therefore received the careful study of medical geographers and statisticians.

I can give but a brief statement of their conclusions. They are to the effect, first, that when the migration takes place along approximately the same isothermal lines, the changes in the system are slight; but as the mean annual temperature rises, the body becomes increasingly unable to resist its deleterious action until a difference of 18° F. is reached, at which continued existence of the

[1] From Daniel G. Brinton, *The Basis of Social Relations*, pp. 194-99. (Courtesy of G. P. Putnam's Sons, New York and London, 1902.)

more northern races becomes impossible.   They suffer from a chemical
change in the condition of the blood cells, leading to anemia in the
individual and to extinction of the lineage in the third generation.

This is the general law of the relation to race and climate.   Like
most laws it has its exceptions, depending on special conditions.   A
stock which has long been accustomed to change of climate adapts
itself to any with greater facility.   This explains the singular readiness
of the Jews to settle and flourish in all zones.   For a similar reason a
people who at home are accustomed to a climate of wide and sudden
changes, like that of the eastern United States, supports others with
less loss of power than the average.

A locality may be extremely hot but unusually free from other
malefic influences, being dry with regular and moderate winds, and
well drained, such as certain areas between the Red Sea and the Nile,
which are also quite salubrious.

Finally, certain individuals and certain families, owing to some
fortunate power of resistance which we cannot explain, acclimate
successfully where their companions perish.   Most of the instances
of alleged successful acclimatization of Europeans in the tropics are
due to such exceptions, the far greater number of the victims being
left out of the count.

If these alleged successful cases, or that of the Jews or Arabs, be
closely examined, it will almost surely be discovered that another
physiological element has been active in bringing about acclimatization, and that is the mingling of blood with the native race.   In the
American tropics the Spaniards have survived for four centuries;
but how many of the *Ladinos* can truthfully claim an unmixed
descent?   In Guatemala, for example, says a close observer, *not any*.
The Jews of the Malabar coast have actually become black, and so
has also in Africa many an Arab claiming direct descent from the
Prophet himself.

But along with this process of adaptation by amalgamation
comes unquestionably a lowering of the mental vitality of the higher
race.   That is the price it has to pay for the privilege of survival
under the new conditions.   But, in conformity to the principles
already laid down as accepted by all anthropologists, such a lowering
must correspond to a degeneration in the highest grades of structure,
the brain cells.

We are forced, therefore, to reach the decision that the human species attains its highest development only under moderate conditions of heat, such as prevail in the temperate zones (an annual mean of 8°–12° C.); and the more startling conclusion that the races now native to the polar and tropical areas are distinctly *pathological*, are types of degeneracy, having forfeited their highest physiological elements in order to purchase immunity from the unfavorable climatic conditions to which they are subject. We must agree with a French writer, that "man is not cosmopolitan," and if he insists on becoming a "citizen of the world" he is taxed heavily in his best estate for his presumption.

The inferences in racial psychology which follow this opinion are too evident to require detailed mention. Natural selection has fitted the Eskimo and the Sudanese for their respective abodes, but it has been by the process of regressive evolution; progressive evolution in man has confined itself to less extreme climatic areas.

The facts of acclimatization stand in close connection with another doctrine in anthropology which is interesting for my theme, that of "ethno-geographic provinces." Alexander von Humboldt seems to have been the first to give expression to this system of human grouping, and it has been diligently cultivated by his disciple, Professor Bastian. It rests upon the application to the human species of two general principles recognized as true in zoölogy and botany. The one is that every organism is directly dependent on its environment (the *milieu*), action and reaction going on constantly between them; the other is, that no two faunal or floral regions are of equal rank in their capacity for the development of a given type of organism.

The features which distinguish one ethno-geographic province from another are chiefly, according to Bastian, meteorological, and they permit, he claims, a much closer division of human groups than the general continental areas which give us an African, a European, and an American subspecies.

It is possible that more extended researches may enable ethnographers to map out, in this sense, the distribution of our species; but the secular alterations in meteorologic conditions, combined with the migratory habits of most early communities, must greatly interfere with a rigid application of these principles in ethnography.

The historic theory of "centres of civilisation" is allied to that of ethno-geographic provinces. The stock examples of such are familiar. The Babylonian plain, the valley of the Nile, in America the plateaus of Mexico and of Tiahuanuco are constantly quoted as such. The geographic advantages these situations offered—a fertile soil, protection from enemies, domesticable plants, and a moderate climate— are offered as reasons why an advanced culture rapidly developed in them, and from them extended over adjacent regions.

Without denying the advantages of such surroundings, the most recent researches in both hemispheres tend to reduce materially their influence. The cultures in question did not begin at one point and radiate from it, but arose simultaneously over wide areas, in different linguistic stocks, with slight connections; and only later, and secondarily, was it successfully concentrated by some one tribe—by the agency, it is now believed, of cognatic rather than geographic aids.

Assyriologists no longer believe that Sumerian culture originated in the delta of the Euphrates, and Egyptologists look for the sources of the civilization of the Nile Valley among the Libyans; while in the New World not one but seven stocks partook of the Aztec learning, and half a dozen contributed to that of the Incas. The prehistoric culture of Europe was not one of Carthaginians or Phoenicians, but was self-developed.

2.   Slavery Defined[1]

In most branches of knowledge the phenomena the man of science has to deal with have their technical names, and, when using a scientific term, he need not have regard to the meaning this term conveys in ordinary language; he knows he will not be misunderstood by his fellow-scientists. For instance, the Germans call a whale *Wallfisch*, and the English speak of shellfish; but a zoölogist, using the word fish, need not fear that any competent person will think he means whales or shellfish.

In ethnology the state of things is quite different. There are a few scientific names bearing a definite meaning, such as the terms "animism" and "survival," happily introduced by Professor Tylor. But most phenomena belonging to our science have not yet been

[1] From Dr. H. J. Nieboer, *Slavery as an Industrial System*, pp. 1-7.   (Martinus Nijhoff, The Hague, 1910.)

investigated, so it is no wonder that different writers (sometimes even the same writer on different pages) give different names to the same phenomenon, whereas, on the other hand, sometimes the same term (e.g., matriarchate) is applied to widely different phenomena. As for the subject we are about to treat of, we shall presently see that several writers have given a definition of slavery; but no one has taken the trouble to inquire whether his definition can be of any practical use in social science. Therefore, we shall try to give a good definition and justify it.

But we may not content ourselves with this; we must also pay attention to the meaning of the term "slavery" as commonly employed. There are two reasons for this. First, we must always rely upon the statements of ethnographers. If an ethnographer states that some savage tribe carries on slavery, without defining in what this "slavery" consists, we have to ask: What may our informant have meant? And as he is likely to have used the word in the sense generally attached to it, we have to inquire: What is the ordinary meaning of the term "slavery"?

The second reason is this. Several theoretical writers speak of slavery without defining what they mean by it; and we cannot avail ourselves of their remarks without knowing what meaning they attach to this term. And as they too may be supposed to have used it in the sense in which it is generally used, we have again to inquire: What is the meaning of the term "slavery" in ordinary language?

The general use of the word, as is so often the case, is rather inaccurate. Ingram says:

Careless or rhetorical writers use the words "slave" and "slavery" in a very lax way. Thus, when protesting against the so-called "Subjection of Women," they absurdly apply those terms to the condition of the wife in the modern society of the west—designations which are inappropriate even in the case of the inmate of Indian zenanas; and they speak of the modern worker as a "wage-slave," even though he is backed by a powerful trade-union. Passion has a language of its own, and poets and orators must doubtless be permitted to denote by the word "slavery" the position of subjects of a state who labor under civil disabilities or are excluded from the exercise of political power; but in sociological study things ought to have their right names, and those names should, as far as possible, be uniformly employed.

But this use of the word **we may** safely regard **as a** metaphor; nobody will assert that these laborers and women are really slaves. Whoever uses the term slavery in its ordinary sense attaches a fairly distinct idea to it. What is this idea? We can express it most generally thus: a slave is one who is not free. There are never slaves without there being freemen too; and nobody can be at the same time a slave and a freeman. We must, however, be careful to remember that, man being a "social animal," no man is literally free; all members of a community are restricted in their behavior toward each other by social rules and customs. But freemen at any rate are relatively free; so a slave must be one who does not share in the common amount of liberty, compatible with the social connection.

The condition of the slave as opposed to that of the freeman presents itself to us under the three following aspects:

First, every slave has his master to whom he is subjected. And this subjection is of a peculiar kind. Unlike the authority one freeman sometimes has over another, the master's power over his slave is unlimited, at least in principle; any restriction put upon the master's free exercise of his power is a mitigation of slavery, not belonging to its nature, just as in Roman law the proprietor may do with his property whatever he is not by special laws forbidden to do. The relation between master and slave is therefore properly expressed by the slave being called the master's "possession" or "property"— expressions we frequently meet with.

Secondly, slaves are in a lower condition as compared with freemen. The slave has no political rights; he does not choose his government, he does not attend the public councils. Socially he is despised.

In the third place, we always connect with slavery the idea of compulsory labor. The slave is compelled to work; the free laborer may leave off working if he likes, be it at the cost of starving. All compulsory labor, however, is not slave labor; the latter requires that peculiar kind of compulsion that is expressed by the word "possession" or "property" as has been said before.

Recapitulating, we may define a slave in the ordinary sense of the word as a man who is the property of another, politically and socially at a lower level than the mass of the people, and performing compulsory labor.

The great function of slavery can be no other than a *division of labor*. Division of labor is taken here in the widest sense, as including not only a qualitative division, by which one man does one kind of work and another a different kind, but also a quantitative one, by which one man's wants are provided for, not by his own work only, but by another's. A society without any division of labor would be one in which each man worked for his own wants, and nobody for another's; in any case but this there is a division of labor in this wider sense of the word. Now this division can be brought about by two means. "There are two ways" says Puchta "in which we can avail ourselves of the strength of other men which we are in need of. One is the way of free commerce, that does not interfere with the liberty of the person who serves us, the making of contracts by which we exchange the strength and skill of another, or their products, for other performances on our part: hire of services, purchase of manufactures, etc. The other way is the subjugation of such persons, which enables us to dispose of their strength in our behalf but at the same time injures the personality of the subjected. This subjection can be imagined as being restricted to certain purposes, for instance to the cultivation of the land, as with soil-tilling serfs, the result of which is that this subjection, for the very reason that it has a definite and limited aim, does not quite annul the liberty of the subjected. But the subjection can also be an unlimited one, as is the case when the subjected person, in the whole of his outward life, is treated as but a means to the purposes of the man of power, and so his personality is entirely absorbed. This is the institution of slavery."

3. Excerpts from the Journal of a West India Slave Owner[1]

Soon after nine o'clock we reached Savannah la Mar, where I found my trustee, and a whole cavalcade, waiting to conduct me to my own estate; for he had brought with him a curricle and pair for myself, a gig for my servant, two black boys upon mules, and a cart with eight oxen to convey my baggage. The road was excellent, and we had not above five miles to travel; and as soon as the carriage entered my gates, the uproar and confusion which ensued sets all description at defiance. The works were instantly all abandoned;

[1] From Matthew G. Lewis, *Journal of a West India Proprietor*, pp. 60-337. (John Murray, 1834.)

everything that had life came flocking to the house from all quarters; and not only the men, and the women, and the children, but, "by a bland assimilation," the hogs, and the dogs, and the geese, and the fowls, and the turkeys, all came hurrying along by instinct, to see what could possibly be the matter, and seemed to be afraid of arriving too late. Whether the pleasure of the negroes was sincere may be doubted; but certainly it was the loudest that I ever witnessed: they all talked together, sang, danced, shouted, and, in the violence of their gesticulations, tumbled over each other, and rolled about upon the ground. Twenty voices at once enquired after uncles, and aunts, and grandfathers, and great-grandmothers of mine, who had been buried long before I was in existence, and whom, I verily believe, most of them only knew by tradition. One woman held up her little naked black child to me, grinning from ear to ear, "Look, Massa, look here! him nice lilly neger for Massa!" Another complained, "So long since none come see we, Massa; good Massa, come at last." As for the old people, they were all in one and the same story: now they had lived once to see Massa, they were ready for dying tomorrow, "them no care."

The shouts, the gaiety, the wild laughter, their strange and sudden bursts of singing and dancing, and several old women, wrapped up in large cloaks, their heads bound round with different-colored hand-kerchiefs, leaning on a staff, and standing motionless in the middle of the hubbub, with their eyes fixed upon the portico which I occupied, formed an exact counterpart of the festivity of the witches in Macbeth. Nothing could be more odd or more novel than the whole scene; and yet there was something in it by which I could not help being affected; perhaps it was the consciousness that all these human beings were my *slaves*;—to be sure, I never saw people look more happy in my life; and I believe their condition to be much more comfortable than that of the laborers of Great Britain; and, after all, slavery, in *their* case, is but another name for servitude, now that no more negroes can be forcibly carried away from Africa and subjected to the horrors of the voyage and of the seasoning after their arrival; but still I had already experienced, in the morning, that Juliet was wrong in saying "What's in a name?" For soon after my reaching the lodging-house at Savannah la Mar, a remarkably clean-looking negro lad presented himself with some water and a

towel—I concluded him to belong to the inn—and, on my returning
the towel, as he found that I took no notice of him, he at length
ventured to introduce himself by saying, "Massa not know me;
me your slave!—and really the sound made me feel a pang at the
heart. The lad appeared all gaiety and good humor, and his whole
countenance expressed anxiety to recommend himself to my notice,
but the word "slave" seemed to imply that, although he did feel
pleasure then in serving me, if he had detested me he must have served
me still. I really felt quite humiliated at the moment, and was
tempted to tell him, "Do not say that again; say that you are my
negro, but do not call yourself my slave."

As I was returning this morning from Montego Bay, about a
mile from my own estate, a figure presented itself before me, I really
think the most picturesque that I ever beheld: it was a mulatto
girl, born upon Cornwall, but whom the overseer of a neighboring
estate had obtained my permission to exchange for another slave,
as well as two little children, whom she had borne to him; but, as yet,
he had been unable to procure a substitute, owing to the difficulty of
purchasing single negroes, and Mary Wiggins is still my slave. However, as she is considered as being manumitted, she had not dared to
present herself at Cornwall on my arrival, lest she should have been
considered as an intruder; but she now threw herself in my way to tell
me how glad she was to see me, for that she had always thought till
now (which is the general complaint) that "*she had no massa;*" and also
to obtain a regular invitation to my negro festival tomorrow. By this
universal complaint, it appears that, while Mr. Wilberforce is lament-
ing their hard fate in being subject to a master, *their* greatest fear is
the not having a master whom they know; and that to be told by the
negroes of another estate that "they belong to no massa," is one of
the most contemptuous reproaches that can be cast upon them. Poor
creatures, when they happened to hear on Wednesday evening that
my carriage was ordered for Montego Bay the next morning, they
fancied that I was going away for good and all, and came up to the
house in such a hubbub that my agent was obliged to speak to them,
and pacify them with the assurance that I should come back on
Friday without fail.

But to return to Mary Wiggins: she was much too pretty not to
obtain her invitation to Cornwall; on the contrary, I *insisted* upon her

coming, and bade her tell her *husband* that I admired his taste very much for having chosen her. I really think that her form and features were the most *statue-like* that I ever met with; her complexion had no yellow in it and yet was not brown enough to be dark—it was more of an ash-dove color than anything else; her teeth were admirable, both for color and shape; her eyes equally mild and bright; and her face merely broad enough to give it all possible softness and grandness of contour: her air and countenance would have suited Yarico; but she reminded me most of Grassini in "La Vergine del Sole," only that Mary Wiggins was a thousand times more beautiful, and that, instead of a white robe, she wore a mixed dress of brown, white, and dead yellow, which harmonized excellently with her complexion; while one of her beautiful arms was thrown across her brow to shade her eyes, and a profusion of rings on her fingers glittered in the sunbeams. Mary Wiggins and an old cotton tree are the most picturesque objects that I have seen for these twenty years.

I really believe that the negresses can produce children at pleasure, and where they are barren, it is just as hens will frequently not lay eggs on shipboard, because they do not like their situation. Cubina's wife is in a family way, and I told him that if the child should live, I would christen it for him, if he wished it. "Tank you, kind massa, me like it very much: much oblige if massa do that for *me*, too." So I promised to baptize the father and the baby on the same day, and said that I would be godfather to any children that might be born on the estate during my residence in Jamaica. This was soon spread about, and, although I have not yet been here a week, two women are in the straw already, Jug Betty and Minerva: the first is wife to my head driver, The Duke of Sully, but my sense of propriety was much gratified at finding that Minerva's husband was called Captain. I think nobody will be able to accuse me of neglecting the religious education of my negroes, for I have not only promised to baptize all the infants, but, meeting a little black boy this morning, who said that his name was Moses, I gave him a piece of silver, and told him that it was for the sake of Aaron; which, I flatter myself, was planting in his young mind the rudiments of Christianity.

On my former visit to Jamaica, I found on my estate a poor woman nearly one hundred years old, and stone blind. She was too infirm to walk, but two young negroes brought her on their backs to the steps of my house, in order, as she said, that she might at least touch massa, although she could not see him. When she had kissed my hand, "that was enough," she said: "now me hab once kiss a massa's hand, me willing to die tomorrow, me no care." She had a woman appropriated to her service and was shown the greatest care and attention; however, she did not live many months after my departure. There was also a mulatto, about thirty years of age, named Bob, who had been almost deprived of the use of his limbs by the horrible cocoa-bay, and had never done the least work since he was fifteen. He was so gentle and humble and so fearful, from the consciousness of his total inability of soliciting my notice, that I could not help pitying the poor fellow; and whenever he came in my way I always sought to encourage him by little presents and other trifling marks of favor. His thus unexpectedly meeting with distinguishing kindness, where he expected to be treated as a worthless incumbrance, made a strong impression on his mind.

4. The Origin of Caste in India[1]

If it were possible to compress into a single paragraph a theory so complex as that which would explain the origin and nature of Indian caste, I should attempt to sum it up in some such words as the following: A caste is a marriage union, the constituents of which were drawn from various different tribes (or from various other castes similarly formed) in virtue of some industry, craft, or function, either secular or religious, which they possessed in common. The internal discipline, by which the conditions of membership in regard to connubial and convivial rights are defined and enforced, has been borrowed from the tribal period which preceded the period of castes by many centuries, and which was brought to a close by the amalgamation of tribes into a nation under a common scepter. The differentia of *caste* as a marriage union consist in some community of function; while the differentia of *tribe* as a marriage union consisted in a common ancestry, or a common worship, or a common totem, or in fact in any kind of common property except that of a common function.

[1] From "Modern Theories of Caste: Mr. Nesfield's Theory," Appendix V, in Sir Herbert Risley, *The People of India*, pp. 407–8. (W. Thacker & Co., 1915.)

Long before castes were formed on Indian soil, most of the industrial classes, to which they now correspond, had existed for centuries, and as a rule most of the industries which they practiced were hereditary on the male side of the parentage. These hereditary classes were and are simply the concrete embodiments of those successive stages of culture which have marked the industrial development of mankind in every part of the world. Everywhere (except at least in those countries where he is still a savage), man has advanced from the stage of hunting and fishing to that of nomadism and cattle-grazing, and from nomadism to agriculture proper. Everywhere has the age of metallurgy and of the arts and industries which are coeval with it been preceded by a ruder age, when only those arts were known or practiced which sufficed for the hunting, fishing, and nomad states. Everywhere has the class of ritualistic priests and lettered theosophists been preceded by a class of less-cultivated worshipers, who paid simple offerings of flesh and wine to the personified powers of the visible universe without the aid of a hereditary professional priesthood. Everywhere has the class of nobles and territorial chieftains been preceded by a humbler class of small peasant proprietors, who placed themselves under their protection and paid tribute or rent in return. Everywhere has this class of nobles and chieftains sought to ally itself with that of the priests or sacerdotal order; and everywhere has the priestly order sought to bring under its control those chiefs and rulers under whose protection it lives.

All these classes had been in existence for centuries before any such thing as caste was known on Indian soil; and the only thing that was needed to convert them into castes, such as they now are, was that the Brāhman, who possessed the highest of all functions— the priestly—should set the example. This he did by establishing for the first time the rule that no child, either male or female, could inherit the name and status of Brāhman, unless he or she was of Brāhman parentage on *both* sides. By the establishment of this rule the principle of marriage unionship was superadded to that of functional unionship; and it was only by the combination of these two principles that a caste in the strict sense of the term could or can be formed. The Brāhman, therefore, as the Hindu books inform us, was "the first-born of castes." When the example had thus been

set by an arrogant and overbearing priesthood, whose pretensions it
was impossible to put down, the other hereditary classes followed in
regular order downward, partly in imitation and partly in self-defence.
Immediately behind the Brāhman came the Kshatriya, the military
chieftain or landlord.   He therefore was the "second-born of castes."
Then followed the bankers or upper trading classes (the Agārwal,
Khattri, etc.); the scientific musician and singer (Kathak); the
writing or literary class (Kāyasth); the bard or genealogist (Bhāt);
and the class of inferior nobles (Taga and Bhuinhār) who paid no
rent to the landed aristocracy.   These, then, were the third-born of
castes.   Next in order came those artisan classes, who were coeval
with the age and art of metallurgy; the metallurgic classes themselves;
the middle trading classes; the middle agricultural classes, who
placed themselves under the protection of the Kshatriya and paid him
rent in return (Kurmi, Kāchhi, Māli, Tāmboli); and the middle
serving classes, such as Napit and Baidya, who attended to the bodily
wants of their equals and superiors.   These, then, were the fourth-
born of castes; and their rank in the social scale has been determined
by the fact that their manners and notions are farther removed than
those of the preceding castes from the Brāhmanical ideal.   Next
came the inferior artisan classes, those who preceded the age and
art of metallurgy (Teli, Kumhār, Kalwār, etc.); the partly nomad
and partly agricultural classes (Jāt, Gūjar, Ahir, etc.); the inferior
serving classes, such as Kahār; and the inferior trading classes, such
as Bhunja.   These, then, were the fifth-born of castes, and their
mode of life is still farther removed from the Brāhmanical ideal than
that of the preceding.   The last-born, and therefore the lowest, of all
the classes are those semisavage communities, partly tribes and partly
castes, whose function consists in hunting or fishing, or in acting as
butcher for the general community, or in rearing swine and fowls, or
in discharging the meanest domestic services, such as sweeping and
washing, or in practicing the lowest of human arts, such as basket-
making, hide-tanning, etc.   Thus throughout the whole series of
Indian castes a double test of social precedence has been in active
force, the industrial and the Brāhmanical; and these two have kept
pace together almost as evenly as a pair of horses harnessed to a
single carriage.   In proportion as the function practiced by any given
caste stands high or low in the scale of industrial development, in

the same proportion does the caste itself, impelled by the general
tone of society by which it is surrounded, approximate more nearly
or more remotely to the Brāhmanical idea of life. It is these two
criteria combined which have determined the relative ranks of the
various castes in the Hindu social scale.

5. Caste and the Sentiments of Caste Reflected in Popular Speech[1]

No one indeed can fail to be struck by the intensely popular
character of Indian proverbial philosophy and by its freedom from
the note of pedantry which is so conspicuous in Indian literature.
These quaint sayings have dropped fresh from the lips of the Indian
rustic; they convey a vivid impression of the anxieties, the troubles,
the annoyances, and the humors of his daily life; and any sympathetic
observer who has felt the fascination of an oriental village would have
little difficulty in constructing from these materials a fairly accurate
picture of rural society in India. The *mise en scène* is not altogether
a cheerful one. It shows us the average peasant dependent upon the
vicissitudes of the season and the vagaries of the monsoon, and
watching from day to day to see what the year may bring forth.
Should rain fall at the critical moment his wife will get golden earrings.
but one short fortnight of drought may spell calamity when "God
takes all at once." Then the forestalling Baniya flourishes by selling
rotten grain, and the Jāt cultivator is ruined. First die the improvi-
dent Musalmān weavers, then the oil-pressers for whose wares there
is no demand; the carts lie idle, for the bullocks are dead, and the
bride goes to her husband without the accustomed rites. But be the
season good or bad, the pious Hindu's life is ever overshadowed by
the exactions of the Brāhman—"a thing with a string round its
neck" (a profane hit at the sacred thread), a priest by appearance,
a butcher at heart, the chief of a trio of tormentors gibbeted in the
rhyming proverb:

> Blood-suckers three on earth there be,
> The bug, the Brāhman, and the flea.

Before the Brāhman starves the king's larder will be empty;
cakes must be given to him while the children of the house may lick

[1] From Sir Herbert Risley, *The People of India*, pp. 130–39. (W. Thacker &
Co., 1915.)

the grindstone for a meal; his stomach is a bottomless pit; he eats so immoderately that he dies from wind. He will beg with a lakh of rupees in his pocket, and a silver begging-bowl in his hand. In his greed for funeral fees he spies out corpses like a vulture, and rejoices in the misfortunes of his clients. A village with a Brāhman in it is like a tank full of crabs; to have him as a neighbor is worse than leprosy; if a snake has to be killed the Brāhman should be set to do it, for no one will miss him. If circumstances compel you to perjure yourself, why swear on the head of your son, when there is a Brāhman handy? Should he die (as is the popular belief) the world will be none the poorer. Like the devil in English proverbial phi-losophy, the Brāhman can cite scripture for his purpose; he demands worship himself but does not scruple to kick his low-caste brethren; he washes his sacred thread but does not cleanse his inner man; and so great is his avarice that a man of another caste is supposed to pray "O God, let me not be reborn as a Brāhman priest, who is always begging and is never satisfied." He defrauds even the gods; Vishnu gets the barren prayers while the Brāhman devours the offerings. So Pan complains in one of Lucian's dialogues that he is done out of the good things which men offer at his shrine.

The next most prominent figure in our gallery of popular portraits is that of the Baniya, money-lender, grain-dealer, and monopolist, who dominates the material world as the Brāhman does the spiritual. His heart, we are told, is no bigger than a coriander seed; he has the jaws of an alligator and a stomach of wax; he is less to be trusted than a tiger, a scorpion, or a snake; he goes in like a needle and comes out like a sword; as a neighbor he is as bad as a boil in the armpit. If a Baniya is on the other side of a river you should leave your bundle on this side, for fear he should steal it. When four Baniyas meet they rob the whole world. If a Baniya is drowning you should not give him a hand: he is sure to have some base motive for drifting down stream. He uses light weights and swears that the scales tip themselves; he keeps his accounts in a character that no one but God can read; if you borrow from him, your debt mounts up like a refuse heap or gallops like a horse; if he talks to a customer he "draws a line" and debits the conversation; when his own credit is shaky he writes up his transactions on the wall so that they can easily be rubbed out. He is so stingy that the dogs starve at his

feast, and he scolds his wife if she spends a farthing on betel-nut
A Jain Baniya drinks dirty water and shrinks from killing ants and
flies, but will not stick at murder in pursuit of gain. As a druggist
the Baniya is in league with the doctor; he buys weeds at a
nominal price and sells them very dear. Finally, he is always a
shocking coward: eighty-four Khatris will run away from four
thieves.

Nor does the clerical caste fare better at the hands of the popular
epigrammatist. Where three Kāyasths are gathered together a
thunderbolt is sure to fall; when honest men fall out the Kāyasth
gets his chance. When a Kāyasth takes to money-lending he is a
merciless creditor. He is a man of figures; he lives by the point of
his pen; in his house even the cat learns two letters and a half.
He is a versatile creature, and where there are no tigers he will become
a shikāri; but he is no more to be trusted than a crow or a snake
without a tail. One of the failings sometimes imputed to the educated
Indian is attacked in the saying, "Drinking comes to a Kāyasth
with his mother's milk."

Considering the enormous strength of the agricultural population
of India, one would have expected to find more proverbs directed
against the great cultivating castes. Possibly the reason may be
that they made most of the proverbs, and people can hardly be
expected to sharpen their wit on their own shortcomings. In two
provinces, however, the rural Pasquin has let out very freely at the
morals and manners of the Jāt, the typical peasant of the eastern
Punjab and the western districts of the United Provinces. You
may as well, we are told, look for good in a Jāt as for weevils in a
stone. He is your friend only so long as you have a stick in your hand.
If he cannot harm you he will leave a bad smell as he goes by. To
be civil to him is like giving treacle to a donkey. If he runs amuck
it takes God to hold him. A Jāt's laugh would break an ordinary
man's ribs. When he learns manners, he blows his nose with a mat,
and there is a great run on the garlic. His baby has a plowtail
for a plaything. The Jāt stood on his own corn heap and called out
to the King's elephant-drivers, "Hi there, what will you take for
those little donkeys?" He is credited with practicing fraternal
polyandry, like the Venetian nobility of the early eighteenth century,
as a measure of domestic economy, and a whole family are said to
have one wife between them.

The Doms, among whom we find scavengers, vermin-eaters, executioners, basket-makers, musicians, and professional burglars, probably represent the remnants of a Dravidian tribe crushed out of recognition by the invading Aryans and condemned to menial and degrading occupations. Sir G. Grierson has thrown out the picturesque suggestion that they are the ancestors of the European gypsies and that Rom or Romany is nothing more than a variant of Dom. In the ironical language of the proverbs the Dom figures as "the lord of death" because he provides the wood for the Hindu funeral pyre. He is ranked with Brāhmans and goats as a creature useless in time of need. A common and peculiarly offensive form of abuse is to tell a man that he has eaten a Dom's leavings. A series of proverbs represents him as making friends with members of various castes and faring ill or well in the process. Thus the Kanjar steals his dog, and the Gūjar loots his house; on the other hand, the barber shaves him for nothing, and the silly Jolāhā makes him a suit of clothes. His traditions associate him with donkeys, and it is said that if these animals could excrete sugar, Doms would no longer be beggars. 'A Dom in a palanquin and a Brāhman on foot" is a type of society turned upside down. Nevertheless, outcast as he is, the Dom occupies a place of his own in the fabric of Indian society. At funerals he provides the wood and gets the corpse clothes as his perquisite; he makes the discordant music that accompanies a marriage procession; and baskets, winnowing-fans, and wicker articles in general are the work of his hands.

In the west of India, Mahārs and Dheds hold much the same place as the Dom. In the walled villages of the Marāthā country the Mahār is the scavenger, watchman, and gate-keeper. His presence pollutes; he is not allowed to live in the village; and his miserable shanty is huddled up against the wall outside. But he challenges the stranger who comes to the gate, and for this and other services he is allowed various perquisites, among them that of begging for broken victuals from house to house. He offers old blankets to his god, and his child's playthings are bones. The Dhed's status is equally low. If he looks at a water jar he pollutes its contents; if you run up against him by accident, you must go off and bathe. If you annoy a Dhed he sweeps up the dust in your face. When he dies, the world is so much the cleaner. If you go to the Dheds' quarter you find there nothing but a heap of bones.

This relegation of the low castes to a sort of ghetto is carried to great lengths in the south of India where the intolerance of the Brāhman is very conspicuous. In the typical Madras village the Pariahs—"dwellers in the quarter" (*pārā*) as this broken tribe is now called—live in an irregular cluster of conical hovels of palm leaves known as the *pārchery*, the squalor and untidiness of which present the sharpest contrasts to the trim street of tiled masonry houses where the Brāhmans congregate. "Every village," says the proverb, "has its Pariah hamlet"—a place of pollution the census of which is even now taken with difficulty owing to the reluctance of the high caste enumerator to enter its unclean precincts. "A palm tree," says another, "casts no shade; a Pariah has no caste and rules." The popular estimate of the morals of the Pariah comes out in the saying, "He that breaks his word is a Pariah at heart"; while the note of irony predominates in the pious question, "If a Pariah offers boiled rice will not the god take it?" the implication being that the Brāhman priests who take the offerings to idols are too greedy to inquire by whom they are presented.

B.   SUBORDINATION AND SUPERORDINATION

1.   The Psychology of Subordination and Superordination[1]

The typical suggestion is given by words. But the impulse to act under the influence of another person arises no less when the action is proposed in the more direct form of showing the action itself. The submission then takes the form of imitation. This is the earliest type of subordination. It plays a fundamental rôle in the infant's life, long before the suggestion through words can begin its influence. The infant imitates involuntarily as soon as connections between the movement impulses and the movement impressions have been formed. At first automatic reflexes produce all kinds of motions, and each movement awakes kinesthetic and muscle sensations. Through association these impressions become bound up with the motor impulses. As soon as the movements of other persons arouse similar visual sensations the kinesthetic sensations are associated and realize the corresponding movement. Very soon the associative

[1] From Hugo Münsterberg, *Psychology, General and Applied*, pp. 259–64. (D. Appleton & Co., 1914.)

irradiation becomes more complex, and whole groups of emotional reactions are imitated. The child cries and laughs in imitation.

Most important is the imitation of the speech movement. The sound awakes the impulse to produce the same vocal sound long before the meaning of the word is understood. Imitation is thus the condition for the acquiring of speech, and later the condition for the learning of all other abilities. But while the imitation is at first simply automatic, it becomes more and more volitional. The child intends to imitate what the teacher shows as an example. This intentional imitation is certainly one of the most important vehicles of social organization. The desire to act like certain models becomes the most powerful social energy. But even the highest differentiation of society does not eliminate the constant working of the automatic, impulsive imitation.

The inner relation between imitation and suggestion shows itself in the similarity of conditions under which they are most effective. Every increase of suggestibility facilitates imitation. In any emotional excitement of a group every member submits to the suggestion of the others, but the suggestion is taken from the actual movements. A crowd in a panic or a mob in a riot shows an increased suggestibility by which each individual automatically repeats what his neighbors are doing. Even an army in battle may become, either through enthusiasm or through fear, a group in which all individuality is lost and everyone is forced by imitative impulses to fight or escape. The psychophysical experiment leaves no doubt that this imitative response releases the sources of strongest energy in the mental mechanism. If the arm lifts the weight of an ergograph until the will cannot overcome the fatigue, the mere seeing of the movement carried out by others whips the motor centers to new efficiency.

We saw that our feeling states are both causes and effects of our actions. We cannot experience the impulse to action without a new shading of our emotional setting. Imitative acting involves, therefore, an inner imitation of feelings too. The child who smiles in response to the smile of his mother shares her pleasant feeling. The adult who is witness of an accident in which someone is hurt imitates instinctively the cramping muscle contractions of the victim, and as a result he feels an intense dislike without having the pain sensations themselves. From such elementary experiences an

imitative emotional life develops, controlled by a general sympathetic
tendency. We share the pleasures and the displeasures of others
through an inner imitation which remains automatic. In its richer
forms this sympathy becomes an *altruistic sentiment;* it stirs the
desire to remove the misery around us and unfolds to a general mental
setting through which every action is directed toward the service
to others. But from the faintest echoing of feelings in the infant to
the highest self-sacrifice from altruistic impulse, we have the common
element of submission. The individual is feeling, and accordingly
acting, not in the realization of his individual impulses, but under the
influence of other personalities.

This subordination to the feelings of others through sympathy
and pity and common joy takes a new psychological form in the
affection of tenderness and especially parental love. The relation
of parents to children involves certainly an element of superordination, but the mentally strongest factor remains the subordination, the
complete submission to the feelings of those who are dependent upon
the parents' care. In its higher development the parental love will
not yield to every momentary like or dislike of the child, but will
adjust the educative influence to the lasting satisfactions and to the
later sources of unhappiness. But the submission of the parents to
the feeling tones in the child's life remains the fundamental principle
of the family instinct. While the parents' love and tenderness mean
that the stronger submits to the weaker, even up to the highest points
of self-sacrifice, the loving child submits to his parents from feelings
which are held together by a sense of dependence. This feeling of
dependence as a motive of subordination enters into numberless
human relations. Everywhere the weak lean on the strong, and
choose their actions under the influence of those in whom they have
confidence. The corresponding feelings show the manifold shades of
modesty, admiration, gratitude, and hopefulness. Yet it is only
another aspect of the social relation if the consciousness of dependence
upon the more powerful is felt with fear and revolt, or with the nearly
related emotion of envy.

The desire to assert oneself is no less powerful, in the social interplay, than the impulse to submission. Society needs the leaders as
well as the followers. Self-assertion presupposes contact with other
individuals. Man protects himself against the dangers of nature,

and man masters nature; but he asserts himself against men who interfere with him or whom he wants to force to obedience. The most immediate reaction in the compass of self-assertion is indeed the *rejection of interference*. It is a form in which even the infant shows the opposite of submission. He repels any effort to disturb him in the realization of the instinctive impulses. From the simplest reaction of the infant disturbed in his play or his meal, a straight line of development leads to the fighting spirit of man, whose pugnaciousness and whose longing for vengeance force his will on his enemies. Every form of rivalry, jealousy, and intolerance finds in this feeling group its source of automatic response. The most complex intellectual processes may be made subservient to this self-asserting emotion.

But the effort to impose one's will on others certainly does not result only from conflict. An entirely different emotional center is given by the mere desire for *self-expression*. In every field of human activity the individual may show his inventiveness, his ability to be different from others, to be a model, to be imitated by his fellows. The normal man has a healthy, instinctive desire to claim recognition from the members of the social group. This interferes neither with the spirit of co-ordination nor with the subordination of modesty. In so far as the individual demands acknowledgement of his personal behavior and his personal achievement, he raises himself by that act above others. He wants his mental attitude to influence and control the social surroundings. In its fuller development this inner setting becomes the ambition for leadership in the affairs of practical life or in the sphere of cultural work.

The superficial counterpart is the desire for *self-display* with all its variations of vanity and boastfulness. From the most bashful submission to the most ostentatious self-assertion, from the self-sacrifice of motherly love to the pugnaciousness of despotic egotism, the social psychologist can trace the human impulses through all the intensities of the human energies which interfere with equality in the group. Each variation has its emotional background and its impulsive discharge. Within normal limits they are all equally useful for the biological existence of the group and through the usefulness for the group ultimately serviceable to its members. Only through superordination and subordination does the group receive the inner firmness which transforms the mere combination of men into working units. They give to human society that strong and yet flexible organization which is the necessary condition for its successful development.

2. Social Attitudes in Subordination: Memories of an Old Servant[1]

Work is a great blessing, and it has been wisely arranged by our divine Master that all his creatures should have a work to do of some kind. Some are weak and some are strong. Old and young, rich and poor, there is that work expected from us, and how much happier we are when we are at our work.

There are so many things to learn, so many different kinds of work that must be done to make the world go on right. And some work is easier than others; but all ought to be well done, and in a cheerful, contented manner. Some prefer working with hands and feet; they say it is easier than the head work; but surely both are heavy work, for it does depend on your ability.

Boys and girls do not leave school so early as they did fifty or sixty years ago. The boys went out quite happy and manly to do their herding at some farm, and would be very useful for some years till they preferred learning some trade, etc.; then a younger boy just filled his place; and by doing this they did learn farming a good bit, and this helped them on in after years if they wanted to go back to farming again. We regret to see that the page-boy is not wanted so much as he used to be; and what a help that used to be for a young boy. He learns a great deal by being first of all a while in the stable yard or garage before he goes into the gentleman's house, and he is neat and tidy at all times for messages. We have seen many of them in our young days; and even the waif has been picked up by a good master, and began in the stables and worked his way up to be a respected valet in the same household, and often and often told the story of his waif life in the servants' hall.

The old servant has seen many changes and in many cases prefers the good old ways; there may be some better arrangements made, we cannot doubt that, but we are surprised at good old practices that our late beloved employers had ignored by their own children

[1] Adapted from *Domestic Service*, by An Old Servant, pp. 10–110. (Houghton Mifflin Co., 1917.)

after they have so far grown up. Servants need the good example from their superiors, and when they hear the world speak well of them they do look for the good ways in the home life. We all like to hold up an employer's good name, surely we do if we are interested at all in our work, and if we feel that we cannot do our duty to them we ought to go elsewhere and not deceive them. We are trusted with a very great deal, and it is well for us if we are doing all we can as faithful servants, and in the end lay down our tools with the feeling that we have tried to do our best.

We must remember that each one is born in his station in life, wisely arranged by "One Who Knows and Who Is Our Supreme Ruler." No one can alter this nor say to him, "What Doest Thou?" so we must each and all keep our station and honor the rich man and the poor man who humbly tries to live a Christian life, and when their faults are seen by us may we at once turn to ourselves and look if we are not human, too, and may be as vile as they.

We have noticed some visitors very rude to the servants and so different to our own employers, and we set a mark on them, for we would not go to serve them. We remember once when our lady's brother was showing a visiting lady some old relics near the front door they came upon the head housemaid who was cleaning the church pew chairs (they were carried in while the church was being repaired), and she was near a very old grand piano. The lady asked in such a jeer, "And is this the housemaid's piano"? The gentleman looked very hard at the housemaid, for we were sure that he was very annoyed at her, but we did not hear his answer; but the housemaid had the good sense to keep quiet, but she could have told her to keep her jeers, for we were not her class of servant, neither was she our class of employer. We heard her character after, and never cared to see her. Some servants take great liberties, and then all are supposed to be alike; but we are glad that all ladies are not like this, for the world would be poor indeed; they would soon ruin all the girls—and no wonder her husband had left her. We heard of a gentleman who fancied his laundry-maid, so he called his servants together and told them that he was to marry her and bring her home as the lady of his house, and he hoped they would all stay where they were; but if they felt that they could not look upon her as their mistress and his wife, they were free to go away. And not one of them left, for they stayed on with them for years.   This is a true story from one who knew them and could show us their London house.   Now we have lived with superior servants, and we would much rather serve them even now in our old age than serve any lady who can never respect a servant.

Nothing brings master and servant closer together than the sudden sore bereavement, and very likely this book could not be written so sad were it not for the many sad days that have been spent in service, and now so very few of the employers are to be seen; and when they are with us we feel that we are still respected by them, for there is the usual welcome—for they would look back the same as we do on days that are gone by.   In our young days the curtsy was fashionable; you would see every man's daughter bobbing whenever they met the lady or gentlemen or when they met their teacher. The custom is gone now, and we wonder why; but the days are changed, and some call it education that is so far doing this; it cannot be education, for we do look for more respect from the educated than from the class that we called the ignorant.

How well off the servants are in these years of war, for they have no rent to worry about and no anxiety about their coal bill, nor how food, etc., is to be got in and paid for, no taxes nor cares like so many poor working men; they are also sure of their wages when quarter day comes round.   It is true she may have a widow mother who requires some help with rent, coals, or food, but there are many who ought to value a good situation, whether in the small comfortable house as general or in larger good situations where a few servants are, for we have seen them all and know what they have been like, and so we say that all as a rule ought to be very thankful that they are the domestic servant and so study to show gratitude by good deeds to all around, as there is work just now for everyone to do.

A great deal more could easily be written, and we hope some old servant may also speak out in favor of domestic service, and so let it be again what it has been, and when both will look on each other as they ought, for there has always been master and servant, and we have the number of servants, or near the number, given here by one who knows, 1,330,783 female domestic servants at the last census in 1911, and so the domestic service is the largest single industry that is; there are more people employed as domestic servants thar any other class of employment. Before closing this book the writer would ask that a kinder interest may be taken in girls who may have at one time been in disgrace; many of them have no homes and we might try to help them into situations. This appeal is from the old housekeeper and so from one who has had many a talk with young girls for their good; but they have often been led far astray. We ought to give them the chance again, by trying to get them situations, and if the lady is not her friend, nor the housekeeper, we pity her.

3. The Reciprocal Character of Subordination and Superordination[1]

Every social occurrence consists of an interaction between individuals. In other words, each individual is at the same time an active and a passive agent in a transaction. In case of superiority and inferiority, however, the relation assumes the appearance of a one-sided operation; the one party appears to exert, while the other seems merely to receive, an influence. Such, however, is not in fact the case. No one would give himself the trouble to gain or to maintain superiority if it afforded him no advantage or enjoyment. This return to the superior can be derived from the relation, however, only by virtue of the fact that there is a reciprocal action of the inferior upon the superior. The decisive characteristic of the relation at this point is this, that the effect which the inferior actually exerts upon the superior is determined by the latter. The superior causes the inferior to produce a given effect which the superior shall experience. In this operation, in case the subordination is really absolute, no sort of spontaneity is present on the part of the subordinate. The reciprocal influence is rather the same as that between a man and a lifeless external object with which the former performs an act for his own use. That is, the person acts upon the object in order that the latter may react upon himself. In this reaction of the object no spontaneity on the part of the object is to be observed, but merely the further operation of the spontaneity of the person. Such an extreme case of superiority and inferiority will scarcely occur among human beings. Rather will a certain measure of independence, a certain direction of the relation proceed also from the self-will and

[1] Adapted from a translation of Georg Simmel by Albion W. Small, "Superiority and Subordination," in the *American Journal of Sociology*, II (1896–97), 169–71.

the character of the subordinate. The different cases of superiority and inferiority will accordingly be characterized by differences in the relative amount of spontaneity which the subordinates and the superiors bring to bear upon the total relation. In exemplification of this reciprocal action of the inferior, through which superiority and inferiority manifests itself as proper socialization, I will mention only a few cases, in which the reciprocity is difficult to discern.

When in the case of an absolute despotism the ruler attaches to his edicts the threat of penalty or the promise of reward, the meaning is that the monarch himself will be bound by the regulation which he has ordained. The inferior shall have the right, on the other hand, to demand something from the lawgiver. Whether the latter subsequently grants the promised reward or protection is another question. The spirit of the relation as contemplated by the law is that the superior completely controls the inferior, to be sure, but that a certain claim is assured to the latter, which claim he may press or may allow to lapse, so that even this most definite form of the relation still contains an element of spontaneity on the part of the inferior.

Still farther; the concept "law" seems to connote that he who gives the law is in so far unqualifiedly superior. Apart from those cases in which the law is instituted by those who will be its subjects, there appears in lawgiving as such no sign of spontaneity on the part of the subject of the law. It is, nevertheless, very interesting to observe how the Roman conception of law makes prominent the reciprocity between the superior and the subordinate elements. Thus *lex* means originally "compact," in the sense, to be sure, that the terms of the same are fixed by the proponent, and the other party can accept or reject it only *en bloc*. The *lex publica populi Romani* meant originally that the king proposed and the people accepted the same. Thus even here, where the conception itself seems to express the complete one-sidedness of the superior, the nice social instinct of the Romans pointed in the verbal expression to the co-operation of the subordinate. In consequence of like feeling of the nature of socialization the later Roman jurists declared that the *societas leonina* is not to be regarded as a social compact. Where the one absolutely controls the other, that is, where all spontaneity of the subordinate is excluded, there is no longer any socialization.

Once more, the orator who confronts the assembly, or the teacher his class, seems to be the sole leader, the temporary superior. Nevertheless everyone who finds himself in that situation is conscious of the limiting and controlling reaction of the mass which is apparently merely passive and submissive to his guidance. This is the case not merely when the parties immediately confront each other. All leaders are also led, as in countless cases the master is the slave of his slaves. "I am your leader, therefore I must follow you," said one of the most eminent German parliamentarians, with reference to his party. Every journalist is influenced by the public upon which he seems to exert an influence entirely without reaction. The most characteristic case of actual reciprocal influence, in spite of what appears to be subordination without corresponding reaction, is that of hypnotic suggestion. An eminent hypnotist recently asserted that in every hypnosis there occurs an actual if not easily defined influence of the hypnotized upon the hypnotist, and that without this the effect would not be produced.

4. Three Types of Subordination and Superordination[1]

Three possible types of superiority present themselves. Superiority may be exercised (a) by an individual, (b) by a group, (c) by an objective principle higher than individuals.

a) *Subordination to an individual.*—The subordination of a group to a single person implies a very decided unification of the group. This is equally the case with both the characteristic forms of this subordination, viz.: (1) when the group with its head constitutes a real internal unity; when the superior is more a leader than a master and only represents in himself the power and the will of the group; (2) when the group is conscious of opposition between itself and its head, when a party opposed to the head is formed. In both cases the unity of the supreme head tends to bring about an inner unification of the group. The elements of the latter are conscious of themselves as belonging together, because their interests converge at one point. Moreover the opposition to this unified controlling power compels the group to collect itself, to condense itself into unity

[1] Adapted from a translation of Georg Simmel by Albion W. Small, "Superiority and Subordination," in the *American Journal of Sociology*, II (1896–97), 172–86.

This is true not alone of the political group. In the factory, the ecclesiastical community, a school class, and in associated bodies of every sort it is to be observed that the termination of the organization in a head, whether in case of harmony or of opposition, helps to effect unification of the group. This is most conspicuous to be sure in the political sphere. History has shown it to be the enormous advantage of monarchies that they unify the political interests of the popular mass. The totality has a common interest in holding the prerogatives of the crown within their boundaries, possibly in restricting them; or there is a common field of conflict between those whose interests are with the crown and those who are opposed. Thus there is a supreme point with reference to which the whole people constitutes either a single party or, at most, two. Upon the disappearance of its head, to which all are subordinate—with the end of this political pressure—all political unity often likewise ceases. There spring up a great number of party factions which previously, in view of that supreme political interest for or against the monarchy, found no room.

Wonder has often been felt over the irrationality of the condition in which a single person exercises lordship over a great mass of others. The contradiction will be modified when we reflect that the ruler and the individual subject in the controlled mass by no means enter into the relationship with an equal *quantum* of their personality. The mass is composed through the fact that many individuals unite fractions of their personality—one-sided purposes, interests and powers, while that which each personality as such actually is towers above this common level and does not at all enter into that "mass," i.e., into that which is really ruled by the single person. Hence it is also that frequently in very despotically ruled groups individuality may develop itself very freely, in those aspects particularly which are not in participation with the mass. Thus began the development of modern individuality in the despotisms of the Italian Renaissance. Here, as in other similar cases (for example, under Napoleon I and Napoleon III), it was for the direct interest of the despots to allow the largest freedom to all those aspects of personality which were not identified with the regulated mass, i.e., to those aspects most apart from politics. Thus subordination was more tolerable.

b) *Subordination to a group.*—In the second place the group may assume the form of a pyramid. In this case the subordinates stand over against the superior not in an equalized mass but in very nicely graded strata of power. These strata grow constantly smaller in extent but greater in significance. They lead up from the inferior mass to the head, the single ruler.

This form of the group may come into existence in two ways. It may emerge from the autocratic supremacy of an individual. The latter often loses the substance of his power and allows it to slip downward, while retaining its form and titles. In this case more of the power is retained by the orders nearest to the former autocrat than is acquired by those more distant. Since the power thus gradually percolates, a continuity and graduation of superiority and inferiority must develop itself. This is, in fact, the way in which in oriental states the social forms often arise. The power of the superior orders disintegrates, either because it is essentially incoherent and does not know how to attain the above-emphasized proportion between subordination and individual freedom; or because the persons comprising the administration are too indolent or too ignorant of governmental technique to preserve supreme power. For the power which is exercised over a large circle is never a constant possession. It must be constantly acquired and defended anew if anything more than its shadow and name is to remain.

The other way in which a scale of power is constructed up to a supreme head is the reverse of that just described. Starting with a relative equality of the social elements, certain elements gain greater significance; within the circle of influence thus constituted certain especially powerful individuals differentiate themselves until this development accommodates itself to one or to a few heads. The pyramid of superiority and inferiority is built in this case from below upward, while in the former case the development was from above downward. This second form of development is often found in economic relationships, where at first there exists a certain equality between the persons carrying on the work of a certain industrial society. Presently some of the number acquire wealth; others become poor; others fall into intermediate conditions which are as dependent upon an aristocracy of property as the lower orders are upon the middle strata; this aristocracy rises in manifold gradations to the magnates, of whom sometimes a single individual is appropriately designated as the "king" of a branch of industry. By a sort of combination of the two ways in which graded superiority and inferiority of the group come into being the feudalism of the Middle Ages arose. So long as the full citizen—either Greek, Roman, or Teutonic—knew no subordination under an individual, there existed for him on the one hand complete equality with those of his own order, but on the other hand rigid exclusiveness toward those of lower orders. Feudalism remodeled this characteristic social form into the equally characteristic arrangement which filled the gap between freedom and bondage with a scale of classes.

A peculiar form of subordination to a number of individuals is determination by vote of a majority. The presumption of majority rule is that there is a collection of elements originally possessing equal rights. In the process of voting the individual places himself in subordination to a power of which he is a part, but in this way, that it is left to his own volition whether he will belong to the superior or the inferior, i.e., the outvoted party. We are not now interested in cases of this complex problem in which the superiority is entirely formal, as, for example, in resolves of scientific congresses, but only with those in which the individual is constrained to an action by the will of the party outvoting him, that is, in which he must practically subordinate himself to the majority. This dominance of numbers through the fact that others, though only equal in right, have another opinion, is by no means the matter of course which it seems to us today in our time of determinations by masses. Ancient German law knew nothing of it. If one did not agree with the resolve of the community, he was not bound by it. As an application of this principle, unanimity was later necessary in the choice of king, evidently because it could not be expected or required that one who had not chosen the king would obey him. The English baron who had opposed authorizing a levy, or who had not been present, often refused to pay it. In the tribal council of the Iroquois, as in the Polish Parliament, decisions had to be unanimous. There was therefore no subordination of an individual to a majority, unless we consider the fact that a proposition was regarded as rejected if it did not receive unanimous approval, a subordination, an outvoting, of the person proposing the measure.

When, on the contrary, majority rule exists, two modes of subordination of the minority are possible, and discrimination between them is of the highest sociological significance. Control of the minority may, in the first place, arise from the fact that the many are more powerful than the few. Although, or rather because, the individuals participating in a vote are supposed to be equals, the majority have the physical power to coerce the minority. The taking of a vote and the subjection of the minority serves the purpose of avoiding such actual measurement of strength, but accomplishes practically the same result through the count of votes, since the minority is convinced of the futility of such resort to force. There exist in the group two parties in opposition as though they were two groups, between which relative strength, represented by the vote, is to decide.

Quite another principle is in force, however, in the second place, where the group as a unity predominates over all individuals and so proceeds that the passing of votes shall *merely give expression to the unitary group will*. In the transition from the former to this second principle the enormously important step is taken from a unity made up merely of the sum of the individuals to recognition and operation of an abstract objective group unity. Classic antiquity took this step much earlier—not only absolutely but relatively earlier—than the German peoples. Among the latter the oneness of the community did not exist over against the individuals who composed it but entirely in them. Consequently the group will was not only not enacted but it did not even exist so long as a single member dissented. The group was not complete unless all its members were united, since it was only in the sum of its members that the group consisted. In case the group, however, is a self-existent structure—whether consciously or merely in point of fact—in case the group organization effected by union of the individuals remains along with and in spite of the individual changes, this self-existent unity—state, community, association for a distinctive purpose—must surely will and act in a definite manner. Since, however, only one of two contradictory opinions can ultimately prevail, it is assumed as more probable that the majority knows or represents this will better than the minority. According to the presumptive principle involved the minority is, in this case, not excluded but included. The subordination of the minority is thus in this stage of sociological development quite different from that in case the majority simply represents the stronger power. In the case in hand the majority does not speak in its own name but in that of the ideal unity and totality. It is only to this unity, which speaks by the mouth of the majority, that the minority subordinates itself. This is the immanent principle of our parliamentary decisions.

c) *Subordination to an impersonal principle.*—To these must be joined, third, those formations in which subordination is neither to an individual nor yet to a majority, but to an impersonal objective principle. Here, where we seem to be estopped from speaking of a *reciprocal influence* between the superior and the subordinate, a sociological interest enters in but two cases: first, when this ideal superior principle is to be interpreted as the psychological consolidation of a real social power; second, when the principle establishes specific and characteristic relationships between those who are subject to it in common. The former case appears chiefly in connection with the moral imperatives. In the moral consciousness we feel ourselves subject to a decree which does not appear to be issued by any personal human power; we hear the voice of conscience only in ourselves, although with a force and definiteness, in contrast with all subjective egoism, which, as it seems, could have had its source only from an authority outside the subject. As is well known, the attempt has been made to resolve this contradiction by the assumption that we have derived the content of morality from social decrees. Whatever is serviceable to the species and to the group, whatever on that account is demanded of the members for the self-preservation of the group, is gradually bred into individuals as an instinct, so that it asserts itself as a peculiar autonomous impression by the side of the properly personal, and consequently often contradictory, impulses. Thus would be explained the double character of the moral command. On the one side it appears to us as an impersonal order to which we have simply to yield. On the other side, however, no visible external power but only our own most real and personal instinct enforces it upon us. Sociologically this is of interest as an example of a wholly peculiar form of reaction between the individual and his group. The social force is here completely grown into the individual himself.

We now turn to the second sociological question raised by the case of subordination to an impersonal ideal principle. How does this subordination affect the reciprocal relation of the persons thus subordinated in common? The development of the position of the *pater familias* among the Aryans exhibits this process clearly. The power of the *pater familias* was originally unlimited and entirely subjective; that is, his momentary desire, his personal advantage, was permitted to give the decision upon all regulations. But this arbitrary power gradually became limited by a feeling of responsibility. The unity of the domestic group, embodied in the *spiritus familiaris*, grew into the ideal power, in relation to which the lord of the whole came to regard himself as merely an obedient agent. Accordingly it follows that morals and custom, instead of subjective preference, determine his acts, his decisions, his judicial judgments; that he no longer behaves as though he were absolute lord of the family property, but rather the manager of it in the interest of the whole; that his position bears more the character of an official station than that of an unlimited right. Thus the relation between superiors and inferiors is placed upon an entirely new basis. The family is thought of as standing above all the individual members. The guiding patriarch himself is, like every other member, subordinate to the family idea. He may give directions to the other members of the family only in the name of the higher ideal unity.

C. CONFLICT AND ACCOMMODATION

1. War and Peace as Types of Conflict and Accommodation[1]

It is obvious that the transition from war to peace must present a more considerable problem than the reverse, i.e., the transition from peace to war. The latter really needs no particular scrutiny. For the situations existing in time of peace are precisely the conditions out of which war emerges and contain in themselves struggle in a diffused, unobserved, or latent form. For instance, if the economic advantage which the southern states of the American Union had over the northern states in the Civil War as a consequence of the slave system was also the reason for this war, still, so long as no antagonism arises from it, but is merely immanent in the existing conditions, this source of conflict did not become specifically a question of war and peace. At the moment, however, at which the antagonism began to assume a color which meant war, an accumulation of antagonisms,

[1] Adapted from a translation of Georg Simmel by Albion W. Small, "The Sociology of Conflict," in the *American Journal of Sociology*, IX (1903–4), 799–802

feelings of hatred, newspaper polemics, frictions between private persons, and on the borders reciprocal moral equivocations in matters outside of the central antithesis at once manifested themselves. The transition from peace to war is thus not distinguished by a special sociological situation. Rather out of relationships existing within a peaceful situation antagonism is developed immediately, in its most visible and energetic form. The case is different, however, if the matter is viewed from the opposite direction. Peace does not follow so immediately upon conflict. The termination of strife is a special undertaking which belongs neither in the one category nor in the other, like a bridge which is of a different nature from that of either bank which it unites. The sociology of struggle demands, therefore, at least as an appendix, an analysis of the forms in which conflict is terminated, and these exhibit certain special forms of reaction not to be observed in other circumstances.

The particular motive which in most cases corresponds with the transition from war to peace is the simple longing for peace. With the emergence of this factor there comes into being, as a matter of fact, peace itself, at first in the form of the wish immediately parallel with the struggle itself, and it may without any special transitional form displace struggle. We need not pause long to observe that the desire for peace may spring up both directly and indirectly; the former may occur either through the return to power of this peaceful character in the party which is essentially in favor of peace; or through the fact that, through the mere change of the formal stimulus of struggle and of peace which is peculiar to all natures, although in different rhythms, the latter comes to the surface and assumes a control which is sanctioned by its own nature alone. In the case of the indirect motive, however, we may distinguish, on the one hand, the exhaustion of resources which, without removal of the persistent contentiousness, may instal the demand for peace; and, on the other hand, the withdrawal of interest from struggle through a higher interest in some other object. The latter case begets all sorts of hypocrisies and self-deceptions. It is asserted and believed that peace is desired from ideal interest in peace itself and the suppression of antagonism, while in reality only the object fought for has lost its interest and the fighters would prefer to have their powers free for other kinds of activity.

The simplest and most radical sort of passage from war to peace is victory—a quite unique phenomenon in life, of which there are, to be sure, countless individual forms and measures, which, however, have no resemblance to any of the otherwise mentioned forms which may occur between persons. Victory is a mere watershed between war and peace; when considered absolutely, only an ideal structure which extends itself over no considerable time. For so long as struggle endures there is no definitive victor, and when peace exists a victory *has been* gained but the act of victory has ceased to exist. Of the many shadings of victory, through which it qualifies the following peace, I mention here merely as an illustration the one which is brought about, not exclusively by the preponderance of the one party, but, at least in part, through the resignation of the other. This confession of inferiority, this acknowledgment of defeat, or this consent that victory shall go to the other party without complete exhaustion of the resources and chances for struggle, is by no means always a simple phenomenon. A certain ascetic tendency may also enter in as a purely individual factor, the tendency to self-humiliation and to self-sacrifice, not strong enough to surrender one's self from the start without a struggle, but emerging so soon as the consciousness of being vanquished begins to take possession of the soul; or another variation may be that of finding its supreme charm in the contrast to the still vital and active disposition to struggle. Still further, there is impulse to the same conclusion in the feeling that it is worthier to yield rather than to trust to the last moment in the improbable chance of a fortunate turn of affairs. To throw away this chance and to elude at this price the final consequences that would be involved in utter defeat—this has something of the great and noble qualities of men who are sure, not merely of their strengths, but also of their weaknesses, without making it necessary for them in each case to make these perceptibly conscious. Finally, in this voluntariness of confessed defeat there is a last proof of power on the part of the agent; the latter has of himself been able to act. He has therewith virtually made a gift to the conqueror. Consequently, it is often to be observed in personal conflicts that the concession of the one party, before the other has actually been able to compel it, is regarded by the latter as a sort of insult, as though this latter party were really the weaker, to whom, however, for some reason or other, there is made a concession without its being really necessary. Behind the objective reasons for yielding "for the sake of sweet peace" a mixture of these subjective motives is not seldom concealed. The latter may not be entirely without visible consequences, however, for the further sociological attitude of the parties. In complete antithesis with the end of strife by victory is its ending by compromise. One of the most characteristic ways of subdividing struggles is on the basis of whether they are of a nature which admits of compromise or not.

2.   Compromise and Accommodation[1]

On the whole, compromise, especially of that type which is brought to pass through negotiation, however commonplace and matter of fact it has come to be in the processes of modern life, is one of the most important inventions for the uses of civilization. The impulse of uncivilized men, like that of children, is to seize upon every desirable object without further consideration, even though it be already in the possession of another. Robbery and gift are the most naïve forms of transfer of possession, and under primitive conditions change of possession seldom takes place without a struggle. It is the beginning of all civilized industry and commerce to find a way of avoiding this struggle through a process in which there is offered to the possessor of a desired object some other object from the possessions of the person desiring the exchange. Through this arrangement a reduction is made in the total expenditure of energy as compared with the process of continuing or beginning a struggle. All exchange is a compromise. We are told of certain social conditions in which it is accounted as knightly to rob and to fight for the sake of robbery; while exchange and purchase are regarded in the same society as undignified and vulgar. The psychological explanation of this situation is to be found partly in the fact of the element of compromise in exchange, the factors of withdrawal and renunciation which make exchange the opposite pole to all struggle and conquest. Every exchange presupposes that values and interest have assumed an objective character. The decisive element is accordingly no longer the mere subjective passion of desire, to which struggle alone corresponds, but the value of the object, which is recognized by both interested parties but which without essential modification may be

[1] Adapted from a translation of Georg Simmel by Albion W. Small, "The Sociology of Conflict," in the *American Journal of Sociology*, IX (1903–4), 804–6.

represented by various objects. Renunciation of the valued object in question, because one receives in another form the quantum of value contained in the same, is an admirable reason, wonderful also in its simplicity, whereby opposed interests are brought to accommodation without struggle. It certainly required a long historical development to make such means available, because it presupposes a psychological generalization of the universal valuation of the individual object, an abstraction, in other words, of the value for the objects with which it is at first identified; that is, it presupposes ability to rise above the prejudices of immediate desire. Compromise by representation, of which exchange is a special case, signifies in principle, although realized only in part, the possibility of avoiding struggle or of setting a limit to it before the mere force of the interested parties has decided the issue.

In distinction from the objective character of accommodation of struggle through compromise, we should notice that conciliation is a purely subjective method of avoiding struggle. I refer here not to that sort of conciliation which is the consequence of a compromise or of any other adjournment of struggle but rather to the reasons for this adjournment. The state of mind which makes conciliation possible is an elementary attitude which, entirely apart from objective grounds, seeks to end struggle, just as, on the other hand, a disposition to quarrel, even without any real occasion, promotes struggle. Probably both mental attitudes have been developed as matters of utility in connection with certain situations; at any rate, they have been developed psychologically to the extent of independent impulses, each of which is likely to make itself felt where the other would be more practically useful. We may even say that in the countless cases in which struggle is ended otherwise than in the pitiless consistency of the exercise of force, this quite elementary and unreasoned tendency to conciliation is a factor in the result—a factor quite distinct from weakness, or good fellowship; from social morality or fellow-feeling. This tendency to conciliation is, in fact, a quite specific sociological impulse which manifests itself exclusively as a pacificator, and is not even identical with the peaceful disposition in general. The latter avoids strife under all circumstances, or carries it on, if it is once undertaken, without going to extremes, and always with the undercurrents of longing for peace. The spirit of conciliation, however, manifests itself frequently in its full peculiarity precisely after complete surrender to the struggle, after the conflicting energies have exercised themselves to the full in the conflict.

Conciliation depends very definitely upon the external situation. It can occur both after the complete victory of the one party and after the progress of indecisive struggle, as well as after the arrangement of the compromise. Either of these situations may end the struggle without the added conciliation of the opponents. To bring about the latter it is not necessary that there shall be a supplementary repudiation or expression of regret with reference to the struggle. Moreover, conciliation is to be distinguished from the situation which may follow it. This may be either a relationship of attachment or alliance, and reciprocal respect, or a certain permanent distance which avoids all positive contacts. Conciliation is thus a removal of the roots of conflict, without reference to the fruits which these formerly bore, as well as to that which may later be planted in their place.

D. COMPETITION, STATUS, AND SOCIAL SOLIDARITY

1. Personal Competition, Social Selection, and Status[1]

The function of personal competition, considered as a part of the social system, is to assign to each individual his place in that system. If "all the world's a stage," this is a process that distributes the parts among the players. It may do it well or ill, but after some fashion it does it. Some may be cast in parts unsuited to them; good actors may be discharged altogether and worse ones retained; but nevertheless the thing is arranged in some way and the play goes on.

That such a process must exist can hardly, it seems to me, admit of question; in fact, I believe that those who speak of doing away with competition use the word in another sense than is here intended. Within the course of the longest human life there is necessarily a complete renewal of the persons whose communication and co-operation make up the life of society. The new members come into the world without any legible sign to indicate what they are fit for, a mystery to others from the first and to themselves as soon as they

[1] Adapted from Charles H. Cooley, "Personal Competition," in *Economic Studies*, IV (1899), No. 2, 78–86.

are capable of reflection: the young man does not know for what he is adapted, and no one else can tell him. The only possible way to get light upon the matter is to adopt the method of experiment. By trying one thing and another and by reflecting upon his experience, he begins to find out about himself, and the world begins to find out about him. His field of investigation is of course restricted, and his own judgment and that of others liable to error, but the tendency of it all can hardly be other than to guide his choice to that one of the available careers in which he is best adapted to hold his own. I may say this much, perhaps, without assuming anything regarding the efficiency or justice of competition as a distributor of social functions, a matter regarding which I shall offer some suggestions later. All I wish to say here is that the necessity of some selective process is inherent in the conditions of social life.

It will be apparent that, in the sense in which I use the term, competition is not necessarily a hostile contention, nor even something of which the competing individual is always conscious. From our infancy onward throughout life judgments are daily forming regarding us of which we are unaware, but which go to determine our careers. "The world is full of judgment days." A and B, for instance, are under consideration for some appointment; the experience and personal qualifications of each are duly weighed by those having the appointment to make, and A, we will say, is chosen. Neither of the two need know anything about the matter until the selection is made. It is eligibility to perform some social function that makes a man a competitor, and he may or may not be aware of it, or, if aware of it, he may or may not be consciously opposed to others. I trust that the reader will bear in mind that I always use the word competition in the sense here explained.

There is but one alternative to competition as a means of determining the place of the individual in the social system, and that is some form of status, some fixed, mechanical rule, usually a rule of inheritance, which decides the function of the individual without reference to his personal traits, and thus dispenses with any process of comparison. It is possible to conceive of a society organized entirely upon the basis of the inheritance of functions, and indeed societies exist which may be said to approach this condition. In India, for example, the prevalent idea regarding the social function of the individual is that it is unalterably determined by his parentage, and the village blacksmith, shoemaker, accountant, or priest has his place assigned to him by a rule of descent as rigid as that which governs the transmission of one of the crowns of Europe. If all functions were handed down in this way, if there were never any deficiency or surplus of children to take the place of their parents, if there were no progress or decay in the social system making necessary new activities or dispensing with old ones, then there would be no use for a selective process. But precisely in the measure that a society departs from this condition, that individual traits are recognized and made available, or social change of any sort comes to pass, in that measure must there be competition.

Status is not an active process, as competition is; it is simply a rule of conservation, a makeshift to avoid the inconveniences of continual readjustment in the social structure. Competition or selection is the only constructive principle, and everything worthy the name of organization had at some time or other a competitive origin. At the present day the eldest son of a peer may succeed to a seat in the House of Lords simply by right of birth; but his ancestor got the seat by competition, by some exercise of personal qualities that made him valued or loved or feared by a king or a minister.

Sir Henry Maine has pointed out that the increase of competition is a characteristic trait of modern life, and that the powerful ancient societies of the old world were for the most part non-competitive in their structure. While this is true, it would be a mistake to draw the inference that status is a peculiarly natural or primitive principle of organization and competition a comparatively recent discovery. On the contrary the spontaneous relations among men, as we see in the case of children, and as we may infer from the life of the lower animals, are highly competitive, personal prowess and ascendency being everything and little regard being paid to descent simply as such. The régime of inherited status, on the other hand, is a comparatively complex and artificial product, necessarily of later growth, whose very general prevalence among the successful societies of the old world is doubtless to be explained by the stability and consequently the power which it was calculated to give to the social system. It survived because under certain conditions it was the fittest. It

was not and is not universally predominant among savages or bar-
barous peoples. With the American Indians, for example, the
definiteness and authority of status were comparatively small, personal prowess and initiative being correspondingly important. The
interesting monograph on Omaha sociology, by Dorsey, published by
the United States Bureau of Ethnology, contains many facts showing
that the life of this people was highly competitive. When the tribe
was at war any brave could organize an expedition against the enemy,
if he could induce enough others to join him, and this organizer
usually assumed the command. In a similar way the managers of
the hunt were chosen because of personal skill; and, in general,
"any man can win a name and rank in the state by becoming 'wacuce'
or brave, either in war or by the bestowal of gifts and the frequent
giving of feasts."

Throughout history there has been a struggle between the principles of status and competition regarding the part that each should
play in the social system. Generally speaking the advantage of
status is in its power to give order and continuity. As Gibbon
informs us, "The superior prerogative of birth, when it has obtained
the sanction of time and popular opinion, is the plainest and least
invidious of all distinctions among mankind," and he is doubtless
right in ascribing the confusion of the later Roman Empire largely
to the lack of an established rule for the transmission of imperial
authority. The chief danger of status is that of suppressing personal
development, and so of causing social enfeeblement, rigidity, and
ultimate decay. On the other hand, competition develops the
individual and gives flexibility and animation to the social order,
its danger being chiefly that of disintegration in some form or other.
The general tendency in modern times has been toward the relative
increase of the free or competitive principle, owing to the fact that
the rise of other means of securing stability has diminished the need
for status. The latter persists, however, even in the freest countries,
as the method by which wealth is transmitted, and also in social
classes, which, so far as they exist at all, are based chiefly upon
inherited wealth and the culture and opportunities that go with it.
The ultimate reason for this persistence—without very serious opposition—in the face of the obvious inequalities and limitations upon

liberty that it perpetuates is perhaps the fact that no other method of transmission has arisen that has shown itself capable of giving continuity and order to the control of wealth.

2. Personal Competition and the Evolution of Individual Types[1]

The ancient city was primarily a fortress, a place of refuge in time of war. The modern city, on the contrary, is primarily a convenience of commerce and owes its existence to the market place around which it sprang up. Industrial competition and the division of labor, which have probably done most to develop the latent powers of mankind, are possible only upon condition of the existence of markets, of money and other devices for the facilitation of trade and commerce.

The old adage which describes the city as the natural environment of the free man still holds so far as the individual man finds in the chances, the diversity of interests and tasks, and in the vast unconscious co-operation of city life, the opportunity to choose his own vocation and develop his peculiar individual talents. The city offers a market for the special talents of individual men. Personal competition tends to select for each special task the individual who is best suited to perform it.

The difference of natural talents in different men is, in reality, much less than we are aware of; and the very different genius which appears to distinguish men of different professions, when grown up to maturity, is not upon many occasions so much the cause, as the effect of the division of labour. The difference between the most dissimilar characters, between a philosopher and a common street porter, for example, seems to arise not so much from nature, as from habit, custom and education. When they came into the world, and for the first six or eight years of their existence, they were perhaps very much alike, and neither their parents nor playfellows could perceive any remarkable difference. About that age, or soon after, they come to be employed in different occupations. The difference of talents comes then to be taken notice of, and widens by degrees, till at last the vanity of the philosopher is willing to acknowledge scarce any resemblance. But without the disposition to truck, barter, and exchange, every man must have procured to himself every necessary and conveniency of life which he wanted. All must have had the same duties to perform, and the same work to do, and there could have been no such difference of

    [1] From Robert E. Park, "The City," in the *American Journal of Sociology*, XX (1915), 584–86.

employment as could alone give occasion to any great difference of talent.

As it is the power of exchanging that gives occasion to the division of labour, so the extent of this division must always be limited by the extent of that power, or, in other words, by the extent of the market. . . . . There are some sorts of industry, even of the lowest kind, which can be carried on nowhere but in a great town.

Success, under conditions of personal competition, depends upon concentration upon some single task, and this concentration stimulates the demand for rational methods, technical devices, and exceptional skill. Exceptional skill, while based on natural talent, requires special preparation, and it has called into existence the trade and professional schools, and finally bureaus for vocational guidance. All of these, either directly or indirectly, serve at once to select and emphasize individual differences.

Every device which facilitates trade and industry prepares the way for a further division of labor and so tends further to specialize the tasks in which men find their vocations.

The outcome of this process is to break down or modify the older organization of society, which was based on family ties, on local associations, on culture, caste, and status, and to substitute for it an organization based on vocational interests.

In the city every vocation, even that of a beggar, tends to assume the character of a profession, and the discipline which success in any vocation imposes, together with the associations that it enforces, emphasizes this tendency.

The effect of the vocations and the division of labor is to produce, in the first instance, not social groups but vocational types—the actor, the plumber, and the lumber-jack. The organizations, like the trade and labor unions, which men of the same trade or profession form are based on common interests. In this respect they differ from forms of association like the neighborhood, which are based on contiguity, personal association, and the common ties of humanity. The different trades and professions seem disposed to group themselves in classes, that is to say, the artisan, business, and professional classes. But in the modern democratic state the classes have as yet attained no effective organization. Socialism, founded on an effort to create an organization based on "class consciousness," has never succeeded in creating more than a political party.

The effects of the division of labor as a discipline may therefore be best studied in the vocational types it has produced. Among the types which it would be interesting to study are: the shopgirl, the policeman, the peddler, the cabman, the night watchman, the clairvoyant, the vaudeville performer, the quack doctor, the bartender, the ward boss, the strike-breaker, the labor agitator, the school teacher, the reporter, the stockbroker, the pawnbroker; all of these are characteristic products of the conditions of city life; each with its special experience, insight, and point of view determines for each vocational group and for the city as a whole its individuality.

3.   Division of Labor and Social Solidarity[1]

The most remarkable effect of the division of labor is not that it accentuates the distinction of functions already divided but that it makes them interdependent. Its rôle in every case is not simply to embellish or perfect existing societies but to make possible societies which, without it, would not exist. Should the division of labor between the sexes be diminished beyond a certain point, the family would cease to exist and only ephemeral sexual relations would remain. If the sexes had never been separated at all, no form of social life would ever have arisen. It is possible that the economic utility of the division of labor has been a factor in producing the existing form of conjugal society. Nevertheless, the society thus created is not limited to merely economic interests; it represents a unique social and moral order. Individuals are mutually bound together who otherwise would be independent. Instead of developing separately, they concert their efforts; they are interdependent parts of a unity which is effective not only in the brief moments during which there is an interchange of services but afterward indefinitely. For example, does not conjugal solidarity of the type which exists today among the most cultivated people exert its influence constantly and in all the details of life? On the other hand, societies which are created by the division of labor inevitably bear the mark of their origin. Having this special origin, it is not possible that they should resemble those societies which have their origin in the attraction of like for like; the latter are inevitably constituted in another

[1] Translated and adapted from Émile Durkheim, *La division du travail social*, pp. 24-209. (Félix Alcan, 1902.)

manner, repose on other foundations, and appeal to other sentiments.

The assumption that the social relations resulting from the division of labor consist in an exchange of services merely is a misconception of what this exchange implies and of the effects it produces. It assumes that two beings are mutually dependent the one on the other, because they are both incomplete without the other. It interprets this mutual dependence as a purely external relation. Actually this is merely the superficial expression of an internal and more profound state. Precisely because this state is constant, it provokes a complex of mental images which function with a continuity independent of the series of external relations. The image of that which completes us is inseparable from the image of ourselves, not only because it is associated with us, but especially because it is our natural complement. It becomes then a permanent and integral part of self-consciousness to such an extent that we cannot do without it and seek by every possible means to emphasize and intensify it. We like the society of the one whose image haunts us, because the presence of the object reinforces the actual perception and gives us comfort. We suffer, on the contrary, from every circumstance which, like separation and death, is likely to prevent the return or diminish the vivacity of the idea which has become identified with our idea of ourselves.

Short as this analysis is, it suffices to show that this complex is not identical with that which rests on sentiments of sympathy which have their source in mere likeness. Unquestionably there can be the sense of solidarity between others and ourselves only so far as we conceive others united with ourselves. When the union results from a perception of likeness, it is a cohesion. The two representations become consolidated because, being undistinguished totally or in part, they are mingled and are no more than one, and are consolidated only in the measure in which they are mingled. On the contrary, in the case of the division of labor, each is outside the other, and they are united only because they are distinct. It is not possible that sentiments should be the same in the two cases, nor the social relations which are derived from them the same.

We are then led to ask ourselves if the division of labor does not play the same rôle in more extended groups; if, in the contemporaneous societies where it has had a development with which we are familiar, it does not function in such a way as to integrate the social body and to assure its unity. It is quite legitimate to assume that the facts which we have observed reproduce themselves there, but on a larger scale. The great political societies, like smaller ones, we may assume maintain themselves in equilibrium, thanks to the specialization of their tasks. The division of labor is here, again, if not the only, at least the principal, source of the social solidarity. Comte had already reached this point of view. Of all the sociologists, so far as we know, he is the first who has pointed out in the division of labor anything other than a purely economic phenomenon. He has seen there "the most essential condition of the social life," provided that one conceives it "in all its rational extent, that is to say, that one applies the conception to the ensemble of all our diverse operations whatsoever, instead of limiting it, as we so often do, to the simple material usages." Considered under this aspect, he says:

It immediately leads us to regard not only individuals and classes but also, in many respects, the different peoples as constantly participating, in their own characteristic ways and in their own proper degree, in an immense and common work whose inevitable development gradually unites the actual co-operators in a series with their predecessors and at the same time in a series with their successors. It is, then, the continuous redivison of our diverse human labors which mainly constitutes social solidarity and which becomes the elementary cause of the extension and increasing complexity of the social organism.

If this hypothesis is demonstrated, division of labor plays a rôle much more important than that which has ordinarily been attributed to it. It is not to be regarded as a mere luxury, desirable perhaps, but not indispensable to society; it is rather a condition of its very existence. It is this, or at least it is mainly this, that assures the solidarity of social groups; it determines the essential traits of their constitution. It follows—even though we are not yet prepared to give a final solution to the problem, we can nevertheless foresee from this point—that, if such is really the function of the division of labor, it may be expected to have a moral character, because the needs of order, of harmony, of social solidarity generally, are what we understand by moral needs.

Social life is derived from a double source: (*a*) from a similarity of minds, and (*b*) from the division of labor. The individual is socialized in the first case, because, not having his own individuality, he is confused, along with his fellows, in the bosom of the same collective type; in the second case, because, even though he possesses a physiognomy and a temperament which distinguish him from others, he is dependent upon these in the same measure in which he is distinguished from them. Society results from this union.

Like-mindedness gives birth to judicial regulations which, under the menace of measures of repression, impose upon everybody uniform beliefs and practices. The more pronounced this like-mindedness, the more completely the social is confused with the religious life, the more nearly economic institutions approach communism.

The division of labor, on the other hand, gives birth to regulations and laws which determine the nature and the relations of the divided functions, but the violation of which entails only punitive measures not of an expiatory character.

Every code of laws is accompanied by a body of regulations purely moral. Where the penal law is voluminous, moral consensus is very extended; that is to say, a multitude of collective activities is under the guardianship of public opinion. Where the right of reparation is well developed, there each profession maintains a code of professional ethics. In a group of workers there invariably exists a body of opinion, diffused throughout the limits of the group, which, although not fortified with legal sanctions, still enforces its decrees. There are manners and customs, recognized by all the members of a profession, which no one of them could infringe without incurring the blame of society. Certainly this code of morals is distinguished from the preceding by differences analogous to those which separate the two corresponding kinds of laws. It is, in fact, a code localized in a limited region of society. Furthermore, the repressive character of the sanctions which are attached to it is sensibly less accentuated. Professional faults arouse a much feebler response than offenses against the mores of the larger society.

Nevertheless, the customs and code of a profession are imperative. They oblige the individual to act in accordance with ends which to him are not his own, to make concessions, to consent to compromises, to take account of interests superior to his own. The consequence is that, even where the society rests most completely upon the division of labor, it does not disintegrate into a dust of atoms, between which there can exist only external and temporary contacts. Every function which one individual exercises is invariably dependent upon functions exercised by others and forms with them a system of interdependent parts. It follows that, from the nature of the task one chooses, corresponding duties follow. Because we fill this or that domestic or social function, we are imprisoned in a net of obligations from which we do not have the right to free ourselves. There is especially one organ toward which our state of dependencies is ever increasing—the state. The points at which we are in contact with it are multiplying. So are the occasions in which it takes upon itself to recall us to a sense of the common solidarity.

There are then two great currents in the social life, collectivism and individualism, corresponding to which we discover two types of structure not less different. Of these currents, that which has its origin in like-mindedness is at first alone and without rival. At this moment it is identified with the very life of the society; little by little it finds its separate channels and diminishes, whilst the second becomes ever larger. In the same way, the segmentary structure of society is more and more overlaid by the other, but without ever disappearing completely.

CHAPTER IX

ASSIMILATION

I. INTRODUCTION

1. Popular Conceptions of Assimilation

The concept assimilation, so far as it has been defined in popular usage, gets its meaning from its relation to the problem of immigration. The more concrete and familiar terms are the abstract noun Americanization and the verbs Americanize, Anglicize, Germanize, and the like. All of these words are intended to describe the process by which the culture of a community or a country is transmitted to an adopted citizen. Negatively, assimilation is a process of denationalization and this is, in fact, the form it has taken in Europe.

The difference between Europe and America, in relation to the problem of cultures, is that in Europe difficulties have arisen from the forcible incorporation of minor cultural groups, i.e., nationalities, within the limits of a larger political unit, i.e., an empire. In America the problem has arisen from the voluntary migration to this country of peoples who have abandoned the political allegiances of the old country and are gradually acquiring the culture of the new. In both cases the problem has its source in an effort to establish and maintain a political order in a community that has no common culture. Fundamentally the problem of maintaining a democratic form of government in a southern village composed of whites and blacks, and the problem of maintaining an international order based on anything but force are the same. The ultimate basis of the existing moral and political order is still kinship and culture. Where neither exist, a political order, not based on caste or class, is at least problematic.

Assimilation, as popularly conceived in the United States, was expressed symbolically some years ago in Zangwill's dramatic parable of *The Melting Pot*. William Jennings Bryan has given oratorical expression to the faith in the beneficent outcome of the process: "Great has been the Greek, the Latin, the Slav, the Celt, the Teuton, and the Saxon; but greater than any of these is the American, who combines the virtues of them all."

359

Assimilation, as thus conceived, is a natural and unassisted process, and practice, if not policy, has been in accord with this laissez faire conception, which the outcome has apparently justified. In the United States, at any rate, the tempo of assimilation has been more rapid than elsewhere.

Closely akin to this "magic crucible" notion of assimilation is the theory of "like-mindedness." This idea was partly a product of Professor Giddings' theory of sociology, partly an outcome of the popular notion that similarities and homogeneity are identical with unity. The ideal of assimilation was conceived to be that of feeling, thinking, and acting alike. Assimilation and socialization have both been described in these terms by contemporary sociologists.

Another and a different notion of assimilation or Americanization is based on the conviction that the immigrant has contributed in the past and may be expected in the future to contribute something of his own in temperament, culture, and philosophy of life to the future American civilization. This conception had its origin among the immigrants themselves, and has been formulated and interpreted by persons who are, like residents in social settlements, in close contact with them. This recognition of the diversity in the elements entering into the cultural process is not, of course, inconsistent with the expectation of an ultimate homogeneity of the product. It has called attention, at any rate, to the fact that the process of assimilation is concerned with differences quite as much as with likenesses.

2. The Sociology of Assimilation

Accommodation has been described as a process of adjustment, that is, an organization of social relations and attitudes to prevent or to reduce conflict, to control competition, and to maintain a basis of security in the social order for persons and groups of divergent interests and types to carry on together their varied life-activities. Accommodation in the sense of the composition of conflict is invariably the goal of the political process.

Assimilation is a process of interpenetration and fusion in which persons and groups acquire the memories, sentiments, and attitudes of other persons or groups, and, by sharing their experience and history, are incorporated with them in a common cultural life. In so far as assimilation denotes this sharing of tradition, this intimate participation in common experiences, assimilation is central in the historical and cultural processes.

This distinction between accommodation and assimilation, with reference to their rôle in society, explains certain significant formal differences between the two processes. An accommodation of a conflict, or an accommodation to a new situation, may take place with rapidity. The more intimate and subtle changes involved in assimilation are more gradual. The changes that occur in accommodation are frequently not only sudden but revolutionary, as in the mutation of attitudes in conversion. The modifications of attitudes in the process of assimilation are not only gradual, but moderate, even if they appear considerable in their accumulation over a long period of time. If mutation is the symbol for accommodation, growth is the metaphor for assimilation. In accommodation the person or the group is generally, though not always, highly conscious of the occasion, as in the peace treaty that ends the war, in the arbitration of an industrial controversy, in the adjustment of the person to the formal requirements of life in a new social world. In assimilation the process is typically unconscious; the person is incorporated into the common life of the group before he is aware and with little conception of the course of events which brought this incorporation about.

James has described the way in which the attitude of the person changes toward certain subjects, woman's suffrage, for example, not as the result of conscious reflection, but as the outcome of the unreflective responses to a series of new experiences. The intimate associations of the family and of the play group, participation in the ceremonies of religious worship and in the celebrations of national holidays, all these activities transmit to the immigrant and to the alien a store of memories and sentiments common to the native-born, and these memories are the basis of all that is peculiar and sacred in our cultural life.

As social contact initiates interaction, assimilation is its final perfect product. The nature of the social contacts is decisive in the process. Assimilation naturally takes place most rapidly where contacts are primary, that is, where they are the most intimate and intense, as in the area of touch relationship, in the family circle and in intimate congenial groups. Secondary contacts facilitate accommodations, but do not greatly promote assimilation. The contacts here are external and too remote.

A common language is indispensable for the most intimate association of the members of the group; its absence is an insurmountable barrier to assimilation. The phenomenon "that every group has its own language," its peculiar "universe of discourse," and its cultural symbols is evidence of the interrelation between communication and assimilation.

Through the mechanisms of imitation and suggestion, communication effects a gradual and unconscious modification of the attitudes and sentiments of the members of the group. The unity thus achieved is not necessarily or even normally like-mindedness; it is rather a unity of experience and of orientation, out of which may develop a community of purpose and action.

3. Classification of the Materials

The selections in the materials on assimilation have been arranged under three heads: (a) biological aspects of assimilation; (b) the conflict and fusion of cultures; and (c) Americanization as a problem in assimilation. The readings proceed from an analysis of the nature of assimilation to a survey of its processes, as they have manifested themselves historically, and finally to a consideration of the problems of Americanization.

a) *Biological aspects of assimilation.*—Assimilation is to be distinguished from amalgamation, with which it is, however, closely related. Amalgamation is a biological process, the fusion of races by interbreeding and intermarriage. Assimilation, on the other hand, is limited to the fusion of cultures. Miscegenation, or the mingling of races, is a universal phenomenon among the historical races. There are no races, in other words, that do not interbreed. Acculturation, or the transmission of cultural elements from one social group to another, however, has invariably taken place on a larger scale and over a wider area than miscegenation.

Amalgamation, while it is limited to the crossing of racial traits through intermarriage, naturally promotes assimilation or the cross-fertilization of social heritages. The offspring of a "mixed" marriage not only biologically inherits physical and temperamental traits from both parents, but also acquires in the nurture of family life the attitudes, sentiments, and memories of both father and mother. Thus amalgamation of races insures the conditions of primary social contacts most favorable for assimilation.

b) *The conflict and fusion of cultures.*—The survey of the process of what the ethnologists call *acculturation*, as it is exhibited historically in the conflicts and fusions of cultures, indicates the wide range of the phenomena in this field.

(1) Social contact, even when slight or indirect, is sufficient for the transmission from one cultural group to another of the material elements of civilization. Stimulants and firearms spread rapidly upon the objective demonstration of their effects. The potato, a native of America, has preceded the white explorer in its penetration into many areas of Africa.

(2) The changes in languages in the course of the contacts, conflicts, and fusions of races and nationalities afford data for a more adequate description of the process of assimilation. Under what conditions does a ruling group impose its speech upon the masses, or finally capitulate to the vulgar tongue of the common people? In modern times the printing-press, the book, and the newspaper have tended to fix languages. The press has made feasible language revivals in connection with national movements on a scale impossible in earlier periods.

The emphasis placed upon language as a medium of cultural transmission rests upon a sound principle. For the idioms, particularly of a spoken language, probably reflect more accurately the historical experiences of a people than history itself. The basis of unity among most historical peoples is linguistic rather than racial. The Latin peoples are a convenient example of this fact. The experiment now in progress in the Philippine Islands is significant in this connection. To what extent will the national and cultural development of those islands be determined by native temperament, by Spanish speech and tradition, or by the English language and the American school system?

(3) Rivers in his study of Melanesian and Hawaiian cultures was impressed by the persistence of fundamental elements of the social structure. The basic patterns of family and social life remained practically unmodified despite profound transformations in technique,

in language, and in religion. Evidently many material devices and formal expressions of an alien society can be adopted without significant changes in the native culture.

The question, however, may be raised whether or not the complete adoption of occidental science and organization of industry would not produce far-reaching changes in social organization. The trend of economic, social, and cultural changes in Japan will throw light on this question. Even if revolutionary social changes actually occur, the point may well be made that they will be the outcome of the new economic system, and therefore not effects of acculturation.

(4) The rapidity and completeness of assimilation depends directly upon the intimacy of social contact. By a curious paradox, slavery, and particularly household slavery, has probably been, aside from intermarriage, the most efficient device for promoting assimilation.

Adoption and initiation among primitive peoples provided a ceremonial method for inducting aliens and strangers into the group, the significance of which can only be understood after a more adequate study of ceremonial in general.

c) *Americanization as a problem of assimilation.*—Any consideration of policies, programs, and methods of Americanization gain perspective when related to the sociology of assimilation. The "Study of Methods of Americanization," of the Carnegie Corporation, defines Americanization as "the participation of the immigrant in the life of the community in which he lives." From this standpoint participation is both the medium and the goal of assimilation. Participation of the immigrant in American life in any area of life prepares him for participation in every other. What the immigrant and the alien need most is an opportunity for participation. Of first importance, of course, is the language. In addition he needs to know how to use our institutions for his own benefit and protection. But participation, to be real, must be spontaneous and intelligent, and that means, in the long run, that the immigrant's life in America must be related to the life he already knows. Not by the suppression of old memories, but by their incorporation in his new life is assimilation achieved. The failure of conscious, coercive policies of denationalization in Europe and the great success of the early, passive phase of Americanization in this country afford in this connection an impressive contrast. It follows that assimilation cannot be promoted directly, but only indirectly, that is, by supplying the conditions that make for participation.

There is no process but life itself that can effectually wipe out the immigrant's memory of his past. The inclusion of the immigrant in our common life may perhaps be best reached, therefore, in cooperation that looks not so much to the past as to the future. The second generation of the immigrant may share fully in our memories, but practically all that we can ask of the foreign-born is participation in our ideals, our wishes, and our common enterprises.

CHAPTER X

SOCIAL CONTROL

I. INTRODUCTION

1. Social Control Defined

Social control has been studied, but, in the wide extension that sociology has given to the term, it has not been defined. All social problems turn out finally to be problems of social control. In the introductory chapter to this volume social problems were divided into three classes: Problems (a) of administration, (b) of policy and polity, (c) of social forces and human nature.[1] Social control may be studied in each one of these categories. It is with social forces and human nature that sociology is mainly concerned. Therefore it is from this point of view that social control will be considered in this chapter.

In the four preceding chapters the process of interaction, in its four typical forms, competition, conflict, accommodation, and assimilation, has been analyzed and described. The community and the natural order within the limits of the community, it appeared, are an effect of competition. Social control and the mutual subordination of individual members to the community have their origin in conflict, assume definite organized forms in the process of accommodation, and are consolidated and fixed in assimilation.

Through the medium of these processes, a community assumes the form of a society. Incidentally, however, certain definite and quite spontaneous forms of social control are developed. These forms are familiar under various titles: tradition, custom, folkways, mores, ceremonial, myth, religious and political beliefs, dogmas and creeds, and finally public opinion and law. In this chapter it is proposed to define a little more accurately certain of these typical mechanisms through which social groups are enabled to act. In the chapter on "Collective Behavior" which follows, materials will be presented to exhibit the group in action.

[1] Chap. i, pp. 46-47.

It is in action that the mechanisms of control are created, and the materials under the title "Collective Behavior" are intended to illustrate the stages, (*a*) social unrest, (*b*) mass movements, (*c*) institutions in which society is formed and reformed. Finally, in the chapter on "Progress," the relation of social change to social control will be discussed and the rôle of science and collective representations in the direction of social changes indicated.

The most obvious fact about social control is the machinery by which laws are made and enforced, that is, the legislature, the courts, and the police. When we think of social control, therefore, these are the images in which we see it embodied and these are the terms in which we seek to define it.

It is not quite so obvious that legislation and the police must, in the long run, have the support of public opinion. Hume's statement that governments, even the most despotic, have nothing but opinion to support them, cannot be accepted without some definition of terms, but it is essentially correct. Hume included under opinion what we would distinguish from it, namely, the mores. He might have added, using opinion in this broad sense, that the governed, no matter how numerous, are helpless unless they too are united by "opinion."

A king or a political "boss," having an army or a political "machine" at his command, can do much. It is possible, also, to confuse or mislead public opinion, but neither the king nor the boss will, if he be wise, challenge the mores and the common sense of the community.

Public opinion and the mores, however, representing as they do the responses of the community to changing situations, are themselves subject to change and variation. They are based, however, upon what we have called fundamental human nature, that is, certain traits which in some form or other are reproduced in every form of society.

During the past seventy years the various tribes, races, and nationalities of mankind have been examined in detail by the students of ethnology, and a comparison of the results shows that the fundamental patterns of life and behavior are everywhere the same, whether among the ancient Greeks, the modern Italians, the Asiatic Mongols, the Australian blacks, or the African Hottentots. All have a form of family life, moral and legal regulations, a religious system, a form of government, artistic practices, and so forth.   An examination of the moral code of any given group, say the African Kaffirs, will disclose many identities with that of any other given group, say the Hebrews.   All groups have such "commandments" as "Honor thy father and mother," "Thou shalt not kill," "Thou shalt not steal."   Formerly it was assumed that this similarity was the result of borrowing between groups.   When Bastian recorded a Hawaiian myth resembling the one of Orpheus and Eurydice, there was speculation as to how this story had been carried so far from Greece.   But it is now recognized that similarities of culture are due, in the main, not to imitation, but to parallel development.   The nature of man is everywhere essentially the same and tends to express itself everywhere in similar sentiments and institutions.[1]

There are factors in social control more fundamental than the mores.   Herbert Spencer, in his chapter on "Ceremonial Government," has defined social control from this more fundamental point of view.   In that chapter he refers to "the modified forms of action caused in men by the presence of their fellows" as a form of control "out of which other more definite controls are evolved."   The spontaneous responses of one individual to the presence of another which are finally fixed, conventionalized, and transmitted as social ritual constitute that "primitive undifferentiated kind of government from which political and religious government are differentiated, and in which they continue immersed."

In putting this emphasis upon ceremonial and upon those forms of behavior which spring directly and spontaneously out of the innate and instinctive responses of the individual to a social situation, Spencer is basing government on the springs of action which are fundamental, so far, at any rate, as sociology is concerned.

2.   Classification of the Materials

The selections on social control have been classified under three heads: (a) elementary forms of social control, (b) public opinion, and (c) institutions.   This order of the readings indicates the development of control from its spontaneous forms in the crowd, in ceremony, prestige, and taboo; its more explicit expression in gossip, rumor, news, and public opinion; to its more formal organization in law,

[1] Robert E. Park and Herbert A. Miller, *Old World Traits Transplanted*, pp. 1-2.   (New York, 1921.)

dogma, and in religious and political institutions. Ceremonial, public opinion, and law are characteristic forms in which social life finds expression as well as a means by which the actions of the individual are co-ordinated and collective impulses are organized so that they issue in behavior, that is, either (a) primarily expressive—play, for example—or (b) positive action.

A very much larger part of all human behavior than we ordinarily imagine is merely expressive. Art, play, religious exercises, and political activity are either wholly or almost wholly forms of expression, and have, therefore, that symbolic and ceremonial character which belongs especially to ritual and to art, but is characteristic of every activity carried on for its own sake. Only work, action which has some ulterior motive or is performed from a conscious sense of duty, falls wholly and without reservation into the second class.

a) Elementary forms of social control.—Control in the crowd, where rapport is once established and every individual is immediately responsive to every other, is the most elementary form of control.

Something like this same direct and spontaneous response of the individual in the crowd to the crowd's dominant mood or impulse may be seen in the herd and the flock, the "animal crowd."

Under the influence of the vague sense of alarm, or merely as an effect of heat and thirst, cattle become restless and begin slowly moving about in circles, "milling." This milling is a sort of collective gesture, an expression of discomfort or of fear. But the very expression of the unrest tends to intensify its expression and so increases the tension in the herd. This continues up to the point where some sudden sound, the firing of a pistol or a flash of lightning, plunges the herd into a wild stampede.

Milling in the herd is a visible image of what goes on in subtler and less obvious ways in human societies. Alarms or discomforts frequently provoke social unrest. The very expression of this unrest tends to magnify it. The situation is a vicious circle. Every attempt to deal with it merely serves to aggravate it. Such a vicious circle we witnessed in our history from 1830 to 1861, when every attempt to deal with slavery served only to bring the inevitable conflict between the states nearer. Finally there transpired what had for twenty years been visibly preparing and the war broke.

Tolstoi in his great historical romance, *War and Peace*, describes, in a manner which no historian has equaled, the events that led up to the Franco-Russian War of 1812, and particularly the manner in which Napoleon, in spite of his efforts to avoid it, was driven by social forces over which he had no control to declare war on Russia, and so bring about his own downfall.

The condition under which France was forced by Bismarck to declare war on Prussia in 1870, and the circumstances under which Austria declared war on Serbia in 1914 and so brought on the world-war, exhibit the same fatal circle. In both cases, given the situation, the preparations that had been made, the resolutions formed and the agreements entered into, it seems clear that after a certain point had been reached every move was forced.

This is the most fundamental and elementary form of control. It is the control exercised by the mere play of elemental forces. These forces may, to a certain extent, be manipulated, as is true of other natural forces; but within certain limits, human nature being what it is, the issue is fatally determined, just as, given the circumstances and the nature of cattle, a stampede is inevitable. Historical crises are invariably created by processes which, looked at abstractly, are very much like milling in a herd. The vicious circle is the so-called "psychological factor" in financial depressions and panics and is, indeed, a factor in all collective action.

The effect of this circular form of interaction is to increase the tensions in the group and, by creating a state of expectancy, to mobilize its members for collective action. It is like attention in the individual: it is the way in which the group prepares to act.

Back of every other form of control—ceremonial, public opinion, or law—there is always this interaction of the elementary social forces. What we ordinarily mean by social control, however, is the arbitrary intervention of some individual—official, functionary, or leader—in the social process. A policeman arrests a criminal, an attorney sways the jury with his eloquence, the judge passes sentence; these are the familiar formal acts in which social control manifests itself. What makes the control exercised in this way social, in the strict sense of that term, is the fact that these acts are supported by custom, law, and public opinion.

The distinction between control in the crowd and in other forms of society is that the crowd has no tradition. It has no point of reference in its own past to which its members can refer for guidance. It has therefore neither symbols, ceremonies, rites, nor ritual; it imposes no obligations and creates no loyalties.

Ceremonial is one method of reviving in the group a lively sense of the past. It is a method of reinstating the excitements and the sentiments which inspired an earlier collective action. The savage war dance is a dramatic representation of battle and as such serves to rouse and reawaken the warlike spirit. This is one way in which ceremonial becomes a means of control. By reviving the memories of an earlier war, it mobilizes the warriors for a new one.

Ernst Grosse, in *The Beginnings of Art*, has stated succinctly what has impressed all first-hand observers, namely, the important rôle which the dance plays in the lives of primitive peoples.

The dances of the hunting peoples are, as a rule, mass dances. Generally the men of the tribe, not rarely the members of several tribes, join in the exercises, and the whole assemblage then moves according to one law in one time. All who have described the dances have referred again and again to this "wonderful" unison of the movements. In the heat of the dance the several participants are fused together as into a single being, which is stirred and moved as by one feeling. During the dance they are in a condition of complete social unification, and the dancing group feels and acts like a single organism. *The social significance of the primitive dance lies precisely in this effect of social unification.* It brings and accustoms a number of men who, in their loose and precarious conditions of life, are driven irregularly hither and thither by different individual needs and desires, to act under one impulse with one feeling for one object. It introduces order and connection, at least occasionally, into the rambling, fluctuating life of the hunting tribes. It is, besides wars, perhaps the only factor that makes their solidarity vitally perceptible to the adherents of a primitive tribe, and it is at the same time one of the best preparations for war, for the gymnastic dances correspond in more than one respect to our military exercises. It would be hard to overestimate the importance of the primitive dance in the culture development of mankind. All higher civilization is conditioned upon the uniformly ordered co-operation of individual social elements, and primitive men are trained to this co-operation by the dance.[1]

[1] Ernst Grosse, *The Beginnings of Art*, pp. 228–29. (New York, 1897.)

The dance, which is so characteristic and so universal a feature of the life of primitive man—at once a mode of collective expression and of collective representation—is but a conventionalized form of the circular reaction, which in its most primitive form is represented by the milling of the herd.

b) Public opinion.—We ordinarily think of public opinion as a sort of social weather. At certain times, and under certain circumstances, we observe strong, steady currents of opinion, moving apparently in a definite direction and toward a definite goal. At other times, however, we note flurries and eddies and countercurrents in this movement. Every now and then there are storms, shifts, or dead calms. These sudden shifts in public opinion, when expressed in terms of votes, are referred to by the politicians as "landslides."

In all these movements, cross-currents and changes in direction which a closer observation of public opinion reveals, it is always possible to discern, but on a much grander scale, to be sure, that same type of circular reaction which we have found elsewhere, whenever the group was preparing to act. Always in the public, as in the crowd, there will be a circle, sometimes wider, sometimes narrower, within which individuals are mutually responsive to motives and interests of one another, so that out of this interplay of social forces there may emerge at any time a common motive and a common purpose that will dominate the whole.

Within the circle of the mutual influence described, there will be no such complete rapport and no such complete domination of the individual by the group as exists in a herd or a crowd in a state of excitement, but there will be sufficient community of interest to insure a common understanding. A public is, in fact, organized on the basis of a universe of discourse, and within the limits of this universe of discourse, language, statements of fact, news will have, for all practical purposes, the same meanings. It is this circle of mutual influence within which there is a universe of discourse that defines the limits of the public.

A public, like a crowd, is not to be conceived as a formal organization like a parliament or even a public meeting. It is always the widest area over which there is conscious participation and consensus in the formation of public opinion. The public has not only a circumference, but it has a center. Within the area within which there is participation and consensus there is always a focus of attention around which the opinions of the individuals which compose the public seem to revolve. This focus of attention, under ordinary circumstances, is constantly shifting. The shifts of attention of the public constitute what is meant by the changes in public opinion. When these changes take a definite direction and have or seem to have a definite goal, we call the phenomenon a social movement. If it were possible to plot this movement in the form of maps and graphs, it would be possible to show movement in two dimensions. There would be, for example, a movement in space. The focus of public opinion, the point namely at which there is the greatest "intensity" of opinion, tends to move from one part of the country to another.[1] In America these movements, for reasons that could perhaps be explained historically, are likely to be along the meridians, east and west, rather than north and south. In the course of this geographical movement of public opinion, however, we are likely to observe changes in intensity and changes in direction (devagation).

Changes in intensity seem to be in direct proportion to the area over which opinion on a given issue may be said to exist. In minorities opinion is uniformly more intense than it is in majorities and this is what gives minorities so much greater influence in proportion to their numbers than majorities. While changes in intensity have a definite relation to the area over which public opinion on an issue may be said to exist, the devagations of public opinion, as distinguished from the trend, will probably turn out to have a direct relation to the character of the parties that participate. Area as applied to public opinion will have to be measured eventually in terms of social rather than geographical distance, that is to say, in terms of isolation and contact. The factor of numbers is also involved in any such calculation. Geographical area, communication, and the number of persons involved are in general the factors that would determine the concept "area" as it is used here. If party spirit is strong the general direction or trend of public opinion will probably be intersected by shifts and sudden transient changes in direction, and these shifts will be in proportion to the intensity of the party spirit. Charles E. Merriam's recent study of political parties indicates that the minority parties formulate most of the legislation in the United States.[2] This is because there is not very great

[1] See A. L. Lowell, *Public Opinion and Popular Government*, pp. 12–13. (New York, 1913.)

[2] *The American Party System*, chap. viii. (New York, 1922.) [In press.]

divergence in the policies of the two great parties and party struggles are fought out on irrelevant issues. So far as this is true it insures against any sudden change in policy. New legislation is adopted in response to the trend of public opinion, rather than in response to the devagations and sudden shifts brought about by the development of a radical party spirit.

All these phenomena may be observed, for example, in the Prohibition Movement. Dicey's study of *Law and Public Opinion in England* showed that while the direction of opinion in regard to specific issues had been very irregular, on the whole the movement had been in one general direction. The trend of public opinion is the name we give to this general movement. In defining the trend, shifts, cross-currents, and flurries are not considered. When we speak of the tendency or direction of public opinion we usually mean the trend over a definite period of time.

When the focus of public attention ceases to move and shift, when it is fixed, the circle which defines the limits of the public is narrowed. As the circle narrows, opinion itself becomes more intense and concentrated. This is the phenomenon of crisis. It is at this point that the herd stampedes.

The effect of crisis is invariably to increase the dangers of precipitate action. The most trivial incident, in such periods of tension, may plunge a community into irretrievable disaster. It is under conditions of crisis that dictatorships are at once possible and necessary, not merely to enable the community to act energetically, but in order to protect the community from the mere play of external forces. The manner in which Bismarck, by a slight modification of the famous telegram of Ems, provoked a crisis in France and compelled Napoleon III, against his judgment and that of his advisers, to declare war on Germany, is an illustration of this danger.[1]

[1] "On the afternoon of July 13, Bismarck, Roon, and Moltke were seated together in the Chancellor's Room at Berlin. They were depressed and moody; for Prince Leopold's renunciation had been trumpeted in Paris as a humiliation for Prussia. They were afraid, too, that King William's conciliatory temper might lead him to make further concessions, and that the careful preparations of Prussia for the inevitable war with France might be wasted, and a unique opportunity lost. A telegram arrived. It was from the king at Ems, and described his interview that morning with the French ambassador. The king had met Benedetti's request for the guarantee required by a firm but courteous refusal; and when the ambassador had sought to renew the interview, he had sent a polite

It is this narrowing of the area over which a definite public opinion may be said to exist that at once creates the possibility and defines the limits of arbitrary control, so far as it is created or determined by the existence of public opinion.

Thus far the public has been described almost wholly in terms that could be applied to a crowd. The public has been frequently described as if it were simply a great crowd, a crowd scattered as widely as news will circulate and still be news.[1] But there is this difference. In the heat and excitement of the crowd, as in the choral dances of primitive people, there is for the moment what may be described as complete fusion of the social forces. Rapport has, for the time being, made the crowd, in a peculiarly intimate way, a social unit.

No such unity exists in the public. The sentiment and tendencies which we call public opinion are never unqualified expressions of emotion. The difference is that public opinion is determined by conflict and discussion, and made up of the opinions of individuals not wholly at one. In any conflict situation, where party spirit is aroused, the spectators, who constitute the public, are bound to take sides. The

---

message through his aide-de-camp informing him that the subject must be considered closed. In conclusion, Bismarck was authorized to publish the message if he saw fit. The Chancellor at once saw his opportunity. In the royal despatch, though the main incidents were clear enough, there was still a note of doubt, of hesitancy, which suggested a possibility of further negotiation. The excision of a few lines would alter, not indeed the general sense, but certainly the whole tone of the message. Bismarck, turning to Moltke, asked him if he were ready for a sudden risk of war; and on his answering in the affirmative, took a blue pencil and drew it quickly through several parts of the telegram. Without the alteration or addition of a single word, the message, instead of appearing a mere 'fragment of a negotiation still pending,' was thus made to appear decisive. In the actual temper of the French people there was no doubt that it would not only appear decisive, but insulting, and that its publication would mean war.

"On July 14 the publication of the 'Ems telegram' became known in Paris, with the result that Bismarck had expected. The majority of the Cabinet, hitherto in favour of peace, were swept away by the popular tide; and Napoleon himself reluctantly yielded to the importunity of his ministers and of the Empress, who saw in a successful war the best, if not the only, chance of preserving the throne for her son. On the evening of the same day, July 14, the declaration of war was signed."—W. Alison Phillips, *Modern Europe, 1815–1899*, pp. 465–66. (London, 1903.)

[1] G. Tarde, *L'opinion et la foule*. (Paris, 1901.)

impulse to take sides is, in fact, in direct proportion to the excitement and party spirit displayed.   The result is, however, that both sides of an issue get considered.   Certain contentions are rejected because they will not stand criticism.   Public opinion formed in this way has the character of a judgment, rather than a mere unmediated expression of emotion, as in the crowd.   The public is never ecstatic.   It is always more or less rational.   It is this fact of conflict, in the form of discussion, that introduces into the control exercised by public opinion the elements of rationality and of fact.

In the final judgment of the public upon a conflict or an issue, we expect, to be sure, some sort of unanimity of judgment, but in the general consensus there will be some individual differences of opinion still unmediated, or only partially so, and final agreement of the public will be more or less qualified by all the different opinions that co-operated to form its judgment.

In the materials which follow a distinction is made between public opinion and the mores, and this distinction is important. Custom and the folkways, like habit in the individual, may be regarded as a mere residuum of past practices.   When folkways assume the character of mores, they are no longer merely matters of fact and common sense, they are judgments upon matters which were probably once live issues and as such they may be regarded as the products of public opinion.

Ritual, religious or social, is probably the crystallization of forms of behavior which, like the choral dance, are the direct expression of the emotions and the instincts.   The mores, on the other hand, in so far as they contain a rational element, are the accumulation, the residuum, not only of past practices, but of judgments such as find expression in public opinion.   The mores, as thus conceived, are the judgments of public opinion in regard to issues that have been settled and forgotten.

L. T. Hobhouse, in his volume, *Morals in Evolution*, has described, in a convincing way, the process by which, as he conceives it, custom is modified and grows under the influence of the personal judgments of individuals and of the public.   Public opinion, as he defines it, is simply the combined and sublimated judgments of individuals.

Most of these judgments are, to be sure, merely the repetition of old formulas.   But occasionally, when the subject of discussion touches us more deeply, when it touches upon some matter in which we have had a deeper and more intimate experience, the ordinary patter that passes as public opinion is dissipated and we originate a moral judgment that not only differs from, but is in conflict with, the prevailing opinion. In that case "we become, as it were, centers from which judgments of one kind or another radiate and from which they pass forth to fill the atmosphere of opinion and take their place among the influences that mould the judgments of men."

The manner in which public opinion issues from the interaction of individuals, and moral judgments are formed that eventually become the basis of law, may be gathered from the way in which the process goes on in the daily life about us.

No sooner has the judgment escaped us—a winged word from our own lips—than it impinges on the judgment similarly flying forth to do its work from our next-door neighbor, and if the subject is an exciting one the air is soon full of the winged forces clashing, deflecting or reinforcing one another as the case may be, and generally settling down toward some preponderating opinion which is society's judgment on the case. But in the course of the conflict many of the original judgments are modified. Discussion, further consideration, above all, the mere influence of our neighbour's opinion reacts on each of us, with a stress that is proportioned to various mental and moral characteristics of our own, our clearness of vision, our firmness, or, perhaps, obstinacy of character, our self-confidence, and so forth. Thus, the controversy will tend to leave its mark, small or great, on those who took part in it. It will tend to modify their modes of judgment, confirming one, perhaps, in his former ways, shaping the confidence of another, opening the eyes of a third. Similarly, it will tend to set a precedent for future judgments. It will affect what men say and think on the next question that turns up. It adds its weight, of one grain it may be, to some force that is turning the scale of opinion and preparing society for some new departure. In any case, we have here in miniature at work every day before our eyes the essential process by which moral judgments arise and grow.[1]

c) *Institutions.*—An institution, according to Sumner, consists of a concept and a structure. The concept defines the purpose, interest, or function of the institution. The structure embodies the idea of the institution and furnishes the instrumentalities through which the

[1] L. T. Hobhouse, *Morals in Evolution, A Study in Comparative Ethics,* pp. 13-14. (New York, 1915.)

idea is put into action. The process by which purposes, whether they are individual or collective, are embodied in structures is a continuous one. But the structures thus formed are not physical, at least not entirely so. Structure, in the sense that Sumner uses the term, belongs, as he says, to a category of its own. "It is a category in which custom produces continuity, coherence, and consistency, so that the word 'structure' may properly be applied to the fabric of relations and prescribed positions with which functions are permanently connected." Just as every individual member of a community participates in the process by which custom and public opinion are made, so also he participates in the creation of the structure, that "cake of custom" which, when it embodies a definite social function, we call an institution.

Institutions may be created just as laws are enacted, but only when a social situation exists to which they correspond will they become operative and effective. Institutions, like laws, rest upon the mores and are supported by public opinion. Otherwise they remain mere paper projects or artefacts that perform no real function. History records the efforts of conquering peoples to impose upon the conquered their own laws and institutions. The efforts are instructive, but not encouraging. The most striking modern instance is the effort of King Leopold of Belgium to introduce civilization into the Congo Free State.[1]

Law, like public opinion, owes its rational and secular character to the fact that it arose out of an effort to compromise conflict and to interpret matters which were in dispute.

To seek vengeance for a wrong committed was a natural impulse, and the recognition of this fact in custom established it not merely as a right but as a duty. War, the modern form of trial by battle, the vendetta, and the duel are examples that have survived down to modern times of this natural and primitive method of settling disputes.

In all these forms of conflict custom and the mores have tended to limit the issues and define the conditions under which disputes might be settled by force. At the same time public opinion, in passing judgment on the issues, exercised a positive influence on the outcome of the struggle.

[1] E. D. Morel, *King Leopold's Rule in Africa*. (London, 1904.)

Gradually, as men realized the losses which conflicts incurred, the community has intervened to prevent them. At a time when the blood feud was still sanctioned by the mores, cities of refuge and sanctuaries were established to which one who had incurred a blood feud might flee until his case could be investigated. If it then appeared that the wrong committed had been unintentional or if there were other mitigating circumstances, he might find in the sanctuary protection. Otherwise, if a crime had been committed in cold blood, "lying in wait," or "in enmity," as the ancient Jewish law books called it, he might be put to death by the avenger of blood, "when he meeteth him."[1]

Thus, gradually, the principle became established that the community might intervene, not merely to insure that vengeance was executed in due form, but to determine the facts, and thus courts which determined by legal process the guilt or innocence of the accused were established.

It does not appear that courts of justice were ever set up within the kinship group for the trial of offenses, although efforts were made there first of all, by the elders and the headmen, to compromise quarrels and compose differences.

Courts first came into existence, the evidence indicates, when society was organized over wider areas and after some authority had been established outside of the local community. As society was organized over a wider territory, control was extended to ever wider areas of human life until we have at present a program for international courts with power to intervene between nations to prevent wars.[2]

Society, like the individual man, moves and acts under the influence of a multitude of minor impulses and tendencies which mutually interact to produce a more general tendency which then dominates all the individuals of the group. This explains the fact that a group, even a mere casual collection of individuals like a crowd, is enabled to act more or less as a unit. The crowd acts under the influence of such a dominant tendency, unreflectively, without

[1] L. T. Hobhouse, *op. cit.*, p. 85.

[2] The whole process of evolution by which a moral order has been established over ever wider areas of social life has been sketched in a masterly manner by Hobhouse in his chapter, "Law and Justice," *op. cit.*, pp. 72-131.

definite reference to a past or a future. The crowd ·has no past and no future. The public introduces into this vortex of impulses the factor of reflection. The public presupposes the existence of a common impulse such as manifests itself in the crowd, but it presupposes, also, the existence of individuals and groups of individuals representing divergent tendencies. These individuals interact upon one another *critically*. The public is, what the crowd is not, a discussion group. The very existence of discussion presupposes objective standards of truth and of fact. The action of the public is based on a universe of discourse in which things, although they may and do have for every individual somewhat different value, are describable at any rate in terms that mean the same to all individuals. The public, in other words, moves in an objective and intelligible world.

Law is based on custom. Custom is group habit. As the group acts it creates custom. There is implicit in custom a conception and a rule of action, which is regarded as right and proper in the circumstances. Law makes this rule of action explicit. Law grows up, however, out of a distinction between this rule of action and the facts. Custom is bound up with the facts under which the custom grew up. Law is the result of an effort to frame the rule of action implicit in custom in such general terms that it can be made to apply to new situations, involving new sets of facts. This distinction between the law and the facts did not exist in primitive society. The evolution of law and jurisprudence has been in the direction of an increasingly clearer recognition of this distinction between law and the facts. This has meant in practice an increasing recognition by the courts of the facts, and a disposition to act in accordance with them. The present disposition of courts, as, for example, the juvenile courts, to call to their assistance experts to examine the mental condition of children who are brought before them and to secure the assistance of juvenile-court officers to advise and assist them in the enforcement of the law, is an illustration of an increasing disposition to take account of the facts.

The increasing interest in the natural history of the law and of legal institutions, and the increasing disposition to interpret it in sociological terms, from the point of view of its function, is another evidence of the same tendency.

CHAPTER XI

COLLECTIVE BEHAVIOR

I. INTRODUCTION

1. Collective Behavior Defined

A collection of individuals is not always, and by the mere fact of its collectivity, a society. On the other hand, when people come together anywhere, in the most casual way, on the street corner or at a railway station, no matter how great the social distances between them, the mere fact that they are aware of one another's presence sets up a lively exchange of influences, and the behavior that ensues is both social and collective. It is social, at the very least, in the sense that the train of thought and action in each individual is influenced more or less by the action of every other. It is collective in so far as each individual acts under the influence of a mood or a state of mind in which each shares, and in accordance with conventions which all quite unconsciously accept, and which the presence of each enforces upon the others.

The amount of individual eccentricity or deviation from normal and accepted modes of behavior which a community will endure without comment and without protest will vary naturally enough with the character of the community. A cosmopolitan community like New York City can and does endure a great deal in the way of individual eccentricity that a smaller city like Boston would not tolerate. In any case, and this is the point of these observations, even in the most casual relations of life, people do not behave in the presence of others as if they were living alone like Robinson Crusoe, each on his individual island. The very fact of their consciousness of each other tends to maintain and enforce a great body of convention and usage which otherwise falls into abeyance and is forgotten. Collective behavior, then, is the behavior of individuals under the influence of an impulse that is common and collective, an impulse, in other words, that is the result of social interaction.

2. Social Unrest and Collective Behavior

The most elementary form of collective behavior seems to be what is ordinarily referred to as "social unrest." Unrest in the individual becomes social when it is, or seems to be, transmitted from one individual to another, but more particularly when it produces something akin to the milling process in the herd, so that the manifestations of discontent in A communicated to B, and from B reflected back to A, produce the circular reaction described in the preceding chapter.

The significance of social unrest is that it represents at once a breaking up of the established routine and a preparation for new collective action. Social unrest is not of course a new phenomenon; it is possibly true, however, that it is peculiarly characteristic, as has been said, of modern life. The contrast between the conditions of modern life and of primitive society suggests why this may be true.

The conception which we ought to form of primitive society, says Sumner, is that of small groups scattered over a territory. The size of the group will be determined by the conditions of the struggle for existence and the internal organization of each group will correspond (1) to the size of the group, and (2) to the nature and intensity of the struggle with its neighbors.

Thus war and peace have reacted on each other and developed each other, one within the group, the other in the intergroup relation. The closer the neighbors, and the stronger they are, the intenser is the warfare, and then the intenser is the internal organization and discipline of each. Sentiments are produced to correspond. Loyalty to the group, sacrifice for it, hatred and contempt for outsiders, brotherhood within, warlikeness without—all grow together, common products of the same situation. These relations and sentiments constitute a social philosophy. It is sanctified by connection with religion. Men of an others-group are outsiders with whose ancestors the ancestors of the we-group waged war. The ghosts of the latter will see with pleasure their descendants keep up the fight, and will help them. Virtue consists in killing, plundering, and enslaving outsiders.[1]

The isolation, territorial and cultural, under which alone it is possible to maintain an organization which corresponds to Sumner's description, has disappeared within comparatively recent times from

[1] W. G. Sumner, *Folkways*. A study of the sociological importance of usages, manners, customs, mores, and morals, pp. 12-13. (Boston, 1906.)

all the more inhabitable portions of the earth. In place of it there has come, and with increasing rapidity is coming, into existence a society which includes within its limits the total population of the earth and is so intimately bound together that the speculation of a grain merchant in Chicago may increase the price of bread in Bombay, while the act of an assassin in a provincial town in the Balkans has been sufficient to plunge the world into a war which changed the political map of three continents and cost the lives, in Europe alone, of 8,500,000 combatants.

The first effect of modern conditions of life has been to increase and vastly complicate the economic interdependence of strange and distant peoples, i.e., to destroy distances and make the world, as far as national relations are concerned, small and tight.

The second effect has been to break down family, local, and national ties, and emancipate the individual man.

When the family ceases, as it does in the city, to be an economic unit, when parents and children have vocations that not only intercept the traditional relations of family life, but make them well nigh impossible, the family ceases to function as an organ of social control. When the different nationalities, with their different national cultures, have so far interpenetrated one another that each has permanent colonies within the territorial limits of the other, it is inevitable that the old solidarities, the common loyalties and the common hatreds that formerly bound men together in primitive kinship and local groups should be undermined.

A survey of the world today shows that vast changes are everywhere in progress. Not only in Europe but in Asia and in Africa new cultural contacts have undermined and broken down the old cultures. The effect has been to loosen all the social bonds and reduce society to its individual atoms. The energies thus freed have produced a world-wide ferment. Individuals released from old associations enter all the more readily into new ones. Out of this confusion new and strange political and religious movements arise, which represent the groping of men for a new social order.

3. The Crowd and the Public

Gustave Le Bon, who was the first writer to call attention to the significance of the crowd as a social phenomenon,[1] said that

[1] Scipio Sighele, in a note to the French edition of his *Psychology of Sects*, claims that his volume, *La Folla delinquente*, of which the second edition was

mass movements mark the end of an old régime and the beginning of a new.

"When the structure of a civilization is rotten, it is always the masses that bring about its downfall."[1] On the other hand, "all founders of religious or political creeds have established them solely because they were successful in inspiring crowds with those fanatical sentiments which have as result that men find their happiness in worship and obedience and are ready to lay down their lives for their idol."[2]

The crowd was, for Le Bon, not merely any group brought together by the accident of some chance excitement, but it was above all the emancipated masses whose bonds of loyalty to the old order had been broken by "the destruction of those religious, political, and social beliefs in which all the elements of our civilization are rooted." The crowd, in other words, typified for Le Bon the existing social order. Ours is an age of crowds, he said, an age in which men, massed and herded together in great cities without real convictions or fundamental faiths, are likely to be stampeded in any direction for any chance purpose under the influence of any passing excitement.

Le Bon did not attempt to distinguish between the crowd and the public. This distinction was first made by Tarde in a paper entitled "Le Public et la foule," published first in *La Revue de Paris* in 1898, and included with several others on the same general theme under the title *L'Opinion et la foule* which appeared in 1901. The public, according to Tarde, was a product of the printing press. The limits of the crowd are determined by the length to which a voice will carry or the distance that the eye can survey. But the public presupposes a higher stage of social development in which suggestions are transmitted in the form of ideas and there is "contagion without contact."[3]

---

published at Turin in 1895, and his article "Physiologie du succès," in the *Revue des Revues*, October 1, 1894, were the first attempts to describe the crowd from the point of view of collective psychology. Le Bon published two articles, "Psychologie des foules" in the *Revue scientifique*, April 6 and 20, 1895. These were later gathered together in his volume *Psychologie des foules*, Paris, 1895. See Sighele *Psychologie des sectes*, pp. 25, 39.

[1] Gustave Le Bon, *The Crowd*. A study of the popular mind, p. 19. (New York, 1900.)

[2] *Ibid.*, p. 83.   [3] *L'Opinion et la foule*, pp. 6-7. (Paris, 1901.)

The fundamental distinction between the crowd and the public, however, is not to be measured by numbers nor by means of communication, but by the form and effects of the interactions. In the public, interaction takes the form of discussion. Individuals tend to act upon one another critically; issues are raised and parties form. Opinions clash and thus modify and moderate one another.

The crowd does not discuss and hence it does not reflect. It simply "mills." Out of this milling process a collective impulse is formed which dominates all members of the crowd. Crowds, when they act, do so impulsively. The crowd, says Le Bon, "is the slave of its impulses."

"The varying impulses which crowds obey may be, according to their exciting causes, generous or cruel, heroic or cowardly, but they will always be so imperious that the interest of the individual, even the interest of self-preservation, will not dominate them."[1]

When the crowd acts it becomes a mob. What happens when two mobs meet? We have in the literature no definite record. The nearest approach to it are the occasional accounts we find in the stories of travelers of the contacts and conflicts of armies of primitive peoples. These undisciplined hordes are, as compared with the armies of civilized peoples, little more than armed mobs. Captain S. L. Hinde in his story of the Belgian conquest of the Congo describes several such battles. From the descriptions of battles carried on almost wholly between savage and undisciplined troops it is evident that the morale of an army of savages is a precarious thing. A very large part of the warfare consists in alarms and excursions interspersed with wordy duels to keep up the courage on one side and cause a corresponding depression on the other.[2]

[1] *The Crowd*, p. 41.

[2] Sidney L. Hinde, *The Fall of the Congo Arabs*, p. 147. (London, 1897.) Describing a characteristic incident in one of the strange confused battles Hinde says: "Wordy war, which also raged, had even more effect than our rifles. Mahomedi and Sefu led the Arabs, who were jeering and taunting Lutete's people, saying that they were in a bad case, and had better desert the white man, who was ignorant of the fact that Mohara with all the forces of Nyange was camped in his rear. Lutete's people replied: 'Oh, we know all about Mohara; we ate him the day before yesterday.'" This news became all the more depressing when it turned out to be true. See also Hirn, *The Origins of Art*, p. 269, for an explanation of the rôle of threats and boastings in savage warfare.

Gangs are conflict groups. Their organization is usually quite informal and is determined by the nature and imminence of the conflicts with other groups. When one crowd encounters another it either goes to pieces or it changes its character and becomes a conflict group. When negotiations and palavers take place as they eventually do between conflict groups, these two groups, together with the neutrals who have participated vicariously in the conflict, constitute a public. It is possible that the two opposing savage hordes which seek, by threats and boastings and beatings of drums, to play upon each other's fears and so destroy each other's morale, may be said to constitute a very primitive type of public.

Discussion, as might be expected, takes curious and interesting forms among primitive peoples. In a volume, *Iz Derevni: 12 Pisem* ("From the Country: 12 Letters"), A. N. Engelgardt describes the way in which the Slavic peasants reach their decisions in the village council.

In the discussion of some questions by the *mir* [organization of neighbors] there are no speeches, no debates, no votes. They shout, they abuse one another—they seem on the point of coming to blows; apparently they riot in the most senseless manner. Some one preserves silence, and then suddenly puts in a word, one word, or an ejaculation, and by this word, this ejaculation, he turns the whole thing upside down. In the end, you look into it and find that an admirable decision has been formed and, what is most important, a unanimous decision. . . (In the division of land) the cries, the noise, the hubbub do not subside until everyone is satisfied and no doubter is left.[1]

4. Crowds and Sects

Reference has been made to the crowds that act, but crowds do not always act. Sometimes they merely dance or, at least, make expressive motions which relieve their feelings. "The purest and most typical expression of simple feeling," as Hirn remarks, "is that which consists of mere random movements."[2] When these motions assume, as they so easily do, the character of a fixed sequence in time, that is to say when they are rhythmical, they can be and inevitably are, as

[1] Robert E. Park and Herbert A. Miller, *Old World Traits Transplanted.* Document 23, pp. 32–33. (New York, 1921.)

[2] Yrjö Hirn, *The Origins of Art.* A psychological and sociological inquiry, p. 87. (London, 1900.)

by a sort of inner compulsion, imitated by the onlookers. "As soon as the expression is fixed in rhythmical form its contagious power is incalculably increased."[1]

This explains at once the function and social importance of the dance among primitive people. It is the form in which they prepare for battle and celebrate their victories. It gives the form at once to their religious ritual and to their art. Under the influence of the memories and the emotions which these dances stimulate the primitive group achieves a sense of corporate unity, which makes corporate action possible outside of the fixed and sacred routine of ordinary daily life.

If it is true, as has been suggested, that art and religion had their origin in the choral dance, it is also true that in modern times religious sects and social movements have had their origin in crowd excitements and spontaneous mass movements. The very names which have been commonly applied to them—Quakers, Shakers, Convulsionaires, Holy Rollers—suggest not merely the derision with which they were at one time regarded, but indicate likewise their origin in ecstatic or expressive crowds, the crowds that *do not act.*

All great mass movements tend to display, to a greater or less extent, the characteristics that Le Bon attributes to crowds. Speaking of the convictions of crowds, Le Bon says:

When these convictions are closely examined, whether at epochs marked by fervent religious faith, or by great political upheavals such as those of the last century, it is apparent that they always assume a peculiar form which I cannot better define than by giving it the name of a religious sentiment.[2]

Le Bon's definition of religion and religious sentiment will hardly find general acceptance but it indicates at any rate his conception of the extent to which individual personalities are involved in the excitements that accompany mass movements.

A person is not religious solely when he worships a divinity, but when he puts all the resources of his mind, the complete submission of his will, and the whole-souled ardour of fanaticism at the service of a cause or an individual who becomes the goal and guide of his thoughts and actions.[3]

[1] *Ibid.,* p. 89. [2] Le Bon, *op. cit.,* p. 82.
[3] *Ibid.,* p. 82.

Just as the gang may be regarded as the perpetuation and permanent form of "the crowd that acts," so the sect, religious or political, may be regarded as a perpetuation and permanent form of the orgiastic (ecstatic) or expressive crowd.

"The sect," says Sighele, "is a crowd *triée*, selected, and permanent; the crowd is a transient sect, which does not select its members. The sect is the *chronic* form of the crowd; the crowd is the *acute* form of the sect."[1]   It is Sighele's conception that the crowd is an elementary organism, from which the sect issues, like the chick from the egg, and that all other types of social groups "may, in this same manner, be deduced from this primitive social protoplasm." This is a simplification which the facts hardly justify.   It is true that, implicit in the practices and the doctrines of a religious sect, there is the kernel of a new independent culture.

5. Sects and Institutions

A sect is a religious organization that is at war with the existing mores.   It seeks to cultivate a state of mind and establish a code of morals different from that of the world about it and for this it claims divine authority.   In order to accomplish this end it invariably seeks to set itself off in contrast with the rest of the world.   The simplest and most effective way to achieve this is to adopt a peculiar form of dress and speech.   This, however, invariably makes its members objects of scorn and derision, and eventually of persecution.   It would probably do this even if there was no assumption of moral superiority to the rest of the world in this adoption of a peculiar manner and dress.

Persecution tends to dignify and sanctify all the external marks of the sect, and it becomes a cardinal principle of the sect to maintain them.   Any neglect of them is regarded as disloyalty and is punished as heresy.   Persecution may eventually, as was the case with the Puritans, the Quakers, the Mormons, compel the sect to seek refuge in some part of the world where it may practice its way of life in peace.

Once the sect has achieved territorial isolation and territorial solidarity, so that it is the dominant power within the region that it occupies, it is able to control the civil organization, establish schools

[1] Scipio Sighele, *Psychologie des sectes*, p. 46.   (Paris, 1898.)

and a press, and so put the impress of a peculiar culture upon all the civil and political institutions that it controls. In this case it tends to assume the form of a state, and become a nationality. Something approaching this was achieved by the Mormons in Utah. The most striking illustration of the evolution of a nationality from a sect is Ulster, which now has a position not quite that of a nation within the English empire.

This sketch suggests that the sect, like most other social institutions, originates under conditions that are typical for all institutions of the same species; then it develops in definite and predictable ways, in accordance with a form or entelechy that is predetermined by characteristic internal processes and mechanisms, and that has, in short, a nature and natural history which can be described and explained in sociological terms. Sects have their origin in social unrest to which they give a direction and expression in forms and practices that are largely determined by historical circumstances; movements which were at first inchoate impulses and aspirations gradually take form; policies are defined, doctrine and dogmas formulated; and eventually an administrative machinery and efficiencies are developed to carry into effect policies and purposes. The Salvation Army, of which we have a more adequate history than of most other religious movements, is an example.

A sect in its final form may be described, then, as a movement of social reform and regeneration that has become institutionalized. Eventually, when it has succeeded in accommodating itself to the 'other rival organizations, when it has become tolerant and is tolerated, it tends to assume the form of a denomination. Denominations tend and are perhaps destined to unite in the form of religious federations— a thing which is inconceivable of a sect.

What is true of the sect, we may assume, and must assume if social movements are to become subjects for sociological investigation, is true of other social institutions. Existing institutions represent social movements that survived the conflict of cultures and the struggle for existence.

Sects, and that is what characterizes and distinguishes them from secular institutions, at least, have had their origin in movements that aimed to reform the mores—movements that sought to renovate and renew the inner life of the community. They have wrought upon

society from within outwardly. Revolutionary and reform movements, on the contrary, have been directed against the outward fabric
and formal structure of society. Revolutionary movements in
particular have assumed that if the existing structure could be
destroyed it would then be possible to erect a new moral order upon
the ruins of the old social structures.

A cursory survey of the history of revolutions suggests that the
most radical and the most successful of them have been religious. Of
this type of revolution Christianity is the most conspicuous example.

6. Classification of the Materials

The materials in this chapter have been arranged under the
headings: (a) social contagion, (b) the crowd, and (c) types of mass
movements. The order of materials follows, in a general way, the
order of institutional evolution. Social unrest is first communicated, then takes form in crowd and mass movements, and finally
crystallizes in institutions. The history of almost any single social
movement—woman's suffrage, prohibition, protestantism—exhibits in
a general way, if not in detail, this progressive change in character.
There is at first a vague general discontent and distress. Then a
violent, confused, and disorderly, but enthusiastic and popular movement arises. Finally the movement takes form; develops leadership,
organization; formulates doctrines and dogmas. Eventually it is
accepted, established, legalized. The movement dies, but the
institution remains.

a) Social contagion.—The ease and the rapidity with which a
cultural trait originating in one cultural group finds its way to other
distant groups is familiar to students of folklore and ethnology. The
manner in which fashions are initiated in some metropolitan community, and thence make their way, with more or less rapidity, to the
provinces is an illustration of the same phenomenon in a different
context.

Fashion plays a much larger rôle in social life than most of us imagine.
Fashion dominates our manners and dress but it influences also our sentiments and our modes of thought. Everything in literature, art or philosophy that was characteristic of the middle of the nineteenth century, the
"mid-Victorian period," is now quite out of date and no one who is intelligent now-a-days practices the pruderies, defends the doctrines, nor shares

the enthusiasms of that period. Philosophy, also, changes with the fashion and Sumner says that even mathematics and science do the same. Lecky in his history of Rationalism in Europe describes in great detail how the belief in witches, so characteristic of the Middle Ages, gradually disappeared with the period of enlightenment and progress.[1] But the enlightenment of the eighteenth century was itself a fashion and is now quite out of date. In the meantime a new popular and scientific interest is growing up in obscure mental phenomena which no man with scientific training would have paid any attention to a few years ago because he did not believe in such things. It was not good form to do so.

But the changes of fashion are so pervasive, so familiar, and, indeed, universal phenomena that we do not regard the changes which they bring, no matter how fantastic, as quite out of the usual and expected order. Gabriel Tarde, however, regards the "social contagion" represented in fashion (imitation) as the fundamental social phenomenon.[2]

The term social epidemic, which is, like fashion, a form of social contagion, has a different origin and a different connotation. J. F. C. Hecker, whose study of the Dancing Mania of the Middle Ages, published in 1832, was an incident of his investigation of the Black Death, was perhaps the first to give currency to the term.[3] Both the Black Death and the Dancing Mania assumed the form of epidemics and the latter, the Dancing Mania, was in his estimation the sequel of the former, the Black Death. It was perhaps this similarity in the manner in which they spread—the one by physical and the other by psychical infection—that led him to speak of the spread of a popular delusion in terms of a physical science. Furthermore, the hysteria was directly traceable, as he believed, to the prevailing conditions of the time, and this seemed to put the manifestations in the world of intelligible and controllable phenomena, where they could be investigated.

It is this notion, then, that unrest which manifests itself in social epidemics is an indication of pathological social conditions, and the

[1] W. E. H. Lecky, *History of the Rise and Influence of the Spirit of Rationalism in Europe.* 2 vols. (Vol. I.) (New York, 1866.)

[2] See Gabriel Tarde, *Laws of Imitation.*

[3] J. F. C. Hecker, *Die Tanzwuth, eine Volkskrankheit im Mittelalter.* (Berlin, 1832.) See Introduction of *The Black Death and the Dancing Mania.* Translated from the German by B. G. Babington. Cassell's National Library. (New York, 1888.)

further, the more general, conception that unrest does not become social and hence contagious except when there are contributing causes in the environment—it is this that gives its special significance to the term and the facts.   Unrest in the social organism with the social ferments that it induces is like fever in the individual organism, a highly important diagnostic symptom.

b) *The crowd.*—Neither Le Bon nor any of the other writers upon the subject of mass psychology has succeeded in distinguishing clearly between the organized or "psychological" crowd, as Le Bon calls it, and other similar types of social groups.   These distinctions, if they are to be made objectively, must be made on the basis of case studies.   It is the purpose of the materials under the general heading of "The 'Animal' Crowd," not so much to furnish a definition, as to indicate the nature and sources of materials from which a definition can be formulated.   It is apparent that the different animal groups behave in ways that are distinctive and characteristic, ways which are predetermined in the organism to an extent that is not true of human beings.

One other distinction may possibly be made between the so-called "animal" and the human crowd.   The organized crowd is controlled by *a common purpose* and acts to achieve, no matter how vaguely it is defined, a common end.   The herd, on the other hand, has apparently no common purpose.   Every sheep in the flock, at least as the behavior of the flock is ordinarily interpreted, behaves like every other.   Action in a stampede, for example, is collective but it is not concerted.   It is very 'difficult to understand how there can be concerted action in the herd or the flock unless it is on an instinctive basis. The crowd, however, responds to collective representations.   The crowd does not imitate or follow its leader as sheep do a bellwether. On the contrary, the crowd *carries out the suggestions of the leader*, and even though there be no division of labor each individual acts more or less in his own way to achieve a common end.

In the case of a panic or a stampede, however, where there is no common end, the crowd acts like a flock of sheep.   But a stampede or a panic is not a crowd in Le Bon's sense.   It is not a psychological unity, nor a "single being," subject to "the mental unity of crowds."[1] The panic is the crowd in dissolution.   All effective methods of

[1] Le Bon, *op. cit.*, p. 26.

dispersing crowds involve some method of distracting attention, breaking up the tension, and dissolving the mob into its individual units.

c) *Types of mass movements.*—The most elementary form of mass movement is a mass migration. Such a mass movement displays, in fact, many of the characteristics of the "animal" crowd. It is the "human" herd. The migration of a people, either as individuals or in organized groups, may be compared to the swarming of the hive. Peoples migrate in search of better living conditions, or merely in search of new experience. It is usually the younger generation, the more restless, active, and adaptable, who go out from the security of the old home to seek their fortunes in the new. Once settled on the new land, however, immigrants inevitably remember and idealize the home they have left. Their first disposition is to reproduce as far as possible in the new world the institutions and the social order of the old. Just as the spider spins his web out of his own body, so the immigrant tends to spin out of his experience and traditions, a social organization which reproduces, as far as circumstances will permit, the organization and the life of the ancestral community. In this way the older culture is transplanted and renews itself, under somewhat altered circumstances, in the new home. That explains, in part, at any rate, the fact that migration tends to follow the isotherms, since all the more fundamental cultural devices and experience are likely to be accommodations to geographical and climatic conditions.

In contrast with migrations are movements which are sometimes referred to as crusades, partly because of the religious fervor and fanaticism with which they are usually conducted and partly because they are an appeal to the masses of the people for direct action and depend for their success upon their ability to appeal to some universal human interest or to common experiences and interests that are keenly comprehended by the common man.

The Woman's Christian Temperance Crusade, referred to in the materials, may be regarded, if we are permitted to compare great things with small, as an illustration of collective behavior not unlike the crusades of the eleventh and twelfth centuries.

Crusades are reformatory and religious. This was true at any rate of the early crusades, inspired by Peter the Hermit, whatever may have been the political purposes of the popes who encouraged them. It was the same motive that led the people of the Middle Ages to make pilgrimages which led them to join the crusades. At bottom it was an inner restlessness, that sought peace in great hardship and inspiring action, which moved the masses.

Somewhat the same widespread contagious restlessness is the source of most of our revolutions. It is not, however, hardships and actual distress that inspire revolutions but hopes and dreams, dreams which find expression in those myths and "vital lies," as Vernon Lee calls them,[1] which according to Sorel are the only means of moving the masses.

The distinction between crusades, like the Woman's Temperance Crusade, and revolutions, like the French Revolution, is that one is a radical attempt to correct a recognized evil and the other is a radical attempt to reform an existing social order.

II.   MATERIALS

A.   SOCIAL CONTAGION

1.   An Incident in a Lancashire Cotton Mill[2]

At a cotton manufactory at Hodden Bridge, in Lancashire, a girl, on the fifteenth of February, 1787, put a mouse into the bosom of another girl, who had a great dread of mice. The girl was immediately thrown into a fit, and continued in it with the most violent convulsions for twenty-four hours. On the following day three more girls were seized in the same manner; and on the seventeenth, six more. By this time the alarm was so great that the whole work, in which 200 or 300 were employed, was totally stopped, and an idea prevailed that a particular disease had been introduced by a bag of cotton opened in the house. On Sunday, the eighteenth, Dr. St. Clare was sent for from Preston; before he arrived three more were seized, and during that night and the morning of the nineteenth, eleven more, making in all twenty-four. Of these, twenty-one were young women, two were girls of about ten years of age, and one man, who had been much fatigued with holding the girls. Three of the number lived

---

[1] Vernon Lee [pseud.], *Vital Lies*. Studies of some varieties of recent obscurantism. (London, 1912.)

[2] Taken from *Gentleman's Magazine*, March, 1787, p. 268.

about two miles from the place where the disorder first broke out, and three at another factory in Clitheroe, about five miles distant, which last and two more were infected entirely from report, not having seen the other patients, but, like them and the rest of the country, strongly impressed with the idea of the plague being caught from the cotton. The symptoms were anxiety, strangulation, and very strong convulsions; and these were so violent as to last without any intermission from a quarter of an hour to twenty-four hours, and to require four or five persons to prevent the patients from tearing their hair and dashing their heads against the floor or walls. Dr. St. Clare had taken with him a portable electrical machine, and by electric shocks the patients were universally relieved without exception. As soon as the patients and the country were assured that the complaint was merely nervous, easily cured, and not introduced by the cotton, no fresh person was affected. To dissipate their apprehension still further, the best effects were obtained by causing them to take a cheerful glass and join in a dance. On Tuesday, the twentieth, they danced, and the next day were all at work, except two or three, who were much weakened by their fits.

2. The Dancing Mania of the Middle Ages[1]

So early as the year 1374, assemblages of men and women were seen at Aix-la-Chapelle who had come out of Germany and who, united by one common delusion, exhibited to the public both in the streets and in the churches the following strange spectacle. They formed circles hand in hand and, appearing to have lost all control over their senses, continued dancing, regardless of the by-standers, for hours together in wild delirium, until at length they fell to the ground in a state of exhaustion. While dancing they neither saw nor heard, being insensible to external impressions through the senses, but were haunted by visions, their fancies conjuring up spirits whose names they shrieked out; and some of them afterward asserted that they felt as if they had been immersed in a stream of blood, which obliged them to leap so high. Others, during the paroxysm, saw the heavens open and the Saviour enthroned with

[1] Adapted from J. F. C. Hecker, *The Black Death, and the Dancing Mania,* pp. 106–11. (Cassell & Co., 1888.)

the Virgin Mary, according as the religious notions of the age were strangely and variously reflected in their imaginations.

Where the disease was completely developed, the attack commenced with epileptic convulsions. Those affected fell to the ground senseless, panting and laboring for breath. They foamed at the mouth, and suddenly springing up began their dance amid strange contortions. Yet the malady doubtless made its appearance very variously, and was modified by temporary or local circumstances, whereof non-medical contemporaries but imperfectly noted the essential particulars, accustomed as they were to confound their observation of natural events with their notions of the world of spirits.

It was but a few months ere this demoniacal disease had spread from Aix-la-Chapelle, where it appeared in July, over the neighboring Netherlands. Wherever the dancers appeared, the people assembled in crowds to gratify their curiosity with the frightful spectacle. At length the increasing number of the affected excited no less anxiety than the attention that was paid to them. In towns and villages they took possession of the religious houses, processions were everywhere instituted on their account, and masses were said and hymns were sung, while the disease itself, of the demoniacal origin of which no one entertained the least doubt, excited everywhere astonishment and horror. In Liège the priests had recourse to exorcisms and endeavored by every means in their power to allay an evil which threatened so much danger to themselves; for the possessed, assembling in multitudes, frequently poured forth imprecations against them and menaced their destruction.

A few months after this dancing malady had made its appearance at Aix-la-Chapelle, it broke out at Cologne, where the number of those possessed amounted to more than five hundred; and about the same time at Metz, the streets of which place are said to have been filled with eleven hundred dancers. Peasants left their plows, mechanics their workshops, housewives their domestic duties, to join the wild revels, and this rich commercial city became the scene of the most ruinous disorder. Secret desires were excited and but too often found opportunities for wild enjoyment; and numerous beggars, stimulated by vice and misery, availed themselves of this new complaint to gain a temporary livelihood. Girls and boys

quitted their parents, and servants their masters, to amuse themselves at the dances of those possessed, and greedily imbibed the poison
of mental infection.   Above a hundred unmarried women were seen
raving about in consecrated and unconsecrated places, and the
consequences were soon perceived.   Gangs of idle vagabonds, who
understood how to imitate to the life the gestures and convulsions
of those really affected, roved from place to place seeking maintenance and adventures, and thus, wherever they went, spreading this
disgusting spasmodic disease like a plague; for in maladies of this
kind the susceptible are infected as easily by the appearance as by
the reality.   At last it was found necessary to drive away these
mischievous guests, who were equally inaccessible to the exorcisms
of the priests and the remedies of the physicians.   It was not, however, until after four months that the Rhenish cities were able to
suppress these impostures, which had so alarmingly increased the
original evil.   In the meantime, when once called into existence, the
plague crept on and found abundant food in the tone of thought which
prevailed in the fourteenth and fifteenth centuries, and even, though
in a minor degree, throughout the sixteenth and seventeenth, causing
a permanent disorder of the mind, and exhibiting, in those cities to
whose inhabitants it was a novelty, scenes as strange as they were
detestable.

B.   THE CROWD

1.   The "Animal" Crowd

a.   The Flock[1]

Understand that a flock is not the same thing as a number of
sheep.   On the stark, wild headlands of the White Mountains, as
many as thirty Bighorn are known to run in loose, fluctuating hordes;
in fenced pastures, two to three hundred; close-herded on the range,
two to three thousand; but however artificially augmented, the flock
is always a conscious adjustment.   There are always leaders, middlers,
and tailers, each insisting on its own place in the order of going.
Should the flock be rounded up suddenly in alarm it mills within
itself until these have come to their own places.

There is much debate between herders as to the advantage of
goats over sheep as leaders.   In any case there are always a few goats

[1] From Mary Austin, *The Flock*, pp. 110–29.   (Houghton Mifflin Co., 1906.)

in a flock, and most American owners prefer them; but the Frenchmen choose bell-wethers. Goats lead naturally by reason of a quicker instinct, forage more freely, and can find water on their own account. But wethers, if trained with care, learn what goats abhor, to take broken ground sedately, to walk through the water rather than set the whole flock leaping and scrambling; but never to give voice to alarm, as goats will, and call the herder.

It appears that leaders understand their office, and goats particularly exhibit a jealousy of their rights to be first over the stepping-stones or to walk the teetering log-bridges at the roaring creeks. By this facile reference of the initiative to the wisest one, the shepherd is served most. The dogs learn to which of the flock to communicate orders, at which heels a bark or a bite soonest sets the flock in motion. But the flock-mind obsesses equally the best-trained, flashes as instantly from the meanest of the flock.

By very little the herder may turn the flock-mind to his advantage, but chiefly it works against him. Suppose on the open range the impulse to forward movement overtakes them, set in motion by some eager leaders that remember enough of what lies ahead to make them oblivious to what they pass. They press ahead. The flock draws on. The momentum of travel grows. The bells clang soft and hurriedly; the sheep forget to feed; they neglect the tender pastures; they will not stay to drink. Under an unwise or indolent herder the sheep going on an unaccustomed trail will overtravel and underfeed, until in the midst of good pasture they starve upon their feet. So it is on the Long Trail you so often see the herder walking with his dogs ahead of his sheep to hold them back to feed. But if it should be new ground he must go after and press them skilfully, for the flock-mind balks chiefly at the unknown.

In sudden attacks from several quarters, or inexplicable man-thwarting of their instincts, the flock-mind teaches them to turn a solid front, revolving about in the smallest compass with the lambs in their midst, narrowing and indrawing until they perish by suffocation. So they did in the intricate defiles of Red Rock, where Carrier lost 250 in '74, and at Poison Springs, as Narcisse Duplin told me, where he had to choose between leaving them to the deadly waters, or, prevented from the spring, made witless by thirst, to mill about until they piled up and killed threescore in their midst. By no urgency of the dogs could they be moved forward or scattered until night fell with coolness and returning sanity. Nor does the imperfect gregariousness of man always save us from ill-considered rushes or strangulous in-turnings of the social mass. Notwithstanding there are those who would have us to be flock-minded.

It is doubtful if the herder is anything more to the flock than an incident of the range, except as a giver of salt, for the only cry they make to him is the salt cry. When the natural craving is at the point of urgency, they circle about his camp or his cabin, leaving off feeding for that business; and nothing else offering, they will continue this headlong circling about a bowlder or any object bulking large in their immediate neighborhood remotely resembling the appurtenances of man, as if they had learned nothing since they were free to find licks for themselves, except that salt comes by bestowal and in conjunction with the vaguely indeterminate lumps of matter that associate with man. As if in fifty centuries of man-herding they had made but one step out of the terrible isolation of brute species, an isolation impenetrable except by fear to every other brute, but now admitting the fact without knowledge, of the God of the Salt. Accustomed to receiving this miracle on open bowlders, when the craving is strong upon them, they seek such as these to run about, vociferating, as if they said, In such a place our God has been wont to bless us, come now, let us greatly entreat Him. This one quavering bleat, unmistakable to the sheepman even at a distance, is the only new note in the sheep's vocabulary, and the only one which passes with intention from himself to man. As for the call of distress which a leader raised by hand may make to his master, it is not new, is not common to flock usage, and is swamped utterly in the obsession of the flock-mind.

b. The Herd[1]

My purpose in this paper is to discuss a group of curious and useless emotional instincts of social animals, which have not yet been properly explained. Excepting two of the number, placed first and last in the list, they are not related in their origin; consequently they are here grouped together arbitrarily, only for the reason that

[1] From W. H. Hudson, "The Strange Instincts of Cattle," in *Longman's Magazine*, XVIII (1891), 389-91.

we are very familiar with them on account of their survival in our domestic animals, and because they are, as I have said, useless; also because they resemble each other, among the passions and actions of the lower animals, in their effect on our minds. This is in all cases unpleasant, and sometimes exceedingly painful, as when species that rank next to ourselves in their developed intelligence and organized societies, such as elephants, monkeys, dogs, and cattle, are seen under the domination of impulses, in some cases resembling insanity, and in others simulating the darkest passions of man.

These instincts are:

(1) The excitement caused by the smell of blood, noticeable in horses and cattle among our domestic animals, and varying greatly in degree, from an emotion so slight as to be scarcely perceptible to the greatest extremes of rage or terror.

(2) The angry excitement roused in some animals when a scarlet or bright red cloth is shown to them. So well known is this apparently insane instinct in our cattle that it has given rise to a proverb and metaphor familiar in a variety of forms to everyone.

(3) The persecution of a sick or weakly animal by its companions.

(4) The sudden deadly fury that seizes on the herd or family at the sight of a companion in extreme distress. Herbivorous mammals at such times will trample and gore the distressed one to death. In the case of wolves, and other savage-tempered carnivorous species, the distressed fellow is frequently torn to pieces and devoured on the spot.

To take the first two together. When we consider that blood is red; that the smell of it is, or may be, or has been, associated with that vivid hue in the animal's mind; that blood, seen and smelt, is, or has been, associated with the sight of wounds and with cries of pain and rage or terror from the wounded or captive animal, there appears at first sight to be some reason for connecting these two instinctive passions as having the same origin—namely, terror and rage caused by the sight of a member of the herd struck down and bleeding, or struggling for life in the grasp of an enemy. I do not mean to say that such an image is actually present in the animal's mind, but that the inherited or instinctive passion is one in kind and in its working with the passion of the animal when experience and reason were its guides.

But the more I consider the point, the more am I inclined to regard these two instincts as separate in their origin, although I retain the belief that cattle and horses and several wild animals are violently excited by the smell of blood for the reason just given—namely, their inherited memory associates the smell of blood with the presence among them of some powerful enemy that threatens their life.

The following incident will show how violently this blood passion sometimes affects cattle, when they are permitted to exist in a half-wild condition, as on the Pampas. I was out with my gun one day, a few miles from home, when I came across a patch on the ground where the grass was pressed or trodden down and stained with blood. I concluded that some thievish Gauchos had slaughtered a fat cow there on the previous night, and, to avoid detection, had somehow managed to carry the whole of it away on their horses. As I walked on, a herd of cattle, numbering about three hundred, appeared moving slowly on to a small stream a mile away; they were traveling in a thin, long line, and would pass the blood-stained spot at a distance of seven to eight hundred yards, but the wind from it would blow across their track. When the tainted wind struck the leaders of the herd they instantly stood still, raising their heads, then broke out into loud, excited bellowings; and finally turning, they started off at a fast trot, following up the scent in a straight line, until they arrived at the place where one of their kind had met its death. The contagion spread, and before long all the cattle were congregated on the fatal spot, and began moving round in a dense mass, bellowing continually.

It may be remarked here that the animal has a peculiar language on occasions like this; it emits a succession of short, bellowing cries, like excited exclamations, followed by a very loud cry, alternately sinking into a hoarse murmur and rising to a kind of scream that grates harshly on the sense. Of the ordinary "cow-music" I am a great admirer, and take as much pleasure in it as in the cries and melody of birds and the sound of the wind in trees; but this performance of cattle excited by the smell of blood is most distressing to hear.

The animals that had forced their way into the center of the mass to the spot where the blood was, pawed the earth, and dug it up with their horns, and trampled each other down in their frantic excitement. It was terrible to see and hear them. The action of those on the border of the living mass, in perpetually moving round in a circle with dolorous bellowings, was like that of the women in an Indian village when a warrior dies, and all night they shriek and howl with simulated grief, going round and round the dead man's hut in an endless procession.

c. The Pack[1]

Wolves are the most sociable of beasts of prey. Not only do they gather in bands, but they arrange to render each other assistance, which is the most important test of sociability. The most gray wolves I ever saw in a band was five. This was in northern New Mexico in January, 1894. The most I ever heard of in a band was thirty-two that were seen in the same region. These bands are apparently formed in winter only. The packs are probably temporary associations of personal acquaintances, for some temporary purpose, or passing reason, such as food question or mating-instinct. As soon as this is settled, they scatter.

An instance in point was related to me by Mr. Gordon Wright of Carberry, Manitoba. During the winter of 1865 he was logging at Sturgeon Lake, Ontario. One Sunday he and some companions strolled out on the ice of the lake to look at the logs there. They heard the hunting-cry of wolves, then a deer (a female) darted from the woods to the open ice. Her sides were heaving, her tongue out, and her legs cut by the slight crust of the snow. Evidently she was hard pressed. She was coming toward them, but one of the men gave a shout which caused her to sheer off. A minute later six timber wolves appeared galloping on her trail, heads low, tails horizontal, and howling continuously. They were uttering their hunting-cry, but as soon as they saw her they broke into a louder, different note, left the trail and made straight for her. Five of the wolves were abreast and one that seemed much darker was behind. Within half a mile they overtook her and pulled her down, all seemed to seize her at once. For a few minutes she bleated like a sheep in distress; after that the only sound was the snarling and the crunching of the wolves as they feasted. Within fifteen minutes nothing was left of the deer but hair and some of the larger bones, and the wolves fighting among themselves for even these. Then they scattered, each going a quarter of a

[1] From Ernest Thompson Seton, "The Habits of Wolves," in *The American Magazine*, LXIV (1907), 636.

mile or so, no two in the same direction, and those that remained in view curled up there on the open lake to sleep. This happened about ten in the morning within three hundred yards of several witnesses.

2. The Psychological Crowd[1]

In its ordinary sense the word "crowd" means a gathering of individuals of whatever nationality, profession, or sex, and whatever be the chances that have brought them together. From the psychological point of view the expression "crowd" assumes quite a different signification. Under certain given circumstances, and only under those circumstances, an agglomeration of men presents new characteristics very different from those of the individuals composing it. The sentiments and ideas of all the persons in the gathering take one and the same direction, and their conscious personality vanishes. A collective mind is formed, doubtless transitory, but presenting very clearly defined characteristics. The gathering has thus become what, in the absence of a better expression, I will call an organized crowd, or, if the term is considered preferable, a psychological crowd. It forms a single being, and is subjected to the law of the mental unity of crowds.

It is evident that it is not by the mere fact of a number of individuals finding themselves accidentally side by side that they acquire the character of an organized crowd. A thousand individuals accidentally gathered in a public place without any determined object in no way constitute a crowd, from the psychological point of view. To acquire the special characteristics of such a crowd, the influence is necessary of certain predisposing causes, of which we shall have to determine the nature.

The disappearance of conscious personality and the turning of feelings and thoughts in a definite direction, which are the primary characteristics of a crowd about to become organized, do not always involve the simultaneous presence of a number of individuals on one spot. Thousands of isolated individuals may acquire at certain moments, and under the influence of certain violent emotions—such, for example, as a great national event—the characteristics of a psychological crowd. It will be sufficient in that case that a mere

[1] Adapted from Gustave Le Bon, *The Crowd*, pp. 1-14. (T. Fisher Unwin, 1897.)

chance should bring them together for their acts at once to assume the characteristics peculiar to the acts of a crowd. At certain moments half a dozen men might constitute a psychological crowd, which may not happen in the case of hundreds of men gathered together by accident. On the other hand, an entire nation, though there may be no visible agglomeration, may become a crowd under the action of certain influences.

It is not easy to describe the mind of crowds with exactness, because its organization varies not only according to race and composition but also according to the nature and intensity of the exciting causes to which crowds are subjected. The same difficulty, however, presents itself in the psychological study of an individual. It is only in novels that individuals are found to traverse their whole life with an unvarying character. It is only the uniformity of the environment that creates the apparent uniformity of characters. I have shown elsewhere that all mental constitutions contain possibilities of character which may be manifested in consequence of a sudden change of environment. This explains how it was that among the most savage members of the French Convention were to be found inoffensive citizens who, under ordinary circumstances, would have been peaceable notaries or virtuous magistrates. The storm past, they resumed their normal character of quiet, law-abiding citizens. Napoleon found amongst them his most docile servants.

It being impossible to study here all the successive degrees of organization of crowds, we shall concern ourselves more especially with such crowds as have attained to the phase of complete organization. In this way we shall see what crowds may become, but not what they invariably are. It is only in this advanced phase of organization that certain new and special characteristics are superposed on the unvarying and dominant character of the race; then takes place that turning, already alluded to, of all the feelings and thoughts of the collectivity in an identical direction. It is only under such circumstances, too, that what I have called above the psychological law of the mental unity of crowds comes into play.

The most striking peculiarity presented by a psychological crowd is the following: Whoever be the individuals that compose it, however like or unlike be their mode of life, their occupations, their character, or their intelligence, the fact that they have been transformed into a crowd puts them in possession of a sort of collective mind which makes them feel, think, and act in a manner quite different from that in which each individual of them would feel, think, and act, were he in a state of isolation. There are certain ideas and feelings which do not come into being or do not transform themselves into acts except in the case of individuals forming a crowd. The psychological crowd is a provisional being formed of heterogeneous elements, which for a moment are combined, exactly as the cells which constitute a living body form by their reunion a new being which displays characteristics very different from those possessed by each of the cells singly.

Contrary to an opinion which one is astonished to find coming from the pen of so acute a philosopher as Herbert Spencer, in the aggregate which constitutes a crowd there is in no sort a summing-up of or an average struck between its elements. What really takes place is a combination followed by the creation of new characteristics, just as in chemistry certain elements, when brought into contact— bases and acids, for example—combine to form a new body possessing properties quite different from those of the bodies that have served to form it.

It is easy to prove how much the individual forming part of a crowd differs from the isolated individual, but it is less easy to discover the causes of this difference. To obtain, at any rate, a glimpse of them it is necessary in the first place to call to mind the truth established by modern psychology that unconscious phenomena play an altogether preponderating part not only in organic life but also in the operations of the intelligence. The conscious life of the mind is of small importance in comparison with its unconscious life. The most subtle analyst, the most acute observer, is scarcely successful in discovering more than a very small number of the unconscious motives that determine his conduct.

The greater part of our daily actions are the result of hidden motives which escape our observation. It is more especially with respect to those unconscious elements that all the individuals belonging to it resemble each other, while it is principally in respect to the conscious elements of their character—the fruit of education, and yet more of exceptional hereditary conditions—that they differ from each other. Men most unlike in the matter of their intelligence possess instincts, passions, and feelings that are very similar. In the case of everything that belongs to the realm of sentiment—religion, politics, morality, the affections and antipathies, etc.—the most eminent men seldom surpass the standard of the most ordinary individuals. From the intellectual point of view an abyss may exist between a great mathematician and his bootmaker, but from the point of view of character the difference is most often slight or non-existent.

It is precisely these general qualities of character, governed by forces of which we are unconscious, and possessed by the majority of the normal individuals of a race in much the same degree, it is precisely these qualities that in crowds become common property. In the collective mind the intellectual aptitudes of the individuals, and in consequence their individuality, are weakened. The heterogeneous is swamped by the homogeneous, and the unconscious qualities obtain the upper hand.

This very fact that crowds possess in common ordinary qualities explains why they can never accomplish acts demanding a high degree of intelligence. The decisions affecting matters of general interest come to by an assembly of men of distinction, but specialists in different walks of life, are not sensibly superior to the decisions that would be adopted by a gathering of imbeciles. The truth is, they can only bring to bear in common on the work in hand those mediocre qualities which are the birthright of every average individual. In crowds it is stupidity and not mother-wit that is accumulated. It is not all the world, as is so often repeated, that has more wit than Voltaire, but assuredly Voltaire that has more wit than all the world, if by "all the world" crowds are to be understood.

If the individuals of a crowd confined themselves to putting in common the ordinary qualities of which each of them has his share, there would merely result the striking of an average, and not, as we have said is actually the case, the creation of new characteristics. How is it that these new characteristics are created? This is what we are now to investigate.

Different causes determine the appearance of these characteristics peculiar to crowds and not possessed by isolated individuals. The first is that the individual forming part of a crowd acquires, solely from numerical considerations, a sentiment of invincible power which allows him to yield to instincts which, had he been alone, he would perforce have kept under restraint. He will be the less disposed to check himself from the consideration that, a crowd being anonymous and in consequence irresponsible, the sentiment of responsibility which always controls individuals disappears entirely.

The second cause, which is contagion, also intervenes to determine the manifestation in crowds of their special characteristics, and at the same time the trend they are to take. Contagion is a phenomenon of which it is easy to establish the presence, but which it is not easy to explain. It must be classed among those phenomena of a hypnotic order. In a crowd every sentiment and act is contagious, and contagious to such a degree that an individual readily sacrifices his personal interest to the collective interest. This is an aptitude very contrary to his nature, and of which a man is scarcely capable except when he makes part of a crowd.

A third cause, and by far the most important, determines in the individuals of a crowd special characteristics which are quite contrary at times to those presented by the isolated individual. I allude to that suggestibility of which, moreover, the contagion mentioned above is neither more nor less than an effect.

The most careful observations seem to prove that an individual immerged for some length of time in a crowd in action soon finds himself—either in consequence of the magnetic influence given out by the crowd or from some other cause of which we are ignorant— in a special state, which much resembles the state of fascination in which the hypnotized individual finds himself in the hands of the hypnotizer.

Such also is approximately the state of the individual forming part of a psychological crowd. He is no longer conscious of his acts. In his case, as in the case of the hypnotized subject, at the same time that certain faculties are destroyed, others may be brought to a high degree of exaltation. Under the influence of a suggestion, he will undertake the accomplishment of certain acts with irresistible impetuosity. This impetuosity is the more irresistible in the case of crowds than in that of the hypnotized subject, from the fact that, the suggestion being the same for all the individuals of the crowd, it gains in strength by reciprocity. The individualities in the crowd who might possess a personality sufficiently strong to resist the suggestion are too few in number to struggle against the current. At the utmost, they may be able to attempt a diversion by means of different suggestions. It is in this way, for instance, that a happy expression, an image opportunely evoked, have occasionally deterred crowds from the most bloodthirsty acts.

We see, then, that the disappearance of the conscious personality, the predominance of the unconscious personality, the turning by means of suggestion and contagion of feelings and ideas in an identical direction, the tendency to immediately transform the suggested ideas into acts; these, we see, are the principal characteristics of the individual forming part of a crowd. He is no longer himself, but has become an automaton who has ceased to be guided by his will.

Moreover, by the mere fact that he forms part of an organized crowd, a man descends several rungs in the ladder of civilization. Isolated, he may be a cultivated individual; in a crowd, he is a barbarian—that is, a creature acting by instinct. He possesses the spontaneity, the violence, the ferocity, and also the enthusiasm and heroism of primitive beings.

An individual in a crowd is a grain of sand amid other grains of sand, which the wind stirs up at will. It is for these reasons that juries are seen to deliver verdicts of which each individual juror would disapprove, that parliamentary assemblies adopt laws and measures of which each of their members would disapprove in his own person. Taken separately, the men of the Convention were enlightened citizens of peaceful habits. United in a crowd, they did not hesitate to give their adhesion to the most savage proposals, to guillotine individuals most clearly innocent, and, contrary to their interest, to renounce their inviolability and to decimate themselves.

The conclusion to be drawn from what precedes is that the crowd is always intellectually inferior to the isolated individual, but that, from the point of view of feelings and of the acts these feelings provoke, the crowd may, according to circumstances, be better or worse than the individual. All depends on the nature of the suggestion to which the crowd is exposed. This is the point that has been completely misunderstood by writers who have only studied crowds from the criminal point of view. Doubtless a crowd is often criminal, but also it is often heroic. It is crowds rather than isolated individuals that may be induced to run the risk of death to secure the triumph of a creed or an idea, that may be fired with enthusiasm for glory and honor, that are led on—almost without bread and without arms, as in the age of the Crusades—to deliver the tomb of Christ from the infidel, or, as in '93, to defend the fatherland. Such heroism is without doubt somewhat unconscious, but it is of such heroism that history is made. Were peoples only to be credited with the great actions performed in cold blood, the annals of the world would register but few of them.

3. The Crowd Defined[1]

A crowd in the ordinary sense of that term is any chance collection of individuals. Such a collectivity becomes a crowd in the sociological sense only when a condition of *rapport* has been established among the individuals who compose it.

Rapport implies the existence of a mutual responsiveness, such that every member of the group reacts immediately, spontaneously, and sympathetically to the sentiments and attitudes of every other member.

The fact that A responds sympathetically toward B and C implies the existence in A of an attitude of receptivity and suggestibility toward the sentiments and attitudes of B and C. Where A, B, and C are mutually sympathetic, the inhibitions which, under ordinary circumstances, serve to preserve the isolation and self-consciousness of individuals are relaxed or completely broken down. Under these circumstances each individual, in so far as he may be said to reflect, in his own consciousness and in his emotional reactions, the sentiments and emotions of all the others, tends at the same time to modify the sentiments and attitudes of those others. The effect is to produce a heightened, intensified, and relatively impersonal state of consciousness in which all seem to share, but which is, at the same time, relatively independent of each.

The development of this so-called "group-consciousness" represents a certain amount of loss of self-control on the part of the individual. Such control as the individual loses over himself is thus automatically transferred to the group as a whole or to the leader.

What is meant by *rapport* in the group may be illustrated by a somewhat similar phenomenon which occurs in hypnosis. In this case a relation is established between the experimenter and his subject

[1] From Robert E. Park, *The Crowd and the Public.* (Unpublished manuscript.)

such that the subject responds automatically to every suggestion of the experimenter but is apparently oblivious of suggestions coming from other persons whose existence he does not perceive or ignores. This is the condition called "isolated rapport."[1]

In the case of the crowd this mutual and exclusive responsiveness of each member of the crowd to the suggestions emanating from the other members produces here also a kind of mental isolation which is accompanied by an inhibition of the stimuli and suggestions that control the behavior of individuals under the conditions of ordinary life. Under these conditions impulses long repressed in the individual may find an expression in the crowd. It is this, no doubt, which accounts for those so-called criminal and atavistic tendencies of crowds, of which Le Bon and Sighele speak.[2]

The organization of the crowd is only finally effected when the attention of the individuals who compose it becomes focused upon some particular object or some particular objective. This object thus fixed in the focus of the attention of the group tends to assume the character of a *collective representation*.[3] It becomes this because it is the focus of the collectively enhanced emotion and sentiment of the group. It becomes the representation and the symbol of what the crowd feels and wills at the moment when all members are suffused with a common collective excitement and dominated by a common and collective idea. This excitement and this idea with the meanings that attach to it are called collective because they are a product of the interactions of the members of the crowd. They are not individual but corporate products.

Le Bon describes the organization thus effected in a chance-met collection of individuals as a "collective mind," and refers to the group, transitory and ephemeral though it be, as a "single being."

The positive factors in determining the organization of the crowd are then:

(1) A condition of *rapport* among the members of the group with a certain amount of contagious excitement and heightened suggestibility incident to it.

[1] Moll, *Hypnotism*, pp. 134–36.

[2] Sighele, *Psychologie des Auflaufs und der Massenverbrechen* (translated from the Italian), p. 79.

[3] Durkheim, *The Elementary Forms of Religious Life*, pp. 432–37.

(2) A certain degree of mental isolation of the group following as a consequence of the *rapport* and sympathetic responsiveness of members of the group.

(3) Focus of attention; and finally the consequent

(4) Collective representation.

C. TYPES OF MASS MOVEMENTS

1. Crowd Excitements and Mass Movements: The Klondike Rush[1]

It was near the middle of July when the steamer *Excelsior* arrived in San Francisco from St. Michael's, on the west coast of Alaska, with forty miners, having among them seven hundred and fifty thousand dollars' worth of gold, brought down from the Klondike. When the bags and cans and jars containing it had been emptied and the gold piled on the counters of the establishment to which it was brought, no such sight had been seen in San Francisco since the famous year of 1849.

On July 18 the *Portland* arrived in Seattle, on Puget Sound, having on board sixty-eight miners, who brought ashore bullion worth a million dollars. The next day it was stated that these miners had in addition enough gold concealed about their persons and in their baggage to double the first estimate. Whether all these statements were correct or not does not signify, for those were the reports that were spread throughout the states. From this last source alone, the mint at San Francisco received half a million dollars' worth of gold in one week, and it was certain that men who had gone away poor had come back with fortunes. It was stated that a poor blacksmith who had gone up from Seattle returned with $115,000, and that a man from Fresno, who had failed as a farmer, had secured $135,000.

The gold fever set in with fury and attacked all classes. Men in good positions, with plenty of money to spend on an outfit, and men with little beyond the amount of their fare, country men and city men, clerks and professional men without the faintest notion of the meaning of "roughing it," flocked in impossible numbers to secure a passage. There were no means of taking them. Even in distant New York, the offices of railroad companies and local agencies were

[1] Adapted from T. C. Down, "The Rush to the Klondike," in the *Cornhill Magazine*, IV (1898), 33–43.

besieged by anxious inquirers eager to join the throng. On Puget Sound, mills, factories, and smelting works were deserted by their employees, and all the miners on the upper Skeena left their work in a body. On July 21 the North American Transportation Company (one of two companies which monopolized the trade of the Yukon) was reincorporated in Chicago with a quadrupled capital, to cope with the demands of traffic. At the different Pacific ports every available vessel was pressed into the service, and still the wild rush could not be met. Before the end of July the *Portland* left Seattle again for St. Michael's, and the *Mexico* and *Topeka* for Dyea; the *Islander* and *Tees* sailed for Dyea from Victoria, and the *G. W. Elder* from Portland; while from San Francisco the *Excelsior*, of the Alaska Company, which had brought the first gold down, left again for St. Michael's on July 28, being the last of the company's fleet scheduled to connect with the Yukon river boats for the season. Three times the original price was offered for the passage, and one passenger accepted an offer of $1,500 for the ticket for which he had paid only $150.

This, however, was only the beginning of the rush. Three more steamers were announced to sail in August for the mouth of the Yukon, and at least a dozen more for the Lynn Canal, among which were old tubs, which, after being tied up for years, were now overhauled and refitted for the voyage north. One of these was the *Williamette*, an old collier with only sleeping quarters for the officers and crew, which, however, was fitted up with bunks and left Seattle for Dyea and Skagway with 850 passengers, 1,200 tons of freight, and 300 horses, men, live stock, and freight being wedged between decks till the atmosphere was like that of a dungeon; and even with such a prospect in view, it was only by a lavish amount of tipping that a man could get his effects taken aboard. Besides all these, there were numerous scows loaded with provisions and fuel, and barges conveying horses for packing purposes.

A frightful state of congestion followed as each successive steamer on its arrival at the head of the Lynn Canal poured forth its crowds of passengers and added to the enormous loads of freight already accumulated. Matters became so serious that on August 10 the United States Secretary of the Interior, having received information that 3,000 persons with 2,000 tons of baggage and freight were then waiting to cross the mountains to Yukon, and that many more were preparing to join them, issued a warning to the public (following that of the Dominion Government of the previous week) in which he called attention to the exposure, privation, suffering, and danger incident to the journey at that advanced period of the season, and further referred to the gravity of the possible consequences to people detained in the mountainous wilderness during five or six months of Arctic winter, where no relief could reach them.

To come now to the state of things at the head of the Lynn Canal, where the steamers discharged their loads of passengers, horses, and freight. This was done either at Dyea or Skagway, the former being the landing-place for the Chilcoot Pass, and the latter for the White Pass, the distance between the two places being about four miles by sea. There were no towns at these places, nor any convenience for landing except a small wharf at Skagway, which was not completed, the workmen having been smitten with the gold fever. Every man had to bring with him, if he wanted to get through and live, supplies for a year: sacks of flour, slabs of bacon, beans, and so forth, his cooking utensils, his mining outfit and building tools, his tent, and all the heavy clothing and blankets suitable for the northern winter, one thousand pounds' weight at least. Imagine the frightful mass of stuff disgorged as each successive vessel arrived, with no adequate means of taking it inland!

Before the end of September people were preparing to winter on the coast, and Skagway was growing into a substantial town. Where in the beginning of August there were only a couple of shacks, there were in the middle of October 700 wooden buildings and a population of about 1,500. Businesses of all kinds were carried on, saloons and low gaming houses and haunts of all sorts abounded, but of law and order there was none. Dyea also, which at one time was almost deserted, was growing into a place of importance, but the title of every lot in both towns was in dispute. Rain was still pouring down, and without high rubber boots walking was impossible. None indeed but the most hardy could stand existence in such places, and every steamer from the south carried fresh loads of people back to their homes.

Of the 6,000 people who went in this fall, 200 at the most got over to the Dawson Route by the White Pass, and perhaps 700 by the Chilcoot. There were probably 1,000 camped at Lake Bennett, and all the rest, except the 1,500 remaining on the coast, had returned home to wait till midwinter or the spring before venturing up again. The question of which was the best trail was still undecided, and men vehemently debated it every day with the assistance of the most powerful language at their command.

As to the crowds who had gone to St. Michael's, it is doubtful whether any of them got through to Dawson City, since the lower Yukon is impassable by the end of September, and, at any rate, in view of the prospects of short rations, it would have been rash to try. The consequence would be that they would have to remain on that desolate island during nine months of almost Arctic winter, for the river does not open again till the end of June. Here they would be absolutely without employment unless they chose to stack wood for the steamboat companies, and their only amusements (save the mark) would be drinking bad rye-whiskey—for Alaska is a "prohibition" country—and poker-playing. For men with a soul above such delights, the heart-breaking monotony of a northern winter would be appalling, and it is only to be understood by those who have had to endure similar experiences themselves on the western prairies.

2. Mass Movements and the Mores: The Woman's Temperance Crusade[1]

On the evening of December 23, 1873, there might have been seen in the streets of Hillsboro, Ohio, persons singly or in groups wending their way to Music Hall, where a lecture on temperance was to be delivered by Dr. Dio Lewis, of Boston, Massachusetts.

Hillsboro is a small place, containing something more than 3,000 people. The inhabitants are rather better educated than is usually the case in small towns, and its society is indeed noted in that part of the country for its quietude, culture, and refinement.

But Hillsboro was by no means exempt from the prevailing scourge of intemperance. The early settlers of Hillsboro were mostly from Virginia, and brought with them the old-fashioned ideas of hospitality. For many years previous to the crusade the professional men, and especially of the bar, were nearly all habitual drinkers, and many of them very dissipated. When a few earnest temperance men, among

[1] Adapted from Mrs. Annie Wittenmyer, *History of the Woman's Temperance Crusade* (1878), pp. 34–62.

whom was Governor Allen Trimble, initiated a total-abstinence movement in or about the year 1830, the pulpit took up arms against them, and a condemnatory sermon was preached in one of the churches.

Thus it was that, although from time to time men, good and true, banded themselves together in efforts to break up this dreadful state of things and reform society, all endeavors seemed to fail of any permanent effect.

The plan laid down by Dr. Lewis challenged attention by its novelty at least. He believed the work of temperance reform might be successfully carried on by women if they would set about it in the right manner—going to the saloon-keeper in a spirit of Christian love, and persuading him for the sake of humanity and his own eternal welfare to quit the hateful, soul-destroying business. The doctor spoke with enthusiasm; and seeing him so full of faith, the hearts of the women seized the hope—a forlorn one, 'tis true, but still a hope—and when Dr. Lewis asked if they were willing to undertake the task, scores of women rose to their feet, and there was no lack of good men who pledged themselves to encourage and sustain the women in their work.

At a subsequent meeting an organization was effected and Mrs. Eliza J. Thompson, a daughter of ex-Governor Trimble of Ohio, was elected chairman. Mrs. Thompson gives the following account of the manner in which the crusade was organized:

My boy came home from Dr. Dio Lewis' lecture and said, "Ma, they've got you into business"; and went on to tell that Dio Lewis had incidentally related the successful effort of his mother, by prayer and persuasion, to close the saloon in a town where he lived when a boy, and that he had exhorted the women of Hillsboro to do the same, and fifty had risen up to signify their willingness, and that they looked to me to help them to carry out their promise. As I'm talking to you here familiarly, I'll go on to say that my husband, who had retired, and was in an adjoining room, raised up on his elbow and called out, "Oh! that's all tomfoolery!" I remember I answered him something like this: "Well, husband, the men have been in the tomfoolery business a long time; perhaps the Lord is going to call us into partnership with them." I said no more. The next morning my brother-in-law, Colonel ——, came in and told me about the meeting, and said, "Now, you must be sure to go to the women's meeting at the church this morning; they look to see you there." Our folks talked it all over, and my husband said, "Well, we all know where your mother'll take this case for counsel," and then he pointed to the Bible and left the room.

I went into the corner of my room, and knelt down and opened my Bible to see what God would say to me. Just at that moment there was a tap on the door and my daughter entered. She was in tears; she held her Bible in her hand, open to the 146th Psalm. She said, "Ma, I just opened to this, and I think it is for you," and then she went away, and I sat down and read

THIS WONDERFUL MESSAGE FROM GOD

"Put not your trust in princes, nor in the son of man, in whom there is no help. Happy is he that hath the God of Jacob for his help, whose hope is in the Lord his God; which keepeth truth forever; which executeth judgment for the oppressed; the Lord looseth the prisoners; the Lord openeth the eyes of the blind; the Lord raiseth them that are bowed down; the Lord loveth the righteous; the Lord relieveth the fatherless and the widow—*but the way of the wicked he turneth upside down.* The Lord shall reign forever, even thy God, O Zion, unto all generations. Praise ye the Lord!"

I knew that was for me, and I got up, put on my shoes, and started. I went to the church, in this town where I was born. I sat down quietly in the back part of the audience room, by the stove. A hundred ladies were assembled. I heard my name—heard the whisper pass through the company, "Here she is!" "She's come!" and before I could get to the pulpit, they had put me "in office"—I was their leader.

Many of our citizens were there, and our ministers also. They stayed a few minutes, and then rose and went out, saying, "This is your work— we leave it with the women and the Lord." When they had gone, I just opened the big pulpit Bible and read that 146th Psalm, and told them the circumstance of my selecting it. The women sobbed so I could hardly go on. When I had finished, I felt inspired to call on a dear Presbyterian lady to pray. She did so without the least hesitation, though it was the first audible prayer in her life. I can't tell you anything about that prayer, only that the words were like fire.

When she had prayed, I said—and it all came to me just at the moment —"Now, ladies, let us file out, two by two, the smallest first, and let us sing as we go, 'Give to the winds thy fears.' "

We went first to John ———'s saloon. Now, John was a German, and his sister had lived in my family thirteen years, and she was very mild and gentle, and I hoped it might prove a family trait, but I found out it wasn't. He fumed about dreadfully and said, "It's awful; it's a sin and a shame to pray in a saloon!" But we prayed right on just the same.

Next day the ladies held another meeting, but decided not to make any visitations, it being Christmas day, and the hotel-keepers more than usually busy and not likely to listen very attentively to our proposition.

On the twenty-sixth, the hotels and saloons were visited; Mrs. Thompson presenting the appeal. And it was on this morning, and at the saloon of Robert Ward, that there came a break in the established routine. "Bob" was a social, jolly sort of fellow, and his saloon was a favorite resort, and there were many women in the company that morning whose hearts were aching in consequence of his wrong-doing. Ward was evidently touched. He confessed that it was a "bad business," said if he could only "afford to quit it he would," and then tears began to flow from his eyes. Many of the ladies were weeping, and at length, as if by inspiration, Mrs. Thompson kneeled on the floor of the saloon, all kneeling with her, even the saloonist, and prayed, pleading with indescribable pathos and earnestness for the conversion and salvation of this and all saloon-keepers. When the amen was sobbed rather than spoken, Mrs. Washington Doggett's sweet voice began, "There is a fountain," etc., in which all joined; the effect was most solemn, and when the hymn was finished the ladies went quietly away, and that was the first saloon prayer meeting.

There was a saloon-keeper brought from Greenfield to H—— to be tried under the Adair law. The poor mother who brought the suit had besought him not to sell to her son—"her only son." He replied roughly that he would sell to him "as long as he had a dime." Another mother, an old lady, made the same request, "lest," she said, "he may some day fill a drunkard's grave." "Madam," he replied, "your son has as good a right to fill a drunkard's grave as any other mother's son." And in one of the Hillsboro saloons a lady saw her nephew. "O, Mr. B——," said she, "don't sell whiskey to that boy: if he has one drink he will want another, and he may die a drunkard." "Madam, I will sell to him if it sends his soul to hell," was the awful reply. The last man is a peculiarly hard, stony sort of man; his lips look as if chiseled out of flint, a man to be afraid of. One morning, when the visiting band reached his door, they found him in a very bad humor. He locked his door and seated himself on the horse block in front in a perfect rage, clenched his fist, swore furiously, and ordered us to go home. Some gentlemen, on the opposite side of the street, afterward said that they were watching the scene, ready to rush over and defend the ladies from an attack, and they were sure it would come; but one of the ladies, a sweet-souled woman, gentle and placid, kneeled just at his feet, and poured out such a tender, earnest prayer for him, that he quieted down entirely, and when she rose and offered him her hand in token of kind feeling, he could not refuse to take it.

During the Crusade, a saloon-keeper (at Ocean Grove) consented to close his business. There was a great deal of enthusiasm and interest, and we women decided to compensate the man for his whiskey and make a bonfire of it in the street. A great crowd gathered about the saloon, and the barrels of whiskey were rolled out to the public square where we were to have our bonfire. Myself and two other little women, who had been chosen to knock in the heads, and had come to the place with axes concealed under our shawls, went to our work with a will.

I didn't know I was so strong, but I lifted that axe like a woodman and brought it down with such force that the first blow stove in the head of a barrel and splashed the whiskey in every direction. I was literally baptized with the noxious stuff. The intention was to set it on fire, and we had brought matches for that purpose, *but it would not burn!* It was a villainous compound of some sort, but we had set out to have a fire, and were determined by some means or other to make it burn, so we sent for some coal oil and poured it on and we soon had a blaze. The man who could sell such liquors would not be likely to keep the pledge. He is selling liquors again.

The crusade began at Washington C.H. only two days later than at Hillsboro. And Washington C.H. was the first place where the crusade was made prominent and successful.

On Friday morning, December 26, 1873, after an hour of prayer in the M.E. Church, forty-four women filed slowly and solemnly down the aisle, and started forth upon their strange mission with fear and trembling, while the male portion of the audience remained at the church to pray for the success of this new undertaking; the tolling of the church-bell keeping time to the solemn march of the women, as they wended their way to the first drug-store on the list. (The number of places within the city limits where intoxicating drinks were sold was fourteen—eleven saloons and three drug-stores.) Here, as in every place, they entered singing, every woman taking up the sacred strain as she crossed the threshold. This was followed by the reading of the appeal and prayer; then earnest pleading to desist from their soul-destroying traffic and sign the dealer's pledge.

Thus, all the day long, they went from place to place, without stopping even for dinner or lunch, till five o'clock, meeting with no marked success; but invariably courtesy was extended to them; not even their reiterated promise, "We will call again," seeming to offend.

No woman who has ever entered one of these dens of iniquity on such an errand needs to be told of the heartsickness that almost overcame them as they, for the first time, saw behind those painted windows or green blinds, or entered the little stifling "back room," or found their way down winding steps into the damp, dark cellars, and realized that into *such places* those they loved best were being landed, through the allurements of the brilliantly lighted drug-store, the fascinating billiard table, or the enticing beer gardens, with their siren attractions. A crowded house at night, to hear the report of the day's work, betrayed the rapidly increasing interest in this mission.

On the twenty-seventh the contest really began, and, at the first place, the doors were found locked. With hearts full of compassion, the women knelt in the snow upon the pavement, to plead for the divine influence upon the heart of the liquor-dealer, and there held their first street prayer meeting.

At night the weary but zealous workers reported at a mass meeting of the various rebuffs, and the success in having two druggists sign the pledge not to sell, except upon the written prescription of a physician.

The Sabbath was devoted to union mass meeting, with direct reference to the work in hand; and on Monday the number of ladies had increased to near one hundred. That day, December 29, is one long to be remembered in Washington, as the day upon which occurred the first surrender ever made by a liquor-dealer, of his stock of liquors of every kind and variety, to the women, in answer to their prayers and entreaties, and by them poured into the street. Nearly a thousand men, women, and children witnessed the mingling of beer, ale, wine, and whiskey, as they filled the gutters and were drunk up by the earth, while the bells were ringing, men and boys shouting, and women singing and praying to God who had given the victory. But on the fourth day, "stock sale-day," the campaign had reached its height, the town being filled with visitors from all parts of the county and adjoining villages. Another public surrender, and another pouring into the street of a larger stock of liquors than on the previous day, and more intense excitement and enthusiasm.

Mass meetings were held nightly, with new victories reported constantly, until on Friday, January 21, one week from the beginning of the work, at the public meeting held in the evening, the secretary's report announced the unconditional surrender of every liquor-dealer, some having shipped their liquors back to wholesale dealers, others having poured them into the gutters, and the druggists as all having signed the pledge. Thus a campaign of prayer and song had, in eight days, closed eleven saloons, and pledged three drug-stores to sell only on prescription. At first men had wondered, scoffed, and laughed, then criticized, respected, and yielded.

Morning prayer and evening mass meetings continued daily, and the personal pledge was circulated till over one thousand signatures were obtained. Physicians were called upon to sign a pledge not to prescribe ardent spirits when any other substitute could be found, and in no case without a personal examination of the patient.

Early in the third week the discouraging intelligence came that a new man had taken out a license to sell liquor in one of the deserted saloons, and that he was backed by a whiskey house in Cincinnati, to the amount of $5,000, to break down this movement. On Wednesday, the fourteenth, the whiskey was unloaded at his room. About forty women were on the ground and followed the liquor in, and remained holding an uninterrupted prayer meeting all day and until eleven o'clock at night. The next day, bitterly cold, was spent in the same place and manner, without fire or chairs, two hours of that time the women being locked in, while the proprietor was off attending a trial. On the following day, the coldest of the winter of 1874, the women were locked out, and stood on the street holding religious services all day long.

Next morning a tabernacle was built in the street, just in front of the house, and was occupied for the double purpose of *watching* and prayer through the day; and before night the sheriff closed the saloon, and the proprietor surrendered; thus ended the third week.

A short time after, on a dying-bed, this four days' liquor-dealer sent for some of these women, telling them their songs and prayers had never ceased to ring in his ears, and urging them to pray again in his behalf; so he passed away.

Thus, through most of the winter of 1874 no alcoholic drinks were publicly sold as a beverage in the county.

During the two intervening years weekly temperance-league meetings have been kept up by the faithful few, while frequent union mass meetings have been held, thus keeping the subject always before the people. Today the disgraceful and humiliating fact exists that there are more places where liquors are sold than before the crusade.

3. Mass Movements and Revolution

a. The French Revolution[1]

The outward life of men in every age is molded upon an inward life consisting of a framework of traditions, sentiments, and moral influences which direct their conduct and maintain certain fundamental notions which they accept without discussion.

Let the resistance of this social framework weaken, and ideas which could have had no force before will germinate and develop. Certain theories whose success was enormous at the time of the Revolution would have encountered an impregnable wall two centuries earlier.

The aim of these considerations is to recall to the reader the fact that the outward events of revolutions are always a consequence of invisible transformations which have slowly gone forward in men's minds. Any profound study of a revolution necessitates a study of the mental soil upon which the ideas that direct its courses have to germinate.

Generally slow in the extreme, the evolution of ideas is often invisible for a whole generation. Its extent can only be grasped by comparing the mental condition of the same social classes at the two extremities of the curve which the mind has followed.

The actual influence of the philosophers in the genesis of the Revolution was not that which was attributed to them. They revealed nothing new, but they developed the critical spirit which no dogma can resist, once the way is prepared for its downfall.

[1] Adapted from Gustave Le Bon, *The Psychology of Revolution*, pp. 147-70. (G. P. Putnam's Sons, 1913.)

Under the influence of this developing critical spirit things which were no longer very greatly respected came to be respected less and less. When tradition and prestige had disappeared, the social edifice suddenly fell. This progressive disaggregation finally descended to the people, but was not commenced by them. The people follow examples, but never set them.

The philosophers, who could not have exerted any influence over the people, did exert a great influence over the enlightened portion of the nation. The unemployed nobility, who had long been ousted from their old functions and who were consequently inclined to be censorious, followed their leadership. Incapable of foresight, the nobles were the first to break with the traditions that were their only *raison d'être*. As steeped in humanitarianism and rationalism as the *bourgeoisie* of today, they continually sapped their own privileges by their criticisms. As today, the most ardent reformers were found among the favorites of fortune. The aristocracy encouraged dissertations on the social contract, the rights of man, and the equality of citizens. At the theater it applauded plays which criticized privileges, the arbitrariness and the incapacity of men in high places, and abuses of all kinds.

As soon as men lose confidence in the foundations of the mental framework which guides their conduct, they feel at first uneasy and then discontented. All classes felt their old motives of action gradually disappearing. Things that had seemed sacred for centuries were now sacred no longer.

The censorious spirit of the nobility and of the writers of the day would not have sufficed to move the heavy load of tradition but that its action was added to that of other powerful influences. We have already stated, in citing Bossuet, that under the *ancien régime* the religious and civil governments, widely separated in our day, were intimately connected. To injure one was inevitably to injure the other. Now even before the monarchical idea was shaken, the force of religious tradition was greatly diminished among cultivated men. The constant progress of knowledge had sent an increasing number of minds from theology to science by opposing the truth observed to the truth revealed.

This mental evolution, although as yet very vague, was sufficient to show that the traditions which for so many centuries had guided men had not the value which had been attributed to them, and that it would soon be necessary to replace them.

But where discover the new elements which might take the place of tradition? Where seek the magic ring which would raise a new social edifice on the remains of that which no longer contented men?

Men were agreed in attributing to reason the power that tradition and the gods seemed to have lost. How could its force be doubted? Its discoveries having been innumerable, was it not legitimate to suppose that by applying it to the construction of societies it would entirely transform them? Its possible function increased very rapidly in the thoughts of the more enlightened, in proportion as tradition seemed more and more to be distrusted.

The sovereign power attributed to reason must be regarded as the culminating idea which not only engendered the Revolution but governed it throughout. During the whole Revolution men gave themselves up to the most persevering efforts to break with the past and to erect society upon a new plan dictated by logic.

Slowly filtering downward, the rationalistic theories of the philosophers meant to the people simply that all the things which had been regarded as worthy of respect were now no longer worthy. Men being declared equal, the old masters need no longer be obeyed. The multitude easily succeeded in ceasing to respect what the upper classes themselves no longer respected. When the barrier of respect was down the Revolution was accomplished.

The first result of this new mentality was a general insubordination. Mme. Vigée Lebrun relates that on the promenade at Longchamps men of the people leaped on the footboards of the carriages, saying, "Next year you will be behind and we shall be inside."

The populace was not alone in manifesting insubordination and discontent. These sentiments were general on the eve of the Revolution. "The lesser clergy," says Taine, "are hostile to the prelates; the provincial gentry to the nobility of the court; the vassals to the seigneurs; the peasants to the townsmen, etc."

This state of mind, which had been communicated from the nobles and clergy to the people, also invaded the army. At the moment the States General were opened, Necker said: "We are not sure of the troops." The officers were becoming humanitarian and philosophical. The soldiers, recruited from the lowest class of th population, did not philosophize, but they no longer obeyed. Ii their feeble minds the ideas of equality meant simply the suppressioi of all leaders and masters, and therefore of all obedience. In 179 more than twenty regiments threatened their officers, and some times, as at Nancy, threw them into prison.

The mental anarchy which, after spreading through all classes o society, finally invaded the army was the principal cause of the dis appearance of the *ancien régime.* "It was the defection of th army affected by the ideas of the Third Estate," wrote Rivarol "that destroyed royalty."

The genesis of the French Revolution, as well as its duratior was conditioned by elements of a rational, affective, mystic, an collective nature, each category of which was ruled by a differen logic. The rational element usually invoked as an explanatio exerted in reality but very slight influence. It prepared the way fc the Revolution, but maintained it only at the outset, while it wa still exclusively middle class. Its action was manifested by man measures of the time, such as the proposals to reform the taxes, th suppression of the privileges of a useless nobility, etc.

As soon as the Revolution reached the people, the influence c the rational elements speedily vanished before that of the affectiv and collective elements. As for the mystic elements, the foundatio of the revolutionary faith, they made the army fanatical and propa gated the new belief throughout the world.

We shall see these various elements as they appeared in event and in the psychology of individuals. Perhaps the most importan was the mystic element. The Revolution cannot be clearly compre hended—we cannot repeat it too often—unless it is considered a the formation of a religious belief. What I have said elsewhere c all beliefs applies equally to the Revolution. They impose themselve on men apart from reason and have the power to polarize men' thoughts and feelings in one direction. Pure reason had never suc a power, for men were never impassioned by reason.

The religious forms rapidly assumed by the Revolution explai its power of expansion and the prestige which it possessed and ha retained. Few historians have understood that this great monumen ought to be regarded as the foundation of a new religion. Th penetrating mind of Tocqueville, I believe, was the first to perceive as much. He wrote:

The French Revolution was a political revolution which operated in the manner of and assumed something of the aspect of a religious revolution. See by what regular and characteristic traits it finally resembled the latter; not only did it spread itself far and wide like a religious revolution, but, like the latter, it spread itself by means of preaching and propaganda. A political revolution which inspires proselytes, which is preached as passionately to foreigners as it is accomplished at home: consider what a novel spectacle was this.

Although the mystic element is always the foundation of beliefs, certain affective and rational elements are quickly added thereto. A belief thus serves to group sentiments and passions and interests which belong to the affective domain. Reason then envelops the whole, seeking to justify events in which, however, it played no part whatever.

At the moment of the Revolution everyone, according to his aspirations, dressed the new belief in a different rational vesture. The peoples saw in it only the suppression of the religious and political despotisms and hierarchies under which they had so often suffered. Writers like Goethe and thinkers like Kant imagined that they saw in it the triumph of reason. Foreigners like Humboldt came to France "to breathe the air of liberty and to assist at the obsequies of despotism." These intellectual illusions did not last long. The evolution of the drama soon revealed the true foundations of the dream.

b. Bolshevism[1]

Great mass movements, whether these be religious or political, are at first always difficult to understand. Invariably they challenge existing moral and intellectual values, the revaluation of which is, for the normal mind, an exceedingly difficult and painful task. Moreover the definition of their aims and policies into exact and comprehensive programs is generally slowly achieved. At their inception and during the early stages of their development there must needs be many crude and tentative statements and many rhetorical exaggerations. It is safe to assert as a rule that at no stage of its history

[1] Adapted from John Spargo, *The Psychology of Bolshevism*, pp. 1–120. (Harper & Brothers, 1919.)

can a great movement of the masses be fully understood and fairly interpreted by a study of its formal statements and authentic expositions only. These must be supplemented by a careful study of the psychology of the men and women whose ideals and yearnings these statements and expositions aim to represent. It is not enough to know and comprehend the creed: it is essential that we also know and comprehend the spiritual factors, the discontent, the hopes, the fears, the inarticulate visionings of the human units in the movement. This is of greater importance in the initial stages than later, when the articulation of the soul of the movement has become more certain and clear.

No one who has attended many bolshevist meetings or is acquainted with many of the individuals to whom bolshevism makes a strong appeal will seriously question the statement that an impressively large number of those who profess to be Bolshevists present a striking likeness to extreme religious zealots, not only in the manner of manifesting their enthusiasm, but also in their methods of exposition and argument. Just as in religious hysteria a single text becomes a whole creed to the exclusion of every other text, and instead of being itself subject to rational tests is made the sole test of the rationality of everything else, so in the case of the average Bolshevist of this type a single phrase received into the mind in a spasm of emotion, never tested by the usual criteria of reason, becomes not only the very essence of truth but also the standard by which the truth or untruth of everything else must be determined. Most of the preachers who become pro-Bolshevists are of this type.

People who possess minds thus affected are generally capable of and frequently indulge in, the strictest logical deduction and analysis. Sometimes they acquire the reputation of being exceptionally brilliant thinkers because of this power. But the fact is that their initial ideas, upon which everything is pivoted, are derived emotionally and are not the results of a deliberate weighing of available evidence. The initial movement is one of feeling, of emotional impulse. The conviction thereby created is so strong and so dominant that it cannot be affected by any purely rational functional factors.

People of this type jump at decisions and reach very positive convictions upon the most difficult matters with bewildering ease. For them the complexities and intricacies which trouble the normal mind do not exist. Everything is either black or white: there are no perplexing intervening grays. Right is right and wrong is wrong; they do not recognize that there are doubtful twilight zones. Ideas capable of the most elaborate expansion and the most subtle intricacies of interpretation are immaturely grasped and preached with naïve assurance. Statements alleged to be facts, no matter what their source, if they seem to support the convictions thus emotionally derived, are received without any examination and used as conclusive proof, notwithstanding that a brief investigation would prove them to be worthless as evidence.

If we take the group of American intellectuals who at present are ardent champions of bolshevism we shall find that, with exceptions so few as to be almost negligible, they have embraced nearly every "ism" as it arose, seeing in each one the magic solvent of humanity's ills. Those of an older generation thus regarded bimetallism, for instance. What else could be required to make the desert bloom like a garden and to usher in the earthly Paradise? The younger ones, in their turn, took up anarchist-communism, Marxian socialism, industrial unionism, syndicalism, birth control, feminism, and many other movements and propagandas, each of which in its turn induced ecstatic visions of a new heaven and a new earth. The same individuals have grown lyrical in praise of every bizarre and eccentric art fad. In the banal and grotesque travesties of art produced by cubists, futurists, *et al.*, they saw transcendent genius. They are forever seeking new gods and burying old ones.

It would be going too far to say that these individuals are all hystericals in the pathological sense, but it is strictly accurate to say that the class exhibits marked hysterical characteristics and that it closely resembles the large class of over-emotionalized religious enthusiasts which furnish so many true hystericals. It is probable that accidents of environment account for the fact that their emotionalism takes sociological rather than religious forms. If the sociological impetus were absent, most of them would be religiously motived to a state not less abnormal.

To understand the spread of bolshevist agitation and sympathy among a very considerable part of the working class in this country, we must take into account the fact that its logical and natural nucleus is the I.W.W. It is necessary also to emancipate our minds from the obsession that only "ignorant foreigners" are affected. This is not a true estimate of either the I.W.W. or the bolshevist propaganda as a whole. There are indeed many of this class in both, but there are also many native Americans, sturdy, self-reliant, enterprising, and courageous men. The peculiar group psychology which we are compelled to study is less the result of those subtle and complex factors which are comprehended in the vague term "race" than of the political and economic conditions by which the group concerned is environed.

The typical native-born I.W.W. member, the "Wobbly" one frequently encounters in our mid-western and western cities, is very unlike the hideous and repulsive figure conjured up by sensational cartoonists. He is much more likely to be a very attractive sort of man. Here are some characteristics of the type: figure robust, sturdy, and virile; dress rough but not unclean; speech forthright, deliberate, and bold; features intelligent, frank, and free from signs of alcoholic dissipation; movements slow and leisurely as of one averse to over-exertion. There are thousands of "wobblies" to whom the specifications of this description will apply. Conversation with these men reveals that, as a general rule, they are above rather than below the average in sobriety. They are generally free from family ties, being either unmarried or, as often happens, wife-deserters. They are not highly educated, few having attended any school beyond the grammar-school grade. Many of them have, however, read a great deal more than the average man, though their reading has been curiously miscellaneous in selection and nearly always badly balanced. Theology, philosophy, sociology, and economics seem to attract most attention. In discussion—and every "Wobbly" seems to possess a passion for disputation—men of this type will manifest a surprising familiarity with the broad outlines of certain theological problems, as well as with the scriptural texts bearing upon them. It is very likely to be the case, however, that they have only read a few popular classics of what used to be called rationalism—Paine's *Age of Reason*, Ingersoll's lectures in pamphlet form, and Haeckel's *Riddle of the Universe* are typical. A surprisingly large number can quote extensively from Buckle's *History of Civilization* and from the writings of Marx. They quote statistics freely—statistics of wages, poverty, crime, vice, and so on—generally derived from the radical press and implicitly believed because so published, with what they accept as adequate authority.

Their most marked peculiarity is the migratory nature of their lives. Whether this is self-determined, a matter of temperament and habit, or due to uncontrollable factors, it is largely responsible for the contempt in which they are popularly held. It naturally brings upon them the reproach and resentment everywhere visited upon "tramps" and "vagabonds." They rarely remain long enough in any one place to form local attachments and ties or anything like civic pride. They move from job to job, city to city, state to state, sometimes tramping afoot, begging as they go; sometimes stealing rides on railway trains, in freight cars—"side-door Pullmans"—or on the rods underneath the cars. Frequently arrested for begging, trespassing, or stealing rides, they are often victims of injustice at the hands of local judges and justices. The absence of friends, combined with the prejudice against vagrants which everywhere exists, subjects them to arbitrary and high-handed injustice such as no other body of American citizens has to endure. Moreover, through the conditions of their existence they are readily suspected of crimes they do not commit; it is all too easy for the hard-pushed police officer or sheriff to impute a crime to the lone and defenseless "Wobbly," who frequently can produce no testimony to prove his innocence, simply because he has no friends in the neighborhood and has been at pains to conceal his movements. In this manner the "Wobbly" becomes a veritable son of Ishmael, his hand against the hand of nearly every man in conventional society. In particular he becomes a rebel by habit, hating the police and the courts as his constant enemies.

Doubtless the great majority of these men are temperamentally predisposed to the unanchored, adventurous, migratory existence which they lead. Boys so constituted run away to sea, take jobs with traveling circuses, or enlist as soldiers. The type is familiar and not uncommon. Such individuals cannot be content with the prosaic, humdrum, monotonous life of regular employment. As a rule we do not look upon this trait in boy or man as criminal.

Many a hardworking, intelligent American, who from choice or from necessity is a migratory worker, following his job, never has an opportunity to vote for state legislators, for governor, for congressman or president.   He is just as effectively excluded from the actual electorate as if he were a Chinese coolie, ignorant of our customs and our speech.

We cannot wonder that such conditions prove prolific breeders of bolshevism and similar "isms."   It would be strange indeed if it were otherwise.   We have no right to expect that men who are so constantly the victims of arbitrary, unjust, and even brutal treatment at the hands of our police and our courts will manifest any reverence for the law and the judicial system.   Respect for majority rule in government cannot fairly be demanded from a disfranchised group. It is not to be wondered at that the old slogan of socialism, "Strike at the ballot-box!"—the call to lift the struggle of the classes to the parliamentary level for peaceful settlement—becomes the desperate, anarchistic I.W.W. slogan, "Strike at the ballot-box with an ax!"   Men who can have no family life cannot justly be expected to bother about school administration.   Men who can have no home· life but only dreary shelter in crowded work-camps or dirty doss-houses are not going to bother themselves with municipal housing reforms.

In short, we must wake up to the fact that, as the very heart of our problem, we have a bolshevist nucleus in America composed of virile, red-blooded Americans, racy of our soil and history, whose conditions of life and labor are such as to develop in them the psychology of reckless, despairing, revengeful bolshevism.   They really are little concerned with theories of the state and of social development, which to our intellectuals seem to be the essence of bolshevism. They are vitally concerned only with action.   Syndicalism and bolshevism involve speedy and drastic action—hence the force of their appeal.

Finally, if we would understand why millions of people in all lands have turned away from old ideals, old loyalties, and old faiths to bolshevism, with something of the passion and frenzy characteristic of great messianic movements, we must take into account the intense spiritual agony and hunger which the Great War has brought into the lives of civilized men.   The old gods are dead and men are everywhere expectantly waiting for the new gods to arise.   The aftermath of the war is a spiritual cataclysm such as civilized mankind has never before known.   The old religions and moralities are shattered and men are waiting and striving for new ones. It is a time suggestive of the birth of new religions. Man cannot live as yet without faith, without some sort of religion. The heart of the world today is strained with yearning for new and living faiths to replace the old faiths which are dead. Were some persuasive fanatic to arise proclaiming himself to be a new Messiah, and preaching the religion of action, the creation of a new society, he would find an eager, soul-hungry world already predisposed to believe.

4. Mass Movements and Institutions: Methodism[1]

The corruption of manners which has been general since the Restoration was combated by societies for "the reformation of manners, which in the last years of the seventeenth century acquired extraordinary dimensions. They began in certain private societies which arose in the reign of James II, chiefly under the auspices of Beveridge and Bishop Horneck. These societies were at first purely devotional, and they appear to have been almost identical in character with those of the early Methodists. They held prayer meetings, weekly communions, and Bible-readings; they sustained charities and distributed religious books, and they cultivated a warmer and more ascetic type of devotion than was common in the Church. Societies of this description sprang up in almost every considerable city in England and even in several of those in Ireland. In the last years of the seventeenth century we find no less than ten of them in Dublin. Without, however, altogether discarding their first character, they assumed, about 1695, new and very important functions. They divided themselves into several distinct groups, undertaking the discovery and suppression of houses of ill fame, and the prosecution of swearers, drunkards, and Sabbath-breakers. They became a kind of voluntary police, acting largely as spies, and enforcing the laws against religious offenses. The energy with which this scheme was carried out is very remarkable. As many as seventy or eighty persons were often prosecuted in London and Westminster for cursing and swearing, in a single week. Sunday markets, which had hitherto been not uncommon, were effectually suppressed. Hundreds of disorderly houses were closed. Forty or fifty night-walkers were

[1] Adapted from William E. H. Lecky, *A History of England in the Eighteenth Century*, III, 33–101. (D. Appleton & Co., 1892.)

sent every week to Bridewell, and numbers were induced to emigrate to the colonies. A great part of the fines levied for these offenses was bestowed on the poor. In the fortieth annual report of the "Societies for the Reformation of Manners" which appeared in 1735, it was stated that the number of prosecutions for debauchery and profaneness in London and Westminster alone, since the foundation of the societies, had been 99,380.

The term Methodist was a college nickname bestowed upon a small society of students at Oxford, who met together between 1729 and 1735 for the purpose of mutual improvement. They were accustomed to communicate every week, to fast regularly on Wednesdays and Fridays, and on most days during Lent; to read and discuss the Bible in common, to abstain from most forms of amusement and luxury, and to visit sick persons and prisoners in the gaol. John Wesley, the future leader of the religious revival of the eighteenth century, was the master-spirit of this society. The society hardly numbered more than fifteen members, and was the object of much ridicule at the university; but it included some men who afterward played considerable parts in the world. Among them was Charles, the younger brother of John Wesley, whose hymns became the favorite poetry of the sect, and whose gentler, more submissive, and more amiable character, though less fitted than that of his brother for the great conflicts of public life, was very useful in moderating the movement, and in drawing converts to it by personal influence. Charles Wesley appears to have originated the society at Oxford; he brought Whitefield into its pale, and besides being the most popular poet he was one of the most persuasive preachers of the movement.

In the course of 1738 the chief elements of the movement were already formed. Whitefield had returned from Georgia, Charles Wesley had begun to preach the doctrine with extraordinary effect to the criminals in Newgate and from every pulpit into which he was admitted. Methodist societies had already sprung up under Moravian influence. They were in part a continuation of the society at Oxford, in part a revival of those religious societies that have been already noticed as so common after the Revolution. The design of each was to be a church within a church, a seedplot of a more fervent piety, the center of a stricter discipline and a more energetic propagandism than existed in religious communities at large. In these societies the old Christian custom of love-feasts was revived. The members sometimes passed almost the whole night in the most passionate devotions, and voluntarily submitted to a spiritual tyranny that could hardly be surpassed in a Catholic monastery. They were to meet every week, to make an open and particular confession of every frailty, to submit to be cross-examined on all their thoughts, words, and deeds. The following among others were the questions asked at every meeting: "What known sin have you committed since our last meeting? What temptations have you met with? How were you delivered? What have you thought, said, or done of which you doubt whether it be sin or not? Have you nothing you desire to keep secret?"

Such rules could only have been accepted under the influence of an overpowering religious enthusiasm, and there was much truth in the judgment which the elder brother of John Wesley passed upon them in 1739. "Their societies," he wrote to their mother, "are sufficient to dissolve all other societies but their own. Will any man of common sense or spirit suffer any domestic to be in a band engaged to relate to five or ten people everything without reserve that concerns the person's conscience how much soever it may concern the family? Ought any married persons to be there unless husband and wife be there together?"

From this time the leaders of the movement became the most active of missionaries. Without any fixed parishes they wandered from place to place, proclaiming their new doctrine in every pulpit to which they were admitted, and they speedily awoke a passionate enthusiasm and a bitter hostility in the Church.

We may blame, but we can hardly, I think, wonder at the hostility all this aroused among the clergy. It is, indeed, certain that Wesley and Whitefield were at this time doing more than any other contemporary clergymen to kindle a living piety among the people. Yet before the end of 1738 the Methodist leaders were excluded from most of the pulpits of the Church, and were thus compelled, unless they consented to relinquish what they considered a Divine mission, to take steps in the direction of separation.

Two important measures of this nature were taken in 1739. One of them was the creation of Methodist chapels, which were intended not to oppose or replace, but to be supplemental and ancillary to, the churches, and to secure that the doctrine of the new birth should be faithfully taught to the people. The other and still more important event was the institution by Whitefield of field-preaching. The idea had occurred to him in London, where he found congregations too numerous for the church in which he preached, but the first actual step was taken in the neighborhood of Bristol. At a time when he was himself excluded from the pulpits at Bristol, and was thus deprived of the chief normal means of exercising his talents, his attention was called to the condition of the colliers at Kingswood. He was filled with horror and compassion at finding in the heart of a Christian country, and in the immediate neighborhood of a great city, a population of many thousands, sunk in the most brutal ignorance and vice, and entirely excluded from the ordinances of religion. Moved by such feelings, he resolved to address the colliers in their own haunts. The resolution was a bold one, for field-preaching was then utterly unknown in England, and it needed no common courage to brave all the obloquy and derision it must provoke, and to commence the experiment in the center of a half-savage population. Whitefield, however, had a just confidence in his cause and in his powers. Standing himself upon a hillside, he took for his text the first words of the sermon which was spoken from the Mount, and he addressed with his accustomed fire an astonished audience of some two hundred men. The fame of his eloquence spread far and wide. On successive occasions, five, ten, fifteen, even twenty thousand were present. It was February, but the winter sun shone clear and bright. The lanes were filled with carriages of the more wealthy citizens, whom curiosity had drawn from Bristol. The trees and hedges were crowded with humbler listeners, and the fields were darkened by a compact mass. The voice of the great preacher pealed with a thrilling power to the outskirts of that mighty throng. The picturesque novelty of the occasion and of the scene, the contagious emotion of so great a multitude, a deep sense of the condition of his hearers and of the momentous importance of the step he was taking, gave an additional solemnity to his eloquence. His rude auditors were electrified. They stood for a time in rapt and motionless attention. Soon tears might be seen forming white gutters down cheeks blackened from the coal mine. Then sobs and groans told how hard hearts were melting at his words. A fire was kindled among the outcasts of Kingswood which burnt long and fiercely, and was destined in a few years to over-spread the land.

But for the simultaneous appearance of a great orator and a great statesman, Methodism would probably have smouldered and at last perished like the very similar religious societies of the preceding century. Whitefield was utterly destitute of the organizing skill which could alone give a permanence to the movement, and no talent is naturally more ephemeral than popular oratory; while Wesley, though a great and impressive preacher, could scarcely have kindled a general enthusiasm had he not been assisted by an orator who had an unrivaled power of moving the passions of the ignorant. The institution of field-preaching by Whitefield in the February of 1739 carried the impulse through the great masses of the poor, while the foundation by Wesley, in the May of the same year, of the first Methodist chapel was the beginning of an organized body capable of securing and perpetuating the results that had been achieved.

From the time of the institution of lay preachers Methodism became in a great degree independent of the Established Church. Its chapels multiplied in the great towns, and its itinerant missionaries penetrated to the most secluded districts. They were accustomed to preach in fields and gardens, in streets and lecture-rooms, in market places and churchyards. On one occasion we find Whitefield at a fair mounting a stage which had been erected for some wrestlers, and there denouncing the pleasures of the world; on another, preaching among the mountebanks at Moorfields; on a third, attracting around his pulpit ten thousand of the spectators at a race course; on a fourth, standing beside the gallows at an execution to speak of death and of eternity. Wesley, when excluded from the pulpit of Epworth, delivered some of his most impressive sermons in the churchyard, standing on his father's tomb. Howell Harris, the apostle of Wales, encountering a party of mountebanks, sprang into their midst exclaiming, in a solemn voice, "Let us pray," and then proceeded to thunder forth the judgments of the Lord. Rowland Hill was accustomed to visit the great towns on market day in order that he might address the people in the market place, and to go from fair to fair preaching among the revelers from his favorite text, "Come out from among them." In this manner the Methodist preachers came in contact with the most savage elements of the population, and there were few forms of mob violence they did not experience. In 1741 one of their preachers named Seward, after repeated ill treatment in Wales, was at last struck on the head while preaching at Mon-mouth, and died of the blow. In a riot, while Wheatley was preaching at Norwich, a poor woman with child perished from the kicks and blows of the mob. At Dublin, Whitefield was almost stoned to death. At Exeter he was stoned in the very presence of the bishop. At Plymouth he was violently assaulted and his life seriously threatened by a naval officer.

Scenes of this kind were of continual occurrence, and they were interspersed with other persecutions of a less dangerous description. Drums were beaten, horns blown, guns let off, and blacksmiths hired to ply their noisy trade in order to drown the voices of the preachers. Once, at the very moment when Whitefield announced his text, the belfry gave out a peal loud enough to make him inaudible. On other occasions packs of hounds were brought with the same object, and once, in order to excite the dogs to fury, a live cat in a cage was placed in their midst. Fire engines poured streams of fetid water upon the congregation. Stones fell so thickly that the faces of many grew crimson with blood. At Hoxton the mob drove an ox into the midst of the congregation. At Pensford the rabble, who had been baiting a bull, concluded their sport by driving the torn and tired animal full against the table on which Wesley was preaching. Sometimes we find innkeepers refusing to receive the Methodist leaders in their inns, farmers entering into an agreement to dismiss every laborer who attended a Methodist preacher, landlords expelling all Methodists from their cottages, masters dismissing their servants because they had joined the sect. The magistrates, who knew by experience that the presence of a Methodist preacher was the usual precursor of disturbance and riot, looked on them with the greatest disfavor, and often scandalously connived at the persecutions they underwent.

It was frequently observed by Wesley that his preaching rarely affected the rich and the educated. It was over the ignorant and the credulous that it exercised its most appalling power, and it is difficult to overrate the mental anguish it must sometimes have produced. Timid and desponding natures unable to convince themselves that they had undergone a supernatural change, gentle and affectionate natures who believed that those who were dearest to them were descending into everlasting fire, must have often experienced pangs compared with which the torments of the martyr were insignificant. The confident assertions of the Methodist preacher and the ghastly images he continually evoked poisoned their imaginations, haunted them in every hour of weakness or depression, discolored all their judgments of the world, and added a tenfold horror to the darkness of the grave. Sufferings of this description, though among the most real and the most terrible that superstition can inflict, are so hidden in their nature that they leave few traces in history; but it is impossible to read the journals of Wesley without feeling that they were most widely diffused. Many were thrown into paroxysms of extreme, though usually transient, agony; many doubtless nursed a secret sorrow which corroded all the happiness of their lives, while not a few became literally insane. On one occasion Wesley was called to the bedside of a young woman at Kingswood. He tells us:

She was nineteen or twenty years old, but, it seems, could not write or read. I found her on the bed, two or three persons holding her. It was a terrible sight. Anguish, horror, and despair above all description appeared in her pale face. The thousand distortions of her whole body showed how the dogs of hell were gnawing at her heart. The shrieks intermixed were scarce to be endured. But her stony eyes could not weep. She screamed out as soon as words could find their way, "I am damned, damned, lost forever: six days ago you might have helped me. But it is past. I am the devil's now. . . . . I will go with him to hell. I cannot be saved." They sang a hymn, and for a time she sank to rest, but soon broke out anew in incoherent exclamations, "Break, break, poor stony hearts! Will you not break? What more can be done for stony hearts? I am damned that you may be saved!" . . . . She then fixed her eyes in the corner of the ceiling, and said, "There he is, ay, there he is! Come, good devil, come! Take me away." . . . . We interrupted her by calling again on God, on which she sank down as before, and another young woman began to roar out as loud as she had done.

For more than two hours Wesley and his brother continued praying over her. At last the paroxysms subsided and the patient joined in a hymn of praise.

In the intense religious enthusiasm that was generated, many of the ties of life were snapped in twain. Children treated with contempt the commands of their parents, students the rules of their colleges, clergymen the discipline of their Church. The whole structure of society, and almost all the amusements of life, appeared criminal. The fairs, the mountebanks, the public rejoicings of the people, were all Satanic. It was sinful for a woman to wear any gold ornament or any brilliant dress. It was even sinful for a man to exercise the common prudence of laying by a certain portion of his income. When Whitefield proposed to a lady to marry him, he thought it necessary to say, "I bless God, if I know anything of my own heart, I am free from that foolish passion which the world calls love." "I trust I love you only for God, and desire to be joined to you only by His commands, and for His sake." It is perhaps not very surprising that Whitefield's marriage, like that of Wesley, proved very unhappy. Theaters and the reading of plays were absolutely condemned, and Methodists employed all their influence with the authorities to prevent the erection of the former. It seems to have been regarded as a divine judgment that once, when *Macbeth* was being acted at Drury Lane, a real thunderstorm mingled with the mimic thunder in the witch scene. Dancing was, if possible, even worse than the theater. "Dancers," said Whitefield, "please the devil at every step"; and it was said that his visit to a town usually put "a stop to the dancing-school, the assemblies, and every pleasant thing." He made it his mission to "bear testimony against the detestable diversions of this generation"; and he declared that no "recreations, considered as such, can be innocent."

Accompanying this asceticism we find an extraordinary revival of the grossest superstition. It was a natural consequence of the essentially emotional character of Methodism that its disciples should imagine that every strong feeling or impulse within them was a direct inspiration of God or Satan. The language of Whitefield—the language in a great degree of all the members of the sect—was that of men who were at once continually inspired and the continual objects of miraculous interposition. In every perplexity they imagined that, by casting lots or opening their Bibles at random, they could obtain a supernatural answer to their inquiries.

In all matters relating to Satanic interference, Wesley was especially credulous. "I cannot give up to all the Deists in Great Britain the existence of witchcraft till I give up the credit of all history, sacred and profane." He had no doubt that the physical contortions into which so many of his hearers fell were due to the direct agency of Satan, who tore the converts as they were coming to Christ. He had himself seen men and women who were literally possessed by devils; he had witnessed forms of madness which were not natural, but diabolical, and he had experienced in his own person the hysterical affections which resulted from supernatural agency.

If Satanic agencies continually convulsed those who were coming to the faith, divine judgments as frequently struck down those who opposed it. Every illness, every misfortune that befell an opponent, was believed to be supernatural. Molther, the Moravian minister, shortly after the Methodists had separated from the Moravians, was seized with a passing illness. "I believe," wrote Wesley, "it was the hand of God that was upon him." Numerous cases were cited of sudden and fearful judgments which fell upon the adversaries of the cause. A clergyman at Bristol, standing up to preach against the Methodists, "was suddenly seized with a rattling in his throat, attended with a hideous groaning," and on the next Sunday he died. At Todmorden a minister was struck with a violent fit of palsy immediately after preaching against the Methodists. At Enniscorthy a clergyman, having preached for some time against Methodism, deferred the conclusion of the discourse to the following Sunday. Next morning he was raging mad, imagined that devils were about him, "and not long after, without showing the least sign of hope, he went to his account." At Kingswood a man began a vehement invective against Wesley and Methodism. "In the midst he was struck raving mad." A woman, seeing a crowd waiting for Wesley at the church door, exclaimed, "They are waiting for their God." She at once fell senseless to the ground, and next day expired. "A party of young men rowed up to Richmond to disturb the sermons of Rowland Hill. The boat sank, and all of them were drowned." At Sheffield the captain of a gang who had long troubled the field-preachers, was bathing with his companions. "Another dip," he said, "and then for a bit of sport with the Methodists." He dived, struck his head against a stone, and appeared no more. By such anecdotes and by such beliefs a fever of enthusiasm was sustained.

But with all its divisions and defects the movement was unquestionably effecting a great moral revolution in England. It was essentially a popular movement, exercising its deepest influence over the lower and middle classes. Some of its leaders were men of real genius, but in general the Methodist teacher had little sympathy with the more educated of his fellow-countrymen. To an ordinarily cultivated mind there was something extremely repulsive in his tears and groans and amorous ejaculations, in the coarse and anthropomorphic familiarity and the unwavering dogmatism with which he dealt with the most sacred subjects, in the narrowness of his theory of life and his utter insensibility to many of the influences that expand and embellish it, in the mingled credulity and self-confidence with which he imagined that the whole course of nature was altered for his convenience. But the very qualities that impaired his influence in one sphere enhanced it in another. His impassioned prayers and exhortations stirred the hearts of multitudes whom a more decorous teaching had left absolutely callous. The supernatural atmosphere of miracles, judgments, and inspirations in which he moved, invested the most prosaic life with a halo of romance. The doctrines he taught, the theory of life he enforced, proved themselves capable of arousing in great masses of men an enthusiasm of piety which was hardly surpassed in the first days of Christianity, of eradicating inveterate vice, of fixing and directing impulsive and tempestuous natures that were rapidly hastening toward the abyss. Out of the profligate slave-dealer, John Newton, Methodism formed one of the purest and most unselfish of saints. It taught criminals in Newgate to mount the gallows in an ecstasy of rapturous devotion. It planted a fervid and enduring religious sentiment in the midst of the most brutal and most neglected portions of the population, and whatever may have been its vices or its defects, it undoubtedly emancipated great numbers from the fear of death, and imparted a warmer tone to the devotion and a greater energy to the philanthropy of every denomination both in England and the colonies.

III. INVESTIGATIONS AND PROBLEMS

1. Social Unrest

The term collective behavior, which has been used elsewhere to include all the facts of group life, has been limited for the purposes of this chapter to those phenomena which exhibit in the most obvious and elementary way the processes by which societies are disintegrated into their constituent elements and the processes by which these elements are brought together again into new relations to form new organizations and new societies.

Some years ago John Graham Brooks wrote a popular treatise on the labor situation in the United States. He called the volume *Social Unrest*. The term was, even at that time, a familiar one. Since then the word unrest, in both its substantive and adjective forms, has gained wide usage. We speak in reference to the notorious disposition of the native American to move from one part of the country to another, of his restless blood, as if restlessness was a native American trait transmitted in the blood. We speak more often of the "restless age," as if mobility and the desire for novelty and new experience were peculiarly characteristic of the twentieth century. We use the word to describe conditions in different regions of social life in such expressions as "political," "religious," and "labor" unrest, and in every case the word is used in a sense that indicates change, but change that menaces the existing order. Finally, we speak of the "restless woman," as of a peculiar modern type, characteristic of the changed status of women in general in the modern world. In all these different uses we may observe the gradual unfolding of the concept which seems to have been implicit in the word as it was first used. It is the concept of an activity in response to some urgent organic impulse which the activity, however, does not satisfy. It is a diagnostic symptom, a symptom of what Graham Wallas calls "balked disposition." It is a sign that in the existing situation some one or more of the four wishes—security, new experience, recognition, and response—has not been and is not adequately realized. The fact that the symptom is social, that it is contagious, is an indication that the situations that provoke it are social, that is to say, general in the community or the group where the unrest manifests itself.

The materials in which the term unrest is used in the sense indicated are in the popular discussions of social questions. The term is not defined but it is frequently used in connection with descriptions of conditions which are evidently responsible for it. Labor strikes are evidences of social unrest, and the literature already referred to in the chapter on "Conflict" shows the conditions under which unrest arises, is provoked and exploited in labor situations. The relation of unrest to routine and fatigue has been the subject of a good deal of discussion and some investigation. The popular conception is that labor unrest is due to the dull driving routine of machine industry. The matter needs further study. The actual mental experiences of the different sexes, ages, temperamental and mental types under the influence of routine would add a much needed body of fact to our present psychology of the worker.

2. Psychic Epidemics

If social unrest is a symptom of disorganization, then the psychic epidemics, in which all the phenomena of social unrest and contagion are intensified, is evidence positive that disorganization exists. Social disorganization must be considered in relation to reorganization. All change involves a certain amount of disorganization. In order that an individual may make new adjustments and establish new habits it is inevitable that old habits should be broken up, and in order that society may reform an existing social order a certain amount of disorganization is inevitable. Social unrest may be, therefore, a symptom of health. It is only when the process of disorganization goes on so rapidly and to such an extent that the whole existing social structure is impaired, and society is, for that reason, not able to readjust itself, that unrest is to be regarded as a pathological symptom.

There is reason to believe, contrary to the popular conception, that the immigrant in America, particularly in the urban environment, accommodates himself too quickly rather than too slowly to American life. Statistics show, particularly in the second generation, a notable increase in juvenile delinquency, and this seems to be due to the fact that in America the relation between parents and children is reversed. Owing to the children's better knowledge of English and their more rapid accommodation to the conditions of American life, parents become dependent upon their children rather than the children dependent upon their parents.

Social epidemics, however, are evidence of a social disintegration due to more fundamental and widespread disorders. The literature has recorded the facts but writers have usually interpreted the phenomena in medical rather than sociological terms. Stoll, in his very interesting but rather miscellaneous collection of materials upon primitive life, disposes of the phenomena by giving them another name. His volume is entitled *Suggestion and Hypnotism in Folk Psychology.*[1] Friedmann, in his monograph, *Über Wahnideen im Völkerleben,* is disposed as a psychiatrist to treat the whole matter as a form of "social" insanity.

3. Mass Movements

In spite of the abundance of materials on the subject of mass movements no attempt has been made as yet to collect and classify them. There have been a number of interesting books in the field of collective psychology, so called mainly by French and Italian writers—Sighele, Rossi, Tarde, and Le Bon—but they are not based on a systematic study of cases. The general assumption has been that the facts are so obvious that any attempt to study systematically the mechanisms involved would amount to little more than academic elaboration of what is already obvious, a restatement in more abstract terms of what is already familiar.

On the other hand, shepherds and cowboys, out of their experience in handling cattle and sheep, have learned that the flock and the herd have quite peculiar and characteristic modes of collective behavior which it is necessary to know if one is to handle them successfully. At the same time, practical politicians who make a profession of herding voters, getting them out to the polls at the times they are needed and determining for them, by the familiar campaign devices, the persons and the issues for which they are to cast their ballots, have worked out very definite methods for dealing with masses of people, so that they are able to predict the outcome with considerable accuracy far in advance of an election and make their dispositions accordingly.

Political manipulation of the movements and tendencies of popular opinion has now reached a point of perfection where it can and will be studied systematically. During the world-war it was studied, and all the knowledge which advertisers, newspaper men, and psychologists possessed was used to win the war.

[1] Otto Stoll, *Suggestion und Hypnotismus in der Völkerpsychologie.* 2d ed. (Leipzig, 1904.)

Propaganda is now recognized as part of the grand strategy of war. Not only political and diplomatic victories, but battles were won during the world-war by the aid of this insidious weapon. The great victory of the Austrian and German armies at Caporetto which in a few days wiped out all the hard-won successes of the Italian armies was prepared by a psychic attack on the morale of the troops at the front and a defeatist campaign among the Italian population back of the lines.

In the battle of Caporetto the morale of the troops at the front was undermined by sending postal cards and letters to individual soldiers stating that their wives were in illicit relations with officers and soldiers of the allies. Copies of Roman and Milanese newspapers were forged and absolute facsimiles of familiar journals were secretly distributed or dropped from Austrian aeroplanes over the Italian lines. These papers contained sensational articles telling the Italians that Austria was in revolt, that Emperor Charles had been killed. Accompanying these were other articles describing bread riots throughout Italy and stating that the Italian government, unable to quell them with its own forces, had sent British and French re-enforcing troops and even Zulus into the cities, and that these troops were shooting down women and children and priests without mercy.

This attack upon the morale of the troops was followed by an unforeseen assault upon a quiet sector, which succeeded in piercing the line at numerous points. In the confusion that followed the whole structure of the defense crumbled, and the result was disastrous.

When the final history of the world-war comes to be written, one of its most interesting chapters will be a description of the methods and devices which were used by the armies on both sides to destroy the will to war in the troops and among the peoples behind the lines. If the application of modern science to war has multiplied the engines of destruction, the increase of communication and the interpenetration of peoples has given war among civilized peoples the character of an internal and internecine struggle. Under these circumstances propaganda, in the sense of an insidious exploitation of the sources of dissension and unrest, may as completely change the character of wars of peoples as they were once changed by the invention of gunpowder.

In this field there is room for investigation and study, for almost all attempts thus far made to put advertising on a scientific basis have been made by students of individual rather than social psychology.

4. Revivals, Religious and Linguistic

For something more than a hundred years Europe has experienced a series of linguistic and literary revivals, that is to say revivals of the folk languages and the folk cultures.   The folk languages are the speech of peoples who have been conquered but not yet culturally absorbed by the dominant language group.   They are mostly isolated rural populations who have remained to a large extent outside of the cosmopolitan cultures of the cities.   These people while not wholly illiterate have never had enough education in the language of the dominant peoples of the cities to enable them to use this alien speech as a medium of education.   The consequence is that, except for a relatively small group of intellectuals, they have been cut off from the main current of European life and culture.   These linguistic revivals have not been confined to any one nation, since every nation in Europe turns out upon analysis to be a mosaic of minor nationalities and smaller cultural enclaves in which the languages of little and forgotten peoples have been preserved.   Linguistic revivals have, in fact, been well-nigh universal.   They have taken place in France, Spain, Norway, Denmark, in most of the Balkan States, including Albania, the most isolated of them all, and in all the smaller nationalities along the Slavic-German border—Finland, Esthonia, Letvia, Lithuania, Poland, Bohemia, Slovakia, Roumania, and the Ukraine.   Finally, among the Jews of Eastern Europe, there has been the Haskala Movement, as the Jews of Eastern Europe call their period of enlightenment, a movement that has quite unintentionally made the Judeo-German dialect (Yiddish) a literary language.

At first blush, it seems strange that the revivals of the folk speech should have come at a time when the locomotive and the telegraph were extending commerce and communication to the uttermost limits of the earth, when all barriers were breaking down, and the steady expansion of cosmopolitan life and the organization of the Great Society, as Graham Wallas has called it, seemed destined to banish all the minor languages, dialects, and obsolescent forms of speech, the last props of an international provincialism, to the limbo of forgotten things.   The competition of the world-languages was already keen; all the little and forgotten peoples of

Europe—the Finns, Letts, Ukrainians, Russo-Carpathians, Slovaks, Slo-
venians, Croatians, the Catalonians of eastern Spain, whose language, by
the way, dates back to a period before the Roman Conquest, the Czechs,
and the Poles—began to set up presses and establish schools to revive and
perpetuate their several racial languages.

To those who, at this time, were looking forward to world-organization
and a universal peace through the medium of a universal language, all this
agitation had the appearance of an anachronism, not to say a heresy. It
seemed a deliberate attempt to set up barriers, where progress demanded
that they should be torn down. The success of such a movement, it seemed,
must be to bring about a more complete isolation of the peoples, to imprison
them, so to speak, in their own languages, and so cut them off from the
general culture of Europe.[1]

The actual effect has been different from what was expected.
It is difficult, and for the masses of the people impossible, to learn
through the medium of a language that they do not speak. The
results of the efforts to cultivate Swedish and Russian in Finland,
Polish and Russian in Lithuania, Magyar in Slovakia and at the same
time to prohibit the publication of books and newspapers in the
mother-tongue of the country has been, in the first place, to create
an artificial illiteracy and, in the second, to create in the minds of
native peoples a sense of social and intellectual inferiority to the
alien and dominant race.

The effect of the literary revival of the spoken language, however,
has been to create, in spite of the efforts to suppress it, a vernacular
press which opened the gates of western culture to great masses of
people for whom it did not previously exist. The result has been
a great cultural awakening, a genuine renaissance, which has had
profound reverberations on the political and social life of Europe.

The literary revival of the folk speech in Europe has invariably been a
prelude to the revival of the national spirit in subject peoples. The sentiment of nationality has its roots in memories that attach to the common
possessions of the people, the land, the religion, and the language, but
particularly the language.

Bohemian patriots have a saying, "As long as the language lives, the
nation is not dead." In an address in 1904 Jorgen Levland, who was
afterward Premier of Norway, in a plea for "freedom with self-government,

[1] Robert E. Park, *Immigrant Press and Its Control*, chap. ii, "Background of
the Immigrant Press." (New York, 1921. In press.)

home, land, and our own language," made this statement: "Political freedom is not the deepest and greatest. Greater is it for a nation to preserve her intellectual inheritance in her native tongue."

The revival of the national consciousness in the subject peoples has invariably been connected with the struggle to maintain a press in the native language. The reason is that it was through the medium of the national press that the literary and linguistic revivals took place. Conversely, the efforts to suppress the rising national consciousness took the form of an effort to censor or suppress the national press. There were nowhere attempts to suppress the spoken language as such. On the other hand, it was only as the spoken language succeeded in becoming a medium of literary expression that it was possible to preserve it under modern conditions and maintain in this way the national solidarity. When the Lithuanians, for example, were condemned to get their education and their culture through the medium of a language not their own, the effect was to denationalize the literate class and to make its members aliens to their own people. If there was no national press, there could be no national schools, and, indeed, no national church. It was for this reason that the struggle to maintain the national language and the national culture has always been a struggle to maintain a national press.

European nationalists, seeking to revive among their peoples the national consciousness, have invariably sought to restore the national speech, to purge it of foreign idioms, and emphasize every mark which serves to distinguish it from the languages with which it tended to fuse.[1]

Investigation of these linguistic revivals and the nationalist movement that has grown out of them indicates that there is a very intimate relation between nationalist and religious movements. Both of them are fundamentally cultural movements with incidental political consequences. The movement which resulted in the reorganization of rural life in Denmark, the movement that found expression in so unique an institution as the rural high schools of Denmark, was begun by Bishop Grundtvig, called the Luther of Denmark, and was at once a religious and a nationalist movement. The rural high schools are for this reason not like anything in the way of education with which people outside of Denmark are familiar. They are not technical schools but cultural institutions in the narrowest, or broadest, sense of that term.[2] The teaching is "scientific," but at the same

[1] *Ibid.*

[2] Anton H. Hollman, *Die dänische Volkshochschule und ihre Bedeutung für die Entwicklung einer völkischen Kultur in Dänemark.* (Berlin, 1909.)

time "inspirational." They are what a Sunday school might be if it were not held on Sunday and was organized as Mr. H. G. Wells would organize it and with such a bible as he would like to have someone write for us.[1]

The popular accounts which we have of religious revivals do not at first suggest any very definite relations, either psychological or sociological, between them and the literary revivals to which reference has just been made. Religious revivals, particularly as described by dispassionate observers, have the appearance of something bizarre, fantastic, and wild, as indeed they often are.

What must strike the thoughtful observer, however, is the marked similarity of these collective religious excitements, whether among civilized or savage peoples and at places and periods remote in time and in space. Frederick Morgan Davenport, who has collected and compared the materials in this field from contemporary sources, calls attention in the title of his volume, *Primitive Traits in Religious Revivals*, to this fundamental similarity of the phenomena. Whatever else the word "primitive" may mean in this connection it does mean that the phenomena of religious revivals are fundamentally human.

From the frantic and disheveled dances of the Bacchantes, following a wine cart through an ancient Greek village, to the shouts and groans of the mourners' bench of an old-time Methodist camp-meeting, religious excitement has always stirred human nature more profoundly than any other emotion except that of passionate love.

In the volume by Jean Pélissier, *The Chief Makers of the National Lithuanian Renaissance (Les Principaux artisans de la renaissance nationale lituanienne)*, there is a paragraph describing the conversion of a certain Dr. Kudirka, a Lithuanian patriot, to the cause of Lithuanian nationality. It reads like a chapter from William James's *The Varieties of Religious Experience.*[2]

It is materials like this that indicate how close and intimate are the relations between cultural movements, whether religious or literary and national, at least in their formal expression. The question that remains to be answered is: In what ways do they differ?

---

[1] H. G. Wells, *The Salvaging of Civilization*, chaps. iv–v, "The Bible of Civilization," pp. 97–140. (New York, 1921.)

[2] See *The Immigrant Press and Its Control*, chap. ii, for a translation of Dr. Kudirka's so-called "Confession."

5. Fashion, Reform and Revolution

A great deal has been written in recent times in regard to fashion. It has been studied, for example, as an economic phenomenon. Sombart has written a suggestive little monograph on the subject. It is in the interest of machine industry that fashions should be standardized over a wide area, and it is the function of advertising to achieve this result. It is also of interest to commerce that fashions should change and this also is largely, but not wholly, a matter of advertising. Tarde distinguishes between custom and fashion as the two forms in which all cultural traits are transmitted. "In periods when custom is in the ascendant, men are more infatuated about their country than about their time; for it is the past which is pre-eminently praised. In ages when fashion rules, men are prouder, on the contrary, of their time than of their country."[1]

The most acute analysis that has been made of fashion is contained in the observation of Sumner in *Folkways*. Sumner pointed out that fashion though differing from, is intimately related to, the mores. Fashion fixes the attention of the community at a given time and place and by so doing determines what is sometimes called the Spirit of the Age, the *Zeitgeist*. By the introduction of new fashions the leaders of society gain that distinction in the community by which they are able to maintain their prestige and so maintain their position as leaders. But in doing this, they too are influenced by the fashions which they introduce. Eventually changes in fashion affect the mores.[2]

Fashion is related to reform and to revolution, because it is one of the fundamental ways in which social changes take place and because, like reform and revolution, it also is related to the mores.

Fashion is distinguished from reform by the fact that the changes it introduces are wholly irrational if not at the same time wholly unpredictable. Reform, on the other hand, is nothing if not rational. It achieves its ends by agitation and discussion. Attempts have been made to introduce fashions by agitation, but they have not succeeded. On the other hand, reform is itself a fashion and has

---

[1] Gabriel Tarde, *The Laws of Imitation*. Translated from the 2d French ed. by Elsie Clews Parsons, p. 247. (New York, 1903.)

[2] Sumner, *Folkways*, pp. 200–201.

largely absorbed in recent years the interest that was formerly bestowed on party politics.

There has been a great deal written about reforms but almost nothing about *reform*. It is a definite type of collective behavior which has come into existence and gained popularity under conditions of modern life. The reformer and the agitator, likewise, are definite, temperamental, and social types. Reform tends under modern conditions to become a vocation and a profession like that of the politician. The profession of the reformer, however, is social, as distinguished from party politics.

Reform is not revolution. It does not seek to change the mores but rather to change conditions in conformity with the mores. There have been revolutionary reformers. Joseph II of Austria and Peter the Great of Russia were reformers of that type. But revolutionary reforms have usually failed. They failed lamentably in the case of Joseph II and produced many very dubious results under Peter.

A revolution is a mass movement which seeks to change the mores by destroying the existing social order. Great and silent revolutionary changes have frequently taken place in modern times, but as these changes were not recognized at the time and were not directly sought by any party they are not usually called revolutions. They might properly be called "historical revolutions," since they are not recognized as revolutions until they are history.

There is probably a definite revolutionary process but it has not been defined. Le Bon's book on the *Psychology of Revolution*, which is the sequel to his study of *The Crowd*, is, to be sure, an attempt, but the best that one can say of it is that it is suggestive.

INDEX

Acclimatization, as a form of accommodation, 306, 311–14

Accommodation: chap. viii, 303–58; and adaptation, 303–5; and assimilation, 360–61; and competition, 304–5; and compromise, 346–48; and conflict, 296–302, 309–10, 343–378; creates social organization, 191; defined, 303–4; distinguished from assimilation, 191; facilitated by secondary contacts, 361–62; in the form of slavery, 314–17, 317–21; forms of 306–7, 311–28; and historic forms of the organization of society, 307; natural issue of conflict, 305; and the origin of caste in India, 321–24, 324–28; and peace, 343–47; in relation to competition, 191–92; in relation to conflict, 191; as subordination and superordination, 307–9. *See* Subordination and superordination

Accommodation groups, classified, 50

Acculturation: and tradition, 67; transmission of cultural elements, 362

Adaptation, and accommodation, 303–5

Advertising. *See* Publicity

Aggregates, social: composed of spatially separated units, 26; and organic aggregates, 25

Amalgamation, fusion of races by intermarriage, 362–63. *See* Miscegenation

Americanization: as a problem of assimilation, 364–65; study of methods of, 364

Anarchy, of political opinion and parties, 2

Anger, analyzed, 70–71

Animal crowd. *See* Crowd, animal

Anthropology, 10

Appreciation: in relation to imitation, 134; and sense impressions, 146–47

Archaeology, as a new social science, 5

Art: as expressive behavior, 368–69; origin in the choral dance, 387

Assimilation: chap. ix, 359–65; and accommodation, 360–61; based on differences, 360; biological aspects of, 362–63; conceived as a "Melting Pot," 359; and democracy, 359; distinguished from accommodation, 191; facilitated by primary contacts, 361–62, 364; final product of social contact, 361–62; fusion of cultures, 362; as like-mindedness, 360; in personal development, 191; popular conceptions of, 359–65; sociology of, 360–62. *See* Amalgamation, Americanization, Cultures, conflict and fusion of, Denationalization

Attention, in relation to imitation, 134, 181–84

Attitudes: complexes of, 57; in subordination and superordination, 332–35

Balked disposition, a result of secondary contacts, 128

Behavior: defined, 105–6; expressive and positive, 128–29

Behavior, collective. *See* Collective behavior

Behavior patterns, and culture, 66

Blushing, communication by, 155–60

Bureau of Municipal Research, of New York City, 46

Caste: as an accommodation of conflict, 246; a form of accommodation group, 50; interpreted by superordination and subordination, 324–28; its origin in India, 321–24; and the limitation of free competition, 285–87

Ceremony: as expressive behavior, 368–69; fundamental form of social control, 368

Character: defined, 78; and instinct, 110–13; related to custom, 112–13

Circle, vicious. *See* Vicious circle

Circular reaction. *See* Reaction, circular

City: an area of secondary contacts, 126–28; aversion, a protection of the person in the, 246–47; and the evolution of individual types, 352–54; growth of, 214–15; physical human type of, 215–18

Civilization: a part of nature, 3; and permanent settlement, 209–10